ACADEMIC LIBRARY RESEARCH:
Perspectives and Current Trends

Edited by Marie L. Radford and Pamela Snelson

Association of College and Research Libraries
A division of the American Library Association
Chicago, 2008

The paper used in this publication meets the minimum requirements of American National Standard for Information Sciences-Permanence of Paper for Printed Library Materials, ANSI Z39.48-1992. ∞

Library of Congress Cataloging-in-Publication Data

Academic library research : perspectives and current trends / edited by Marie L. Radford and Pamela Snelson.
    p. cm. -- (ACRL publications in librarianship ; no. 59)
    Includes bibliographical references and index.
    ISBN 978-0-8389-0983-6 (pbk. : alk. paper) 1. Academic libraries. 2. Academic libraries--United States. I. Radford, Marie L. II. Snelson, Pamela.
    Z675.U5A3528 2008
    027.7--dc22

                              2008035286

Printed in the United States of America.

12 11 10 09 08   5 4 3 2 1

Table of Contents

Introduction

The original idea for this book came from John M. Budd, then editor of ACRL's Publications in Librarianship series, who had asked Marie if she would be interested in working on a volume that would update *Academic Libraries: Research Perspectives* edited by Mary Jo Lynch and Arthur P. Young, published by ACRL in 1990. The Lynch and Young book provided a summary of research in academic libraries that was useful both for practitioners seeking access to the scholarly literature and for researchers. The chapters of that volume covered the following topics: collection development and management, bibliographic control, access services, instructional services, bibliometrics, advanced technology, analysis and library management, and management theory and organizational structure. Since the publication by Lynch and Young in 1990, no update had been done and was highly desirable, especially due to the unprecedented changes that had occurred in academic libraries in the interim.

Upon reflection, Marie decided to seek the help of a co-editor and asked Pamela Snelson, a friend and colleague whose research interests and expertise in methods complemented hers, if she would join the project. Pamela agreed, and this book is the result of this collaboration. Enlisting well-known and qualified author and pulling together all seven chapters of this book has taken much more time than first anticipated, and John Budd's term as editor came to an end before the book was complete. Tony Schwartz took over as editor of Publications in Librarianship, and it has been under his competent and patient guidance and that of co-editor Craig Gibson that the work on this book has been completed.

Without a doubt, since 1990 there has been rapid and vast change in academic libraries. This change has been driven by advances in information technology, networked systems, and especially the advent of the Web. Almost every aspect of library work has been dramatically impacted by the Web, which enabled greatly enhanced remote access to collections and services and prompted innovations such as virtual reference, e-book and e-journal collection development, and digitized archives. This volume, although not intended to be exhaustive of all areas of research in academic librarianship, extends the Lynch and Young work, reaching into new areas that have developed since 1990 (e.g., the library evaluation chapters on usability and LibQUAL+), while updating more traditional topics that have undergone exceptional, and in some cases unexpected, change. This review combines theoretical scholarship and research designed to inform practice, often conducted by library practitioners: case studies and user surveys. Part I highlights significant perspectives and trends in five chapters, including reference service, information literacy, collection management, knowledge organization, and leadership. Part II features two chapters on recently developing evaluation methods: usability testing and measuring library service quality through LibQUAL+. Several overarching themes have emerged as challenges in the seven chapters:

- **Budget concerns and the need to do more with less funding.** The financial picture of the academic library has been worsening since 1990. Tightened budgets have enormous impact on all areas in higher education and libraries, especially on the nature and size of library collections, as noted in Casserly's collection development chapter. Budget concerns drive increased attention to accountability. Casserly identifies the most influential and useful studies in collection management and discovers limits in methodology and scope. Budget concerns also impact the provision and sustainability of library services such as reference, as discussed in the Radford and Mon chapter, and information literacy, as revealed in the Ondrusek chapter.

- **Collaboration/partnerships have proliferated and become critical to academic library survival and success.** The research reported here reflects increased collaboration between practitioners and researchers, between faculty and librarians, and across different types of institutions (such as public and academic libraries). As budgets become smaller, academics have leveraged collaboration and consortial arrangements to increase purchasing power and reduce demands on staff, as discussed by Casserly. Vellucci discusses international cooperative projects that seek to standardize the description and organization of electronic resources. The Radford and Mon chapter provides an overview of reference service, both traditional and virtual, noting that the most visible change is the expansion into Web technology that has enabled development of live chat reference consortia, as well as individual chat and instant messaging (IM) services.

- **The impact of technology is pervasive, and change is rapid and relentless.** Winston points out, in his chapter on leadership, that there has been an unprecedented proliferation of communication and information technology in design and provision of information service. Vellucci's review of knowledge organization reveals a varied research agenda where new technologies reshape and stretch the classification and organization of information. This theme is further discussed as a pervasive influence in academic libraries in each of the chapters in this book.

- **From Millennials to Baby Boomers, generation gaps have gotten wider.** Users have shifted from Gen Y to the media-immersed Millennial Generation (also known as the Net Generation). Several chapters, including Ondrusek on information literacy, Winston on leadership, and Radford and Mon on reference services, discuss the changing nature of today's college and university students. The impact that their communication and information-seeking behaviors have on library use and student learning is growing in importance to academic libraries. In addition, Winston notes that there is a looming crisis in leadership as our library and information science (LIS) faculty, as well as practitioners, are graying (many of them members of the Baby Boom generation). There seems to be reluctance on the part of entering or mid-career librarians to seek positions of broader responsibility. He also notes that LIS degree programs need to address this crisis through heavier emphasis on leadership education.

- **Assessment efforts have been intensified.** Part II of the book, as noted above, is devoted to recently developing evaluation applications for college and university libraries. Outcomes assessment and strategic planning activities have also become commonplace. Academic libraries face the need to justify spending, as well as to connect their missions directly to student learning. Usability testing, as highlighted in the Prasse and Connaway chapter, is becoming increasingly important in today's Web-based environment. Because of the relatively recent adoption of usability testing by academic libraries, as well as the increasing emphasis on our virtual presence—the library Web site—this chapter takes a different approach from the others. It provides detailed information on how to conduct usability testing, as well as a review of published research using this technique. In addition, Kyrillidou, Cook, and Rao discuss service quality in academic libraries through the development and use of LibQUAL+.

This volume has developed as a critically important overview of research and development in academic libraries. Many of the studies reported herein will serve as benchmarks as academic librarians face the excitement of changing times, users, and environments, as well as the challenges that this fast-paced era has produced.

Marie L. Radford & Pamela Snelson
April 7, 2008

Reference Service in Face-to-Face and Virtual Environments

Marie L. Radford and Lorri M. Mon

Reference services in academic libraries have changed profoundly and rapidly since 1990 as information retrieval technology, information sources and systems, and library users have become more sophisticated. This chapter provides an overview of studies of the reference interaction in the traditional, face-to-face mode as well as in digital environments. Perhaps the most noticeable change in reference work in academe centers on the newly expanded variety and reach of services being offered via library Web pages. Remote users, as well as those in the library building, now often have access to a number of different virtual services, frequently on a 24-7-365 schedule. The research summaries below offer glimpses into major findings and their implications for practitioners as well as the scholarly community. A broad range of methods, including user surveys (online and paper-based), chat and e-mail transcript analysis, individual and focus group interviews, meta-analyses, case studies, and unobtrusive or participant observations, have been utilized by the researchers. An overarching theme of this research is the ongoing commitment to understanding the complex reference environment and to improving services to users. The future outlook for reference promises to be exciting as academic libraries continue to be in the forefront of innovation and to be early adopters of emerging technologies, including Web 2.0 social networking applications.

Introduction

There is no doubt that since 1990, as information retrieval technology has continued to evolve and mature and information sources as well as systems have become more complex, reference work in academic libraries has undergone swift and revolutionary changes of an unprecedented nature. In 1997, Koutnik posed the question "The World Wide Web Is Here: Is the End of Printed Reference Sources Near?"[1] Although printed reference sources have not yet totally disappeared, many print reference collections have shrunk considerably, and face-to-face (FtF) reference question statistics showed a decrease in many academic libraries.[2]

Driven by user demand and the shift to electronic formats for reference sources, reference services have also changed profoundly and rapidly.

Some have speculated that the ubiquitous nature of Web search engines such as Google (http://www.google.com) and freely available information resources such as Wikipedia (http://www.wikipedia.org) portend the death of reference since academic library users now can more often find what they need without the help of reference librarians. A more optimistic academic librarian, Zabel, has declared that we are in a time of "Reference Renaissance" because of the increased attention to service excellence and the myriad ways we are responding to serve rising demand by developing an increasing array of reference service points.[3]

End-user searching of burgeoning free Web-based resources, coupled with a rising number of distance-learning degree programs, have accelerated the development of virtual reference services (VRS), also known as "digital reference services." Academic libraries have been proactive pioneers in the development and adoption of VRS, with the first asynchronous e-mail services beginning in the mid-1980s and then the launching of synchronous live chat in the late 1990s.[4] Instant messaging (IM) and phone text messaging (short message service, or SMS) have appeared as reference options in the early 2000s in response to user preferences as well as technological advances. An intriguing array of Web-based reference services are developing with the advent of social networking software, blogs, and other Web 2.0 applications. Academic libraries want to serve members of the "Net Gen" (also known as the Millennial Generation, Nintendo Generation, Echo Boomers, etc.) and so are increasingly investigating and offering nontraditional online approaches to reference services that seek to meet the students in cyberspace or in social networking sites rather than across the traditional reference desk.[5]

Tech-savvy students and faculty members demand instant gratification, expecting access to full-text collections, global resources, and 24/7/365 services.[6] However, collection budgets are tight, electronic resources are becoming ever more expensive, and human resources are also scarce. In this environment of unrelenting and fast-paced change coupled with limited resources, research that evaluates reference services is playing a more critical role, as Jacoby and O'Brien observe:

> Finding effective and meaningful methods for demonstrating the impact of library services has become increasingly important as almost every library faces reduced budgets that affect services.

Systematic evaluation and assessment of reference services can help demonstrate how library services contribute to broader educational goals and provide an opportunity to examine how well locally defined service goals are being met.[7]

Implementation of VRS also "has necessitated a certain amount of adjustment in academic libraries and the need for this adjustment points up the importance of assessment and evaluation in the planning, implementing, and provision of digital services."[8]

This chapter provides a synopsis of research in all the areas mentioned above, with particular emphasis on academic libraries and studies published since 1990. For those seeking additional overviews of research related to reference services, standard reference textbooks published during the past 15 years provide excellent summaries,[9] as do several monographs on the reference interview process and interpersonal communication[10] and a number of texts on VRS.[11] Richardson provides an excellent summation of the research on reference transactions, including academic settings.[12]

Researchers have utilized a broad range of methods, including user surveys (online and paper-based), chat and e-mail transcript analysis, individual and focus group interviews, meta-analyses, case studies, and unobtrusive observations. An overarching theme of the research featured here is the ongoing commitment to understanding the complex reference environment and seeking to improve services to users.

Reference Encounter as Interpersonal Interaction

Research on the interpersonal communication aspects of reference services has recently blossomed. This body of work uses a number of theoretical frameworks and a variety of perspectives, including approaches that are user-centered, approaches that are librarian-centered, and approaches that compare user and librarian viewpoints. One monograph that compares viewpoints and provides an in-depth discussion of research in the interpersonal communication aspects of academic reference is Radford's *The Reference Encounter: Interpersonal Communication in the Academic Library*, based on her doctoral dissertation.[13] Radford applied communication theory and the theoretical framework of Watzlawick, Beavin, and Jackson to the analysis of academic reference interactions.[14] In conducting observation and interviews with librarians and library users at three academic libraries, Radford found:

- "Interpersonal relationships and communication are of great importance in librarian and user perceptions of reference interactions.
- Library users in academic settings place a high degree of significance on the attitude and personal qualities of the librarian giving reference service.
- Some users valued interpersonal aspects more than their receipt of information.
- Librarians were more likely than users to evaluate the reference encounter from content dimensions that involve the transfer of information.
- Librarians also perceive relationship qualities to be important in the success of reference interactions (although to a lesser degree than users)."[15]

Radford used qualitative methods including the critical incident technique to identify interpersonal aspects that functioned as facilitators (such as positive attitude, relationship quality, and approachability) and barriers (such as negative attitude, poor relationship quality, and lack of approachability) to successful reference interactions.[16]

Radford also studied nonverbal approachability at two academic libraries, one university and one predominately undergraduate college, observing 155 library users in their reference desk interactions with 34 librarians and interviewing users on how they made their decision as to which librarian to approach.[17] Applying the theoretical framework of Mehrabian's immediacy behaviors (such as eye contact, forward lean, movement towards)[18] in a qualitative analysis of the users' responses revealed five categories employed by users in their decision-making process. In order of frequency, the five categories were:

1. **Initiation.** Users felt that the librarian chose them by using eye contact or other immediacy behaviors including a vocal component such as "May I help you?"
2. **Availability.** Users felt that the librarian was available for an encounter, again through observation of immediacy behaviors.
3. **Proximity.** Users chose the librarian they perceived to be physically closest, although observation revealed that the

librarian chosen was not always actually the closest.

4. **Familiarity.** Users chose a librarian they were already acquainted with through a previous interaction or library use instruction.

5. **Gender.** Several users chose a female librarian over a male librarian.

Additionally, Radford identified positive and negative approachability behaviors. Eye contact was the most often mentioned positive nonverbal behavior in the user's decision to approach.

Jacoby and O'Brien employed a variation of the critical incident technique in studying how undergraduate students perceived reference services and staff, utilizing paper and e-mail surveys administered as soon as possible after the reference interaction was finished, with a random selection of participants undergoing a follow-up interview.[19] Findings showed that reference assistance can help students become more confident and more independent in their information-seeking strategies. Friendliness of reference personnel was one of the "best predictors of students' confidence in their ability to find information on their own."[20] Jacoby and O'Brien also found that "When undergraduates perceive the staff to be approachable, they have crossed the first barrier to getting whatever assistance they might need. A friendly and approachable staff helps ensure that students will ask for help when they need it."[21] The majority of those surveyed by Jacoby and O'Brien learned something new regarding specific resources, new ways to approach their search for information, or new reference resources or facilities during their reference interactions: "This suggests that the reference interaction in college and university libraries can be an effective means of teaching students not only about specific library resources, but also about the process of finding, evaluating, and using information."[22] They conclude:

> Reference services clearly can play a significant role in helping students become confident, independent information seekers. Considerable attention has been given to this aspect of library services in the vast literature on information literacy, but the present study findings suggest that the reference interaction is also an important locus for producing lifelong learners able to navigate a complex information environment.[23]

The FtF environment has continued to offer challenges to reference librarians. Research, such as the studies featured above, has helped to inform practice in academic libraries. The interpersonal interaction between users and librarians is a complex process. Virtual environments have added another layer to that complexity, as demonstrated in the research described in the following section.

Librarians and Users in VRS Encounters

The swiftly changing landscape of reference services has been dominated by the impact of new technologies. Many academic libraries led the field in rolling out new virtual reference (VR) initiatives at an unprecedented rate during the late 1990s and early 2000s. In 1999, Goetsch reported that 96% of large academic research libraries had already adopted e-mail digital reference,[24] and a study by Janes, Carter, and Memmott of 150 academic libraries found that 68 (45%) offered e-mail VRS, but none yet offered chat.[25] White reported in 2000 that 63 (45%) of 140 masters' comprehensive level academic libraries were observed to have adopted some form of VRS, increasing to 76% in a subsequent study published in 2006.[26] In 2001, Cardina and Wicks conducted a survey of 68 academic librarians, in which 43 (63%) reported plans for changes to reference services in the near future, with many reporting innovative changes that had already occurred.[27] De Groote, Dorsch, Collard, and Scherrer asserted in 2005 that "over the past several years, digital reference has become an integral part of the services offered by academic libraries."[28] By 2006, Dee and Allen observed among 116 academic health science libraries that 21 (18%) offered chat services and 100 (86%) offered e-mail services.[29] By 2007, almost without exception, academic libraries offered some form of VR, with many providing a range of choices (including chat, e-mail, and IM).[30]

E-Mail Reference Services

In the mid-1990s, VRS research explored e-mail, including Abels, who published research in 1996 on an e-mail question-answering service provided by LIS graduate students for clients including students and faculty at the University of Maryland and from other universities and libraries.[31] Five different styles of e-mail reference interview emerged: piecemeal (asking questions as they occurred to the intermediary), feedback (providing preliminary search results with questions), bombardment (sending a long series of questions in a single e-mail), assumption (acting on the request as initially stated), and systematic (creating a structured form with questions). The systematic approach was found to be the most effective.

Other researchers who looked at e-mail reference services included Carter and Janes, and Ryan, who studied the Internet Public Library (IPL, http://ipl.org), a virtual library founded at the University of Michigan (later moved to Drexel University in 2007), which offers free e-mail reference.[32] Carter and Janes analyzed 3,022 transcripts of e-mail reference interactions received during 1999. A Perl script was written to extract data from the transcripts based on actions logged in the transcript, such as assignment of the subject of the question by the administrator, assignment of the question to a librarian, and thanks sent back by the user. Automatic time and date stamping of each action in the transcripts also allowed tracking of data such as elapsed time to answer. The technique of automatic analysis not only provided data on the question-answering speed by reference librarians, such as an average time to answer of 2.26 days (median 1.07 days), but also tracked reference administrators' processing and triaging of questions, such as responding with a standard Frequently Asked Reference Question (FARQ) answer (9.8% of responses). Ryan studied 254 IPL transcripts of e-mail questions received during 1995, especially focusing on the questions not answered. Many unanswered questions were in the subject areas of business and government, some were vague, some asked about obscure historical figures, while others were extremely specific and technical. This analysis of failures by subject identified areas of weakness that could then be addressed to improve performance.

Many researchers have examined the types of questions asked and patterns of user access to academic library e-mail services. Duff and Johnson evaluated 361 e-mail reference transcripts received from users by 11 archives (including university archives).[33] Questions were coded as administrative/directional, fact-finding, material-finding, specific form, known item, service request, consultation, and user education, as well as for the described information need (coded as "wanted") and the user's knowledge about the need (coded as "given"). The largest groups of questions by type were reported to be service requests (27%) and material-finding (17%), and the major "wanteds" were biographical information, general information, and particular forms that the user needed to fill out.

In 1996, Bushallow-Wilbur, DeVinney, and Whitcomb evaluated 485 e-mail reference transcripts from the State University of New York at Buffalo libraries, noting a 32% rate of returning users in their sample (56 users).[34] They found that 70% of users' e-mail questions ($n = 338$) were considered "reference," and the other 30% consisted of book renewals, borrowing request questions, and requests for book holds. A study of IPL e-mail users at the University of Michigan reported that users had difficulty characterizing their question topic.[35] When given a drop-down list of subjects, 28.8% of users selected the question topic "other/misc" and another 26.3% had no selected subject. The highest subject category chosen by users was "education" at 6.5%.

Diamond and Pease coded types of questions in 450 e-mail transcripts from California State University at Chico.[36] Eleven question categories generated in the analysis included catalog lookup and use, connectivity questions, database mechanics, questions answered using standard reference resources (factual ready reference), specific factual but not ready reference, starting points for term papers and assignments, library policies/procedures and collection scope, information literacy, non-library questions/referrals and non-questions. The top categories were: questions answered using standard reference resources (97 questions), starting points for term papers and assignments (76 questions), factual but not ready reference (54 questions), and catalog lookup and use (49 questions). In a similar in-depth study of question types for e-mail reference in an academic health sciences library environment, Powell and Bradigan found that questions most often related to assignments (22%), holdings information (19%), library services and policies (15%), and consumer health (15%).[37]

Researchers also examined the impact of culture on users and librarians in e-mail reference interactions in academic libraries.[38] In studies published in 2007, Shachaf, Meho, and Hara studied 146 e-mail reference transcripts from three university libraries in Israel, Japan, and Lebanon. They observed culturally influenced differences in both librarian and user behavior, such as a higher incidence of collaborative work in answering reference questions among the Japanese librarians and a lower number of subject-search requests by Japanese users. In a content analysis study of 94 e-mail transactions at a university library, half from African American students and half from Caucasian students, Shachaf and Snyder observed that the African American students asked more questions on follow-up in second and third messages to librarians than the Caucasian students did. These interesting results suggest that additional research needs to be done on cross-cultural information-seeking preferences in virtual environments.

Live Chat Reference—Transcript Analysis

Live chat VRS emerged in the late 1990s as a synchronous "real-time" alternative to e-mail reference. Adoption of chat reference had started slowly, but picked up speed as consortial arrangements among academic and public libraries have proliferated.[39] As academic libraries began offering chat services, researchers examined its impact on the reference interaction between librarians and users. Unlike traditional FtF reference, live chat produces an artifact—an exact transcript that can be used by researchers willing to take on the rewarding, but time-consuming and arguably daunting, task of analyzing these rich documents. Transcript analysis has some drawbacks (e.g., personal or demographic information is unavailable or deleted from transcripts for privacy concerns), but as can be seen in the following examples, it provides an unobtrusive data collection method for analysis of reference questions (such as question types, topics, or accuracy determinations) and revealing aspects of interpersonal communication processes.

Radford applied communication theory to an exploration of relational (socioemotional, interpersonal) aspects of live chat reference, reporting results from two studies.[40] The first was a pilot study that analyzed 44 transcripts nominated for the Green Award given twice a year by Library Systems and Services, LLC (LSSI) in honor of Samuel S. Green, a pioneer in advocating excellent service to users. Radford followed the pilot study with an analysis of 245 transcripts from the Maryland AskUsNow! statewide chat reference service. Results revealed that interpersonal skills important to FtF reference success are present (although modified) in VRS. These included techniques for rapport building, compensation for lack of nonverbal cues, strategies for relationship development, evidence of deference and respect, face-saving tactics, as well as greeting and closing rituals.

Interpersonal dynamics present in the VRS environment were identified, as well as differences in client versus librarian patterns. One difference revealed in the transcript analysis was that clients displayed more deference (e.g., showed respect or agreed to follow suggestions) to librarians, as might be expected. Another difference was that interpersonal barriers created by clients (e.g., rudeness, impatience) were, for the most part, very different from those created by librarians (e.g., negative closure). A rich array of strategies for re-representing nonverbal cues was discovered, with clients showing more informality and willingness to use chat shortcuts, abbreviations, and emoticons. Some mirroring of informality on the librarians' part included the use of emoticons, use of the ellipsis to indicate "more to come," and integration of some shortcuts and abbreviations (such as "info"). This work emphasized the need for librarians to develop strategies for cultivating excellent interpersonal relationships with users in digital environments that mirrors that of FtF reference encounters. Radford included her classification schemes as appendices.

Radford further analyzed the Maryland AskUsNow! transcripts to identify the behaviors of rude and/or impatient users.[41] She found a low number of difficult interactions, with evidence of impatience (e.g. client typing "hurry up!") in 24 (10%) of the 245 transcripts. Poor attitude, rudeness, FLAMING, or insults were only found in 10 (4%) of the transcripts. Radford believed that librarians, in addition to answering questions, were teaching clients how to use VRS and what behaviors were expected. One implication to consider is that the success of VRS may be contingent upon building positive relationships with all clients. If positive relationships are not formed at early, impressionable ages, clients may increasingly turn elsewhere (such as free Web sites) to meet their information needs. To assist practitioners in their encounters with rude or impatient chat clients, research-based guidelines were presented for VRS librarians.[42]

In a related thread of research, Westbrook analyzed 402 chat transcripts at an academic library, using politeness theory to discover techniques used by the librarians and users to raise or lower the formality level in interactions. Techniques observed included brevity through use of abbreviations and informality through self-disclosure, humor, apologies, and self-deprecation. Westbrook emphasizes the relationship between librarian and user as an important aspect of the interaction.[43]

Librarians' perceptions of chat were studied by Ozkaramanli through a qualitative methodology using the critical incident technique. She interviewed 40 academic librarians from 10 libraries in Ohio and Pennsylvania that offered chat reference. Librarians were asked to identify successful and unsuccessful chat interactions and to suggest improvements for these services. A list of chat reference evaluative criteria was generated from analysis of their critical incidents. She found that the librarians perceived successful interactions to be depending primarily on users' positive attitudes and skills.[44]

Ellis explored the extent to which chat interactions at Baruch College's library reflected teaching of the Association of College and Research Library's (ACRL) Information Literacy Competency Standards by analyzing 138 chat transcripts from 2001.[45] Ellis found that standards 1 and 2 (determining information needed and accessing information) were taught most often in the chat interactions, while the other three standards (evaluating information; using information effectively; and understanding economic, legal, and social issues surrounding information) were rarely or never taught.

In the spring of 2001, Kibbee, Ward, and Ma assessed 611 chat transactions at the University of Illinois-Urbana Champaign Library (UIUC).[46] They also explored questions of who uses the service by user-identified status, finding that the majority of users (71.2%) were locally affiliated students. In a 2006 study by Kibbee of unaffiliated users at UIUC, e-mail was observed to be used in asking questions by 61% of unaffiliated users as compared to 39% choosing chat/IM.[47]

Researchers at Carnegie Mellon University analyzed 425 chat transcripts from 2000 to 2001. Marsteller and Mizzy categorized questions from users as directional/policy/procedure, known item, facts/ready reference, reference, or technical problem; they include their classification scheme as an appendix.[48] Librarian responses were categorized as no question, closed question, and open question, and user responses as favorable, unfavorable, or not applicable. In 37% of the interactions, no question was asked by the librarian ($n = 155$); 46% ($n = 197$) of the interactions included a closed question; 17% ($n = 73$) included an open question. Directional/policy questions were the largest category ($n = 141$, 34%), followed by known item ($n = 120$, 28%), and by the ready reference and reference categories, which were equal in size (both $n = 82$, 19%).

As can be seen from the above research, transcript analysis is a fruitful approach to better understanding user behaviors and identifying their information-seeking needs, as well as suggesting areas for training and improving service quality.

Comparison of Different Reference Environments

As reference has moved rapidly to encompass new online communication modes, research has sought to explore the relationship between reference services in various online and FtF environments. Differences and similarities between traditional reference desk questions and questions asked in VRS environments were studied by De Groote at the Library of the Health Sciences reference desk at the University of Illinois at Chicago.[49] She analyzed statistics compiled from July 1997 to June 2003. All groups of library users (graduate students, undergraduates, faculty, staff, and unaffiliated users) were found to use the traditional reference desk to ask questions the majority of the time. Interestingly, she also reports that 35% of the undergraduates said that they use chat reference most often, 34% of the graduate students chose e-mail reference most often, while 35% of faculty/staff chose phone reference most often. Types of questions (ready reference, holdings, etc.) were found to be the same regardless of the venue.[50]

In her doctoral dissertation, Ford compares FtF and VRS interactions (e-mail and live chat) at an academic library.[51] She used unobtrusive methods to analyze how the types of questions asked by users varied in the different media, examining 125 e-mail, 111 chat, and 114 FtF reference interactions. She found that FtF users asked more questions than VRS users, but found similarities in the types of substantive questions asked. She found that the proportions of research, factual, or other types of questions did not vary across the different venues. However, she did find differences in librarian behavior. Librarians asked more questions in the FtF environment than in VRS and were more likely to use print resources and less likely to use online sources. Although fewer words were exchanged, the VRS interactions took more time than FtF encounters and had a more balanced librarian-to-user ratio of words. FtF exchanges were found to be richer in interpersonal aspects, and recommendations included urging librarians to be more creative in adapting their strategies to assist users in VRS settings.

In another dissertation that compared VRS formats in a university library, Mon conducted telephone and in-person interviews with 22 chat and 11 e-mail users, including undergraduates, master's students, doctoral students, staff, faculty, and members of the general public, and also analyzed their chat and e-mail transcripts to explore factors influencing users' perceptions of digital reference services.[52] She found that users positively mentioned librarian behaviors noted in the American Library Association's Reference and User's Service Association (RUSA) recommended behavioral guidelines for information professionals, such as restating users' questions and inviting users to return.[53] Users also referred negatively to impersonal and automated responses such as FAQ and "cut and paste" answers and spoke positively about personalized answers, such as librarians addressing users by name and sharing with users their own names and e-mail addresses.[54] Issues in how users responded to reference evaluation questions were also noted, such as answers that were *"used* but not *useful"* as well as answers that users perceived as complete but which did not solve their problems.[55] Redundancy, in which librarians repeated searches users had already done and presented the duplicate results in answers, was reported by 11 users, with six users describing their answers as entirely redundant.[56] Mon's research pointed to the need to better understand how users interpret and respond to standard digital reference assessment questions.

Nilsen compared users' perspectives of in-person reference and VR through analysis of written accounts and questionnaires completed by University of Western Ontario (UWO) MLIS graduate students on 261 in-person reference interactions (including 79 in academic libraries, 182 in public libraries, and 85 chat and e-mail reference interactions).[57] She found that reference interviews were conducted in 51% of the in-person reference interactions and 20% of the VR interactions, with interviewing least observed in e-mail interactions (10% of 60 e-mails).

De Groote and others report the results of a study of collaborative digital reference at the University of Illinois at Chicago completed in 2004.[58] They found that having one centralized service, even given the complexity of a large university, is feasible and that "having one contact point relieves the burden of choice for library users looking for real-time and expedient assistance and places the decision with the librarian, who is best equipped to triage the request to the most appropriate person."[59] The authors also analyzed who used the service, the types of questions asked, and the librarians' subject expertise. They found that

> The majority of questions were submitted by persons affiliated with the university, that ready reference and directional questions

predominated, and that the librarians were able to successfully share the duty of answering the general reference questions while ensuring that the questions requiring subject expertise were answered by the appropriate subject specialists.[60]

De Groote and others include their "Virtual Reference Coding System," which specifies coding categories and definitions as a model for other universities wishing to replicate their study.[61]

Beyond chat and e-mail, a variety of different types of services have been explored by academic libraries, including MOOs (Multi-user Object Oriented environment in 1995–2001 at the Internet Public Library (IPL) at the University of Michigan and in 1997 at the University of Arkansas at Little Rock.[62]

IM has emerged as a new venue for VRS services among academic libraries. Steiner and Long explored academic librarians' attitudes toward IM with a Web-based survey of 302 librarians at 226 institutions, finding that 80% of the librarians had used IM, with 42% of them having engaged in IM with library users.[63] They also note that in 48 of the 57 libraries offering IM services in the sample, the service had started with the efforts of one individual librarian at the institution.

Ruppel and Fagan compared user perceptions of the physical reference desk with VR using IM software at Southern Illinois University.[64] They found that users were extremely positive about the IM service. Of the users surveyed, 23% said that they preferred IM because they did not want to get up from the computer, suggesting that many users of VRS are present in the library building.[65] It was further observed that 64% of conversations originated from within the library building, while 35% came from outside the library, but on a campus network such as a dormitory or computer lab.

Academic libraries continue to explore new technology in reference services, with cell phone text messaging (SMS) as one of the most recent variants to be adapted. Southeastern Louisiana University's library added text messaging to its reference service options, finding, in a study completed in 2006, that out of 1,447 digital reference requests, 954 were received via chat, 410 via e-mail, and 83 via text messaging.[66] Questions asked by users via text messaging were observed to differ from phone, e-mail, and chat in being geared toward short answers, as one might expect.

Reference Satisfaction and Success

A large body of research exists on studies of user satisfaction, reference accuracy, and quality assessment. In 1995, the American Library Association published *The Reference Assessment Manual* (RAM), which offers a large number of instruments for conducting reference evaluation.[67] Hults also provides an overview of reference evaluation, especially highlighting studies that used unobtrusive testing methods, building on the work of Childers and Crowley, who first reported that reference staff correctly answered about 50% to 55% of the questions posed.[68] Another monograph of interest is by Hernon and Dugan, *An Action Plan for Outcomes Assessment in Your Library*, which discusses experimental design and the research process, with a focus in chapter 9 on "Service Quality and Satisfaction."[69]

Novotny also provides an overview of methods of assessment for reference, including virtual environments, surveys, usability studies, case studies, cost-benefit analysis, focus groups, individual interviews, observation studies, surveys, and Web log analysis.[70] He raises the issue of equity in comparing quality of services to VRS users to those offered to FtF reference desk users. Sandstrom and Sandstrom describe the use of ethnographic research methods in library and information science (LIS), including systematic direct observation, unstructured and semi-structured interviewing, mapping, questionnaires, surveys, network analysis, and other techniques.[71] Also featured is a section on "methodological issues in studies of reference service performance," which discusses qualitative and quantitative research design on the process of asking and answering reference questions. Richardson advocates a systems approach to analysis of the reference interaction, noting that this differs from a process-oriented approach: "systems analysis encourages one to identify explicitly the system's users, goals, and requirements in contrast to process."[72] He recommends the following measures of long-term user satisfaction: "Two appropriate tests would be whether the inquirer says yes to 'Was the answer useful?' one or two weeks later, and perhaps most important, whether he or she returns with another question."[73]

Many researchers sought to ascertain the failure or success of reference encounters through assessing aspects such as librarian and/or user perceptions of the completeness of answers, accuracy of answers, levels of satisfaction, and expressed willingness to return. An earlier survey by Van House, Weil, and McClure used a seven-item survey to measure satisfaction with reference services, which used a five-point Likert-type scale for ratings of relevance of information provided, amount of information provided, completeness of answer, helpfulness of staff, and overall satisfaction, and also included two questions on demographic affiliation with the university and planned use of the information.[74] A nine-item survey to measure satisfaction with intermediated online searching was also provided, which included ratings for searcher's understanding, thoroughness of search, relevance of information, amount of information, currency of information, time taken, and overall satisfaction, and also included two questions on demographic affiliation with the university and planned use of the information.

Throughout a series of often cited articles exploring user perceptions of librarian behaviors in the reference interaction, Dewdney and Ross used unobtrusive/participant observation techniques in which 77 MLIS students at UWO asked questions that mattered to them personally in a library of their choice, filled out questionnaires rating their experiences, produced a detailed step-by-step account, and summarized aspects they found most and least helpful.[75] Of the students, 52 out of 76 (68.4%) visited public libraries while 24 out of 76 (31.6%) went to academic libraries; in one case, the type of library visited was not reported. The students filled out a brief questionnaire that used a seven-point scale to rate staff as friendly or pleasant, how well the staff member understood the question, the helpfulness of the answer provided, their satisfaction with the overall experience, and their willingness to return. Satisfaction levels were relatively low for the total of 128 questions asked, with 45 (35%) rated at low levels of satisfaction, 29 (23%) rated at medium satisfaction and 54 (42%) rated at high satisfaction. (Low was a score of 3 or less on the 7-point scale; 4–5 was medium, and 6–7 was high). When asked how willing they were to return to the same staff member who had provided reference assistance, 46 (60%) of the 77 students said they were willing to return, 21 (27%) said they would not return, and another 10 (13%) were unsure. A significant difference between users' willingness to return and all other variables was found, supporting Durrance's view of willingness to return as a global outcome measure.[76]

Using similar methods with MLIS graduate students again at UWO, Ross and Nilsen examined the question "Has the Internet changed anything in reference?"[77] Willingness to return was again used as a success measure, with 50 (74%) of the academic library users responding yes. In 50 academic library visits, 28 (56%) were found to include a reference interview, 32 (64%) users were given an unmonitored referral, and 38 (76%) users were given a follow-up question or invitation to return for more help (e.g., "Are you finding what you are looking for?") Use of electronic sources or Internet sources was also examined, and 21 (42%) of the academic library responses included electronic sources such as the Internet ($n = 8$) or other databases/electronic sources ($n = 13$).

Comparisons between the perceptions of librarians and users emerged in a study with 10 librarians in public libraries, in which Michell and Dewdney conducted 33 librarian-user interviews to examine how librarians and users perceived the level of difficulty of reference questions.[78] They used a five-point rating scale from *extremely difficult* to *extremely easy*. Perhaps not surprisingly, they found a significant difference in the perceptions of users and librarians, with users tending to believe their questions were easier than librarians believed them to be. The study raises the possibility of using a mental models approach to analyzing users' and librarians' perceptions of reference questions and services.

Reference Accuracy Research

Elzy and others conducted a study of reference accuracy in which 20 undergraduate students asked questions of 19 librarians at Illinois State University's Milner Library using a pool of 58 preselected questions, resulting in 190 reference interactions.[79] Students filled out forms after the interactions including details of the answer, and researchers scored answers for completeness and correctness. Fifteen points were given for "student provided with complete and correct answer," with fewer points given for other outcomes such as "student led to a single source which provided a complete and correct answer" (14 points), "student led to several sources, one of which provided a complete and correct answer" (13 points), and other lower-scored variations, such as being directed to a source or sources, being given appropriate or inappropriate referrals, and being given inappropriate sources or incorrect answers. Students also rated librarian helpfulness and approachability. No relationship was found between answer quality and time spent with the student, and a complete and correct answer did not predict students' positive perceptions of how they were treated by the librarian, although librarians who spent more time with students tended to be viewed more positively. The authors include their scoring method in the article.

Stacy-Bates unobtrusively evaluated accuracy in e-mail question answering at 111 members of the Association of Research Libraries (ARL).[80] For each of the 98 libraries that accepted questions from nonaffiliates, the same three e-mail questions were sent during 2001, with responses received from 96 libraries, with the majority of answers received within one day. Among the 98 libraries, 74 (76%) responded to all three questions. Accuracy rates ranged from 99% to 65%. Evaluation of the reference services and responses was completed using a set of 21 questions listed within the article.

At UIUC, Ward conducted an unobtrusive study exploring answer completeness in which five proxies asked a total of 72 chat questions during 2003, including specific format requests such as "two books," "two scholarly journal articles," or "one book and one scholarly journal article."[81] Proxies recorded the date, start and end times of the interaction, and numbers and types of sources provided, and completed a five-question evaluation of the librarian's actions, followed by a rating of the completeness of the librarian's answer. Of the answers to the 72 questions, 47% ($n = 34$) were rated "complete" and 32% ($n = 23$) were "mostly complete." Chats averaged 15 minutes in length, but the less complete chats tended to be longer. The authors suggested using "complete answer fill rate" as an assessment measure and included the evaluation instrument.

Accuracy in live chat reference was investigated by Arnold and Kaske through analysis of 351 live chat transcripts (comprising 419 questions) at the University of Maryland (UM).[82] They found a high level of accuracy, with correct answers at 92%. The most frequently asked types of questions were found to be policy and procedural (41%), specific search (20%), holdings / do you own (16%), and ready reference (14%). Questions were asked by students (41%), outsiders (25%), other UM individuals (22%), unidentified (6%), staff (3%), and faculty (2%). No significant differences were found between user types and proportion of different types of questions. "From reading the comments made by customers about this chat service, one advantage stands out—it saves them time and that is a big reason they use the service."[83] White, Abels, and Kaske also conducted a pilot study that evaluated quality in live chat reference (both university and public library services) through unobtrusive methods and similarly found a high level of accuracy.[84]

In an interesting comparative study, both public and academic librarians rated the completeness and correctness of academic librarians' consortial chat reference answers lower than answers provided by public librarians, possibly due to a greater tendency among the academic librarians to give sources rather than directed answers in promoting student research efforts.[85]

User Satisfaction

Kwon analyzed 420 chat reference transcripts and user questionnaires and tracked user satisfaction by investigating occasions when a librarian "refers" a user without checking the validity of the redirection.[86] Results indicated that unmonitored referrals constituted approximately 30% of the total transactions, with user satisfaction (perhaps not unexpectedly) significantly lower when compared to satisfaction for completed transactions. Kwon demonstrated that "generic reference questions, such as simple factual and subject-based research questions, are more effectively answered than locality-specific questions."[87] Kwon also found that "patrons did not value referrals to a great extent;" suggesting that librarians should thus not "regard all referrals as equally good alternatives to completed answers."[88]

As noted above, data on user satisfaction with IM reference was collected by Ruppel and Fagan at Southern Illinois University's library from 2001 to 2002 via two surveys.[89] At the end of an IM interaction, a short survey was administered with questions such as, "Were the answer(s) you received helpful?" and "Is Online Reference (chat) a good way to get help?" A longer survey of 15 questions was also administered in paper format to a library instruction class, with questions such as, "What features would you add to this service? (List some)." Researchers analyzed 340 short survey responses and 52 long-form survey responses, finding that 82% of short survey respondents rated the IM chat service as a "very" good method of getting help and described answers as "very" helpful. Among long-form responses to a question on adding new service features, the most frequent request was for "more hours of service" (16 of 51 responses); another 11 of 51 recommended "more staff on at the same time."

Issues of completeness and willingness to return were examined in a survey (also briefly discussed above) of 130 users of chat reference at UIUC by Kibbee, Ward, and Ma, who found that 74% of questions were completely answered. Of respondents, 84.5% were definitely willing to return, and 63.6% found that the service was very welcoming. The researchers observed that 33.2% of chat questions asked were for finding specific library materials; 30.5% were about the library and services; 20.2% were about subject research; 9.1% were ready reference; 5.3% were technical problems; and 1.7% were about the chat service.[90]

Mon and Janes used content analysis in examining a sample of 810 e-mail transcripts from 2002 in the IPL at the University of Michigan. They identified 558 e-mail interactions for which users had spontaneously sent thank-you messages to librarians at the conclusion of e-mail interactions, and 252 "non-thanked" interactions. This research explored whether user thank-you messages might be useful in VRS assessment.[91] They found that users tended to send fewer thank-you responses when answered with Frequently Asked Questions (FAQ) type prewritten standard answers. Users also tended to respond quickly with their thank-you messages, with over 75% of the "thanking" users responding by the day after the answer was sent, raising questions as to whether users had fully evaluated the librarians' answers before sending back a thank-you response.

User satisfaction with e-mail reference was also explored by Vande-Creek through surveys of 167 users of the Northern Illinois University Library's service.[92] Users were asked about reason for using the service, promptness of the response, helpfulness of the response, rating of the service *(Excellent, Good, Only Fair, Poor)*, adequacy of 48-hour response time, and suggestions for improvement. Results indicate that 91% received the needed information, and 75% rated the response *Very Helpful*. In addition, 65% rated the 48-hour response time as adequate, and about one-third of the users wanted a faster e-mail response. This finding raises the important issue of urgency of information need in users' service evaluations.

Nilsen reports on 42 UWO MLIS students' perceptions of VRS encounters in academic as well as public library services.[93] She found that relational (interpersonal) factors are important to the clients and concluded that "simply answering user queries is not enough. User satisfaction with reference services depends on consistent use of best reference behavior."[94]

Reference Service Assessment

In addition to studies that have explored user and librarian perceptions and behaviors, researchers have also tackled a variety of other issues, including the cost of reference interactions and the efficiency of a range of staffing models. Abels, Kantor, and Saracevic compared the cost of providing different types of reference services at five academic libraries.[95] They included traditional FtF reference desk service and reference consultation services in which appointments are made for in-depth assistance, with cost per interaction found to be $1.16 for traditional reference service as compared to $18.80 for a reference consultation. They provided methods for applying functional cost analysis to analyze information services. Coffman and Saxton also examined staffing and suggested ways to improve efficiency and reduce costs.[96] The authors found that use of a call-center model could reduce staff costs by 42% and that paraprofessionals could be used more effectively.

Whitlatch explored librarian and user judgments of service value in five academic libraries with 62 participating librarians, who distributed questionnaires to users upon every fifth question asked at the reference desk.[97] Librarians completed a separate questionnaire, and 257 paired surveys were completed. Variables studied included librarian perceptions of service value, user perceptions of service value, user report of success or failure, client socialization, task-related knowledge, service orientation, librarian job satisfaction/motivation, time constraints, feedback, and type of assistance. Factor analysis was used to determine concepts within these measures, and stepwise regression was used in comparing relationships between dependent and independent variables. Influences on service outcomes that emerged in the analysis were knowledge, social skills/feedback, and constraints (e.g., time, resources, and system).

One research thread has explored how libraries are setting policies about the provision of VRS. Janes, Carter, and Memmott used unobtrusive observation of Web sites of a sample of 150 academic libraries to determine the proportion providing VRS and found that 67 (44.7%) offered e-mail reference services in 1999.[98] Only 18 of the 67 libraries did not have posted policies regarding services, and typical policy areas were limiting the service to specific users, kinds of questions answered or not answered, and turnaround time.[99] Kern and Gillie conducted a survey on the policies of 135 VRS, including those offered by academic libraries, public libraries, and consortia.[100] They report that 118 (87%) of these services had VRS policies that could be accessed via the Web. These policies related to "user restrictions, question restrictions, privacy, and user behavior."[101] Academic libraries were found to be the most restrictive of user affiliation and the least likely to communicate VRS policy to their users. Kern and Gillie recommend, "Where virtual policies differ from in-person policies, the reasons should be clear to the staff and the users. The virtual reference policy should make sense within the institution and relate to broader reference policies."[102]

McClure and Lankes present an overview of assessing VR quality. In addition, Lankes, Gross, and McClure review the development of standards to support VRS.[103] McClure and Lankes define a quality standard as "a specific statement of the desired or expected level of performance that should be provided regarding a service or some aspect of that service."[104] McClure and Lankes propose six quality standards for VRS: (1) courtesy, (2) accuracy, (3) satisfaction, (4) repeat users, (5) awareness, and (6) cost. McClure and Lankes also include a table of utilization standards for each performance measure. Kasowitz, Bennett, and Lankes provide quality standards for VR consortia with notes on observed practice and suggested future goals toward which services should strive in improving quality.[105] The standards were based on discussion among experts and VRS representatives. An example was the suggested turnaround time for answering questions, with observed practice of answering 50% or fewer e-mail questions in two to five days, and a goal of answering 100% of "in-scope" questions within two business days. Twelve "facets of quality" are identified, including authoritative, accessible, fast turnaround of response, private, consistent with good reference practice, clear in user expectations, and specifics of observed practice. Recommended goals are given for each area.

Another framework is offered by White for analyzing and evaluating VRS, with questions in 18 categories grouped into four broad areas: purpose of the service, structure and responsibilities to the client, core functions, and quality control.[106] The framework was tested in a comparative analysis of 20 VRS. Questions examine characteristics such as the policies and practices of the service and the presence of publicly available answered question archives.

Bertot provides a detailed list of quality statistics and performance measures for networked libraries, including reference-related performance measures such as number of VR transactions, total reference activity, and the percentage of total reference questions that were VR.[107]

Both qualitative and quantitative methodologies were identified, and this framework was developed through research that included public and academic libraries. Whitlatch also discusses evaluation techniques such as surveys and questionnaires, observation, individual interviews, focus group interviews, and case studies.[108] She concludes that "case studies that focus on evaluating experimental digital reference services and employ a variety of research methods may have the greatest promise to enhance our knowledge."[109] Whitlatch additionally points to the issue of low response rates as having been a very serious problem with surveys given via the Web. Low response concerns are raised by other researchers as well, including Hyde and Tucker-Raymond, who note a 20% response rate to their Web-based user satisfaction surveys.[110]

LibQUAL+, in which disconfirmation of expectations is used to explore user perceptions of the quality of libraries and library services, has been developed as a major initiative for assessing service quality by the ARL libraries. As applied to reference services, the "Gaps Model" was designed to reflect the disparity between users' expectations of service as compared to their perceptions of the service as actually delivered. Researchers such as Hernon and Nitecki[111] and Cook and Heath[112] provide quantitative and qualitative discussions of LibQUAL+ as applied to assessment in academic libraries. In this era of tight fiscal situations, the academic library community has sought to encourage assessment as a basis for decision making in the development and provision of services.

Another standardized instrument, Wisconsin-Ohio Reference Evaluation Program (WOREP), was used by the Pennsylvania State University Libraries. In 2005, Paster, Fescemyer, and Henry reported on a project at the Life Sciences Library that used the WOREP instrument; 102 paired users and librarians completed surveys on the success of their reference interaction.[113] The study found users and librarians agreed on the success of the interaction 60% of the time, with the two most common problems reported by users as "Too much information found" and "Staff only partly, or not at all, knowledgeable." Novotny and Rimland reported on two additional studies at Pennsylvania State University that again used WOREP, this time in the George and Sherry Middlemas Arts and Humanities Library. They note:

> An important feature of the WOREP is that it not only records user satisfaction, but it also gathers data on aspects of the encoun-

ter that may contribute to the success (or failure) of the reference interaction. Users report on factors such as the quantity of information provided, the amount of attention they received, and the perceived knowledge of the staff member assisting them.[114]

In addition, library staff also reported on factors including depth of the collection on the topic and level of desk activity. These data helped to "identify specific environmental and behavioral factors that influence patron outcomes."[115] Results indicated that service improvements were needed, so a training program was developed to address areas of concern. A follow-up study revealed that significant improvements were made in increasing satisfaction for users. The WOREP provided user feedback that allowed the staff to focus training efforts to improve performance and was recommended for use by academic libraries desiring to make similar service assessment and to have a research-based focus for training.

Reference Problems and Failures

As seen above, while much attention in academic libraries has focused on successes and best practices, assessment projects have also studied problems, failures, and "worst practices." Olszak conducted interviews and observations in an academic library with librarians, paraprofessionals, and student assistants and used Bosk's categories of mistakes[116] to identify commonly observed reference errors as consisting of *technical errors,* in which skills fall short of what the task requires; *judgment errors,* in which the service provider chooses an incorrect strategy; *normative errors,* in which the norms of the profession are violated; and *quasi-normative errors,* which are idiosyncratic individual mistakes not necessarily associated with a professional group.[117] Olszak concludes:

> Although the reference staff wants to provide correct answers to patrons' questions, they also have the competing goals of instructing patrons on how to be self-sufficient and of limiting the time that they spend with any single patron. Often these goals conflict. Consequently, the desire to provide a correct answer may not be the most important goal the reference staff has for every reference transaction.[118]

One study by Ross and Dewdney, of 100 MLIS students at UWO, focused on the impact of librarian behaviors for ending reference encounters. They identified 10 negative closure strategies used by librarians to end interactions without answering the user's question and 11 counterstrategies of users to keep reference interactions from ending prematurely. Ross and Dewdney employed unobtrusive/participant observation techniques, in which students asked questions in libraries and completed questionnaires evaluating user experience of the reference interaction.[119] Incidents of "negative closure" in the reports were categorized to identify problematic reference staff behaviors such as giving unmonitored referrals, claiming the information is not in the library, and going off to find a document and never returning. Olszak's, as well as Ross and Dewdney's, work suggested the possibility of utilizing research findings on service mistakes and "worst practices" to identify reference education and training needs.

Despite efforts to provide clear and effective reference help, verbal communication was seen as frequently ambiguous, which can result in problematic situations. In a study of reference encounters in academic, public, and special libraries, Dewdney and Michell found that most "communication accidents" resulted from misunderstandings or miscommunications of key words in the users' description of the information need. Their typology of errors included "no harm done" accidents, such as user communications not being heard, resolved by the librarian asking the user to repeat the information; "unrecognized" errors of interpretation, such as soundalikes misheard by the librarian or mispronounced by the user ("volume nine"/"value line," "whales"/"Wales"); "secondhand communication," in which the user relays previously misheard information ("oranges and peaches"/"On the Origin of Species"); and "creative reconstruction" errors, in which the user incorrectly recalls words but correctly expresses the meaning ("animal graveyard" for "pet cemetery").[120]

Dewdney and Michell's theme of "secondhand communication" exemplified problems resulting from what Gross has termed the "imposed query." Gross pointes out that traditional reference models assume that all inquiries originate with the questioner, which fails to take into account questions asked on behalf of other people.[121] Gross suggests the need to consider imposed queries when considering variables such as library use per capita, since the person asking an imposed query is not the person who will finally use the information. In a study of 1,107 FtF reference interactions in public libraries, fully 25% of observed questions were being asked on behalf of someone else, such as children, family members, friends, and employers.[122] Imposers may include populations who never or rarely visit the library, e.g., homebound, institutionalized, elderly, illiterate, non-English-speaking, or academic faculty who send graduate assistants to ask questions. Gross also considered queries related to academic coursework to be imposed, since they were initiated by faculty assignments, not by students.

Another study had a similar finding: that cultural differences and language barriers for non-native English speakers can also result in lack of success for academic library users. At San Jose State University, Liu and Redfern examined the attitudes and information-seeking behaviors of multicultural students.[123] The population they studied was 50.7% "minority," including Hispanics, Asians, African Americans, and Pacific Islanders. They found that success level for these students depended upon the students' English proficiency as well as their frequency of library use. Further, they found that those who were unsuccessful seldom asked reference questions and avoided the reference desk. They kept away from the librarians because of lack of knowledge of available services or the role of the reference librarian. These students may have never thought of asking a reference question or were afraid. Their fears centered on worries of asking stupid questions, of their English not being good enough to formulate their query, and fear that they would not be able to understand the librarian's answer.[124]

These findings resonate with the often cited Swope and Katzer article that found academic users are frequently afraid to admit that they do not know something.[125] FtF communication in reference encounters can frequently be seen as daunting for some users. VRS reference is a bit less threatening than the FtF venue, but comes with a different set of problems.[126] Some of these issues surface in the research presented in the next section.

Technical Problems and Viability of Live Chat

By its very nature, success in VR interactions hinge on whether or not the technology works properly, especially in live chat, where connectivity, slow response time, difficulty co-browsing, and dropped chats have become concerns. At Murdoch and Macquarie Universities in Australia,

Lee used both qualitative and quantitative elements in analyzing 47 e-mail and 47 chat interactions in Voice over Internet Protocol (VoIP) in Microsoft NetMeeting and found that establishing a working connection was a problem for 34% of users, who could not connect to the service.[127] Stoffel and Tucker made a similar finding of technical issues, including premature and mysterious session endings, at Milner Library at Illinois State University in the reports of one in three respondents to a chat survey.[128] Technical problems were found in 278 (32%) of 865 chat transcripts collected from 2000 to 2001 at Carnegie Mellon University by Marsteller and Mizzy.[129] Additionally, Lupien found at the University of Guelph that many technical problems, including issues with browser or hardware incompatibilities, pop-up blockers, firewalls, and software upgrades, could impact chat reference services.[130] Stormont provides an overview of technical challenges in VR, noting that complex features are problematic and that co-browsing is "withering" because it was a good idea that was "never fully realized" and that "librarians seem to want … more than patrons. Our patrons gravitate to the more simple interfaces of IM."[131] All these authors raise questions regarding the extent to which technology serves not only as a facilitator, but also as a barrier for users seeking access to remote reference services.

In some cases, academic libraries have launched a VRS that has ultimately failed and been discontinued. Steiner and Long surveyed 302 academic librarians and found that the main reason described for canceling use of commercial chat software was dissatisfaction with "clunky" or "complicated" software, followed by other issues such as financial expense, lack of users, and difficulties with staffing.[132]

Steiner and Long's findings resonate with those of Radford and Kern, who used the multiple case study method to investigate the reasons why nine public, academic, and consortial chat reference services were discontinued.[133] Through structured e-mail and phone interviews with decision makers and analysis of available reports, they found that the major reason for discontinuation was funding problems, followed by low volume. Other reasons for the VRS chat services being closed were staffing problems, technical problems, and clashes in institutional culture (for consortia). Staffing issues included the need for comfortable staffing patterns, maintenance of sufficient volume to maintain proficiency, and cultivation of positive attitudes. Technical problems centered on software malfunctions and connectivity difficulties. Within two of the consortia, different patterns of funding, staffing, and mission posed difficulties for blended cultures that caused the consortia to break up. The researchers included recommendations for libraries planning to start live chat services or to form VRS consortia.

One question that has been raised by researchers has to do with the need for, and feasibility of, synchronous reference services, such as chat and IM, which place a high demand on staffing. Lankes and Shostack polled users of AskERIC regarding whether asynchronous e-mail services were satisfactorily timely for their needs, finding that 95% felt the service was timely and 97% would recommend the service to others.[134]

Researchers at Washington State University surveyed their students to understand low usage of the academic library's chat service, finding that about three quarters of the students did not know the chat service existed; when asked to rank preferred modes for reference services, chat ranked as the least favored. Users also indicated preferred times for accessing chat that were at times when the library was closed, such as evenings and early mornings.[135]

In a two-part series, Coffman and Arret discuss research findings from Janes's Census of Digital Reference study, which found that in a three-day sample of question answering in 2003 by 162 libraries (including 80 academic libraries), 8,106 total questions were answered, of which 5,657 were chat questions; the median numbers of questions answered were 16 in the three-day period, fewer than six per day.[136] Coffman and Arret raise the question of whether chat reference had achieved usage levels sufficient to warrant costs of staffing and of service provision and maintenance.[137]

Education of Reference Librarians

As can be seen above, the complex nature of today's reference landscape, along with its technological challenges, makes research in LIS education ever more critical to the continuing success and sustainability of reference services of all types. Librarians providing VR assistance must learn technical skills in addition to mastering reference techniques.

Dewdney tested the effect of skills training on reference performance by assigning 24 librarians randomly to three groups. One group of eight was trained in "microskills" such as using encouragers, e.g., "uh huh"; another group of eight was trained in neutral questioning techniques; the final group was the control group, which received no training.[138] Prior to the training, 166 reference interviews were recorded; after librarians completed their training, 851 reference interactions were recorded and compared.

> Librarians trained in neutral questioning … demonstrated in-
> creased levels of skill in avoiding premature diagnosis, asking
> open questions, both in comparison with their own pretraining
> levels and in comparison with the posttraining levels of librarians
> from the control group. Librarians trained in microskills showed
> significant increases in the use of open questions, but not, surpris-
> ingly, in the use of other skills.[139]

This research indicated that interpersonal communication skills can be taught, even to those perhaps not previously user-centered in their orientation.

In 2002, Kawakami and Swartz assessed chat librarians at UCLA Library, using a 36-item competencies checklist, observing problems such as librarians accidentally toggling off the "escort" button and finding that only 16 of 22 librarians knew how to "push" a Web page to the user.[140] At California State University at Chico, a 2001 e-mail study by Diamond and Pease analyzing 450 e-mail transcripts recommended that librarians use a nine-point checklist in responding to e-mail questions to ensure that the answer contains all the proper elements, such as a restatement of the question, specific URLs and call numbers, and an invitation to follow up with more questions.[141]

Westbrook provides a synthesis of current practice and recommendations for training librarians in the second decade of providing VRS.[142] She discusses four "overarching guidelines and essential training principles" for VRS librarians in the stages of the reference interview. Her approach is interdisciplinary, recommending the incorporation of the latest research from fields such as psychology, education, communication, and computer-mediated communication. Additional researchers who address issues in training for VRS include Abels and Ruffner, along with Harris.[143]

Inventing the Future—New Models for Reference Services

In seeking creative solutions to managing limited resources while enhancing or expanding online services, academic librarians have reinvented reference with multi-institution consortial reference service arrangements and innovative hybrids, such as the Dr. Martin Luther King Jr. Library, a joint-use facility run by both San Jose State University Library and the San Jose Public Library.[144] Conaway describes a study by Childers in which 32 San Jose academic and public librarians were paired in reference service shadowing to better understand similarities and differences prior to implementing a merged academic/public library service environment. Results of a follow-up survey found perceptions among the academic librarians that public library interactions were largely similar to academic libraries and that there already was overlap noted among some user groups using both the academic and public libraries.[145] After assessment and planning efforts, the merged King Library opened in August 2003.

Another emerging model in the academic libraries is that of the "information commons," in which the library combines with the campus computer center to provide a space in which students have access to technology, reference and help desk assistance, and collaborative work spaces. The information commons concept suggests a new paradigm for libraries as not only planning to accommodate the efforts of individual researchers *seeking* information, but also the work involved in *using* the information through provision of computer spaces and collaborative working and learning areas. Beagle provides a handbook that focuses on the information commons concept of shared space between libraries and computing centers.[146] Elmborg and Hook feature a collection of case studies on collaborations between writing centers and academic libraries, with issues of shared spaces for tutors and collaborative teaching and learning projects.[147] In an individual case study, Dallis and Walters describe the implementation of an information commons at Indiana University Library. They report impacts on reference services such as reductions in technical and computer questions fielded by librarians and an anecdotal perception by librarians of increased complexity of research questions posed by the students.[148] Franks and Tosko discuss the planning process for implementing a learning commons at University of Akron's library.[149]

The arrangement of spaces within libraries to support collaborations has also been suggested as an important area of research. In an academic library in New England in Fall 2005, researchers observed usage patterns of 1,937 library users and conducted interviews with 403 users. They found that 71% of the library users were in groups, with 63% of those engaged in collaborations, including 24% who were studying together and 39% who were working on group projects. The study emphasized the importance of library spaces supporting collaborative work and shared learning in addition to support for the individual academic library user.[150]

Cottrell and Eisenberg used an unobtrusive observation method that consisted of having librarians at a state university document 293 reference desk interactions over the course of two semesters.[151] They applied the Big6 problem-solving framework, an information and technology literacy model and curriculum (see http://www.big6.com/), to analyze the stages at which students asked questions. Major findings were, "(1) location and access activities were observed in many encounters; (2) synthesis activities (Stage 5) were observed in very few encounters; and (3) in many encounters, only one stage of the model was observed."[152] Cottrell and Eisenberg concluded that the lack of questions at the synthesis stage is due to the lack of working tools in the reference area for synthesis efforts: "workstations in the reference area do not support application software such as word processing, database management, spreadsheet, or graphics packages ... students often use such tools during synthesis."[153] The information commons model was suggested as an alternative reference area design.

Other innovative models, such as removing the reference desk or initiating roving reference, have challenged the traditional design of services by using technologies such as portable notebook computers, personal digital assistants (PDAs), and wireless communication devices. These devices allow librarians to walk away from reference desks and bring services to users in the library stacks and at computer terminals. Roving reference services have been implemented in Texas A&M University and Harvard College libraries.[154]

Academic libraries have been experimenting with moving out of the library building as well as away from the reference desk. One pilot project offered a satellite reference location at the information desk in a student union building during the busiest part of the spring semester of 2002 at Rutgers University. An Outpost Service Team was formed to explore the demand for reference services outside of the library. Statistics, such as number of students served and types of questions asked, were collected. In addition, paper surveys were distributed to students and faculty at the outpost, asking them to evaluate the satellite and to describe their library needs. Findings revealed that the outpost was a good public relations move as it drew the attention of students and faculty and also presented an opportunity to promote awareness and use of library services. The librarians were also able to engage with students in a less formal setting to learn more about their information needs and preferences.[155]

Consortia and collaborative reference efforts have further changed the landscape of reference services. Curtis and Mann surveyed seven consortia with cooperative reference agreements, finding e-mail to be the most common means of communication among consortium members.[156] Collaborative models have similarly leveraged new technologies in providing reference services. Pomerantz discusses the emergence of collaborative models for reference services, including the Stumpers discussion list, the Internet Public Library, and chat or e-mail consortia for providing VRS.[157]

One challenge to consortial reference arrangements is the difficulty in answering queries requiring locally based information. In an analysis of 577 randomly selected live chat transcripts from the QuestionPoint service, Radford and Connaway found that questions about holdings or local procedures answered by the consortium rather than by the local chat service took the longest to answer (16.6 minutes per session [$n = 25$], compared to a mean of 12.42 minutes for the entire transcript sample [$n = 577$]).[158] Kwon reports that in a collaborative chat reference service, "local questions were less completely answered compared to non-local, generic questions" and "patrons who ask local questions tend to be less satisfied with the service than the patrons who ask non-local, generic questions."[159] As more local information can be retrieved on Web sites, this problem may lessen in impact, especially for academic libraries that are now regularly posting local information (such as hours of operation) and providing remote access to their online catalogs.

An innovative approach that may eventually help to solve the local information dilemma, as well as to reduce staff time, was increasing standardization and automating of services through FAQs (Frequently Asked Questions) or "knowledge bases" of collected answers mined from chat and e-mail reference transcripts. Nicholson and Lankes surveyed 49 organizations (with more than half of the responses from academic libraries) in order to establish which types of data were currently collected or that institutions might be willing to collect and created an "archival schema for digital reference" that could be used in constructing a "data warehouse" for VR interactions.[160]

Another important new model for reference services leveraged student interest in social networking sites (SNS), such as MySpace or Facebook, or in 3-D worlds such as Second Life. The need to overcome the resistance of experienced librarians who may not be familiar with the potential for these new reference initiatives was revealed in a study by Charnigo and Barnett-Ellis, who surveyed 126 academic librarians regarding their perceptions and attitudes toward Facebook, including attitudes about utilizing it as a means for providing information to users. They found that, while 114 of the 126 librarians surveyed were aware of Facebook, 54% did not feel that Facebook served any academic purpose.[161]

Although published research in academic initiatives in using SNS for reference has been scarce because of its recent appearance in the reference repertoire, articles are appearing that provide an overview of Web 2.0 and the growing importance of service initiatives in this area. For example, in a 2006 publication, Maness suggests that future directions for the incorporation of Web 2.0 technologies into library services include synchronous online reference services, streaming media, blogs, wikis, and use of social networking sites.[162] Similarly, Bolan, Canada, and Cullen describe particularly important Web 2.0 services for young adults, with additional inclusion of photo-sharing services, gaming, and podcasting.[163]

Beyond Web 2.0 enterprises, Web 3.0 library applications have already surfaced in the literature. In 2006, Pope and others of the Alliance Library System in Illinois, a consortium of 259 libraries, launched an exploration of "Library 3D," or what has sometimes also been referred to as "Library 3.0," in establishing library and reference services within the virtual world Second Life. In 2007, Second Life Library volunteer librarians handled 6,769 reference queries from avatars within the virtual world.[164]

One extraordinary research project was undertaken by the University of Rochester to discover the technologies that are most popular for today's university students and to recommend changes that academic libraries can adopt in order to leverage these emerging applications. The university hired an anthropologist to study the behaviors and information-seeking preferences of members of the "Net Gen." These findings were published in a monograph by Gibbons, who concludes that academic libraries are risk-averse and are having trouble keeping up with the fast pace and flux of Web 2.0 developments. She recommends that libraries adopt a research and development (R&D) mind-set:

In an academic library setting, an R&D culture takes the form of continually evaluating, examining, and assessing your services, resources, and staffing to ensure that they meet the teaching, learning, and research needs of your academic institution.[165]

If academic libraries are to survive and flourish in this technological landscape through more intense research, as Gibbons suggests, and if they are to develop reference approaches that embrace merging and emerging technologies, what might a relevant research agenda encompass?

Forecasting the Reference Research Agenda

The earlier part of this chapter reveals an already rich array of ongoing research in reference services using an assortment of quantitative, qualitative, and combined methods. However, several authors have, along with Gibbons, embraced the idea of a more pervasive research culture, especially highlighting an urgency to learn more about reference realities and possibilities in virtual environments.[166] Ruppel and Fagan note that there is a lack of qualitative study and recommended that there be more analysis of chat reference conversations.[167] Kwon has recommended increased research in VRS referrals.[168] Arnold and Kaske believe that there should be further research on the percent of correct answers and exploration of user expectations.[169] They also want research to answer the question of whether "library customers think about the advantages and limitations of different communication modes before selecting one through which to have their questions addressed."[170]

Lankes describes a detailed research agenda for VR that encompasses conceptual "lenses" of policy (including training), systems, evaluation (including assessment and standards), and behavior of users and librarians within a mapping of research questions in a research agenda matrix.[171]

Another extensive research agenda has been proposed by Pomerantz, especially designed for chat-based VR and urging development of an overarching theoretical framework that is conceived as a process model. He details important focal points for chat reference research, including the individual's choice and use of chat, queuing behavior, the reference transaction (including query negotiation and opening questions), and the archiving of the transaction (including privacy issues).[172]

One shortcoming in reference research was revealed by Saxton, who performed a meta-analysis of reference service evaluation, reviewing 59 research studies that identified 162 different variables.[173] He found that only 12 variables could be compared across studies. Saxton points to the need for studies that go beyond reports from individual locations, including more broad-based or longitudinal studies that can be generalized. These works document the well-established trend towards a user-centered paradigm of research and a culture of continuous assessment. A more recent overview of the evaluation of reference services was completed by Kuruppu in 2007.[174]

Trends That Will Impact Future Reference Service and Research

A number of trends have surfaced that hold a good deal of potential for having an impact on the future of reference and evolving research directions. Some of these include:

- **Distance education.** Growing numbers of online distance education programs in colleges and universities have accelerated academic reference expansion beyond the FtF reference desk to provide services to users who pay tuition but cannot visit the library in person.
- **Technological innovation.** Continuing change in information and communication technologies have brought academic libraries into new areas from chat and e-mail to IM, cell phone text messaging, social networking (including Facebook and MySpace), and virtual worlds.
- **Cell phones and other handheld devices.** As has been said, "What's old is new again"—given that these devices have become ubiquitous, especially with younger students, telephone reference service, particularly text messaging (SMS), will definitely be an important trend for the future, and perhaps VoIP as well.
- **E-book digitization.** Massive book digitization projects are growing in number and are sure to prompt additional need for online reference assistance.
- **Complexity of information landscape.** The complexity and sophistication of the present and future information landscape continue to grow, which will lead more users to seek and to value the expert help that reference librarians can provide.

- **Assessment culture.** Assessment initiatives at academic libraries will prompt increased attention to student learning outcomes and to figuring out how to measure reference success, how to accurately count reference encounters, and how to use limited staff and budget resources effectively.
- **Portable wireless services.** Faster, smaller, more powerful portable (wearable?) computers will free the reference librarian from being tied to the physical reference desk. More kiosk-type reference and satellite reference points will be made available.
- **Greater collaboration and increased consortial involvement.** Diminishing budgets for human resources coupled with the rise in the number of VRS modes will drive this already growing trend. Software will enable more difficult questions to be routed easily and transparently to subject experts who will enjoy the challenge and opportunity to use their specialized skills.

There is no doubt that reference research in academic libraries will intensify as technological innovations enable development of numerous new venues for reaching users both within the library and from remote locations. Virtual formats will continue changing and growing in importance, while traditional reference work will also endure and evolve in ways that are yet to be imagined. Research, such as that reported above, will be highly significant in reaffirming practice and in suggesting new insights and approaches for informed practitioners and evidence-based planning.

References

1. Chuck Koutnik, "The World Wide Web Is Here: Is the End of Printed Reference Sources Near?" *Reference Quarterly* 36, no. 3 (1997): 422–425.
2. Jana Ronan and Carol Turner, *Chat Reference* (Washington, DC: Association of Research Libraries, 2002); Martha Kyrillidou and Mark Young, comps., *ARL Statistics, 2004–05,* (Washington, DC: Association of Research Libraries, 2006), http://www.arl.org/bm~doc/arlstat05.pdf (accessed February 7, 2008); Carol A. Tenopir and Lisa Ennis, "Reference Services in the New Millennium," *Online* 25, no. 4 (2001): 40–45; Carol A. Tenopir and Lisa Ennis, "A Decade of Digital Reference, 1991–2001," *Reference and User Services Quarterly* 41, no. 3 (2002): 265–273.
3. Diane Zabel, "A Reference Renaissance," *Reference and User Services Quarterly* 47, no. 2 (2007): 108–110.
4. Jeffrey Pomerantz and others, "The Current State of Digital Reference: Validation of a General Digital Reference Model through a Survey of Digital

Reference Services," *Information Processing and Management* 40, no. 2 (2004): 347–363.

5. Susan Gibbons, *The Academic Library and the Net Gen Student: Making the Connections,* (Chicago: American Library Association, 2007).

6. Carol Tenopir, "The Impact of Digital Reference on Librarians and Library Users," *Online* 22, no. 6 (1998): 84–88.

7. JoAnn Jacoby and Nancy P. O'Brien, "Assessing the Impact of Reference Services Provided to Undergraduate Students," *College and Research Libraries* 66, no. 4 (2005): 324.

8. Sandra L. De Groote, Josephine L. Dorsch, and Scott Collard, "Quantifying Cooperation: Collaborative Digital Reference Service in the Large Academic Library," *College and Research Libraries* 66, no. 5 (2005): 436.

9. See Kay A. Cassell and Uma Hiremath, *Reference and Information Services in the 21st Century: An Introduction* (New York: Neal-Schuman, 2006); Robert E. Bopp and Linda C. Smith, *Reference and Information Services: An Introduction,* 3rd ed. (Englewood, CO: Libraries Unlimited, 2001); William A. Katz, *Introduction to Reference Work,* 8th ed. (New York: McGraw-Hill, 2002).

10. See Marie L. Radford, *The Reference Encounter: Interpersonal Communication in the Academic Library* (Chicago: Association of College and Research Libraries, 1999); Catherine Sheldrick Ross, Kirsti Nilsen, and Patricia Dewdney, *Conducting the Reference Interview: A How-to-Do-It Manual for Librarians* (New York: Neal-Schumann, 2002); Catherine Sheldrick Ross and Patricia Dewdney, *Communicating Professionally: A How-to-Do-It Manual for Library Applications,* 2nd ed. (New York: Neal-Schumann, 1998); Elaine Zaremba Jennerich and Edward J. Jennerich, *Reference Interview as a Creative Art* (Englewood, CO: Libraries Unlimited, 1997).

11. Buff Hirko, *Virtual Reference Training* (Chicago: American Library Association, 2004); Joseph Janes, *Introduction to Reference Work in the Digital Age* (New York, Neal-Schuman, 2003); R. David Lankes and others, eds., *The Virtual Reference Experience: Integrating Theory into Practice* (New York: Neal-Schuman, 2004); R. David Lankes and others, eds., *The Virtual Reference Desk: Creating a Reference Future* (New York: Neal-Schuman, 2006); R. David Lankes and others, eds., *Virtual Reference Service: From Competencies to Assessment* (New York: Neal- Schuman, 2008); Anne G. Lipow, *The Virtual Reference Librarian's Handbook* (New York: Neal-Schuman, 2003).

12. John V. Richardson, "The Current State of Research on Reference Transactions," in *Advances in Librarianship,* vol. 26, ed. Fredreck Lynden (San Diego: Academic Press, 2002).

13. Radford, *Reference Encounter.*

14. Marie L. Radford, "Relational Aspects of Reference Interactions: A Qualitative Investigation of the Perceptions of Users and Librarians in the Academic Library," Ph.D. diss., Rutgers University, 1993; Paul Watzlawick, Janet Beavin, and Don D. Jackson, *Pragmatics of Human Communication* (New York: Norton,

1967).

15. Radford, *Reference Encounter,* 104.

16. On the critical incident technique, see J. C. Flanagan, "The Critical Incident Technique," *Psychological Bulletin* 51, no. 4 (1954): 327–358; Marie L. Radford, "Communication Theory Applied to the Reference Encounter: An Analysis of Critical Incidents," *Library Quarterly* 66, no. 2 (1996):123–137. For additional information about the application of the critical incident technique in studying library services and programs, see Marie L. Radford, "Encountering Virtual Users: A Qualitative Investigation of Interpersonal Communication in Chat Reference," *Journal of the American Society for Information Science and Technology* 57, no. 8 (2006): 1046–1059; Charlotte Ford, "An Exploratory Study of the Differences between Face-to-Face and Computer-Mediated Reference Interaction," Ph.D. diss., Indiana University, 2003.

17. Marie L. Radford, "Approach or Avoidance? The Role of Nonverbal Communication in the Academic Library User's Decision to Initiate a Reference Encounter," *Library Trends* 46, no. 4 (1998): 699–717.

18. Albert Mehrabian, *Silent Messages* (Belmont, CA: Wadsworth, 1971).

19. Jacoby and O'Brien, "Accessing the Impact."

20. Ibid., 324.

21. Ibid., 326. See also Marie L. Radford, "Approach or Avoidance?"

22. Jacoby and O'Brien, "Accessing the Impact," 335.

23. Ibid.

24. Lori A. Goetsch, *Electronic Reference Service* (Washington, DC: Association of Research Libraries, 1999).

25. Joseph W. Janes, David Carter, and Patricia Memmott, "Digital Reference Services in Academic Libraries," *Reference and User Services Quarterly* 39, no. 2 (1999): 145–150.

26. Marilyn Domas White, "Diffusion of an Innovation: Digital Reference Service in Carnegie Foundation Master's (Comprehensive) Academic Institution Libraries," *Journal of Academic Librarianship* 27, no. 3 (2001): 173–187; Marilyn Domas White, "Conclusion: Looking to the Future," in *The Virtual Reference Desk: Creating a Reference Future,* ed. R. David Lankes and others, 203–208 (New York: Neal-Schuman, 2006), 203.

27. Christen Cardina and Donald Wicks, "The Changing Roles of Academic Reference Librarians over a Ten-Year Period," *Reference and User Services Quarterly* 44, no. 2 (2004): 133–142.

28. De Groote and others, "Quantifying Cooperation," 436.

29. Cheryl Dee and Maryellen Allen, "A Survey of the Usability of Digital Reference Services on Academic Health Science Library Web Sites," *Journal of Academic Librarianship* 32, no. 1 (2006): 69–78.

30. De Groote and others, "Quantifying Cooperation."

31. Eileen G. Abels, "The E-Mail Reference Interview," *Reference Quarterly* 35,

no. 3 (1996): 345–358.

32. David S. Carter and Joseph W. Janes, "Unobtrusive Data Analysis of Digital Reference Questions and Service at the Internet Public Library: An Exploratory Study," *Library Trends* 49, no.2 (2000): 251–265; Sara Ryan, "Reference Service for the Internet Community: A Case Study of the Internet Public Library Reference Division," *Library and Information Science Research* 18, no. 3 (1996): 241–259.

33. Wendy M. Duff and Catherine A. Johnson, "A Virtual Expression of Need: An Analysis of E-Mail Reference Questions," *American Archivist* 64, no. 1 (2001): 43–60.

34. Lara Bushallow-Wilbur, Gemma S. DeVinney, and Fritz Whitcomb. "Electronic Mail Reference Service: A Study," *Reference Quarterly* 35, no. 3 (1996): 359–371.

35. Carter and Janes, "Unobtrusive Data Analysis," 255.

36. Wendy Diamond and Barbara Pease, "Digital Reference: A Case Study of Question Types in an Academic Library," *Reference Services Review* 29, no. 3 (2001): 210–218.

37. Carol A. Powell and Pamela S. Bradigan, "E-Mail Reference Services: Characteristics and Effects on Overall Reference Services at an Academic Health Services Library," *Reference and User Services Quarterly* 41, no. 2 (2001): 170–178.

38. Pnina Shachaf, Lokman I. Meho, and Noriko Hara, "Cross-Cultural Analysis of E-Mail Reference," *Journal of Academic Librarianship* 33, no. 2 (2007): 243–253; Pnina Shachaf and Mary Snyder, "The Relationship between Cultural Diversity and User Needs in Virtual Reference Services," *Journal of Academic Librarianship* 33, no. 3 (2007): 361–367.

39. Bernie Sloan, "Twenty Years of Virtual Reference," *Internet Reference Services Quarterly* 11, no. 2 (2006): 91–95.

40. Radford, "Encountering Virtual Users."

41. Marie L. Radford, "Interpersonal Communication in Chat Reference: Encounters with Rude and Impatient Users," in *The Virtual Reference Desk: Creating a Reference Future,* ed. R. David Lankes and others, 23–46 (New York: Neal-Schuman, 2006).

42. See also Marie L. Radford and Joseph Thompson, "Yo Dude! Y R U Typin So Slow? Interpersonal Communication in Chat Reference Encounters" (paper presented at 6th annual Virtual Reference Desk conference, Cincinnati, OH, November 8–9, 2004), online proceedings at http://www.webjunction. org/do/DisplayContent;jsessionid=2F065F4145C99626F5134FE3194A762 0?id=12499 (accessed July 14, 2008).

43. Lynn Westbrook, "Chat Reference Communication Patterns and Implications: Applying Politeness Theory," *Journal of Documentation* 63, no. 5 (2007): 638–658.

44. Eylem Ozkaramanli, "Librarian's Perceptions of Quality Digital Reference

Services by Means of Critical Incidents," Ph.D. diss., University of Pittsburgh, 2005, 79, 86–89.

45. Lisa Ellis, "Approaches to Teaching through Digital Reference," *Reference Services Review* 32, no. 2 (2004): 103–119.

46. Jo Kibbee, David Ward, and Wei Ma, "Virtual Service, Real Data: Results of a Pilot Study," *Reference Services Review* 30, no. 2 (2002): 25–36.

47. Jo Kibbee, "Librarians without Borders? Virtual Reference Service to Unaffiliated Users," *Journal of Academic Librarianship* 32, no. 5 (2006): 467–473.

48. Matthew R. Marsteller and Danianne Mizzy, "Exploring the Synchronous Digital Reference Interaction for Query Types, Question Negotiation, and Patron Response," *Internet Reference Services Quarterly* 8, no. 1/2 (2003): 149–165.

49. Sandra L. De Groote, "Questions Asked at the Virtual and Physical Health Sciences Reference Desk: How Do They Compare and What Do They Tell Us?" *Medical Reference Services Quarterly* 24, no. 2 (2005): 11–23.

50. See also the review of De Groote's research by Suzanne P. Lewis, "The Majority of Library Clients Still Use Person-to-Person Interaction When Asking Reference Questions," *Evidence Based Library and Information Practice* 1, no. 1 (2006): 92–95.

51. Ford, "Exploratory Study."

52. Lorri Mon, "User Perceptions of Digital Reference Services," Ph.D. diss., University of Washington, 2006.

53. Reference and User Services Association, *Guidelines for Behavioral Performance of Reference and Information Services Providers* (Chicago: Reference and User Services Association, 2004), http://www.ala.org/ala/rusa/protools/referenceguide/guidelinesbehavioral.cfm (accessed July 14,,\ 2008).

54. Mon, "User Perceptions," 140–141.

55. Ibid., 149, 160–161.

56. Ibid., 196.

57. Kirsti Nilsen, "Comparing Users' Perspectives of In-Person and Virtual Reference," *New Library World* 107, no. 3/4 (2006): 91–104.

58. De Groote and others, "Quantifying Cooperation."

59. Ibid., 451.

60. Ibid., 436.

61. Ibid., 453–454.

62. Elizabeth Shaw, "Real-Time Reference in a MOO: Promise and Problems," April 25, 1996, Internet Public Library, http://www.ipl.org/div/iplhist/moo.html (accessed March 31, 2008); Barbara D'Angelo and Barry Maid, "Virtual Classroom, Virtual Library: Library Services for an Online Writing Laboratory," *Reference and User Services Quarterly* 39, no. 3 (2000): 278–283.

63. Sarah K. Steiner and Casey M. Long, "What Are We Afraid Of? A Survey of Librarian Opinions and Misconceptions Regarding Instant Messenger,"

Reference Librarian 47, no. 1 (2007): 31–50.

64. Margie Ruppel and Jody Condit Fagan, "Instant Messaging Reference: Users' Evaluation of Library Chat," *Reference Services Review* 30, no. 3 (2002):183–197.

65. See also similar findings in Marianne Foley, "Instant Messaging Reference in an Academic Library: A Case Study," *College and Research Libraries* 63, no. 1 (2002): 36–45.

66. J. B. Hill, Cherie Madarash Hill, and Dayne Sherman, "Text Messaging in an Academic Library: Integrating SMS into Digital Reference," *Reference Librarian* 47, no. 1 (2007): 17–29.

67. American Library Association, *The Reference Assessment Manual* (Ann Arbor, MI: Pierian Press, 1995). In this volume, Krylladou, Cook, & Rao review LibQUAL research; see also the following for more about assessing reference quality using LibQUAL: Colleen Cook and Fred M. Heath, "Users' Perceptions of Library Service Quality: A LibQUAL+ Qualitative Study," *Library Trends* 49, no. 4 (2001): 548–584; Wanda Dole, "LibQUAL+ and the Small Academic Library," *Performance Measurement and Metrics* 3, no. 2 (2002): 85–95; Peter Hernon and Ellen Altman, *Assessing Service Quality: Satisfying the Expectations of Library Customers* (Chicago: American Library Association, 1998); Peter Hernon and Danuta A. Nitecki, "Service Quality: A Concept Not Fully Explored," *Library Trends* 49, no. 4 (2001): 687–708; Danuta Nitecki and Peter Hernon, "Measuring Service Quality at Yale University's Libraries." *Journal of Academic Librarianship* 26, no. 4 (2000): 259–273.

68. Patricia Hults, "Reference Evaluation: An Overview," in *Assessment and Accountability in Reference Work,* ed. Susan Griswold Blandly, Lynne M. Martin, and Mary L. Strife, 141–150 (New York: Haworth,1992); Terence Crowley and Thomas Childers, *Information Service in Public Libraries: Two Studies* (Metuchen, NJ: Scarecrow Press, 1971).

69. Peter Hernon and Robert E. Dugan, *An Action Plan for Outcomes Assessment in Your Library* (Chicago: American Library Association, 2002).

70. Eric Novotny, *Reference Service Statistics & Assessment: SPEC Kit 268* (Washington, DC: Association of Research Libraries, Office of Leadership and Management Services, 2002).

71. Alan R. Sandstrom and Pamela Effrein Sandstrom, "The Use and Misuse of Anthropological Methods in Library and Information Science Research," *Library Quarterly* 65, no. 2 (1995): 161–199.

72. John V. Richardson, "Understanding the Reference Transaction: A Systems Analysis Perspective," *College and Research Libraries* 26, no. 3 (1999): 212.

73. Ibid., 219.

74. Nancy A. Van House, Beth Weil, and Charles R. McClure, *Measuring Academic Library Performance: A Practical Approach* (Chicago: Association of College and Research Libraries, 1990).

75. Patricia Dewdney and Catherine Sheldrick Ross, "Best Practices: An Analysis

of the Best (and Worst) in Fifty-Two Public Library Reference Transactions," *Public Libraries* 33, no. 5 (1994): 261–266.

76. Joan Durrance, "Reference Success: Does The 55 Percent Rule Tell the Whole Story?" *Library Journal* 114, no. 7 (1989): 31–36.

77. Catherine Sheldrick Ross and Kirsti Nilsen, "Has the Internet Changed Anything in Reference? The Library Visit Study, Phase 2," *Reference and User Services Quarterly* 40, no. 2 (2000): 147–155.

78. Gillian Michell and Patricia Dewdney, "Mental Models Theory: Applications for Library and Information Science," *Journal of Education for Library and Information Science* 39, no. 4 (1998): 275–281.

79. Cheryl Elzy and others, "Evaluating Reference Service in a Large Academic Library," *College and Research Libraries* 52, no. 5 (1991): 454–465.

80. Kristine Stacy-Bates, "E-Mail Reference Responses from Academic ARL Libraries: An Unobtrusive Study," *Reference and User Services Quarterly* 43, no. 1 (2003): 59–70.

81. David Ward, "Measuring the Completeness of Reference Transactions in Online Chats: Results of an Unobtrusive Study," *Reference and User Services Quarterly* 44, no. 1 (2004): 46–56.

82. Julie Arnold and Neal Kaske, "Evaluating the Quality of a Chat Service," *portal: Libraries and the Academy* 5, no. 2 (2005): 177–193.

83. Ibid., 191.

84. Marilyn Domas White, Eileen G. Abels, and Neal Kaske, "Evaluation of Chat Reference Service Quality," *D-Lib Magazine* 9, no. 2 (2003): 1–13.

85. Jeffrey Pomerantz, Lili Luo, and Charles R. McClure, "Peer Review of Chat Reference Transcripts: Approaches and Strategies," *Library and Information Science Research* 28, no. 1 (2006): 24–48.

86. Nahyun Kwon, "User Satisfaction with Referrals at a Collaborative Virtual Reference Service," *Information Research* 11, no. 2 (2006), http://InformationR.net/ir/11-2/paper246.html (accessed March 31, 2008).

87. Ibid., paragraph 50.

88. Ibid.

89. Ruppel and Fagan, "Instant Messaging Reference."

90. Kibbee, Ward, and Ma, "Virtual Service."

91. Lorri Mon and Joseph W. Janes, "The Thank You Study: User Feedback in E-mail 'Thank You' Messages," *Reference and User Services Quarterly* 46, no. 4 (2007): 53–59.

92. Leanne M. VandeCreek, "E-Mail Reference Evaluation Using the Results of a Satisfaction Survey," *Reference Librarian* 45, no. 93 (2006): 99–108.

93. Kirsti Nilsen, "The Library Visit Study: User Experiences at the Virtual Reference Desk," *Information Research* 9, no. 2 (2004), http://informationr.net/ir/9-2/paper171.html (accessed March 31, 2008).

94. Ibid., 16.

95. Eileen G. Abels, Paul B. Kantor, and Tefko Saracevic, "Studying the Cost and Value of Library and Information Services: Applying Functional Cost Analysis to the Library in Transition," *Journal of the American Society for Information Science* 47, no. 3 (1996): 217–227.

96. Steve Coffman and Matthew L. Saxton, "Staffing the Reference Desk in the Largely-Digital Library," *Reference Librarian* 31, no. 66 (1999): 141–163.

97. Jo Bell Whitlatch, "Reference Service Effectiveness," *Reference Quarterly* 30, no. 2 (1990): 205–215.

98. Janes, Carter, and Memmott, "Digital Reference Services in Academic Libraries."

99. Ibid., 148.

100. M. Kathleen Kern and Esther Gillie, "Virtual Reference Policies: An Examination of Current Practice," in *The Virtual Reference Experience*, ed. Joseph Janes, Linda C. Smith, and R. David Lankes, 165–184 (New York: Neal-Schuman, 2004).

101. Ibid., 165.

102. Ibid. 182.

103. Charles R. McClure and R. David Lankes, "Assessing Quality in Digital Reference Services: A Research Prospectus," draft dated January 12, 2001, Information Institute of Syracuse, http://quartz.syr.edu/quality/Overview. htm (accessed March 31, 2008); R. David Lankes, Melissa Gross, and Charles R. McClure, "Cost, Statistics, Measures, and Standards for Digital Reference Services: A Preliminary View," *Library Trends,* 51, no. 3 (2003): 401–413.

104. McClure and Lankes, "Assessing Quality," paragraph 10.

105. Abby Kasowitz, Blythe Bennett, and R. David Lankes, "Quality Standards for Digital Reference Consortia," *Reference and User Services Quarterly* 39, no. 4 (2000): 355–363.

106. Marilyn Domas White, "Digital Reference Services: Framework for Analysis and Evaluation," *Library and Information Science Research* 23, no. 3 (2001): 211–231.

107. John Carlo Bertot, "Measuring Service Quality in the Networked Environment: Approaches and Considerations," *Library Trends* 49, no. 4 (2001): 758–775.

108. Jo Bell Whitlatch, "Evaluating Reference Services in the Electronic Age," *Library Trends* 50, no. 2 (2001): 207–217.

109. Ibid., 215.

110. Loree Hyde and Caleb Tucker-Raymond, "Benchmarking Librarian Performance in Chat Reference," *Reference Librarian* 46, no. 95/96 (2006): 5–19.

111. Hernon and Nitecki, "Service Quality."

112. Cook and Heath, "Users' Perceptions of Library Service Quality."

113. Amy Paster, Kathy Fescemyer, and Nancy Henry, "Assessing Reference Using the Wisconsin-Ohio Reference Evaluation Program in an Academic Science

Library," *Issues in Science and Technology Librarianship,* no. 46 (2006), unp.

114. Eric Novotny and Emily Rimland, "Using the Wisconsin-Ohio Reference Evaluation Program (WOREP) to Improve Training and Reference Services," *Journal of Academic Librarianship* 33, no. 3 (2007): 384.

115. Ibid.

116. Charles L. Bosk, *Forgive and Remember: Managing Medical Failure* (Chicago: University of Chicago Press, 1979).

117. Lydia Olszak, "Mistakes and Failures at the Reference Desk," *Reference Quarterly* 31, no. 1 (1991): 39–49.

118. Ibid., 48.

119. Catherine Sheldrick Ross and Patricia Dewdney, "Negative Closure: Strategies and Counter-Strategies in the Reference Transaction," *Reference and User Services Quarterly* 38, no. 2 (1998): 151–163.

120. Patricia Dewdney and Gillian Michell, "Oranges and Peaches: Understanding Communication Accidents in the Reference Interview," *Reference Quarterly* 35, no. 4 (1996): 520–536.

121. Melissa Gross, "The Imposed Query: Implications for Library Service Evaluation," *Reference and User Services Quarterly* 37, no. 3 (1998): 290–299.

122. Melissa Gross and Matthew L. Saxton, "Who Wants to Know? Imposed Queries in the Public Library," *Public Libraries* 40, no. 3 (2001): 170–176.

123. Mengxiong Liu and Bernice Redfern, "Information-Seeking Behavior of Multicultural Students: A Case Study at San Jose State University," *College and Research Libraries* 58, no. 4 (1997): 348–354.

124. On the fear of asking stupid questions, see also Mary Jane Swope and Jeffrey Katzer, "The Silent Majority: Why Don't They Ask Questions?" *Reference Quarterly* 12, no. 2 (1972): 161–166.

125. Ibid.

126. Marie L. Radford and Lynn Silipigni Connaway, "'Screenagers' and Live Chat Reference: Living Up to the Promise," *Scan* 26, no. 1 (2007): 31–39.

127. Ian J. Lee, "Do Virtual Reference Librarians Dream of Digital Reference Questions?: A Qualitative and Quantitative Analysis of E-Mail and Chat Reference," *Australian Academic and Research Libraries* 35, no. 2 (2004): 95–110.

128. Bruce Stoffel and Toni Tucker, "E-Mail and Chat Reference: Assessing Patron Satisfaction," *Reference Services Review* 32, no. 2 (2004): 120–140.

129. Marsteller and Mizzy, "Exploring the Synchronous Digital Reference Interaction," 156.

130. Pascal Lupien, "Virtual Reference in the Age of Pop-Up Blockers, Firewalls, and Service Pack 2," *Online* 30, no. 4 (2006): 14–19, http://www.infotoday.com/online/jul06/Lupien.shtml (accessed March 31, 2008).

131. Sam Stormont, "Looking to Connect: Technical Challenges That Impede the Growth of Virtual Reference," *Reference and User Services Quarterly* 47, no. 2 (2007): 116.

132. Steiner and Long, "What Are We Afraid Of?"

133. Marie L. Radford and M. Kathleen Kern, "A Multiple-Case Study Investigation of the Discontinuation of Nine Chat Reference Services," *Library and Information Science Research* 28, no. 4 (2006): 24–48.

134. R. David Lankes and Pauline Shostack, "The Necessity of Real Time: Fact and Fiction in Digital Reference Systems," *Reference and User Services Quarterly* 41, no. 4 (2002): 350–355.

135. Joel Cummings, Lara Cummings, and Linda Frederiksen, "User Preferences in Reference Services: Virtual Reference and Academic Libraries," *portal: Libraries and the Academy* 7, no. 1 (2007): 81–96.

136. Joseph W. Janes, "Global Census of Digital Reference" (paper presented at the 5th annual Virtual Reference Desk conference, San Antonio, TX, November 17–18, 2003), online proceedings at http://www.webjunction. org/do/Navigation?category=11844 (accessed March 31, 2008).

137. Steve Coffman and Linda Arret, "To Chat Or Not to Chat—Taking Another Look at Virtual Reference, Part 1," *Searcher* 12, no. 7 (2004), http://www. infotoday.com/searcher/jul04/arret_coffman.shtml; Steve Coffman and Linda Arret, "To Chat or Not to Chat—Taking Yet Another Look at Virtual Reference, Part 2," *Searcher* 12, no. 8 (2004), http://www.infotoday.com/ searcher/sep04/arret_coffman.shtml (accessed March 31, 2008).

138. Patricia Dewdney, "Recording the Reference Interview," in *Qualitative Research in Information Management,* ed. Jack D. Glazier and Ronald R. Powell, 122–150 (Englewood, CO: Libraries Unlimited, 1992).

139. Ibid., 134.

140. Alice Kawakami and Pauline Swartz, "Digital Reference: Training and Assessment for Service Improvement," *Reference Services Review* 31, no. 3 (2003): 227–236.

141. Diamond and Pease, "Digital Reference."

142. Lynn Westbrook, "Virtual Reference Training: The Second Generation," *College and Research Libraries* 67, no. 3 (2006): 249–259.

143. Eileen G. Abels and Malissa Ruffner, "Training for Online Virtual Reference: Measuring Effective Techniques," in *The Virtual Reference Desk: Creating a Reference Future,* ed. R. David Lankes and others, 49–74 (New York: Neal-Schuman, 2006); Lydia Eato Harris, "Software Is Not Enough: Teaching and Training Digital Reference Librarians" in *The Virtual Reference Experience: Integrating Theory into Practice* ed. R. David Lankes and others, 109–120 (New York: Neal-Schuman, 2004).

144. Danianne Mizzy, "Yours, Mine, and Ours: Reinventing Reference At San Jose," *College and Research Libraries News* 66, no. 8 (2005): 598–599.

145. Peggy Conaway, "One Reference Service for Everyone?" *Library Journal* 125, no. 12 (2000): 42–44.

146. James Beagle, *The Information Commons Handbook* (New York: Neal-Schuman,

2006).

147. James K. Elmborg and Sheril Hook, *Centers for Learning: Writing Centers and Libraries in Collaboration* (Chicago: Association of College and Research Libraries, 2005).

148. Diane Dallis and Carolyn Walters, "Reference Services in the Commons Environment," *Reference Services Review* 34, no. 2 (2006): 248–260.

149. Jeffrey A. Franks and Michael P. Tosko, "Reference Librarians Speak for Users: A Learning Commons Concept That Meets the Needs of a Diverse Student Body," *Reference Librarian* 47, no. 1 (2007): 105–118.

150. Howard Silver, "Use of Collaborative Spaces in an Academic Library" (paper presented at Library Research Seminar IV, London, Ontario, October 10–12, 2007), http://lrs4.fims.uwo.ca/abstracts/lrsiv_silver.pdf (accessed February 8, 2008).

151. Janet R. Cottrell and Michael B. Eisenberg, "Applying an Information Problem-Solving Model to Academic Reference Work: Findings and Implications," *College and Research Libraries* 62, no. 4 (2001): 334–346.

152. Ibid., 343–344.

153. Ibid., 344.

154. Michael M. Smith and Barbara A. Pietraszewski, "Enabling the Roving Reference Librarian: Wireless Access with Tablet PCs," *Reference Services Review* 32, no. 3 (2004): 249–255; see also Stephanie Orphan, "News from the Field: Harvard Takes Reference on the Road," *College and Research Libraries News* 64, no. 7 (2003): 441.

155. Triveni Kuchi, Laura Bowering Mullen, and Stephanie Tama-Bartels," Librarians without Borders: Reaching Out to Students at a Campus Center," *Reference and User Services Quarterly* 43, no. 4 (2004): 310–317.

156. Susan Curtis and Barbara Mann, "Cooperative Reference: Is There a Consortium Model?" *Reference and User Services Quarterly* 41, no. 4 (2002): 344–349.

157. Jeffrey Pomerantz, "Collaboration as the Norm in Reference Work," *Reference and User Services Quarterly* 46, no. 1 (2006): 45–55.

158. Marie L. Radford and Lynn Silipigni Connaway, "Reflections of Reference Practice: Analyzing Virtual Reference Transcripts" (paper presented at the Association for Library and Information Science Education Annual Conference, Seattle, WA, January 16–19, 2007), http://www.oclc.org/research/projects/synchronicity/ (accessed March 31, 2008).

159. Nahyun Kwon, "Public Library Patrons' Use of Collaborative Chat Reference Service: The Effectiveness of Question Answering by Question Type," *Library and Information Science Research* 29, no. 1 (2007): 83–84.

160. Scott Nicholson and R. David Lankes, "The Digital Reference Electronic Warehouse Project Creating the Infrastructure for Digital Reference Research through a Multidisciplinary Knowledge Base," *Reference and User Services*

Quarterly 46, no. 3 (2007): 45–59.

161. Laurie Charnigo and Paula Barnett-Ellis, "Checking Out Facebook.com: The Impact of a Digital Trend on Academic Libraries," *Information Technology and Libraries* 26, no. 1 (2007), 23–34.

162. Jack M. Maness, "Library 2.0: The Next Generation of Web-Based Library Services," *LOGOS: Journal of the World Book Community* 17, no. 3 (2006): 139–145.

163. Kimberly Bolan, Meg Canada, and Rob Cullin, "Web, Library, and Teen Services 2.0," *Young Adult Library Services* 5, no. 2 (2007): 40–43.

164. Kitty Pope and others, *Alliance Second Life Library End of Year Report 2007* (Alliance Library System and Alliance Second Life Library, 2007), http://www.alliancelibraries.info/slendofyearreport2007.pdf (accessed March 31, 2008).

165. Gibbons, *Academic Library and the Net Gen Student,* 92.

166. See, for example, Ibid; Kasowitz, Bennett, and Lankes, "Quality Standards"; McClure and Lankes, "Assessing Quality"; Nilsen, "Comparing Users' Perspectives"; Eric Novotny, "Evaluating Electronic Reference Services: Issues, Approaches and Criteria," *Reference Librarian* 35, no. 74 (2001): 103–120; Jana Smith Ronan, "The Reference Interview Online," *Reference and User Services Quarterly* 43, no. 1 (2003): 43–47; Whitlatch, "Evaluating Reference Services."

167. Ruppel and Fagan, "Instant Messaging Reference."

168. Kwon, "User Satisfaction."

169. Arnold and Kaske, "Evaluating the Quality."

170. Ibid., 191.

171. R. David Lankes, "The Digital Reference Research Agenda," *Journal of the American Society for Information Science and Technology* 55, no. 4 (2004): 301–311.

172. Jeffrey Pomerantz, "A Conceptual Framework and Open Research Questions for Chat-Based Reference," *Journal of the American Society for Information Science and Technology* 56, no. 12 (2005): 1288–1302.

173. Matthew L. Saxton, "Reference Service Evaluation and Meta-Analysis: Findings and Methodological Issues," *Library Quarterly* 67, no. 3 (1997): 267–289.

174. Pali U. Kuruppu, "Evaluation of Reference Services—A Review," *Journal of Academic Librarianship* 33, no. 3 (2007): 368–381

Information Literacy

Anita Ondrusek

Why the information literacy movement has gained momentum in academic library circles and the effects of that movement on agendas of higher education are the theme of this essay. Using Kuhn's philosophy on paradigm shifts in scientific thought, an argument is developed showing that the growing acceptance of the information literacy model represents a series of shifts in academic governance. Six case studies highlight specific theories and practices associated with the information literacy model. Resources that will help librarians "retool" for teaching according to information literacy standards are included, and future directions for information literacy research are suggested.

Introduction

The final decade of the 20th century marked a beginning rather than an ending for developments in library-user education. An old name, information literacy, took on a new meaning as librarians began to use it to describe a model for preparing the citizenry of the information age. On a grand scale, information literacy is viewed as part of a modern social dynamic, taking as its central goal the "cultivat[ion] of necessary abilities and skills that ensure the individual's ... continued functioning in society through effective navigation, evaluation, and use of information."[1] Its forerunners date back to the library instruction and bibliographic instruction movements that started in the 1970s. The emergence of the term *information literacy* in the early 1990s was marked by discussions noting the distinctions between a literacy model and an instruction model.

Arp was one of the first librarians to explicate the differences between bibliographic instruction and information literacy. She pointed out that the acceptance of the term *information literacy* had political and philosophical implications. The notion of literacy implies a *standard that must be achieved* and an *expected product* in the form of the literate individual, Arp posited. Bibliographic instruction could be equated with teaching methodology, whereas information literacy implied that librarians could be held responsible for what students learned. To meet that responsibility, Arp felt librarians would have to "support research in information-seeking," teach information access and management skills, and become more versed in assessing the level of information literacy attainment.[2]

In current academic circles, information literacy has become the centerpiece for the continuing discourse on the role that librarians should assume in the educational spheres of instruction, curriculum, and faculty development. Although information literacy is treated as a philosophy by some of its proponents in the library and information science world, practitioners tend to focus on the instructional aspects of information literacy, using terms such as *information literacy skills* or *information literacy instruction* when discussing this topic. Those individuals who have forged the information literacy framework see a bigger picture, in which information literacy "focuses on student empowerment to do independent, self-directed research ... [and] must be learned by students through experiences shaped by librarians and faculty."[3]

A major change brought about by the shift to information literacy's broad-based goals was the articulation of definitions and standards that now form the foundation for the information literacy movement in higher education programs. In 1989, the American Library Association (ALA) Presidential Committee on Information Literacy released its *Final Report*, stressing achievement of information literacy through a new learning model. Information-literate individuals are defined as those who could "recognize when information is needed and have the ability to locate, evaluate and use effectively the needed information."[4] Two years earlier, in 1987, the Association of College and Research Libraries (ACRL) revised its "Model Statement of Objectives for Academic Bibliographic Instruction" into four areas that set the stage for the guidelines released in 2000 entitled *Information Literacy Competency Standards for Higher Education.*[5] The *Standards* associate five main goals with distinct performance indicators and outcomes. By 2002, educators in academe were "seeing a push for information literacy" in areas such as mandates from accrediting agencies.[6]

Among rank-and-file librarians and researchers in the library and information science (LIS) disciplines, there are signs of a collective commitment to information literacy. Professionals from both camps have produced dozens of books and hundreds of journal articles on the subject. On the other hand, a check of the major indexes of the LIS literature reveals that the term itself is not yet a subject heading consistently assigned to those works. In standard LIS encyclopedias, the term *information literacy* was the designated subject of only one article. This type of disconnect may actually be a symptom of change within a profession.

In his examination of scientific revolutions, Kuhn refers to a lack of acknowledgment of a new standard as the "invisibility of revolutions." He laments that the "sources of authority" in a discipline typically "address themselves to an already articulated body of problems, data, and theory ... to which the scientific community is committed."[7] What matters more is that librarians are writing about the concept and treating it as a framework for their teaching. As Kuhn points out, the real change occurs when the collective vision of those with the power to shape policies aligns with the new paradigm.

The Information Literacy Vision

To fulfill the goals of the information literacy vision, teaching librarians must be involved on many fronts. First, the library needs a teaching force composed of librarians who strive to understand learning itself. A familiarity with basic learning theories is a start, but must expand into deeper understandings of how learning differs among whatever audiences the library serves. Librarians with a strong teaching mind-set are apt to form partnerships with an institution's teaching faculty. Such collaborative relationships are essential for implementing an information literacy program. Finally, assessment of learning must be integrated into the program at some juncture, ideally from the beginning of the program. The next sections present insights from librarians and educators who have pondered these tenets as they apply to the information literacy vision.

Learning about Learning

In reviewing library instruction from the 1980s, George credits the work of learning theorists Jerome Bruner and Robert Gagne as being "cited repeatedly."[8] The adoption of information literacy as part of a library's mission has encouraged heightened interest in a much broader spectrum of theoretical approaches to instruction. For example, Grassian and Kaplowitz devote an entire chapter to learning theories in their book on information literacy instruction.[9] The authors cover specific theorists (e.g.,

Piaget, Bruner, Bandura, Ausubel, and Keller), along with summaries of behaviorist theory, the cognitive science movement, and humanist psychology. An additional chapter highlights research on learning styles (e.g., Keefe's categorization of styles and Kolb's experiential learning).[10]

The growing interest in the theoretical underpinnings of learning is also echoed in journal articles. The following (abbreviated) titles exemplify how far-reaching these interests are. "Learning Theories and Library Instruction"[11] is an article that compares Perry's intellectual developmental theories conducted at Harvard to the female-based study at Wellesley. In "Sense-Making in a Database Environment,"[12] the author examines online searching obstacles using Dervin's sense-making theory. "Breaking the Mold"[13] introduced McCarthy's 4MAT System as a library instruction mode. A librarian had her students create their own "Radical Syllabus"[14] using Freire's participatory education approach. An analysis of strategies that boost motivation using Keller's ARCS (Attention, Relevance, Confidence, and Satisfaction) model and Small and Arrone's Motivation Overlay is the focus of "Motivational Aspects of Information Literacy."[15]

Complementing the interest in learning theory among information literacy advocates is a push for learner-centered instruction. The term *active learning* surfaces in many information literacy articles. Grassian and Kaplowitz equate active learning with the use of participatory learning activities (e.g., group discussions, collaborative learning, and learning communities).[16] Gearing instruction to higher-level cognition (e.g., critical thinking and problem solving) is also a theme in the information literacy literature.[17] To achieve these goals, librarians are turning to the instructional design field for guidelines that can be adapted to their purposes.[18]

In 2007, a documented essay by Jackson appeared in the LIS literature; it outlined the nine positions (i.e., markers or stages) of cognitive development that Perry identified in college students. Perry's study and several subsequent studies on this phenomenon found that most first-year college students operate on the lowest two to four positions when carrying out assignments. Very few students ever reach the highest positions. Then Jackson analyzed the ACRL *Standards* for information literacy, looking for matching points between these developmental positions and the performance expectations implicit in the *Standards*. She concluded that the information literacy standards may include many competencies that are beyond the level of the students librarians encounter, especially from classes like freshman composition or basic communication.[19]Among other things, her analysis shows the depth of understanding of student learning that is needed to place information literacy within a realistic context in teaching situations. Her conclusions also raise questions about whether information literacy in a college setting can be premised upon the *Standards* in their current form.

A pilot study that incorporated information literacy skills into a course designed for problem-based learning (PBL) offers an example of what the librarians involved "learned about learning" among one group of first-year students. The endeavor in its entirety is described in a series of four articles published in *portal* in 2004.[20] By reading all the articles, librarians get a sense of the fundamental elements that differentiate PBL from other small-group methods. PBL sessions must be planned out with the teacher, both the librarian and the course instructor must be present to coach students through the process, materials for the activities must be preselected, and questions assigned to students must be uniform and based on solutions that the students in the course are capable of figuring out. Telling or showing students how to reach the solution is not allowed. Taking the students through the process is what the teacher does. On an interesting note, the librarians originally based the PBL session on the ACRL Standard Two (… the student accesses needed information effectively and efficiently). However, the fulfillment of this standard depended upon the students developing a well-articulated search strategy, and this was not achieved by many of the students. The session was refocused on Standard One (… the student determines the nature and extent of the information needed).[21]

Teaching the Net Generation
Librarians who are stepping into the role of instructional architects for information literacy are also discovering another characteristic of the populations they teach—information-seeking behaviors of students are changing. Snavely and Wright cite the findings of the OCLC White Paper on the Information Habits of College Students (http://www5.oclc.org/downloads/community/informationhabits.pdf) and the Pew report from 2000 (http://www.pewinternet.org/report_display.asp?r=39) as evidence that the Internet is influencing young people's study habits in ways not seen before.[22]

The Pew Internet and American Life Project continues to post reports on education on its Web site (http://www.pewinternet.org/PPF/c/10/topics.asp). It is a reliable source for tracking updated findings on the use of the Internet by teenagers. For example, a report entitled *Teens, Technology, and School* is based on a survey conducted in Fall 2004 that collected data in some of the same categories used in the 2000 survey. Comparisons of responses from these two surveys found that from 2000 to 2004, Internet use by youth between the ages of 12 and 17 rose from 73% (2000) to 87% (2004), and Internet use at schools increased by 45%. These reports also probe for perceptions from students on issues relating the Internet to academics such as the use of the Internet as a major source for school projects and how prevalent teenagers feel cheating is via the Web. Many of the students in the 2004 survey sample were born between 1990 and 1992. These youngsters are on the cusp of what may become a new and different generation of information-seekers.[23]

The members of the generation born between 1980 and 1994 are referred to alternatively as the Millennial Generation, Generation Y, or the Net Generation. Librarians are now observing the information-seeking behavior of these early adults and are searching for ways to gear teaching to their unique learning styles. In 2002, they made up about 20% of college students who began using computers between the ages of five and eight.[24] They prefer communication media such as instant messaging over e-mail; they are mobile and want information to come to them; they can handle multitasking; they like teamwork.[25] They are primarily visual learners, prefer hands-on activities, are task-oriented, and are extremely focused on saving time.[26] They are readers—a shift from students in the X Generation, who wanted information delivered in as few words as possible.[27] They are highly engaged by programmable media such as cell phones and video games.[28] In a small focus group study of Generation Y college students, findings showed that those students were beginning to question the validity of information on the Web and considered "infoglut" an obstacle to finding information.[29] Overall, these "Gen Nexters" are better educated than preceding generations of library users.[30]

The media-savvy nature of the Net Generation is a recurring theme in the research. In 2006, the John D. and Catherine T. MacArthur Foundation set aside $50 million for studies on digital media and learning. One project funded by this grant may be of particular interest to developers of information literacy instruction. The investigators, headed by Henry Jenkins, delved into an exploration of how the Internet provides "an entirely different communication landscape" for young learners. Jenkins sees youngsters engaging in a "participatory culture" that provides venues for artistic expression, along with opportunities for sharing, connecting, and garnering support for their media creations. He exhorts educators to include activities in school work that encourage and reward participatory, media-based learning. In fact, there is a "What Might Be Done" segment at the end of each skill section that describes such activities.[31] Media literacy is addressed somewhat in the ACRL *Standards*, but Jenkins offers a philosophical framework that meshes media creation with the societal goals of information literacy.

Using the Web as a platform for teaching takes a different turn in an article by Swanson. He outlines a shift in instruction based upon prolific electronic information accessibility via the Internet. He posits that online sources "are not collected into some physical object" to be introduced by librarians as appropriate resources. Therefore, the once-effective print-based, training-based model does not fit a "Web-based world."[32] To define a new model, Swanson draws upon the tenets of Ira Shor's critical literacy theory, where knowledge reflects changing views and the instructor directs learning based on student input and experiences.[33] In Swanson's critical information literacy model, information evaluation comes first in instruction and evokes demands that students become adept at prediction, critical thinking, relevance judging and decision-making skills. For this to happen, the teaching focus must shift away from isolating the Web as a format and steer students towards evaluating the qualities of information published on the Web.[34]

There are grounds for many research questions relating to the information-seeking behavior of the Net Generation and creating an information literacy model by which they will learn best. There are also questions of whether this new generation of students can rise to the tasks as sophisticated as those outlined by Swanson and Jenkins. In light of Perry's research on limitations in cognitive development, instructors may have to concentrate more on preliminary activities that build up to proposed higher-level activities. However, it is possible that the Net

Generation students with their multitasking abilities and strong reading skills may be ready for these more rigorous models.

Collaborating with Faculty

As the information literacy movement subsumes preceding instructional movements, shifts in various practices associated with librarians who teach are occurring. One rather obvious shift has been in the scheduling of instruction conducted by librarians. Under the traditional bibliographic instruction model, students' exposure to information use skills was incidental, dependent upon a professor's willingness to allow a librarian to teach such a class. Under the information literacy model, the faculty and librarians assume joint responsibility for incorporating information use competencies into course requirements. Thompson advocates for a shift from course-related instruction to information literacy embedded into courses. Referring to the ACRL *Standards*, he writes, "[t]hese standards call for colleges to consider how students should acquire information competencies over their four years and how the skills should be distributed across the curriculum," and compares this change to the writing across the curriculum model that replaced the once prevalent stand-alone composition class.[35]

Norgaard, a director of a writing and rhetoric program, takes this interest in pedagogical reform shared by the Council of Writing Program Administrators (WPA) and the framers of the ACRL *Standards* a step further. He suggests that both librarians and writing faculty need to rid themselves of old "pedagogical ghosts"—namely the low-level research paper assignments "that ask students for informational reports on a topic … not inquiry into a problem."[36] Of information literacy as a change agent, he writes:

> So, the key to communicating the relevance of information literacy is to convey the broad intellectual playing field on which it moves. That in itself would be a welcome antidote to the narrow instruction and schoolhouse assignments that have distorted impressions of information literacy for our students.[37]

Besides calling for refocusing pedagogies, Norgaard's essay also emphasizes the importance of faculty and librarian collaboration, a theme primary to realizing the information literacy vision.

Canadian LIS educators Leckie and Fullerton published an essay on how pedagogical discourses used by academic faculties differ from those of academic librarians. They used their own research on this topic to explain why librarians are experiencing difficulties in integrating information literacy into academic courses. In essence, they discovered:

> Faculty are participating in discourses that serve to protect their disciplines, preserve their own disciplinary expertise and academic freedom, and uphold self-motivated, individualistic learning. Librarians are employing the pedagogical discourses related to meeting user needs, teaching important generic skills and providing efficient service.[38]

The researchers also uncovered distinct "counter" faculty discourses among a significant percentage of faculty members interviewed, including an openness to integrated learning, a belief that information literacy is important to student learning, and a willingness to collaborate with librarians. Leckie and Fullerton recommend that librarians "start to identify and listen to the faculty discourses on their campus" and capitalize upon opportunities to collaborate with faculty.[39]

Listening to colleagues as a key to transcending the disciplinary boundaries that can separate librarians from faculty resonates with the writings on faculty-librarian collaborations of Raspa and Ward. They foresee a "new information universe" evolving in higher education settings. "It will be a world where change is the constant and flux is the norm, where novel instructional pairings and collaborations between members of the academic community will be commonplace."[40] Within this future universe, the information retrieval knowledge of librarians enjoys equal standing with the content expertise of the faculty. The authors term the current state of affairs as a transitional phase. The shift from librarians and faculty thinking of themselves in independent roles to embracing a collaborative, interdisciplinary partnership model is by no means complete.[41] However, their collaborations (Raspa is a humanities professor and Ward is a coordinator of instruction in a university library system) and the case studies of similar faculty-librarian collaborations documented in their book offer compelling evidence that a shift in this direction parallels the development of information literacy standards in the last decade of the twentieth century.

Assessing Performance

Along with new models for teaching and learning, the information literacy movement has precipitated increased librarian participation in assessment projects. Evaluation of instruction has always been a difficult undertaking for librarians, especially in the area of constructing and administering performance assessments.[42] In the past, librarians relied heavily upon surveys composed of self-reports on satisfaction with, or usefulness of, instructional sessions. This format carried over into the early information literacy assessment projects such as the survey administered to selected students at the University of California campuses at Berkeley and Los Angeles.[43] However, the emphasis that higher education agencies now place on learning outcomes has served as an impetus to involve librarians in the assessment process. The Middle States Commission on Higher Education has issued a handbook entitled *Developing Research and Communication Skills: Guidelines for Information Literacy in the Curriculum* (http://www.msche.org/publications/devskill050208135642.pdf). The book includes a whole chapter on information literacy assessment, characterizing assessment as a "reflective, integrative, and iterative process." Avery describes how the information literacy paradigm is moving librarians away from "traditional assessment of a course or an instructor" and into assessments "designed to inform about the acquisition of skills and thought processes by students."[44] Thompson proposes a complementary assessment model as one in which "[f]aculty and librarians can start to assess at different intervals how much students have learned in terms of information competencies"[45] Sonntag and Meulmans discuss Ianuzzi's concept of four levels of assessment (library, classroom, department or program, and institution) and reinforce her stand that assessment of information literacy should be a collaborative effort involving the entire institution.[46]

Two monographs that provide detailed explanations of how to insert assessment measures into teaching programs have recently been published. In *Information Literacy Assessment: Standards-Based Tools and Assignments*, Teresa Y. Neely and her co-authors outline assignments followed by assessment "queries" (e.g., test items and exercises) articulated specifically to align with ACRL's *Standards*.[47] The final chapters cover garnering institutional support, developing assessment instruments, and automating assessment measures. In the other book, *A Practical Guide to Information*

Literacy Assessment for Academic Librarians,[48] the emphasis is on the "tools" for assessment, ranging from informal measures that can be carried out at the end of a class to formal research methods. A chapter is devoted to an explanation of each formal method (e.g., surveys, interviewing, focus groups, and knowledge tests) and highlights planning considerations such as time, funding, institutional involvement, key characteristics, and what learning domains the assessment would measure.

Librarians interested in implementing a standardized assessment measure for information literacy skills have at least two points of reference to guide their efforts. Project SAILS (Standard Assessment of Information Literacy Skills) grew from an initiative proposed by librarians from Kent State University that was funded by a grant from the Institute of Museum and Library Services (IMLS) in 2002 and also supported by 82 participating institutions. The test component of the project is based on item response theory and is administered by participating sites (https://www.project-sails.org/sails/aboutSAILS.php?page=aboutSAILS).

Perhaps the most far-reaching information literacy assessment effort to date is the Information and Communication Technology (ICT) Literacy Assessment. It was developed collaboratively by the Educational Testing Service (ETS) and a cadre of partners from many spheres of education. The project grew from an International ICT Literacy Panel that convened in 2001. Next, a report establishing a framework for the test was released for consideration by the academic community. Subsequently, a consortium of colleges and universities contributed to the design of the test. The assessment is now marketed by ETS as a product called iSkills (http://www.ets.org). It measures seven competences, somewhat paralleling the ACRL *Standards*, using short and long tasks. This project has helped to establish the validity of the concept that information literacy is measurable. It may also serve as a guidepost for the development of more localized assessments.

Rethinking roles

The information literacy movement has precipitated much thought on how the roles of academic librarians have changed since the late 1980s. An associate university librarian referred to information literacy as "a catalyst for change," also noting that "academic librarians … are rethinking their roles in relation to potential partners in the academy, and have begun to understand the cultural shift that is required to implement information literacy at a deep, enterprise-wide level on their campuses."[49] The word *enterprise* denotes entry into the university culture at a level that goes beyond teaching.

Yet it is the teaching emphasis of information literacy upon which many librarians focus. A dramatic change in a librarian's professional role is embodied in the notion that professional responsibilities should be restructured in order to realize a truly effective information literacy program. In his essay dealing with a movement toward a new paradigm, Owusu-Ansah argues that the custodial conception of the library no longer serves the societal good and suggests that teaching be established as the central role of college and university librarians. He states:

> Teaching, an evolving part of the duties of the academic library, cannot be sporadic, with each institution deciding how far to go. Nor should this teaching activity be on a limited basis, open to only those who elect to take library orientation classes. Instruction in the retrieval, evaluation, and use of information must be provided to all those who graduate from a college or university. This is the least that the current demand on an information society forces on its institutions of higher learning.[50]

All the examples included in the discussion so far point to a desire on the part of many representatives from the library and information science field and from higher education to institute information literacy as the new paradigm for preparing students to enter the information-rich settings they will encounter in scholarly endeavors, the workplace, and society at large. Since a number of information literacy proponents lay claim to a paradigm shift in progress, a burning question is: Have information literacy initiatives achieved the momentum necessary to enact such a change? Are we indeed witnessing a paradigm shift in progress?

Signs of an Information Literacy Paradigm Shift

A paradigm is an accepted model or pattern, so a paradigm shift, in its simplest form, denotes a change to a different model. In the world of natural science, Kuhn pointed to paradigms embodied in works such as Newton's *Principia* and *Opticks* and Lyell's *Principles of Geology*. These works defined the problems and methods in their research fields and remained intact as long as they could be used to explain and solve problems. When anomalies arose that could not be explained by these paradigms, competing schools of explanations (e.g., quantum mechanics and tectonics) gained a following. Kuhn returned to this notion time and again, stating in one passage that "the single most prevalent claim advanced by the proponents of a new paradigm is that they can solve the problems that have led the old one to a crisis."[51]

The new information literacy initiatives offer solutions to the inherent problems highlighted in the previous section. First, there is the demand for accountability that is implicit in the higher education accreditation process. Under the single-incident library class paradigm, neither students nor teaching librarians could be held accountable for the efficacy of the instruction because it was not consistently administered. Second, the cognitive science revolution changed the way educators view learners and approach teaching. Librarians who teach want to experiment with pedagogies that engage learners and thereby increase students' learning. Opportunities to do this are extremely limited in the one-shot library class model. In a trend that is related to both accountability and learning gains, librarians either want to, or are requested to, assess the impact of their programs. The old paradigm restricted assessment to surveys and self-reports, often of untested reliability. Finally, to achieve all of the above, librarians need more time with students and integration of what is to be taught into a motivating learning scenario. This requires collaboration with faculty. The old paradigm paved the way for faculty-librarian partnerships, but the ACRL *Information Literacy Competency Standards* provide a framework for meshing information literacy with content areas.

In his postscript to the second edition of *The Structure of Scientific Revolutions*, Kuhn tried to clarify his concept of a paradigm using the term *disciplinary matrix* and enumerating the components of such a matrix as (1) symbolic generalizations, (2) shared commitments to beliefs, and (3) values (which may be viewed as having differing applications). The information literacy vision contains all these components within its paradigmatic boundaries. Where shared commitments and values translate fairly directly, the notion of symbolic generalizations requires a bit of a stretch to connect it to information literacy. Kuhn used this term to refer to "expressions, deployed without question or dissent by group members."[52] In a scientific group, a symbolic generalization could be a notated formula ($E = mc^2$) or a stated law (an object at rest tends to stay at rest). As members of a discipline become more expert in their fields, these generalizations become the keys to solving many differing problems. Kuhn calls these "shared examples" and considers these important because solving a variety of exemplary problems enables a group member to "assimilate ... a way of seeing."[53]

In the LIS professions, more and more group members are seeing their mission through an information literacy prism. Since the purpose of this discussion is to place information literacy in the context of research perspectives, what Kuhn had to say about how a scientific revolution changes a group's world view seems pertinent. One can substitute *librarians* for *scientists* in his observation:

> Led by a new paradigm, scientists adopt new instruments and look in new places. Even more important, during revolutions scientists see new and different things when looking with familiar instruments in places they have looked before... paradigm changes do cause scientists to see the world of their research-engagement differently.[54]

Shared Examples from Information Literacy Research

The previous discussions presented information literacy as a paradigm arising from a discipline in flux, resulting in its members seeking new models. Identifying exemplary models, therefore, can help to actualize the ideas that support the new paradigm. Kuhn's proposition was that shared examples materialize when a paradigm shift is occurring within a scientific community. Implicit in these shared examples are the tools (e.g., terminology and processes) for explaining and, ultimately, solving the problems of the discipline.

In the final section of this essay, six shared examples from the information literacy research literature will be presented. The first three cases are theoretical investigations conducted by researchers from LIS schools who have produced models and conceptual frameworks that cast new light on the questions surrounding the education of the information-literate individual. The second three examples represent research carried out by practicing librarians to evaluate their own information literacy programs.

Theme 1: Theories, Models, and Conceptual Frameworks

At the heart of the information literacy movement is a change in how teaching librarians view themselves. Once engineers of individual learning activities, they have evolved into architects of blueprints that promote learning. To evoke learning first requires an understanding of how the various aspects of planning for learning fit together. Theories of learning provide explanations of how and why individuals behave in certain learning situations; theories help to inform educators as to what to expect in terms of student performance. Models translate abstract notions into concrete representations and aid teachers in organizing a learning plan into a logical sequence of events. Conceptual frameworks bring structure to the concepts to be included in the instructional process and guide instructors in matching standards or principles to appropriate content and teaching techniques. For a movement to take hold, proponents need all three guideposts (i.e., theories, models, and conceptual frameworks) to shape new educational programs.

Kuhlthau's Information Seeking Process Model

By far, the theorist with the most staying power in the information literacy realm has been Carol Kuhlthau. Her theory conceptualizes the Information Seeking Process (ISP), composed of six stages, that she extrapolated from observations of high school students researching term paper topics. Testing these stages with other cohorts followed. Five studies later, Kuhlthau developed her theory into the ISP model.[55] She summarized her project as follows:

> Beginning in 1983 and working with high school students, Kuhlthau described and refined a model of the information search process that correlates the user's thoughts, feelings, and search behaviors. In these qualitative and longitudinal studies, common patterns in the experience of participants were noted and could be articulated and documented. While the pace of a search varied among individuals, certain aspects in the experience and the sequence remained relatively constant. Students' feelings about themselves, the library, the task, and the topic changed as their understanding of the topic deepened. The critical point of the search process (the turning point when the subjects shifted

from uncertainty to confidence) frequently was associated with forming a focus, defined as a personal point of view, about a topic. The focus was evidence of cognitive movement toward sense-making. Failure to form a focus within the search process often resulted in difficulty in writing because a personal understanding of the topic had not been achieved. In such cases, little or no shift in feelings was noted. A model of the search process was developed from these findings, incorporating affective experience with cognitive movement.[56]

Kuhlthau's work, taken in its entirety, has given the information literacy movement guideposts on many levels. The ISP theory itself and the resulting model revolutionized the way that librarians view information seekers. Kuhlthau's research findings have provided a unified theory on how the affective domain, especially feelings of confidence, can influence a student's ability to organize information. Her article explaining the uncertainty principle inherent in her ISP theory adds a constructivist view to her conceptual framework.[57] The rigorous research designs applied to each of her studies—combinations of journals, search logs, questionnaires, classroom teacher assessments, case studies based on interviews, process surveys, and content analysis—have raised the bar in subsequent information science behavioral studies.

Finally, the Kuhlthau model has been tested in numerous applied research settings by other librarians. One such study, conducted by Holliday and Li, was based on an analysis of written statements of 27 students at the beginning, middle, and end of their research process to fulfill term paper requirements for English writing classes. Their research question focused upon whether Kuhlthau's model holds true with the Millennial Generation, (i.e., students born after 1982) who have had extensive exposure to the Web as an information source. The small student sample precluded any firm conclusions, but observations suggested that this generation's cognitive and affective search behaviors may alter the ISP model. Holliday and Li's extensive literature review identifies other studies based on the ISP model conducted since 1990.[58]

Nahl's Affective-Cognitive Online Searching Dynamic
Since the earliest days of the computerization of information storage

and retrieval, librarians have been interested in how people searched these systems. Crawford and Feldt analyzed 791 articles on instruction in academic libraries published between 1971 and 2002.[59] They found that 11.6% of these articles dealt with searching catalogs, databases, and CD-ROMs. An additional 3.2% of the articles were on research about the Internet. Researchers in this field have mostly observed what people do during an online search. Many questions remain unanswered about what people are thinking while they are searching. Very few researchers have ventured into studies that examine the implications of self-concept and online searching. Attempts to develop a unified theory on online searching behavior are even rarer.

Diane Nahl has taken the theories of Kuhlthau, Bandura, and other researchers interested in the affective side of human behavior and tied these into her research on online information-searching performance. Many of her studies are based on the premise that "cognitive skills cannot be acquired and performed without a corresponding affective motivation or grounding."[60] In her dissertation study, Nahl examined the effects of two variations of Boolean search instructions on novice searchers. One instruction set contained Venn diagrams, search statements, examples, and brief explanations. The other instruction set contained "affectively elaborated" instructions, i.e., additional statements providing the user with orientation, advice, and reassurance. Quantitative measures of Boolean scores, instruction ratings, confidence scores, and self-efficacy beliefs were all significantly higher among the students using the elaborated instructions. The study pointed out, among other things, the need for user-centered instructions written to mitigate feelings of frustration and uncertainty among new searchers.[61]

In a later study of how novices use Web search engines, Nahl used ethnographic techniques (self-reports and content analysis) to track changes in students' feelings. Each week, the students answered the same six questions dealing with difficulty, negative emotion, value of content, improvement, satisfaction, and effort. Self-efficacy judgments were collected through responses to statements such as "I can competently use the Internet." Students with low self-efficacy scores showed a higher dropout rate. Among students who completed the 16-week training, difficulty and negative emotion responses diminished over time, whereas ratings for value, improvement, satisfaction, and effort increased.[62] Nahl also indexed the affective and cognitive responses gathered from students in the first session. A major finding from this exercise was: "Search acts appear to be governed by an affective filter that organizes incoming information and provides criteria for ranking cognitive relevance to search goals."[63]

Nahl's research strengthens the information literacy paradigm in several ways. Her studies offer explanations of why college students react to online systems as they do. Understanding the interplay between the cognitive and affective domains will help practitioners to create user-sympathetic learning opportunities on online systems. Her methods for monitoring and indexing search acts provide meaning to the elusive term *assessing thought processes*. Like Bloom's taxonomy, Nahl's indices can be used to chart learning objectives and performance measures for online searching. Ultimately, Nahl believes there is a common conceptual framework that explains information behavior. She continues to explore this theory using her knowledge of how affective, cognitive, and sensorimotor domains interact and her skills in showing these relationships using taxonomies.[64]

Bruce's Seven Faces of Information Literacy

Probably the most provocative information literacy model of the 1990s came from the Australian library educator Christine S. Bruce, who identified seven *faces* of information literacy.[65] To conduct her research, Bruce used phenomenography, a methodology that elicits people's conceptions or experiences on a particular phenomenon. In this case, 60 higher education professionals from eight Australian universities were asked a series of questions centering upon the information literacy phenomenon. The seven faces refer to varying conceptions of the elements of information literacy as expressed by the educators. Bruce delineated these as:

- Category 1: The Information Technology Conception
- Category 2: The Information Sources Conception
- Category 3: The Information Process Conception
- Category 4: The Information Control Conception
- Category 5: The Knowledge Construction Conception
- Category 6: The Knowledge Extension Conception
- Category 7: The Wisdom Conception

Bruce then interpreted the interrelations among these conceptual categories. She depicted these relationships as circular models, placing the focal elements in the center of each circle and the marginal elements farther away from the circle's core. Three of these models (Categories 5, 6, and 7) show information use as a central information literacy element; three other models (Categories 2, 3, and 4) picture varying elements in the core position (information sources, information processes, and information control); and only one model (Category 1) places information technology as the primary information literacy element. Bruce sees her work as providing a "framework for the adoption of a relational approach … [in which] teaching and learning information literacy would stress not skills acquisition but the growth of learners in coming to understand and experience information literacy in different ways."[66]

Bruce's ideas are highly conceptual. She set out to create a relational model that explains how professionals in education experience information literacy. However, three Australian librarians from Central Queensland University created a more concrete information literacy conceptual framework modeled upon Bruce's foundations. Using charts, they clearly showed how a framework helped them to map specific resources, teaching and learning processes, and faculty-librarian responsibilities to information literacy principles.[67]

How students experience information literacy is a research question addressed most recently in two companion studies conducted by Maybee, an academic librarian in California. Using the same phenomenographic approach employed by Bruce, Maybee examined the perceptions of a selection of undergraduate students at the California Polytechnic State University[68] and later repeated his study at Mills College, a pool of students contrasting those from CalPoly.[69] In both studies, he found that three conceptions of information literacy from an undergraduate student viewpoint coincided with three of Bruce's faces of information literacy. These three categories were Sources (Bruce's Category 2), Processes (Bruce's Category 3), and Knowledge Base (coalescing into Bruce's Categories 5, 6, and 7). Responses from the Mills College students also indicated a Technology category (corresponding to Bruce's Category 1). From a qualitative research view, Maybee's findings "support the phenomenographic premise that there are a limited number of ways that a phenomena is experienced."[70] From an educational view, his findings indicate that students share common perceptions with those educators controlling the curriculum. Maybee's literature review is particularly valuable as an overview of research on studies examining student perceptions of information literacy in the United States and the United Kingdom.[71]

Theme 2: Practice-Based Research Exemplars

What characterizes the information literacy "community" in the field, and by extension, what issues are driving the research among practitioners? Kuhn might respond that its members "work from a single paradigm"[72] and communicate using the accepted symbolic generalizations of that paradigm. In a review of the literature on information literacy research projects conducted by practicing librarians, these words (or equivalents thereof) form the basis of their research lexicons:

opportunity	instruction
collaboration	integration
learning	teamwork
pedagogy	program
curriculum	technology
objectives	methodology
standards	assessment
outcomes	change

It is the combinations of these terms that better impart the themes which librarians in the field are addressing in their quests to test the information literacy paradigm. Some of these expressions were introduced earlier in this essay—*librarian-faculty collaboration* and *outcomes assessment* are two examples. Other terms, such as *integrative teaching methodologies,* are coined by researchers as the information literacy vernacular expands to describe its distinctive variables. In addition to using this shared vocabulary, academic librarians orient their research to their particular circumstances—their subjects are students, their methods center upon teaching and learning, and their research questions stem from programmatic needs. It is within this disciplinary matrix that information literacy research occurs. The most compelling studies are those that combine multiple concepts from this matrix in the examination of a research problem. Three such examples follow.

A Distance Education Graduate Course in Multimedia Literacy

The librarians at Austin Peay State University (APSU) have a long history of teaching students through integrated course instruction. In APSU's

Heritage Program (an alternative interdisciplinary core of courses), librarians have team-taught with faculty and helped to develop courses. In their article "Integrating Information Literacy into the Virtual University: A Course Model," two librarians (the user education librarian and the library's Web master) and a professor of a communications course collaborated to create and co-teach a Web-based distance education module on multimedia literacy. The instruction was developed for a master's degree level course in communication arts, and the professor had experience in distance education course delivery. Fourteen graduate students participated. The librarians integrated all five of the ACRL *Standards* into the course's content, although the "Information Literacy block was still presented as a separate unit at the beginning of the course ... and the students still saw it as the 'library' part of the course."[73] Standard Five (addressing economic, legal, and social issues of information use) was introduced first through readings, followed by threaded discussion sessions. Web site evaluation exercises and discussions came next in order to help students prepare for a group project on creating their own Web site. In the professor-led segments, students learned how to present multimedia on the Web, and this fulfilled the standard on a student's ability to use information to accomplish a specific purpose.

Active learning could not be evaded. Students were required to collaborate on creating group Web sites and also developed individual Web portfolios. They learned to work together, share technical knowledge, brainstorm, and critique each other's work. One exercise, viewing "bad" Web sites using the Lynx text-based browser, was deliberately designed to create disequilibrium. Assessment of information literacy was based on evaluations of discussions, Web site annotations, and a capstone comprehensive exam question. A 16-item online anonymous survey gave students the opportunity to voice their opinions on grading, materials, course design, and content. The librarians felt that, when the course was taught again, concepts such as Web evaluation criteria should be introduced in tandem with Web design issues. The authors also addressed issues related to group work and planning time as these relate to development of a distance education course.

The Contribution of Library Instruction Using English class Portfolios
At the University of New Mexico, library instruction had been taught

as a series of workshops linked to the English 102 course "Analysis and Argument," the second in a two-course composition sequence, for many years. When the course was revised, the librarians saw an opportunity to change the tool-based approach used previously in their teaching to a rhetorical emphasis treating writing as an inquiry process. An instruction librarian with a background in literature was instrumental is articulating this new role. The library's head of instruction and an English professor teamed together to conduct a study comparing papers written before implementation of the inquiry-oriented instruction to papers submitted after this change in instruction. The profile of this project is drawn from the article "Engaging Conversation: Evaluating the Contribution of Library Instruction to the Quality of Student Research."[74]

In English 102, student performance is assessed partly on portfolios that include two revised papers. Groups of instructors evaluate these portfolios using a rubric tied to course objectives and incorporate their findings into the English program's outcomes assessment. From this stockpile of student work, the researchers extracted a sample of unmarked portfolios from 10 semesters divided equally between before and after the introduction of inquiry-based research instruction. In all, the bibliographies of 250 research papers were analyzed for number of citations; variety in format, source, and time frame; and citation accuracy. A detailed rubric was applied to a sample of 60 papers (30 each from before and after the change in instruction). This rubric evaluated the writer's use of research sources based on relevance, credibility, and engagement criteria. Three independent readers (teaching assistants in the writing program) scored each paper using the rubric.

Results from a statistical analysis of the bibliography variables showed a significant increase in referencing scholarly journals and a reduction in citations to textbooks and other materials as effects of the inquiry-based teaching methods. This result was expected due to a teaching emphasis on primary versus secondary sources. In the use-of-sources sphere, students receiving the inquiry-based instruction showed a greater range of relevance scores (the top scores were significantly higher and the bottom scores were noticeably lower) than reflected in the scores of students who had attended traditional library research workshops.

This study helped the researchers to isolate areas of teaching that need to be further explored. They identified these as consistency of instruction, follow-up to the initial instruction, and greater cooperation among content professors and librarians. One proposed solution was team learning in which new librarians and faculty are introduced to the inquiry-based methods together. Scores on the credibility and engagement rubrics "indicate that students continue to view the researched essay as an academic exercise more than a quest for knowledge" and "[i]t looks as though many students continue to work with broad topics rather than with focused research questions."[75] The latter concern fits with Kuhlthau's findings that most students never reach the focusing stage when writing papers. This is an area where Nahl's research on affective guidance might be tied to instructor preparation training.

A Virtual Online Information Literacy Assessment Model
At Hunter College (part of the City University of New York, CUNY), the administration has long recognized the first-year experience as pivotal in helping students adapt to college life. To this end, undergraduate students attended weekly Orientation Seminars (ORSEMs) during their first semester on campus. When discussions about changing this format to a mandatory one-credit course began, a group of reference librarians proposed the development of a suite of virtual presentations to orient students to information literacy prerequisites. This concept was expanded to include an online quiz, and the VOILA! (Virtual Online Information Literacy Assessment) program was born. A contingent from the library (led by the library's ORSEM liaison and the heads of instruction and reference) met with members of the ORSEM steering committee to pitch VOILA! as a component to be included on the ORSEM syllabus. Their proposal was accepted. This event marked the beginning of an intensive review of the design and administration of the quiz. The following profile of that process is derived from the article "A Longitudinal Study of the Development and Evaluation of an Information Literacy Test."[76] VOILA!'s assessment component was actually the forerunner to the project itself. The librarians who provided face-to-face library orientations as part of the original ORSEMs program often ended those sessions with informal performance evaluations. Those librarians knew from years of experience that many students entering Hunter had little previous exposure to library use. Therefore, the learning objectives that formed the basis for the quiz centered upon knowledge prerequisites of using an academic

library, including a student's ability to (1) identify library-use concepts by name, (2) distinguish one material type from another, (3) recall concepts and rules relating to material arrangement, and (4) apply rules related to using the online catalog. These objectives coordinated well with ACRL's Standard Two on accessing information.

Many factors dictated that the quiz be constructed as an objective test, including the large number of students (well over 1,200 each academic year), its online format, and scoring issues. A reference librarian with a background in instructional design developed the test questions. Maintaining congruency between quiz items and the information presented in VOILA!'s online tour and tutorials proved to be the most challenging task. For example, concepts illustrated in the tutorial by images (e.g., a facsimile of a book spine or OPAC screen) had to be tested in the quiz using different but comparable images. The quiz was subjected to two years of pilot testing, during which time the number of items were reduced from 42 to 32, problem items (those missed by 60% or more of the students) were modified, and items covering moot concepts (e.g., microforms as a format declined in use during this period) were dropped. The pilots also showed that parts of the instructional material had to be enhanced in order to provide the detail needed for students to answer corresponding test questions.

Evaluation of the quiz was a group effort. Debriefings were conducted after each quiz administration with the full complement of teaching librarians (some from outside the reference department). ORSEM instructors and students were polled. Reliability and validity of the third and fourth versions of the quiz were determined through statistical analyses—a project largely overseen by the library's computer center coordinator, who had forged strong ties with the reference librarians. The specifics on each step in this project are illustrated and can be used as guides by librarians considering the development of objective assessment measures.

Combining the Theoretical and Practice-Based Themes

Taken together, the themes, representing both the theoretical perspectives and the stances of practitioners in academic libraries, show a steady movement from traditional library instruction to teaching and research frameworks based on the tenets of information literacy. In five of the six examples in this section, the studies included methods for measuring the performances of students. The three practice-based studies all described collaboration between librarians and faculty. In addition, the learning objectives of those three studies were expressed in terms of advancing the students' abilities to perform in a learning environment, not just in a library setting. The study by Bruce emphasized the interest of librarians in aligning information literacy with elements in the "big picture" in education—information, technology, knowledge, and wisdom. Perhaps for the first time in the history of the library profession, we are seeing research on how learning transpires coming from librarians and applications of that research reaching into academic circles beyond library and information science. Librarians advocating for information literacy now have a repertoire of "shared examples," and these are growing.

Professional Resources

The number of resources on information literacy available to academic librarians is vast. The leading source for material geared to United States initiatives is the ACRL. This division of ALA provides materials on its Information Literacy Web site (http://www.ala.org/ala/mgrps/divs/acrl/issues/infolit/informationliteracy.cfm), at annual conferences and preconference programs, and in its publications. ACRL's Instruction Section (IS) has broadened its coverage from "bibliographic instruction" to include information literacy, as reflected in the materials linked to IS Web pages (http://www.ala.org/ala/mgrps/divs/acrl/about/sections/is/welcome/welcome.cfm).

Research on information literacy is often channeled through ACRL and carried out by ranking members. One example is the most recent National Information Literacy Survey, developed by ACRL and supported by the American Association of Higher Education. The survey was distributed to 2,700 higher education institutions in May 2001. It is the sequel to a 1994–1995 survey of 3,236 comparable institutions.[77]

ACRL's journal, *College and Research Libraries*, seeks out articles on information literacy research projects, and its bulletin, *College and Research Libraries News*, contains regular columns such as "ACRL Standards and Guidelines" and "Partnerships and Connections" that highlight model programs, collaborative efforts, best practices, guidelines for instructional programs, and research agendas. The Association also publishes monographs such as *Assessing Student Learning Outcomes for Information Literacy Instruction in Academic Institutions*. This book is a compilation of advice from ACRL information literacy leaders combined with summaries of notable assessment projects carried out by 24 librarians who received grants from IMLS. Grant recipients developed information literacy assessment plans with faculty members in a variety of settings (research universities, four-year colleges, and community colleges).[78]

Librarians interested in formal training in information literacy will find that ACRL has again taken the lead. Its formation of the Institute for Information Literacy (IIL) and particularly the success of the IIL's Immersion Institute in training next-generation library educators have been well documented.[79] In conjunction with the Teaching Learning and Technology Group (TLT), a nonprofit organization that promotes teaching and learning with technology, ACRL offers online seminar series. These programs are generally formatted as one- to three-week WebCT-based instruction or as live Webcasts. Continuing education programs such as those mentioned have been developed in response to a lack of attention paid to information literacy diffusion by library schools. The ACRL/Instruction Section Web site shows that, as of May 2005, 27 of the 48 United States accredited LIS schools included courses on library instruction, but only about a half dozen of these courses used the term *information literacy* in the title.[80] The ACRL/IS community continues to press for information literacy to be placed in the constellation of curricular electives and offered regularly in LIS schools.

For librarians yearning to conduct their own research or simply to acquaint themselves with the current information literacy research scene, journal reading will meet that need. An analysis of journals that publish articles on instruction in academic libraries produced a list of journals that contributed the most articles to this subject from 1971 to 2002. The top seven journals were *Reference Services Review (RSR)*, *Journal of Academic Librarianship (JAL)*, *College and Research Libraries (C&RL)*, *Reference and User Services Quarterly (RUSQ)*, its predecessor *Reference Quarterly (RQ)*, *Reference Librarian*, *Library Trends*, and *Research Strategies* (which has ceased publication).[81] These titles coincide with the journals from which the majority of the sources for this chapter were drawn. Each journal features information literacy topics in the form of special issues and regular columns. Since 1973, *RSR* has issued an annual bibliography, currently titled "Library Instruction and Information Literacy," and has reported on every LOEX (Library Orientation and EXchange) conference. *RUSQ* includes an "Information

Literacy and Instruction" column written by information literacy "guest celebrities."

This chapter has focused mostly on developments in information literacy in the United States, with the exception of Bruce's research in Australia. On the international scene, a number of initiatives should be recognized as important contributions to the information literacy agenda. University libraries and major national libraries in the United Kingdom and Ireland are part of the Society of College, National, and University Libraries (SCONUL). In 1999, SCONUL issued a position paper entitled "Information Skills in Higher Education" that introduced a model depicting the competencies through which a person with basic library and information technology skills must pass to attain information literacy. The model was based on seven competencies and became known as the Seven Pillars of Information Literacy (http://www.sconul.ac.uk/groups/information_literacy/sp/papers/Seven_pillars.html).

SCONUL established a Working Group on Information Literacy in 2005 to refine and promote the Seven Pillars of Information Literacy.

The International Federation of Library Associations (IFLA) has embraced the information literacy paradigm with enthusiasm. An outpouring of equal interest from countries around the globe seemed to follow IFLA's lead. The following chronology of "information literacy milestones" illustrates the extent of the international commitment to the information literacy movement.

- 2002—IFLA changed the name of its User Education Roundtable to the Information Literacy Section (http://www.ifla.org/VII/s42/).
- 2003—IFLA adopted as its presidential theme for 2003–2005 "Libraries for Lifelong Learning" (http://www.ifla.org/III/gb/prtheme03-05.htm).
- 2003—The International Conference of Information Literacy Experts was held in Prague, the Czech Republic. Invited leaders from 23 countries proposed "The Prague Declaration—Towards an Information Literate Society" (http://www.nclis.gov/libinter/infolitconf&meet/post-infolitconf&meet/PragueDeclaration.pdf).
- 2005—The High-Level International Colloquium on Information Literacy and Lifelong Learning, sponsored

by the same organizations as the Prague convocation, met in Alexandria, Egypt. Leaders issued "The Alexandria Proclamation on Information Literacy and Lifelong Learning" (http://www.ifla.org/III/wsis/BeaconInfSoc.html).

- 2006—"Guidelines on Information Literacy for Lifelong Learning" were reviewed, revised, and released (http://www.ifla.org/VII/s42/pub/IL-Guidelines2006.pdf). These were based on a set of "International Guidelines on Information Literacy" that were drafted by the Information Literacy Section in Buenos Aires at the 2004 IFLA conference.

Conclusion

The shared examples from the information literacy research literature offered for consideration in this chapter reveal two dimensions important to a paradigm shift. First, the information literacy movement is generating new models and frameworks derived from research of a theoretical nature. Second, there is an increasing interest in conducting applied research in the real-world situations in which librarians practice. The impetus for the latter circumstance has been the establishment of national standards and organizational sponsorship of support mechanisms such as institutes in teaching and assessment. What kinds of research will add to the momentum of the information literacy movement or define issues in need of further investigation? Two recurring themes in the practice-based research that could be used as starting points for developing an information literacy research agenda are the testing of innovative pedagogies and the investigation of faculty-librarian collaboration.

In the area of teaching through an information literacy focus, research comparing the effectiveness of distinctive pedagogies in varying settings and with varying learners is sorely needed. Many questions have not been explored, such as "What forms of active learning fit best with particular skill acquisition?" or "Are there circumstances in which individualized learning is preferable to collaborative learning?" Librarians from institutions similar in demographics, curriculum, and information literacy missions might team together to teach toward the same ACRL Standard in a particular content area with matched student groups but different teaching methods. The resulting patterns in student learning outcomes would help librarians understand *when* certain teaching strategies are more effective.

A grant similar to the IMLS Outcomes Assessment project could be used to identify participants, fund activities, and publish the findings.

Formal studies of faculty-librarian collaborations examining how and why some faculty members enter into sustained relationships with librarians while other faculty members resist this engagement are also key to the ultimate acceptance of the new information literacy paradigm. A national research project to investigate this question conducted on the same scale as the "UK Academics' Conceptions of, and Pedagogy for, Information Literacy" project is an approach that might answer many nagging questions about the overall limited success librarians have had in integrating with faculties. This project, spearheaded by Webber and Johnson, is outlined on their Web site (http://dis.shef.ac.uk/literacy/project/index.html). However, the authors have subsequently completed their research and reported their findings in the literature.[82]

Finally, the concerns that some librarians have voiced about the applicability of the ACRL *Standards* might serve as an impetus for a comprehensive review of how to best apply those standards in teaching environments. As they are currently stated, the *Standards* contain no recommendations on a sequence by which to present the competencies that are enumerated. However, librarians who have applied the *Standards* to their teaching could contribute "lessons learned" directed at when to introduce each competency. Recasting the *Standards* into a "continuum of learning" would greatly enhance their value.

As the information literacy paradigm matures, the assumptions upon which it was founded will continue to be tested. Meanwhile, the research generated over the past two decades shows a definitive community of members with a shared commitment to the tenets of this new model.

References

1. Edward Owusu-Ansah, "The Academic Library in the Enterprise of Colleges and Universities: Toward a New Paradigm," *Journal of Academic Librarianship* 27, no. 4 (2001): 284.

2. Lori Arp, "Information Literacy or Bibliographic Instruction: Semantics or Philosophy?" *Reference Quarterly* 30, no. 1 (1990): 49.

3. Patricia Senn Breivik, "Take II—Information Literacy: Revolution in Education," *Reference Services Review* 27, no. 3 (1999): 272.

4. American Library Association, *Presidential Committee on Information Literacy: Final Report* (Chicago: American Library Association, 1989). Available online from http://www.ala.org/ala/mgrps/divs/acrl/publications/whitepapers/presidential.cfm.

5. Association of College and Research Libraries, *Information Literacy Competency Standards for Higher Education*, (Chicago: Association of College and Research Libraries, 2000). Available online from http://www.ala.org/ala/mgrps/divs/acrl/standards/informationliteracycompetency.cfm

6. Gary B. Thompson, "Information Literacy Accreditation and Mandates: What They Mean for Faculty and Librarians," *Library Trends* 51, no.2 (2002): 222.

7. Thomas S. Kuhn, *The Structure of Scientific Revolutions*, 2nd ed., (Chicago: University of Chicago Press, 1970), 136.

8. Mary W. George, "Instructional Services," in *Academic Libraries: Research Perspectives*, ed. Mary Jo Lynch and Arthur Young (Chicago: American Library Association, 1990), 128.

9. Esther S. Grassian and Joan R. Kaplowitz, "A Brief Introduction to Learning Theory" in *Information Literacy Instruction: Theory and Practice* (New York: Neal-Schuman, 2001), 33–57.

10. Esther S. Grassian and Joan R. Kaplowitz, "An Overview of Learning Styles" in *Information Literacy Instruction: Theory and Practice* (New York: Neal-Schuman, 2001), 59–87.

11. Elizabeth J. McNeer, "Learning Theories and Library Instruction," *Journal of Academic Librarianship* 17, no. 5 (1991): 294–297.

12. Thomas Jacobson, "Sense-Making in a Database Environment," *Information Processing and Management* 27, no. 6 (1991): 647–657.

13. Naomi Harrison, "Breaking the Mold: Using Educational Pedagogy in Designing Library Instruction of Adult Learners," *Reference Librarian* 33, no. 69/70 (2000): 287–298.

14. Sherri B. Saines, "The Radical Syllabus: A Participatory Approach to Bibliographic Instruction," *Journal of Library Administration* 36, no. 1/2 (2002): 167–175.

15. Ruth V. Small, Nasriah Zakaria, and Houria El-Figuigul, "Motivational Aspects of Information Literacy Skills Instruction in Community College Libraries," *College and Research Libraries* 65, no. 2 (2004): 96–121.

16. Grassian, and Kaplowitz, *Information Literacy Instruction*, 116.

17. Cerise Oberman, "Avoiding the Cereal Syndrome, or Critical Thinking in the Electronic Environment," *Library Trends* 39, no. 3 (1991): 198.

18. Alexius S. Macklin, "Theory into Practice: Applying David Jonassen's Work in Instructional Design to Instruction Programs in Academic Libraries," *College and Research Libraries* 64, no. 6 (2003): 494–511.

19. Rebecca Jackson, "Cognitive Development: The Missing Link in Teaching Information Literacy Skills," *Reference and User Services Quarterly* 46, no. 4 (2007): 28–32.

20. Larry Spence, "The Usual Doesn't Work: Why We Need Problem-Based Learning," *portal: Libraries and the Academy* 4, no. 4 (2004): 485–494; Debora

Cheney, "Problem-Based Learning: Librarians as Collaborators and Consultants," *portal: Libraries and the Academy* 4, no. 4 (2004): 495–508; Michael Pelikan, "Making Problem-Based Learning Work: Evolving a Realistic Approach," *portal: Libraries and the Academy* 4, no. 4 (2004): 509–520; Loanne Snavely, "Making Problem-Based Learning Work: Institutional Challenges," *portal: Libraries and the Academy* 4, no. 4 (2004): 521–531.

21. Pelikan, "Making Problem-Based Learning Work," 517.

22. Loanne L. Snavely and Carol A. Wright, "Research Portfolio Use in Undergraduate Honors Education: Assessment Tool and Model for Future Work," *Journal of Academic Librarianship* 29, no. 5 (2003): 298–303. (Retrieved electronically from Business Source Premier, April 15, 2005).

23. Paul Hitlin and Lee Rainie, *Teens, Technology, and School,* Data Memo (Washington DC: Pew Internet and American Life Project, August 2005). Available online from http://www.pewinternet.org/PPF/r/163/report_display.asp (accessed February 5, 2008).

24. Steve Jones and Mary Madden, *The Internet Goes to College: How Students Are Living in the Future with Today's Technology* (Washington, DC: Pew Internet and American Life Project, 2002). Available online from www.pewinternet.org/PPF/r/71/report_display.asp (accessed February 5, 2008).

25. Susan L. Gibbons, *The Academic Library and the Net Gen Student: Making the Connections* (Chicago: American Library Association, 2007), 14–20.

26. Angela Weiler, "Information-Seeking Behavior in Generation Y Students: Motivation, Critical Thinking, and Learning Theory," *Journal of Academic Librarianship* 31, no. 1 (2004): 51–52.

27. Ron Zemke and Claire Raines, "Generation Gaps in the Classroom," *Training* 36, no. 11 (1999): 48–52. (Retrieved electronically from Business Source Premier January 19, 2008).

28. Gibbons, *Academic Library and the Net Gen Student,* 23–30; 76–78.

29. Weiler, "Information-Seeking Behavior in Generation Y Students," 50.

30. Gibbons, *Academic Library and the Net Gen Student,* 14.

31. Henry Jenkins and others, *Confronting the Challenges of Participatory Culture: Media Education for the 21st Century* (Chicago: The MacArthur Foundation, 2006). Available online from http://digitallearning.macfound.org/atf/cf/%7B7E45C7E0-A3E0-4B89-AC9C-E807E1B0AE4E%7D/JENKINS_WHITE_PAPER.PDF (accessed January 3, 2008)

32. Troy A. Swanson, "A Radical Step: Implementing a Critical Information Literacy Model," *portal: Libraries and the Academy* 4, no. 2 (2004): 259–273. (Retrieved electronically from ProQuest Research Library, April 30, 2005)

33. Ira Shor, *Empowering Education: Critical Teaching for Social Change* (Chicago: University of Chicago Press, 1992).

34. Swanson, "Radical Step."

35. Thompson, "Information Literacy Accreditation and Mandates," 222.

36. Rolf Norgaard, "Writing Information Literacy in the Classroom: Pedagogical Enactments and Implications," *Reference and User Services Quarterly* 43, no. 3 (2004): 222.

37. Ibid. 225.

38. Gloria Leckie and Anne Fullerton, "The Roles of Academic Librarians in Fostering a Pedagogy for Information Literacy," in *Racing Toward Tomorrow: Proceedings of the Ninth National Conference of the Association of College and Research Libraries,* ed. Hugh H. Thompson (Chicago: Association of College and Research Libraries, 1999), 7.

39. Ibid.

40. Richard Raspa and Dane Ward, *The Collaborative Imperative: Librarians and Faculty Working Together in the Information Universe* (Chicago: Association of College and Research Libraries, 2000), 16.

41. Ibid. 15.

42. Richard H. Werking, "Evaluating Bibliographic Education: A Review and Critique," *Library Trends* 29, no. 1 (1980): 153–172.

43. Patricia D. Maughan, "Assessing Information Literacy among Undergraduates: A Discussion of the Literature and the University of California-Berkeley Assessment Experience," *College and Research Libraries* 62, no. 1 (2001): 71–85.

44. Elizabeth F. Avery, *Assessing Student Learning Outcomes for Information Literacy Instruction in Academic Institutions* (Chicago: Association of College and Research Libraries, 2003), 2.

45. Thompson, "Information Literacy Accreditation and Mandates," 228.

46. Gabriela Sonntag and Yvonne Meulmans, "Planning for Assessment" in *Assessing Student Learning Outcomes for Information Literacy Instruction in Academic Institutions,* ed. Elizabeth F. Avery (Chicago: Association of College and Research Libraries, 2003), 6.

47. Teresa Y. Neely, ed., *Information Literacy Assessment: Standards-Based Tools and Assignments* (Chicago: Association of College and Research Libraries, 2006).

48. Carolyn J. Radcliff and others, *A Practical Guide to Information Literacy Assessment for Academic Librarians.* (Westport, CT: Libraries Unlimited, 2007).

49. Craig Gibson, "Information Literacy and IT Fluency: Convergences and Divergences," *Reference and User Services Quarterly* 46, no. 3 (2007): 23–26.

50. Owusu-Ansah, "Academic Library in the Enterprise of Colleges and Universities," 286.

51. Kuhn, *Structure of Scientific Revolutions,* 153.

52. Ibid., 182.

53. Ibid., 189.

54. Ibid., 111.

55. Carol C. Kuhlthau, "Inside the Search Process: Information Seeking from

the User's Perspective," *Journal of the American Society for Information Science* 42, no. 5 (1991): 361–371.

56. Carol C. Kuhlthau and others, "Validating a Model of the Search Process: A Comparison of Academic, Public and School Library Users" *Library and Information Science Research* 12, no. 1 (1990): 6.

57. Carol C. Kuhlthau, "A Principle of Uncertainty for Information Seeking," *Journal of Documentation* 49, no. 4 (1993): 339–355.

58. Wendy Holliday and Qin Li, "Understanding the Millennials: Updating Our Knowledge About Students," *Reference Services Review* 32, no. 4 (2004): 356–366.

59. Gregory A. Crawford and Jessica Feldt, "An Analysis of the Literature on Instruction in Academic Libraries," *Reference and User Services Quarterly* 46, no. 3 (2007): 77–87.

60. Diane Nahl, "Affective Elaborations in Boolean Search Instructions for Novices: Effects on Comprehension, Self-Confidence and Error Type" in *Forging New Partnerships in Information. Proceedings of the 58th ASIS Annual Meeting,* ed. Tom Kinney (Medford, NJ: Information Today, 1995): 69.

61. Ibid.

62. Diane Nahl, "Ethnography Affective Monitoring of Internet Learners: Perceived Self-Efficacy and Success" in *Global Complexity: Information, Chaos and Control. Proceedings of the 59th ASIS Annual Meeting,* ed. Steve Hardin (Medford, NJ: Information Today, 1996): 100–109

63. Diane Nahl, "Ethnography of Novices' First Use of Web Search Engines: Affective Control in Cognitive Processing," *Internet Reference Services Quarterly* 3, no. 2 (1998): 51.

64. Diane Nahl, "A Conceptual Framework for Explaining Information Behavior," *SIMILE* 1, no. 2 (2001): unp. Available online at http://www.utpjournals.com/simile/

65. Christine S. Bruce, "The Phenomenon of Information Literacy," *Higher Education Research and Development* 17, no. 1 (1998): 25–43.

66. Christine S. Bruce, "Information Literacy Research: Dimensions of the Emerging Collective Consciousness." *Australian Academic and Research Libraries* 31, no. 2 (2000): 40.

67. Debbie Orr, Margaret Appleton, and Margie Wallin, "Information Literacy and Flexible Delivery: Creating a Conceptual Framework and Model," *Journal of Academic Librarianship* 27, no. 6 (2001): 457–463.

68. Clarence Maybee, "Undergraduate Perceptions of Information Use: The Basis for Creating User-Centered Student Information Literacy Instruction," *Journal of Academic Librarianship* 32, no. 1 (2006): 79–85.

69. Clarence Maybee, "Understanding Our Student Learners," *References Services Review* 35, no. 3 (2007):452–462.

70. Ibid. 460.

71. Maybee, "Undergraduate Perceptions of Information Use," 80.

72. Kuhn, *Structure of Scientific Revolutions,* 162.

73. Lori E. Buchanan, DeAnne L. Luck, and Ted C. Jones, "Integrating Information Literacy into the Virtual University: A Course Model," *Library Trends* 51, no. 2 (2002): 161.

74. Mark Emmons and Wanda Martin, "Engaging Conversation: Evaluating the Contribution of Library Instruction to the Quality of Student Research," *College and Research Libraries* 63, no. 6 (2002): 545–560.

75. Ibid. 559.

76. Anita Ondrusek and others, "A Longitudinal Study of the Development and Evaluation of an Information Literacy Test," *Reference Services Review* 33, no. 4 (2005): 388–417.

77. Gabriela Sonntag, "Report on the National Information Literacy Survey," *College and Research Libraries News* 62, no. 10 (2001): 996–1001.

78. Avery, *Assessing Student Learning Outcomes.*

79. Elizabeth B. Lindsay and Sara Baron, "Leading Information Literacy Programs: Immersion and Beyond," *Journal of Library Administration* 36, no. 1/2 (2002): 143–165.

80. Professional Education Committee, "Library Instruction Courses Offered by Accredited Master's Programs in Library and Information Studies," Association of College and Research Libraries, http://www.ala.org/ala/mgrps/divs/acrl/about/sections/is/iscommittees/webpages/educationa/libraryschools.cfm

81. Crawford and Feldt, "An Analysis of the Literature on Instruction in Academic Libraries." 81.

82. Sheila Webber, Stuart Boon, and Bill Johnson, "A Comparison of UK Academics' Conceptions of Information Literacy in Two Disciplines: English and Marketing." *Library and Information Research News* 29, no. 93 (2005): 4–15.

Research in Academic Library Collection Management

Mary F. Casserly

This chapter describes the empirical quantitative and qualitative research and case studies pertaining to collection management practice in academic libraries published between 1990 and 2007. The topics covered include collection size and growth, material cost, library expenditures, budgets and budgeting, collection development policies, collection composition, organization and staffing for collection management, selection, and the evaluation of the collection development process and the collection itself. The chapter identifies the most influential and useful studies and the most active areas of research. The collection management research literature was limited in the methodologies employed (surveys and case studies), statistical analyses applied (basic and descriptive), and the scope of the problems addressed (inputs and processes). More studies that focus on effectiveness, outcomes, and impact are needed.

Introduction

This chapter continues the review of academic library collection management research conducted and published in 1990 by Osburn.[1] Like Osburn, the author consulted annual and multiyear reviews of the collection management literature published between 1990 and 2007.[2] These proved to be very useful both for identifying reports of research and for the analyses of findings. Beyond these, the author conducted literature searches, followed citations, and browsed the tables of contents of prominent collection management journals. The majority of the works cited in this chapter were published in the profession's monographs, journals, and conference proceedings. All were published in English, and most document academic library practice in the United States. In order to make manageable the voluminous literature, some limitations were placed on the breadth of collection management–related subjects included. For this reason, with a few exceptions, the literatures of selection for storage, preservation, weeding, scholarly communication, resource sharing, and acquisitions have been excluded.

The focus of this chapter, like that of the book as a whole, is on research. One of the problems that emerged almost as soon as the author began to consider this writing project was the question of how to define *research*. The editors did not offer a definition, wisely allowing authors wide latitude in the selection of literature to be included. This author's goal was to examine the way those in the library profession have employed research methods to investigate the questions, issues, and problems relative to the academic library collection. Therefore, in addition to the empirical quantitative and qualitative research projects identified and discussed here, she has included selected local studies. Although they vary greatly in sophistication and quality, these serve as case studies and are important because they reflect the types of recent challenges those in the trenches faced and the strategies they used to address them.

Technological and economic factors have transformed academic library collection development from a largely solitary effort conducted within the library to one that, with growing frequency, requires collaboration with a wide range of library and campus units, as well as with other libraries. Likewise, the collection itself has been redefined by the placelessness and volatility of electronic resources, the changing landscape of scholarly communication, and user expectations of any time / any place access. Collection management research, with its successes and limitations, was both the product of, and a contributor to, this transformation.

Size and Growth of Collections

Rightly or wrongly, collection size has long been considered an indicator of collection quality. By the early 1980s, collection managers generally understood that the goal of a "comprehensive" collection was unrealistic. But during the 1990s and early 21st century, it was the concept of a shrinking national collection and local collection loss that provided the context in which collection management was practiced and research on it conducted.

University Libraries and Scholarly Communication, or "The Mellon Report," set the framework for its discussion of the principles of scholarly communication and the role of research libraries by identifying historical trends in collections, expenditures, and publishing. The analysis it offered of the 1912–1991 collection expenditure data of 24 members of the Association of Research Libraries (ARL) documented the volatility of collection growth, the declining percentage of library expenditures vis-à-vis university budgets, and a growing crisis in serial pricing.[3] Other ARL publications provided further evidence of the shrinking aggregate print research library collection. "Research Libraries in a Global Context: An Exploratory Paper" described an increase in worldwide book publication, increases in serials prices, a weakening U.S. dollar, and a resulting decline in the percentage of published foreign resources purchased by research libraries annually.[4] Reed-Scott's background paper on foreign acquisitions characterized the coverage of foreign materials in U.S. research libraries as "deteriorating."[5] The authors of both papers observed and expressed concern about the trend toward collection homogeneity. *Changing Global Book Collection Patterns in ARL Libraries* provided a profile of the holdings of all ARL libraries, based on a snapshot of the WorldCat database, by publication date and world regions. The average number of ARL library holdings decreased for nine of the most widely held countries between 1980 and 2004, suggesting that libraries were acquiring fewer books from these countries than they had in the early 1980s. This study raised questions about the meaning of this downward trajectory and provided a baseline for future studies.[6] In addition, ARL tracked trends in research library acquisitions and collection growth in its annual compilations of data on member libraries.[7]

Other studies furthered the concern about the national collection's size and diversity. Using 1967–1987 data on volumes held by the Bowdoin List (of 40 liberal arts colleges) and ARL libraries, Werking found that, contrary to Fremont Rider's widely accepted thesis on collection growth, three quarters of the college libraries and one half of ARL libraries had not doubled in size every 16 years.[8] Perrault analyzed the growth of non-serial imprints based on data from 72 ARL libraries. She found an overall decline in monographic acquisitions among these libraries, as well as significant declines in the numbers of nonserial imprints by broad subject groups and decreases in the percent of total imprints acquired. Perrault also documented a shift toward the acquisition of science and English language nonserial materials. Her data on the mean number of libraries owning titles supported the conclusion that the aggregate collection was becoming less diverse in subject coverage and language.[9]

National trends in serials collections were explored by Chrzastowski and Schmidt by studying ARL library serial holdings records for 1992–1994. This research built on their previous studies of cancellations by five ARL libraries, in which they found that the overlap of serials titles cancelled had grown from 4.3% to 7.2%.[10] Recognizing the need to look at serials collections collectively, the researchers created an aggregate library based on serials records from 10 ARL libraries, which they then used to analyze collection and cancellation rates and characteristics. Their findings included an accelerating rate of cancellation; a 63% overlap in domestic serials, with 37% of titles unique to only one library; and a cancellation overlap rate of 8.3%.[11] Chrzastowski's closer look at the science serials in the aggregated collection documented similar patterns of collection shrinkage, with higher subscription overlap and serials cancellations as measured in dollars among the science serials than had been found in the aggregate collection.[12]

A number of studies that were smaller in scope provided additional evidence of shrinking serials collections. For example, Rowley documented the erosion of the Iowa academic libraries' aggregated serials collection, and Burnam found that the collections of scientific literature were not growing at the majority of the private liberal arts college libraries that participated in his study.[13] Most recently, in a study of print science serials in 75 Illinois academic libraries, Chrzastowski, Naun, Norman, and Schmidt found 59% of these titles to be unique in that they were held by only one library, with another 14% owned by only two of the libraries included in the study.[14]

Researchers have only recently begun to focus on the size and growth of the national *digital* collection. In 2007, Lavoie, Connaway, and O'Neill examined the aggregate digital collection as reflected in the combined digital holdings in WorldCat. Their analysis revealed that this aggregate collection is small but growing rapidly and at a much faster pace than the WorldCat database as a whole. They identified the widely held items as government documents and netLibrary e-books and analyzed these digital resources by holdings patterns and material types.[15]

Cost of Information Resources

Rising prices of materials were one of the chief reasons for the shrinking national collection. Periodical price surveys based on data from EBSCO Subscription Services continued to be published each spring in *Library Journal*. These annual analyses typically included average cost per title by subject area and country of origin, as well as price projections for the coming year.[16] Annual price analyses for periodicals and serials based on data provided by Faxon, and more recently Swets, included average prices by subject area and cumulative price increases over multiples years. The periodical price increases were also presented by LC Classification categories.[17] *The Bowker Annual* included data on prices paid by academic libraries, including average prices and price indices for U. S. and foreign publications, books, periodicals, and other material types.[18]

Collection managers also had access to a number of longitudinal studies and analyses of serial prices by subject. Price increases for journals for academic veterinary medical libraries were published from 1990 to 2000. Analyses included annual price increases and comparisons with 1983 and 1997 prices.[19] Marks, Neilsen, and Petersen published a longitudinal price study focused on scientific journals. The data for this study were the 1967–1987 prices for 370 titles. In addition to measuring price increases, this study also analyzed titles by price per page and publisher nationality. The authors found that prices from foreign commercial publishers were higher and had risen faster than domestic titles.[20] Sapp conducted an analysis of mathematics journal prices with similar findings.[21] Schmidle and Via analyzed the pricing trends for library and information science (LIS) journals from 1997 to 2002. They identified variations between commercial and professional and academic presses and documented price increases related to commercial publisher acquisitions of established journals.[22] These authors also calculated cost per citation for selected LIS journals as a measure of return on investment of acquisitions dollars.[23]

Library Expenditures

In addition to data on the prices of information resources, collection managers needed reliable data on what other academic libraries and, in particular, what their peer institution libraries were spending. As previously noted, The Mellon Report provided a historical look at expenditures, as did the Werking study.[24] In addition, Prabha and Ogden analyzed expenditures by ARL and ACRL libraries between 1982 and 1992 and found increases in overall expenditures and growth in the proportion of expenditures that were being used for serials.[25] Petrick's study of expenditures by SUNY libraries indicated that between 1994 and 2000 expenditures for electronic resources increased, although the increases were not consistent in that period. He found that the funding to support these increased expenditures did not come from funding for print and audiovisual materials and concluded that e-resources were "augmenting rather than replacing" traditional formats. Like Werking, Petrick noted difficulties encountered in comparing expenditure data.[26] Annual expenditure data, in the aggregate and institution-specific, were made available by ARL and ACRL.[27] *The Bowker Annual* reported the academic library acquisitions expenditures by state and material type.[28] In 1998, *Library Journal* surveyed 1,000 academic libraries and analyzed their expenditures by size and type of institution.[29] The survey was repeated in 2001, and the researchers identified changes in the percent of spending on types of materials and in subject areas.[30]

Acquisitions Budgets

Academic libraries have faced ever-increasing materials costs and acquisitions budgets that were not growing as fast as those of their parent institutions. Despite this, very little research was conducted on how, or how successfully, collection managers advocated for additional or inflation funding. Jenkins published a case study that described the University of Dayton Library's experience using benchmarking to advocate for acquisitions fund increases.[31] A 1994 survey of 230 academic libraries conducted by Allen showed that, as a group, libraries relied on university entitlements for their acquisitions budgets and generated very few independent funds. Allen also found that libraries at private institutions were more successful at fundraising for acquisitions than those at public institutions.[32]

New information resource formats and services, as well as the need for hardware and software, put additional pressure on already stretched acquisitions budgets. In 1990, 99% of the ARL libraries responding to a SPEC Kit survey reported that they used their materials budgets to acquire, not only books and serials, but other formats such as microforms, videos, and sound recording. Eighty-seven percent reported acquiring bibliographic files, and 15% computer hardware.[33] Seventy percent of the respondents in Allen's study agreed that certain technology costs should be charged to the library materials budget. Almost 84% agreed that funding such costs in this manner continued a long-standing trend.[34]

The research on methods used by library collection managers to allocate the funds available to them focused on identifying defendable criteria for making these allocations. In his 1990 review of the literature of allocation formulas, Budd commented that while academic libraries use allocation as a means of distributing acquisitions funds, the use of allocation formulas "appears not to be as pervasive as it was a relatively short time ago."[35] Indeed, the research literature suggests that the majority of academic libraries did not use allocation formulas. In 1990, only 14% of the libraries completing a SPEC Kit survey reported that they used a numerical formula to allocate and there was "little consistency among the formula elements."[36] A survey published by ACRL four years later indicated that about 40% of small college and university libraries used allocation formulas. The variables most frequently included in these formulas were book prices and number of faculty and students per department; course level was the most frequent weighting factor.[37]

From 1990 to 2007, a handful of methodological studies—i.e., studies designed and conducted for the purpose of testing an allocation method, formula, or formula variable(s)—were published. Brownson tried to quantify the library's selection policy and use it, along with shelf counts and circulation data, to construct a model that explained variation in expenditure by subject.[38] Based on deviations from the 80/20 Rule, which states that 80% of collection use will be from only 20% of the materials in that collection, Britten quantified "relative levels of use" in selected LC subject classes and discussed the use of this measure as a basis for allocating book acquisitions funds.[39]

Crotts explored the relationships among expenditures, enrollment, and circulation, determined that circulation was the best indicator of relative demand for books, and developed an allocation model based on his findings.[40] Young applied seven allocation formulas to the same data and compared the results. For four science departments he then compared allocations calculated from these formulas with the average expenditures of 60 libraries. He found that the formula allocations were fairly consistent for the broad subject areas of humanities, social sciences, and sciences but varied when applied to more specific science subject areas. The mean allocations from the formulas and the survey libraries were also very similar.[41] Wise and Perushek tested an allocation methodology using lexicographic linear goal programming and determined that it successfully allocated funding within the context of multiple, incommensurable, and conflicting collection development goals.[42] Canepi conducted a meta-analysis of 75 fund allocation formulas, identified the variables used and their frequency of use, and employed factor analysis to identify related variables and variables found within the same formula.[43]

Case studies consisted of descriptions of local efforts to develop formulas for effectively allocating funds. Bandelin and Payne described the process of developing an allocation formula in a collaborative, rather than faculty-driven, collection development program.[44] German and Schmidt developed a formula to allocate new money and then described the process by which the Library Allocation Steering Committee addressed the issue of how well the collections budget supported campus priorities and how responsive it was to change.[45] Arora and Klabjan described their efforts to develop a formula that would maximize journal usage over library units and branch libraries.[46] Sorgenfrei presented a failure analysis of the development and use of an allocation formula at the Colorado School of Mines Library.[47] Lowry described the development of a matrix formula for budget allocation that was the product of cooperation among three academic libraries and that allowed individual libraries to select variables appropriate to their situations.[48] Lafferty, Warning, and Vlies reported on their efforts at the University of Technology in Sydney to incorporate literature dependence into their formula.[49] Kalyan, Weston, and Evans described the development of budget allocation formulas at Seton Hall, Portland State, and Monash University libraries.[50] Bailey, Lessels, and Best used data from Georgia's University Borrowing Program to allocate monograph funds at Auburn University Library.[51]

Collection Development Policies

The literature pertaining to collection development policies included calls to rethink the need for, and purpose and content of, the collection development policy.[52] At the same time, numerous manuals, articles, and texts offering assistance with writing traditional collection development policies appeared.[53] The body of published research on collection development policies is relatively modest in both the number of studies published and the variety of research methods employed. Those who conducted research on this topic relied heavily on the survey approach, the methodology that characterized this literature in the 1980s.

The survey conducted by Futas for the third edition of *Collection Development Policies and Procedures* asked whether libraries had collection development policies, where they were written, by whom, and how often they were reviewed.[54] Vignau and Maneses surveyed academic libraries in Cuba regarding the status of, and need for, collection development policies.[55] College libraries were surveyed about their audiovisual policies in 1991 by Brancolini, and community colleges about their collection development policies by Boyarkski and Hickey.[56] Sayles studied collection policies covering textbooks and found a disconnect between policy and practice.[57] Hsieh and Runner surveyed collection development policies and collection development and acquisitions practices for textbooks and leisure reading materials.[58] E-journal policies were the subject of a 1994 SPEC Kit survey; Straw surveyed the Web pages of the ARL libraries to determine the presence of collection development policy statements; and based on their survey of SPARC member web pages, Hahn and Schmidt described how libraries used their pages to convey information about their collections, collecting policies and scholarly communication issues.[59]

The case studies on policy development described the process of revising the collection development policy statement at St. Johns University and developing policies for electronic resources, communications materials, and materials on contemporary topics.[60] Intner, a faculty member at Simons College Graduate School of Library and Information Science, presented the structure of the model policy based on her course on collection development and management and described how the course assignments could be used by a practitioner to create a collection development policy and procedures manual.[61]

Collection Composition

As previously described, the research on collection growth documented the decrease in collection subject and language diversity as changes in collection composition. Other research focused on the extent to which library collections included specific subject matter and material types. More recent research related to collection composition was dominated by concerns about electronic resources.

In 1993, Brancolini and Provine conducted a SPEC Kit survey that focused on video and multimedia (CD-ROMs) collection policies and procedures.[62] In 1997, Brancolini presented the results of that survey along with the findings of one conducted in 1995 that covered all facets of selecting, budgeting, and managing these types of materials.[63]

Crawford and Harris studied ownership of 110 fiction and 120 nonfiction best sellers published from 1940 to1990 and concluded that future scholars may not have access to these popular culture materials.[64] They also surveyed ownership of religious texts and found that, while texts in English were widely held, those in their original languages were not.[65] Krieger's survey of popular Catholic periodicals indicated that they are not widely collected, and Schwartz reported on the gap between book publication output and holdings in 71 ARL libraries in the area of Judaic studies.[66] Stoddart and Kiser conducted an informal survey of 20 libraries that collected self-published magazines or "zines" and provided some information about how they were collected, cataloged, accessed, and preserved.[67] Marinko and Gerhard studied holdings of alternative press titles by ARL libraries and called for the expansion of national holdings of these materials.[68] Mulcahy found that library holdings of award-winning science fiction novels varied widely in ARL libraries, with few collecting science fiction comprehensively.[69] A survey of ARL libraries by Pellack revealed that as of 2003, about half of the respondents acquired and maintained a collection of historic industry standard, and 60% reported that they acquired standards on demand.[70] The 2005 SPEC Kit survey, *Spatial Data Collections and Services,* revealed that 89% of the responding ARL libraries collected digital data sets.[71]

Many of the large research libraries began investigating and defining their roles regarding e-journals early in the 1990s, and these reports were collected in *Electronic Journals in ARL Libraries.* A survey conducted for that 1994 SPEC Kit identified the challenges libraries faced and the trends in making e-journals available.[72] Another SPEC Kit survey conducted in 1994 revealed that a significant numbers of ARL members were at the stage of either investigating or offering local and remote access to e-journals and that they were following traditional methods for selecting, acquiring, processing, and cataloging them.[73] In 1999, Ashcroft and Langdon found that all but one of the research libraries they surveyed included e-journals in their collections.[74] Ninety-six percent of the UK and North American academic libraries surveyed by Ashcroft in 2002 made e-journals available to their users.[75] ARL surveys reported by Case indicted that 75% of a small sample of ARL libraries reported that they were selectively cancelling print journals in favor of electronic versions.[76] An information survey conducted by DeVoe in 2005 revealed that 85% of the respondents had canceled print and kept the electronic versions of journals.[77] Robbins, McCain, and Scrivener found evidence that ARL libraries were gradually shifting from print reference materials to their electronic counterparts.[78] The research on the access to free scholarly e-journals conducted by Fosmire and Young suggested that, as of 2000, libraries were not "collecting" these types of resources. Almost half of the 213 e-journals in their sample had no holding symbols attached to their OCLC bibliographic record.[79] However, seven years later a SPEC Kit survey on open access resources revealed that 97% of the respondents provided links to open access journals, and Lavoie, Connaway, and O'Neill found that the number of digital materials in WorldCat was growing faster than the database as a whole.[80]

Organization and Staffing for Collection Management

The research literature on organization and staffing illustrated the many variations on the ways in which academic libraries translated collection management into practice.

Organization and Administration

The *Guide to Collection Development and Management Administration, Organization, and Staffing* provided an overview of the organizational models used in all types of libraries.[81] *Organization of Collection Development*, a SPEC Kit published in 1995, described the organizational models employed at ARL libraries and found only subtle changes in the formal organization of collection development since the 1987 SPEC Kit survey. These changes included an increase in the number of part-time professional staff involved in collection management and some organizational changes in response to the increase in information resources in electronic format.[82] Kenselaar conducted interviews about collection development administration with librarians at selected research libraries. Topics covered included the use of advisory committees, manner and frequency of communication with selectors, use of full-time bibliographers, collection development policies, budget allocation, assessment, and preservation.[83] Bryant compared the interview data she collected on collection development organizational structures in 1989–1990 with responses to an inquiry about changes in 1995 and found that collection development officers were losing their separate identity within the library organization and that collection development librarians' responsibilities were broadening in terms of the range of material formats they selected and the types of activities assigned to them. She also found that these changes were occurring in a wide variety of organizational structures.[84] Fisher conducted a survey of multitype libraries, of which the overwhelming majority of respondents were from academic libraries, and did not find consensus about collection development and acquisitions organizational structures. More than half of his respondents indicated that their organizational structures had not changed over the previous six years.[85]

Although the research indicated that change was not widespread in this period, some academic libraries did experiment with major organizational change in collection management and these experiences were reported in the literature as case studies. Webb reported on combining the collections and systems functions at Washington State University Libraries.[86] The team management approach to collection management was taken at the University of Nevada Las Vegas Library and documented by Biery.[87] Eckwright and Bolin described the organizational benefits at the University of Idaho resulting from the creation of a hybrid position that included both collection management and cataloging responsibilities.[88]

Collection Management Responsibilities and Requirements

A number of important theoretical, personal opinion, and prescriptive articles on the changing responsibilities of those involved in collection management were published since 1990.[89] Earlier, the research that examined collection management responsibilities and requirements consisted of analyses of position announcements. In more recent years, researchers used surveys to identify and document changing roles and responsibilities.

Robinson reviewed 433 collection management position announcements that appeared in *College and Research Libraries News* between 1980 and 1991 and found that the majority of these advertised positions had combined responsibilities, generally with reference, and required a strong subject background but not an advanced degree. Forty-six percent of the positions required or preferred foreign language competence, but few required supervisory or budget experience or knowledge of automation. Robinson also found little change in the responsibilities and qualifications included in announcements during the decade studied.[90] Haar examined the 35 advertisements for bibliographer positions that appeared in the *Chronicle of Higher Education* between March and October 1990 and found that liaison and reference duties, bibliographic instruction, and online searching were the most frequently listed responsibilities. He also found that the LIS master's degree, advanced subject degree, foreign language ability, and collection management experience were the qualifications most often required and preferred, and that few advertisements required reference or budget skills or experience.[91] In his study of position announcements for academic subject specialists in business, social sciences, and science from 1990 to 1998, White found that the majority included collection development, reference, and bibliographic instruction responsibilities, and he identified a trend toward including technology-related responsibilities.[92]

In 1999 and 2000, Intner used surveys and interviews to investigate how the Internet had affected the work of collection development librarians. Her findings included an extensive list of activities for which these librarians used the Internet, and her data indicated that their responsibilities included collecting Internet resources. She also interviewed library administrators from six academic libraries, who confirmed that the importance of Internet resources was growing and that these resources were causing changes in the types of materials they bought, how they made the materials available, and the patrons they served.[93] McAbee and Graham surveyed 138 librarians in medium-sized academic libraries to determine subject specialist responsibilities, how much time they spent on their tasks, whether they had enough time, and the value to their position of the tasks they performed.[94] Wilson and Edelman focused on the effect of increasing interdisciplinarity on the selector/bibliographer. Their analysis of the intellectual endeavors of the faculty of one library science graduate program illustrated the difficulties a selector would have in establishing selection parameters.[95] Hardy and Corrall surveyed 32 English, law, and chemistry subject/liaison librarians at universities in the United Kingdom and found that they carried out a wide range of similar responsibilities and required similar competencies.[96]

The most ambitious study of the changing roles of collection managers was published by Dorner in 2004. Using data from four focus groups, he developed a Web-based survey to which he received responses from collection managers at academic and special libraries in five major English-speaking countries. The study found that over the previous five years, collection managers had increased responsibilities that were primarily related to digital resources in an environment where funding remained static. They reported spending more time on collection management related to digital resources, including on activities related to physical access and technology issues, and on attending education and training sessions. Collection managers involved in consortial work reported increases in time spent liaising about such activities.[97]

Education and Training for Collection Management

A number of collection management texts were published between 1990 and 2007, while the research on education for collection management included surveys of practitioners and reviews of LIS graduate programs.[98] Haar reviewed twelve 1990–1991 program bulletins and found that only half of these programs offered collection development courses.[99] Budd and Brill surveyed LIS educators and practitioners in 1994 regarding specific aspects of course instruction. Although both groups agreed on what needed to be taught, practitioners indicated that their formal instruction in collection management had not been adequate. Practitioners also ranked the value of on-the-job training higher than did the educators.[100] Metz conducted an informal review of 10 LIS program catalogs and found that most did not require a course on collection development. He also compared the content of the courses with an earlier study of fundamental elements of a basic course in collection development and found that topics such as organization and arrangement, history of publishing, and distribution infrastructure had been replaced by resource sharing and fund allocation. Based on this review, he called for such curricular additions as access vs. ownership, electronic and digital resources, and organizational structure for collection development.[101]

In their review and discussion of the status of and challenges facing collection management education, Blake and Surprenant cited Blake's finding that 87.4% of the ALA-accredited schools had at least one faculty member with an interest in collection management. In his review of catalog descriptions of collection management courses, Blake found fewer programs in which collection management courses were required than did Metz, but his review of topics covered in those courses yielded a similar list.[102] Liu and Allen addressed the need for subject-specific training/education for business information specialists. Their interviews of 147 academic business librarians indicated that the majority did not have the level of business and economics expertise that they would have if they had academic degrees in those disciplines. The researchers also surveyed instructors of business information resources courses in ALA-accredited LIS programs and determined that their courses covered major business topics, including management, marketing, and finance.[103]

Given that collection management was not necessarily required for those enrolled in LIS master's programs and that bibliographer responsibilities were changing, it is not surprised that many guides and handbooks for collection practitioners were published.[104] However, research on training and professional development was scant. Casserly and Hegg surveyed 246 academic libraries in four-year educational institutions to determine how those who participated in collection development were trained and evaluated. They found that more than half of the respondents were given training and that the most common type was the orientation program. The researchers developed a profile of the libraries most likely to have training programs.[105] Forte and others offered a case study of the development of a collection manager training program and manual at the UC–Santa Barbara Library. The training sessions consisted of a series of panel discussions on topics included in the ALA *Guide for Training Collection Development Librarians*. It had an evaluation component and was found to benefit both new and seasoned collection managers.[106] Lyons compared the relevancy of two professional development opportunities, the annual conference of the ALA and that of the American Political Science Association (APSA), from the point of view of librarians with collection development responsibilities and found strong evidence of the importance of academic conferences.[107] Using case studies and a survey of experts, Dilevko and others provided evidence that by carefully reading and analyzing scholarly book reviews, academic librarians can derive significant knowledge about the intellectual and historical context of a subject area in which they may not have formal training, but for which they may have reference, instruction, or collection development responsibilities.[108]

Evaluation of Collection Management Librarians

Evaluation of those involved in the collection management process is an important, yet infrequently addressed, topic. Casserly and Hegg found that librarians responsible for collection development in academic libraries tended to be involved in the evaluation of their bibliographers / subject specialists as a colleague during the peer review process and, outside that process, only when these individuals were evaluated for promotion or tenure.[109] The survey that served as the basis for a 1992 SPEC Kit found that supervisors of those involved in collection management conducted annual performance reviews and that peer review was used by only 32% of the respondents. The survey identified the types of documentation bibliographers/selectors provided as part of their peer review process and indicated that some libraries required selectors and bibliographers to submit monthly reports and obtain input from faculty in their assigned academic departments as part of that evaluation process.[110] Kenselaar's interview subjects described their approaches to meeting with, but not necessarily evaluating, selectors.[111]

A methodology for evaluating the effectiveness of selectors was developed by Dennison, who compared library monographic and journal holdings with subject-specific, tiered checklists and applied a goodness of fit statistical test to the results.[112] Based on a very small number of interviews, Gonzalez-Kirby identified attributes of bibliographers associated with effective collection development, including specialized subject knowledge, research, and support for and contact with faculty.[113]

The Selection Process

The research that examined selection focused on partnerships with faculty, the identification of selection criteria, and the tools and data that informed the process.

Working with Faculty Partners

The question of *who* should select reflected an awareness that collection managers and faculty need to work together to build collections and that collection managers need to know more than they typically do about how their faculty partners selected materials.

Jenkins found that faculty at the College of Mount St. Joseph ranked selection fifth out of a list of seven secondary activities, which included serving on campus committees, advising students, and miscellaneous duties assigned by their department chair.[114] In a later study at the same institution, he found that faculty used reviews to select materials less frequently than did librarians.[115]

At Kean University, Kuo found that faculty most often used publisher catalogs and journal book reviews to inform their selection, that those with one to five years of ordering experience were the most active selectors, and that faculty most often ordered books for undergraduates, employing the criteria of "good for students" and "good for teaching."[116] Kushkowski surveyed business faculty at three Iowa universities and found that faculty perceived their own areas as more important to their institution's business curriculum than other business subjects.[117] Chu's study focused on the lateral relationship between academic faculty and librarians who share responsibilities for collection development and underscored these groups' differing understandings of collaboration, constraints, and possibilities.[118] Neville, Williams, and Hunt described the College of Charleston's liaison program and offered case studies of how it worked in departments at opposite ends of the spectrum of faculty involvement in the collection development process. The researchers also conducted a survey of their faculty liaisons and identified issues concerning selection of these liaisons, training, and recognition of effort.[119] White's case study of the development and evolution of the selection and assessment process for electronic resources to support the College of Business Administration at Pennsylvania State University revealed that a strong partnership in collection building carried over into enhanced support for faculty research and instruction.[120] University of Manitoba researchers found that most librarians believed that their interactions with faculty substantially impacted the collection, improved communications with faculty, and helped the librarians become aware of new resources and identify areas in which the collections were inadequate.[121] Walther used a Web-based survey to explore the librarian-faculty relationship at one urban academic institution from the perspective of journal cancellations. He found that the factors used by librarians and faculty for identifying journals to be cancelled were similar and that librarians used input from faculty rather than acting arbitrarily.[122]

Lee conducted a historical case study of collection development for women's studies, using analyses of historical documents and archival records as well as personal interviews. She found that the personal ideologies of those involved in collection development influenced their determination of information needs and the means by which to address those needs and that collection development had been influenced by institutional bureaucracy and politics, especially with respect to operating structures, the politics of interdisciplinarity, personnel deployment, and aspiration for prestige.[123]

Criteria Used for Selection

In studying the strategies used by academic libraries to mitigate the impact of price discrimination, Haley and Talaga found that libraries selected and deselected journals based on factors other than price alone and therefore were vulnerable to price discrimination.[124] Spencer and Millson-Martula identified the factors considered important by college and small university libraries when cancelling print serials. The top five factors considered were indexing, cost, evaluation, availability in print locally or in electronic format, and use.[125] Metz and Stemmer surveyed heads of collection management at ARL and Oberlin Group libraries and found strong positive correlations among their familiarity with publishers, opinions about a publisher's academic relevance, and their perceptions of a publisher's intellectual and editorial quality. The researchers also found that selectors used publisher reputation as an evaluation criterion, especially when other information, such as a review, was not available.[126] Lewis asked 56 members of the ACRL Law and Political Science Section with responsibilities for selecting political science materials to evaluate the quality of political science books published by 62 publishers and compared their responses with the results of a similar survey of faculty who were members of the APSA. She found that university press titles were more highly ranked by librarians and that textbook publishers were more highly ranked by APSA members.[127] Sweetland and Christensen surveyed 33 Wisconsin academic libraries about their languages and literatures collection practices and compared their holdings with the *Choice* list of outstanding academic books. They found that selection in most libraries was based on faculty suggestions and curriculum-related needs, while criteria that addressed future needs or availability at other libraries were not considered.[128]

More recently, concerns about burgeoning electronic resources resulted in research on criteria for selecting these types of materials. In 2001, the Digital Library Federation (DLF) published Jewell's study of library practices related to the selection and presentation of commercially available electronic resources. Based on interviews and discussions with academic librarians involved with electronic resources, reviews of Web sites, and quantitative data, Jewell identified best practices.[129] That same year, the DLF also issued a report by Pitschmann on free Web resources. Pitschmann used data gathered from interviews, Web sites, and subject gateways to identify practices to help libraries develop and sustain collections of free third-party Web resources.[130]

Collection-Building Tools and Data

The tools that facilitate and the data that inform collection development range from approval plans to publisher-generated use statistics for electronic resources. This review indicated ongoing interest in the traditional tools and a growing interest in usage data.

Mechanical Selection

Loup and Snoke conducted a survey of 28 ARL libraries to determine how they supplemented their approval plans in the areas of philosophy and political science. They found that the responding libraries used standing orders and, to a lesser extent, retrospective purchasing. The researchers also collected data on approval plan expenditures.[131] In 1996, 93% of the respondents to an ARL SPEC Kit survey indicated that they used approval plans and that they spent at least $100,000 on these plans. The survey also indicated that use of such plans to acquire foreign or specialized materials had not decreased since a similar survey was conducted in the 1980s. Respondents identified advantages and disadvantages of such plans and described how their plans were administered.[132] Calhoun, Bracken, and Firestein developed a method to determine the publishers that should be included in a core collection for large- and medium-sized research libraries based on the 80/20 rule and estimated the costs of approval plans that would supply core materials.[133] Dali and Dilevko surveyed Slavic collection development specialists to determine the extent to which academic libraries in North American acquired books in Slavic and other Eastern European languages through approval plans and to identify the extent to which they used other collection strategies, including bookstores, gifts, exchanges, independent book agents, and book fairs.[134]

Several case studies illustrated the range of approaches that were taken to evaluate and improve blanket order and approval plans. Pulikuthiel conducted an evaluation of the approval plan used by the Centre for Development Studies in terms of faculty participation, subject and publisher distribution of books received, expenditures, and imprints.[135] Galbraith's case study was motivated by an engineering library's need to reduce its approval plan return rate. She compared the effectiveness of selection using Blackwell's Collection Manager database with the approval plan and, based on the results, discontinued the plan.[136] Sennyey assessed the performance of two blanket-order vendors that supplied French and Spanish books to the University of Illinois Library based on both the number of materials they supplied and the quality of those materials. Sennyey proposed this methodology as a way of evaluating blanket-order suppliers on an ongoing basis.[137] Calhoun analyzed a core collection for the libraries in the California State University system in terms of reviews, holdings, and publishers and presses to develop strategies to improve approval plan effectiveness.[138] Brush compared the circulation rate of engineering approval plan books with that of books in the engineering section of the collection—i.e. the books classified in the *Ts*—and found that the approval books were much more heavily used.[139]

Reviews

Much of the research into reviews and reviewing focused on small or alternative press titles and *Choice* as the providers. Serebnick's study of reviewing patterns of small press titles indicated that the percentage of small press books reviewed had decreased since 1980 and that a small number of journals published the majority of reviews.[140] Dilevko and Dali also addressed the availability of reviews of alternative or small press titles and found that titles featured in *Counterpoise* were frequently reviewed in other sources. The researchers also analyzed favorable reviews and characterized the books featured only in *Counterpoise*.[141]

Carlo and Natowitz used content analysis to study a sample of *Choice* reviews of titles in American history, geography, and area studies and found that the majority received favorable ratings and were recommended for purchase. They also found that reviewers most frequently applied criteria of quality or originality of analysis, completeness of research, and readability or quality of narrative.[142] Jordy, McGrath, and Rutledge used *Book Review Digest* to assess the quality of publishers' output and developed a profile of *Choice* as a source of book reviews. They found that *Choice* opinions were similar to those from other sources in their sample, that *Choice* and other reviewers were equally likely to judge a book to be outstanding, but that *Choice* reviewers were significantly more likely to judge a book to be "very good."[143] Sweetland compared criteria for evaluating Web sites developed by the Southern California Online Users Group, the University of Georgia, and Rettig and Laguardia with *Choice* reviews and found that *Choice* did not generally include information on authority, reliability, and other traditional measures of quality.[144] Williams and Best determined that *Choice* could not be used to predict circulation for political science, public administration, and law books at Auburn University.[145]

Integrated Library System (ILS) Data

Chief collection development officers at 108 ARL libraries were surveyed by Carrigan regarding the availability and usefulness of data from their ILSs. His research indicated that less than half of the libraries regularly used the data produced by their systems to inform collection development decisions. Carrigan then analyzed how the data were used and why they were not used.[146] Casserly and Ciliberti surveyed collection management librarians at small- and medium-sized institutions using DRA and Innovative Interfaces Inc. ILSs about the availability and usefulness of 18 types of collection management data. They found that the data were less useful than available.[147] Kraemer and Markwith reported on the integration of subscription agent and ILS data to inform collection-building decisions at the Medical College of Wisconsin.[148]

E-Journal and Database Publisher Data

By the beginning of the present decade, collection managers were all too aware of the shortcomings of vendor-supplied use data and of the incompatibility of use measures across information resources. In a white paper sponsored by the Council on Library and Information Resources, Luther identified library and publisher issues surrounding e-journal usage statistics.[149] In 1999, Dawson compared the variety of use statistics from the BUBL Journals service and developed a search-to-browse ratio as a means of comparing use of individual titles.[150] Two years later, Blecic, Fiscella, and Wiberley compared the use data supplied by 51 vendors with the International Coalition of Library Consortia's categories of data, identified additional useful measures, and made recommendations to vendors and libraries about generating, analyzing, and interpreting use data.[151] Shim and McClure reported and made recommendations based on efforts to standardize vendor usage statistics as part of the ARL's E-Metrics Project. E-Metrics Project studies included surveys of libraries about problems associated with usage reports and field tests of vendor statistics.[152] Hahn and

Faulkner derived three metrics to evaluate the value and performance of e-journals based on use statistics provided by High Wire Press and used these to develop benchmarks for evaluating potential purchases. After applying these benchmarks to two test titles, the researcher concluded that they were reliable.[153]

Evaluating the Collection Development Process

Only a few researchers chose to tackle the problem of assessing the collection development program, or as Carrigan characterized it "to determine how effectively collection developers allocate the resources at their disposal."[154]

Bias was investigated by Harmeyer, who evaluated one aspect of the collection development process in California academic and public libraries. His survey of library holdings of eight prochoice and prolife books indicated that non–religiously affiliated academic and public libraries were three times as likely to hold prochoice than prolife books.[155] Ochola and Jones reported the results of their survey of teaching faculty and librarian assessments of the Baylor University's library liaison program. The data were used to develop recommendations to help invigorate the program.[156] Mozenter, Sanders, and Welch described the restructuring of the liaison program at the University of North Carolina at Charlotte and their survey of teaching faculty to assess the effectiveness of their assigned subject librarians. The researchers identified program planning, responsibility, training, evaluation, and communication characteristics that were associated with an effective liaison program.[157] Yang also approached the evaluation of the library liaison program by surveying the faculty. Faculty at Texas A&M University identified updates about the services available, consulting on supporting instructional needs, and ordering books or serials as the primary services they needed. These services were compared with those offered by the library, and library services were found to be fairly consistent with faculty expectations. However, faculty were unaware of some of the services the library provided.[158] Dinkins evaluated library and faculty selection at Stetson University by comparing the percent of selections that circulated at least once during the period of the study.[159] As part of an evaluation of George Washington University Libraries' monograph acquisitions program, Stebelman compared the titles acquired by the library with those reviewed by *Choice* and analyzed the findings by subject and publisher type.[160]

Cooperative Collection Development

Much as been written about cooperative collection development both pre- and post-1990. In recent years, electronic resources and the resulting increased importance of consortia have provided a wealth of opportunities for cooperation and collaboration. A number of authors provided the historical, theoretical, and organizational contexts in which to consider cooperative collection development efforts.[161] The research literature included efforts to quantify cooperative efforts and characterize and measure their success. Case studies reflected the range of these efforts.

The majority of respondents to the 1998 ARL survey on cooperative collection management programs had at least one collaborative relationship and one consortium membership. The most common reason for collaboration was to expand services and collections, and the acquisition of materials—usually electronic—was the most common form of collaboration. The researchers noted that cooperative efforts for print resources occurred most frequently in area studies.[162] A working group formed by the Center for Research Libraries (CRL) surveyed libraries in order to "map" cooperative collection development activities and also found that cooperative projects for print materials frequently focused on area studies. The working group identified 89 projects, most of which began after 1990, and the majority of survey respondents reported that at least one of their cooperative activities was the shared purchase of electronic resources.[163]

A number of qualitative studies and analyses that identified factors related to successful programs mostly focused on print-based cooperative programs. Dominguez and Swindler researched the history of the Triangle Research Libraries Network's cooperative programs from the 1930s to the early 1990s and identified seven factors that promoted successful collection development.[164] Butler described seven law library cooperative collection development programs and identified institutional culture, economic incentives, and increased interlibrary loan efficiency and effectiveness as factors that had contributed to program success.[165] Hightower and Soete reviewed the physical science translation journal collaborative collection development project at the University of California. Based on the experiences and the problems encountered by the participating libraries they identified 12 strategies for successful collaborative collection management.[166] Dannelly provided cases studies of OhioLINK and the Committee on Institutional Cooperation and identified characteristics common to productive programs.[167] Based on his analysis of Latin American studies cooperative collection development projects, Hazen identified seven conditions for success.[168] The projects studied by the CRL Best Practices Working Group included those that focused on electronic as well as print materials and on access, storage, and preservation. The group found best practices in the areas of communication and consultation, goals and focus, flexibility and adaptability, and technological structure.[169]

Only a handful of researchers presented quantitative analysis of the benefits of cooperative programs. Erickson described the Tri-College University's cooperative collection development program for books. He then presented the results of three historical studies in which effectiveness was measured by the savings resulting from the number of consortially purchased titles that each library did not need to purchase.[170] The California State University Libraries' study of their multicampus shared e-book collection included an analysis of use statistics and a user survey. The researchers identified strategies for expanding the e-book cooperative acquisitions program.[171] Kingma compared the cost of interlibrary loan in one research library consortium with the savings that could be achieved through cooperative collection development and concluded that the savings would not cover the costs of coordinating consortium collection development.[172] Scigliano's analysis compared the costs and benefits of a database acquired through a consortial purchase with those of its paper counterpart. She calculated benefits in terms of the value of time saved by the users of the electronic resource and net library savings for the electronic versions.[173] CRL's Working Group for Qualitative Evaluation of Cooperative Collection Development developed performance measures for evaluating a cooperative project in terms of reduced costs, increased access to information, and increased use and user satisfaction.[174] Kohl and Sanville provided evidence that OhioLINK had improved cost-effectiveness for member libraries as measured by expanding access to, and use of, journal literature.[175]

The literature of the period also included case studies of how consortia and cooperative projects operated and functioned. Gammon and Zeoli reported on the "Not Bought in Ohio" cooperative collection development program for books.[176] Curl and Zeoli reported on the CONSORT Libraries' cooperative collection development project, which is based on a shared approval plan. They presented a list of lessons learned based on their experiences with its development and implementation.[177] Rohe, O'Donovan, and Hanawalt described three PORTAL libraries' projects, the most extensive of which was an effort to expand access to titles listed in *Books for College Libraries* at the 12 participating academic libraries.[178] Dole and Chang described the use of the OCLC / AMIGOS Collection Analysis System to compare the monographic holding of the State University of New York (SUNY) University Center libraries.[179] Dwyer described the California State University libraries' cooperative buying program and the process by which electronic resources were identified and evaluated for the core collection.[180] A number of collection assessments for cooperative projects employed strategies and frameworks adapted from the Conspectus, a tool developed in the 1980s by RLG to facilitate the identification of collection strengths and weaknesses with the ultimate goal of coordinating regional and national collection development. Cochenour and Rutstein reviewed the Colorado Alliance of Research Libraries' (CARL) experience conducting overlap studies, documenting collecting levels, and creating collection management reports in order to create a cooperative collection development environment.[181]

Medina and Highfill documented the history and development of the Network of Alabama Academic Libraries and that network's use of collection assessment methodologies based on the RLG Conspectus.[182] The Alaska multitype library collection assessment project, described by Stephens, employed a modified Conspectus framework that evolved into the WLN Conspectus.[183]

Collection Evaluation and Assessment

All vital academic libraries employ some methods of collection assessment, and since 1990, interest in these efforts has been intense. A number of very useful reviews of the large body of collection evaluation and assessment literature were published, as were evaluation and assessment guides and manuals aimed at the practitioner.[184] Most of the accounts of collection evaluation and assessment published since 1990 reported on the process of conducting evaluations on the local level and their outcomes. These local studies often employed multiple methodologies, included both collection-based and user-based assessments, and were conducted to inform decisions about subscription renewals, cancellations, and storage.

The literature included fewer reports of collection managers' efforts to develop or improve collection evaluation and assessment methodologies.

Local Holdings Studies

Many of the local holdings studies were facilitated by access to the National/North American Title Count, the OCLC/Amigos Collection Analysis System, and recently by R. R. Bowker's Ulrich's Serials Analysis System (USAS). Practitioners analyzed and compared all holdings, or holdings in selected subject areas, as the basis of their local collection assessments. Dole used the OCLC/AMIGOS Collection Analysis System to compare monograph holdings of one ARL library with those of a peer group chosen by the university president and a peer group consisting of similarly ranked ARL libraries. Her analysis yielded information on overlap with these peer groups and identified collecting patterns that needed to be changed.[185] Perrault and others conducted an evaluation of the monograph holdings at 28 community college libraries in Florida and found that the overall median age of their materials was 24 years. They also calculated the median age and provided a distribution analysis of date of publication by subject area.[186] The researchers conducted a follow-up survey to assess the impact of their analysis.[187] Paskoff and Perrault sampled the shelflist to profile the Louisiana State University library collection by age and language of publication, duplication, and subject distribution.[188] Metz and Gasser used USAS to analyze serials subscriptions held by the members of the Virtual Library of Virginia and used their data to identify potential new publisher partners.[189]

Pancheshnikov compared the percentage of books and serials pertaining to agricultural sciences courses in the University of Saskatchewan Library with the percentage available in the National Agriculture Library.[190] Webster assigned National Title Count Classification categories to history courses offered at the University of Central Arkansas and compared that library's holding in those categories with holdings of peer institutions. He then compared the results with student enrollment data in order to identify collection strengths and weaknesses.[191]

Dodd and Gyeszly compared the business collection shelflist count at Texas A&M University with ARL peer institution holdings to identify collection gaps.[192] Grover used data from the National Shelflist Count to analyze Brigham Young University Library's foreign language and area studies collections. He compared holding with five randomly selected libraries and with all participating libraries and then compared the circulation of these materials with that of the total collection.[193] Ciliberti reported on the use of the OCLC/AMIGOS Collection Analysis System as part of a pilot methodology to assesses special education and counseling monographs.[194] Lotlikar employed list checking, along with circulation data, to assess the political science collection at Millersville University.[195]

Use

Use studies employed a wide range of measures, including circulation, in-house use, interlibrary loan data, and vendor-supplied use statistics. Green used the slip method to record use of current journal issues and factored in the length of time each title had been available in order to develop a usage index for science and engineering journals.[196] Chrzastowski and Olesko reported the results of three studies conducted between 1988 and 1996 at the University of Illinois in which use data were collected from reshelving counts, interlibrary loan returns, and circulation returns.[197] The sweep method was used by McBride and Behm to gather data for their year-long study of print and microfilm journal use. The results helped them identify titles for retention, storage, and cancellation.[198] Dole and Chang reported on the journal use surveys and analyses conducted in the early 1990s at SUNY Stony Brook. The methods they used to measure collection demand included reshelving counts, faculty rankings of journals to which the libraries subscribed, and analyses of titles cited by faculty and doctoral students.[199] Ruppel analyzed monographs borrowed through interlibrary loan at the University of Southern Indiana Library and determined that the majority were indicators of subject needs, favorably reviewed, recent publications, and easy to obtain. She concluded that a buy-on-demand program would be appropriate.[200]

Several other researchers incorporated faculty rankings or other measures of faculty evaluation into their use studies. Lent's study of the women's studies journal collection at the University of New Hampshire focused on faculty reading habits. Her analysis compared data from a faculty survey of journal titles they read and browsed with subscribed titles, titles included in databases heavily used by students, and interlibrary loan statistics.[201] Bustion and Eltinge asked faculty at George Washington University to rank journals on a scale of 1 to 5, with 1 being essential to instruction and research and 5 being not related to the instruction and research program. The researchers compared rankings by department with price data and used these findings to identify titles for cancellation.[202] At Louisiana State University Medical Center, Tucker surveyed faculty to identify the importance of subscribed titles to the department's work. She used these data, along with use, cost, and impact factor to cancel subscriptions.[203]

Knievel, Wicht, and Connaway analyzed the English language monograph collection at the University of Colorado at Boulder, using interlibrary loan and circulation in combination with holdings data. Their findings demonstrated the importance of combining different types of data for collection development decision making.[204]

Ochola employed "percentage of expected use" and "ratio of borrowings to holdings" measures to analyze interlibrary loan and circulation data to evaluate the monograph collection at Baylor.[205] Littman and Connaway compared the use of print and electronic versions of books in the libraries at Duke University and found that, although the patterns of use by subject were similar, the electronic versions were used 11% more than the print.[206] Bailey found that between 2003 and 2004 the use of netLibrary books increased while the use of print materials decreased.[207] Chrzastowski, Blobaum, and Welshmer studied the use of Beilstein's *Handbuch der Organischen Chemie* at the University of Illinois and University of Delaware. Based on the low level of use they found and the title's high subscription price, they concluded that it was cost-ineffective.[208] Black analyzed the cost effectiveness of the College of St. Rose library's journal collection in terms of price per use, expenditure per enrollment, enrollment per subscription, and journal use per enrollment.[209] Samson, Derry, and Eggleston reported on efforts at the University of Montana–Missoula to review the networked resources collection using cost, subject coverage, and content overlap as well as usage data.[210]

Citation Analysis

Practitioners used citations from theses and dissertations, student papers, faculty publications, and textbooks and other course materials to help assess the adequacy of their collections. Herubel compared serial citations in philosophy dissertations written at Purdue University with library holdings to determine the extent to which the library provided in-house support for dissertation research.[211] Sylvia and Lesher used citations in psychology and counseling theses and dissertations, along with cost-per-use and shelving statistics, to evaluate the collection at St. Mary's University in San Antonio.[212] Smith conducted a longitudinal study of the usefulness of the University of Georgia Library collection to graduate students by analyzing dissertation and theses citations and comparing cited works to works held by the libraries.[213] Haycock investigated citations to monographs and journals included in 43 education dissertations written at the University of Minnesota and used the data to determine journal retentions and cancellations. She also calculated the serial-monograph citation ratio and compared it to ratios found by other researchers.[214] In order to develop a rank-ordered list of serials, Waugh and Ruppel explored citations from dissertations and theses on workforce education and applied a weighting formula to reflect the frequency with which each title was cited across all of the source documents included in the study.[215] Sylvia conducted an analysis of citations in graduate and undergraduate student psychology papers.[216] Leiding analyzed the citations in advanced undergraduate research papers written at James Madison University in terms of material type, publication date, format, and discipline. She compared citations with library holdings to determine levels of local availability.[217] Using undergraduate papers written at four institutions, St. Clair and Magrill analyzed citations by subject of paper, formats cited, numbers of citations, and publication date.[218]

By and large, researchers who studied citations in faculty publications focused on science and, to a lesser extent, social science disciplines. Hughes used journal titles cited by molecular and cellular biologists at Pennsylvania State University, titles in which these faculty published, and Journal Citation Report data to create a core list of titles as part of a larger collection assessment project.[219] Lascar and Mendelsohn examined citations in publications by structural biologists, along with anecdotal data on journal use from these faculty, and used the results to support a proposal for additional journal subscriptions.[220] Crotteau reviewed citations in biology faculty publications and Journal Citation Reports to evaluate library support for these researchers. He then conducted a survey to determine how these faculty authors obtained cited titles not held in the library.[221] Haas and Lee assessed the adequacy of the forestry journal collection at the University of Florida by studying titles faculty cited and the journals in which they published.[222]

Lightman and Manilov used faculty citations to and in their publications, along with comparisons to standardized lists and availability at other libraries, to assess Northwestern's economics collection.[223] Similarly, Dykeman investigated citations to monographs, periodicals, proceedings, other serials, technical reports, theses, and government documents included in publications authored by Georgia Institute of Technology faculty, and Schaffer examined citations in psychology faculty publications at Texas A&M University by material type, subject, date, availability as electronic full text, and source of electronic full text.[224] Gao and Yu's study of citations in publications by faculty in the departments of surveying and mapping at Wuhan University enabled them to identify collection strengths and gaps.[225] Stelk and Lancaster evaluated the religious studies collection at the University of Illinois by checking the bibliographic references in the religious studies course textbooks.[226] Rupp-Serrano based a needs assessment of social work students on materials cited in course syllabi.[227]

Student Surveys

Prior to the introduction of LibQUAL+, which measures student expectations and perceptions about, among other things, collection adequacy, very few local collection evaluations included a student opinion component. Weaver administered a survey to undergraduate students in selected social sciences, humanities, and life science courses and conducted follow-up interviews with course instructors as a means of assessing the library's local book collection.[228] At Oakland University, Condic surveyed students about the types of materials they would purchase in a tight budget environment and their satisfaction with the library's book and journal collection.[229] At the University of Northern Colorado, Rathe and Blankenship gathered patron opinions about the importance and usefulness of the recreational reading collection.[230]

Methodological Studies

The researchers conducting methodological studies tested the effectiveness, usefulness, and/or accuracy of collection evaluation methods. In some cases, their purpose was to better understand what they were measuring, and in others, it was to develop better evaluation tools.

Holdings

In an effort to develop a core list of titles for undergraduate libraries, Hardesty and Mak performed an overlap study of the holdings of 427 undergraduate libraries. The wide divergence they found in the titles owned led them to conclude that such a core list did not exist.[231] Siverson developed a method of scaling standard bibliographies in order to introduce local collecting priorities into the interpretation of the results of the checklist collection evaluation method.[232]

Using the measures of existing collection strength specified in the Music Conspectus documents of 17 RLG libraries, McGrath and Nuzzo tested the hypotheses that "existing collection strength" can serve as a proxy for shelflist counts. After correlating 138 LC ranges across the libraries and within individual libraries, they concluded that the existing collection strength measure can be used as a proxy for shelflist within individual libraries but cannot be used to compare libraries.[233] White developed "brief tests of collection strength," a methodology for assigning or verifying Conspectus collection levels without conducting extensive holdings comparisons and analyses.[234] Twiss conducted two "brief tests" on the Soviet history collections in five libraries and compared the results with the levels these libraries had assigned to their collections. His findings supported the validity of White's methodology and illustrated the ease with which it could be applied.[235] To identify the strengths and weaknesses of both evaluation methods, Benedetto Beals and Gilmour used the "brief test" method and OCLC's WorldCat Analysis System to analyze the zoology collections in three academic libraries.[236] In his study of the composition of WorldCat records, Bernstein provided evidence that the range of holdings for the Conspectus' Research Level should be revised.[237]

Use

Britten and Webster identified characteristics of books that actively circulated to develop an assessment methodology that could serve as an alternative to costly, time-consuming use studies.[238] Banks also studied relationships between several characteristics of books and circulation. She found shelf level to be the strongest determinant of circulation.[239] Selth, Koller, and Briscoe studied the circulation and in-house use of books in a large research library and found evidence to contradict the results of previous studies in which the two types of use were highly correlated.[240] In a test of widely held assumptions about how often students browse to identify useful library resources and about the need to develop just-in-case collections, Ridley and Weber found that student browsing was uncommon.[241] Use of transaction log data to describe e-book use was explored by Connaway and Snyder. They identified unobtrusiveness and the ability to conduct both micro and macro analyses as advantages to this method, but identified the large quantity of data in these logs and other issues related to how they collect and store data as drawbacks to their use.[242]

A study of the use of current issues of journals by Sauer found that unused titles continue to receive little or no use after they are bound or replaced with microfilm.[243] Naylor compared the results of a journal reshelving study and a self-reported use study conducted at the same research library and discovered that the reshelving method reported higher use.[244]

Although research on the meaning and validity of vendor-generated use statistics is still in its infancy, the literature includes a small body of methodological studies. Davis studied title use reported by HighWire Press and found that the user population could be estimated based on the number of downloads and that this relationship was consistent over time and across institutions.[245] Culpepper compared the usage reports generated by three database vendors with locally produced usage reports and faculty assessments of the utility of specific databases in order to demonstrate the usefulness of the vendor reports.[246] In response to concern over the lack of standardization of vendor-supplied use measures, Bauer developed two indexes, one to measure change in print usage and another to measure change in electronic resource usage based on statistics the library tracked in house, rather on data obtained from publishers and vendors.[247]

Duy and Vaughan addressed the need for standardized vendor statistics by studying the relationship between locally collected usage data of electronic resources at North Carolina State University and the vendor-supplied usage data. Findings indicated that over the course of a year, the data collected by the libraries' Web server logs and those provided by the vendors showed similar use patterns, but that the quantitative measures were not the same.[248] In their study of vendor-supplied usage data for electronic journals, these authors found a statistically significant correlation between these data and print usage data for journals in chemistry, biology and related fields.[249] McDowell and Gorman found no correlation between the types of vendor-supplied use statistics with those preferred by New Zealand academic collection development librarians. Their data support the need for customizable usage statistics.[250]

Citation Analysis

Beile, Botte, and Killingsworth explored the validity of using doctoral dissertation citations to evaluate collections by comparing citations in dissertations written at three institutions in terms of their quality and availability in the home libraries. They found that the quality of the sources cited varied and that doctoral students tended to cite materials available to them. The researchers concluded that citations studies could be used to identify local use but advised caution when using them to assess collection adequacy.[251] Zipp determined that theses and dissertation citations could serve as surrogates for faculty publication citations in evaluating research collections.[252] Millson-Martula and Watson compared the effectiveness of determining undergraduate serial needs by using citations from student papers, reshelving and ILL data, and surveys and concluded that the citation method was the most effective indicator of met and unmet needs.[253]

Nisonger demonstrated the bias inherent in averaging Impact Factor data from multiple years and proposed an adjusted Impact Factor as an alternative.[254] He also addressed the question of whether the rate of self-citation affected journal rankings and concluded that it did not.[255] Altmann and Gorman studied the relationship between Impact Factor and journal use to determine if Impact Factor data could substitute for the more costly-to-collect use data. They concluded that it was not an effective predictor of use.[256] Chung found that Impact Factors could not be used as substitutes for local citation scores and developed a method of combining these two scores to measure the cost-effectiveness of a journal collection.[257] Working only with mathematics journals, Moline concluded that there was no relationship between price per character and Impact Factor.[258] Dilevko and Atkinson developed a procedural model for determining the quality of journals without Impact Factors.[259] Kreider correlated the global citation data from Journal Citation Reports with the Local Journal Utilization Report for the University of British Columbia and found that high global citation counts correlated with local citation counts but that this correlation became weaker as the number of counts decreased.[260] Goldstein found that impact factors and ranking were correlated with, and therefore could predict, local use of chemistry journals in a small departmental library.[261] Coleman calculated measures of journal affinity, association, and consumption factor for the *Journal of Education for Library and Information Science* and contrasted these with the journal's Impact Factor in order to illustrate the limitations of the Impact Factor as a measure of journal value.[262] An and Qiu found a statistically significant correlation between Journal Impact Factors and the Web Impact Factors of the journal Web sites for 42 Chinese engineering journals.[263]

Lancaster and others explored the possibility of using the relationship between scatter and journal availability to evaluate collections in departmental libraries, the library system to which they belong, and an overarching library network.[264] Calhoun developed a model of an academic library serial collection using titles included in several abstracting and indexing services and explored the correlation between journal subject category rank and union holdings rank in order to determine if the correlation could be extended to the arts and humanities literature.[265]

Conclusion

The studies that exerted the most influence during the past decade and a half were those that documented the shrinking national and local collections. These were conducted early in the 1990s, and none of the later studies matched their impact. They quantified what collection managers intuitively knew was happening, and the jolt they gave to the profession affected immediate collection management practice and laid the foundation for the profession's interest in changing the scholarly communication process.

The most useful studies for collection manager's day-to-day work were those that provided data on collection growth, prices, and expenditures over time. These also contained some analyses, but they were primarily important as sources of reliable, comparable data that collection managers could use to advocate for new funding and plan for ubiquitous budget reductions. Studies that described the way collection management was carried out at other academic libraries were also valuable to practitioners. Since 1990, surveys and, to a lesser extent, other types of quantitative studies provided snapshots of how member libraries were organized for collection management, trained their bibliographers, selected their information resources, documented their collection practices, and allocated their acquisitions funds. Qualitative studies were also published that described how libraries managed their collections of electronic resources and participated in cooperative collection development. Unfortunately, the literature included far fewer studies that could help practitioners measure the *effectiveness* of these collection management processes.

Collection evaluation and assessment was arguably the most active collection management research category. Much of this research employed multiple methodologies or at least multiple methods of measuring the variables under study. Researchers conducted both user- and collection-centered evaluations. Collection evaluations and assessments were predominantly local efforts motivated by budgetary considerations, and most operationalized "collection value" as "use." However, this category also included research on the evaluation methods themselves, the purpose of which was to improve assessment accuracy, the quantity and quality of data that could be collected, and/or the ease or efficiency with which evaluations could be conducted. As a group, these studies, along with those that addressed collection size and growth, constituted the best-designed and most methodologically sophisticated and interesting research.

The previous examples not withstanding, overall the collection management research literature was limited in the breadth of methodologies and statistical analyses employed, as well as in the scope of problems addressed. It was predominantly survey- and case study–based and, with the exception of annual statistics on library operations and industry sales, most studies were conducted only once; the literature included few reports of follow-up or replication studies. The majority of researchers used only basic descriptive statistics to analyze their data. Many never fully explored the relationships among the variables in their studies, even when the data they would have needed to do so were presented in the results of the study. The research literature was also limited in scope in that most of it focused on collection management inputs and processes. Collection managers conducted most of their research in order to gather the information they needed to continue to function within a climate of unrelenting change. However, what they learned frequently had a short shelf-life. As Peter Hernon observed:

[W]ith the pace of change so great, it can be difficult to produce research having long-term value—conceptually and practically. *Change and managerial needs may outpace the ability of researchers to deliver insights useful to the future, let alone the present.* In some instances, by the time that researchers have gathered and presented the data, a new culture with new needs and solutions may have emerged.[266]

In an environment in which colleges and universities are increasingly under pressure to demonstrate and quantify the value of the educational experience they offer, the agenda for future collection management research must focus on effectiveness, outcomes, and impact. At the very least, collection managers will need to move from describing the components of the collection management process to assessing process effectiveness, a task that will grow increasingly more complicated as new information resource formats, open-access content, and mass digitization projects alter the concept of the academic library collection. Beyond that, they will need to employ sophisticated research designs and data analysis to learn more about student and faculty information needs and preferences, and their use of the information resources available to them. Data from this type of research will more effectively inform collection managers' day-to-day decision making and longer range planning and will enable them to contribute to library-wide efforts to identify outcomes and assess the impact of collections and services.

References

1. Charles B. Osburn, "Collection Development and Management," in *Academic Libraries: Research Perspectives,* ed. Mary Jo Lynch, 1–37 (Chicago: American Library Association, 1990).

2. Literature reviews consulted included those for 1990–1992 by David S. Sullivan, William S. Monroe, Stephen Lehmann, and James H. Spohrer that appeared in volumes 35–37 of *Library Resources and Technical Services;* those for 1996 and 1997 by Thomas E. Nisonger that appeared in volumes 17–18 of *Collection Building;* and Linda L. Phillips and Sara R. Williams, "Collection Development Embraces the Digital Age: A Review of the Literature, 1997–2003," *Library Resources and Technical Services* 48, no. 4 (2004): 273–299.

3. Anthony M. Cummings and others, *University Libraries and Scholarly Communication: A Study Prepared for the Andrew W. Mellon Foundation* (Washington, DC: Association of Research Libraries, 1992).

4. Association of Research Libraries Committee on Collection Development, "Research Libraries in a Global Context: An Exploratory Paper," rev. ed. (Washington, DC: Association of Research Libraries, 1992), http://www.arl.org/resources/pubs/aau/fa/background.shtml (accessed March 31, 2008).

5. Jutta Reed-Scott, *Scholarship, Research Libraries, and Global Publishing: The Result of a Study Funded by The Andrew W. Mellon Foundation* (Washington, DC: Association of Research Libraries, 1996).

6. Mary E. Jackson and others, *Changing Global Book Collection Patterns in ARL Libraries* (Washington, DC: Association of Research Libraries, 2006), http://www.arl.org/bm~doc/grn_global_book.pdf (accessed March 31, 2008).

7. The Association of Research Libraries has issued annual compilations of member statistics since 1961–1962. The most recent edition is Martha Kyrillidou and Mark Young, eds., *ARL Statistics 2004–2005* (Washington, DC: Association of Research Libraries, 2006).

8. Richard Hume Werking, "Collection Growth and Expenditures in Academic Libraries: A Preliminary Inquiry," *College and Research Libraries* 52, no. 1 (1991): 5–23.

9. Anna H. Perrault, "The Shrinking National Collection: A Study of the Effects of the Diversion of Funds from Monographs to Serials on the Monograph Collections of Research Libraries," *Library Acquisitions: Practice and Theory* 18, no. 1 (1994): 3–22.

10. Tina E. Chrzastowski and Karen A. Schmidt, "Surveying the Damage: Academic Library Serial Cancellations 1987–88 through 1989–90," *College and Research Libraries* 54, no. 2 (1993): 93–102; Tina E. Chrzastowski and Karen A. Schmidt, "Collections at Risk: Revisiting Serial Cancellations in Academic Libraries," *College and Research Libraries* 57, no. 4 (1996): 351–364.

11. Tina E. Chrzastowski and Karen A. Schmidt, "The Serials Cancellation Crisis: National Trends in Academic Library Serial Collections," *Library Acquisitions: Practice and Theory* 21, no. 4 (1997): 431–443.

12. Tina E. Chrzastowski, "National Trends in Academic Chemistry Serial Collections, 1992–1994," *Science and Technology Libraries* 16, no. 3/4 (1997): 191–207.

13. Gordon Rowley, "Academic Libraries in Iowa Cope with Serials Cutbacks," *Collection Building* 14, no. 2 (1995): 24–28; Paul D. Burnam, "Private Liberal Arts Colleges and the Costs of Scientific Journals: A Perennial Dilemma," *College and Research Libraries* 59, no. 5 (1998): 406–420.

14. Tina E. Chrzastowski and others, "Feast AND Famine: A Statewide Science Serial Collection Assessment in Illinois," *College and Research Libraries* 68, no. 6 (2007): 517–532.

15. Brian F. Lavoie, Lynn Silipigni Connaway, and Edward T. O'Neill, "Mapping WorldCat's Digital Landscape," *Library Resources and Technical Services* 51, no. 2 (2007):106–115.

16. Annual price data and analyses based on data provided by EBSCO were published in the April 15 issue of *Library Journal*. The most recent is Lee Van Orsdel and Kathleen Born, "Serials Wars," *Library Journal* 132, no. 7 (2007): 43–48.

17. Annual periodical and serial data and analysis based on data provided by

Faxon and Swets were published in *Library Acquisitions: Practice and Theory*, *American Libraries,* and *Library Resources and Technical Services*. The most recent are available on the ALCTS Web site: Barbara Dingley, "U.S. Periodical Prices—2005," Association for Library Collections and Technical Services, http://www.ala.org/ala/alcts/pubs/pubresources/resources.cfm (accessed March 31, 2008); Nancy Chaffin and Ajaye Bloomstone. "U.S. Serial Services Price Index for 2003–2004," Association for Library Collections and Technical Services, http://www.ala.org/ala/alcts/pubs/pubresources/resources.cfm (accessed March 31, 2008).

18. *The Bowker Annual* included statistics and analyses of book output and prices. The most recent edition is: Dave Bogart, ed., *The Bowker Annual: Library and Book Trade Almanac,* 52nd ed. (Medford, NJ: Information Today, Inc., 2007).

19. Annual price increase studies for journals in veterinary medicine were conducted for a 17-year period. All studies published prior to 1990 are cited in David C. Anderson, "Journals for Academic Veterinary Medical Libraries: Price Increases, 1977–1990 and 1983–1990," *Serials Librarian* 18, no. 3/4 (1990): 73–86. All studies published thereafter are cited in Victoria T. Kok and Eleanor P. Garrison, "Journals for Academic Veterinary Medical Libraries: Price Increases, 1983–2000," *Serials Librarian* 41, no. 1 (2001): 21–30.

20. Kenneth E. Marks, Steven P. Neilsen, and Craig H. Petersen, "Longitudinal Study of Scientific Journal Prices in a Research Library," *College and Research Libraries* 52, no. 2 (1991): 125–138.

21. Gregg Sapp, "A Cost/Inflation Model for Mathematics Research Journals," *Serials Librarian* 18, no. 1/2 (1990): 155–172.

22. Deborah J. Schmidle and Barbara J. Via, "Physician Heal Thyself: The Library and Information Science Serials Crisis," *portal: Libraries and the Academy* 4, no. 2 (2004): 167–203.

23. Barbara J. Via and Deborah J. Schmidle, "Investing Wisely: Citation Rankings as a Measure of Quality in Library and Information Science Journals," *portal: Libraries and the Academy* 7, no. 3 (2007): 333–373.

24. Cummings and others, *University Libraries and Scholarly Communication*; Werking, "Collection Growth and Expenditures in Academic Libraries."

25. Chandra Prabha and John E. Ogden, "Recent Trends in Academic Library Materials Expenditures," *Library Trends* 42, no. 3 (1994): 499–513.

26. Joseph Petrick, "Electronic Resources and Acquisitions Budget: SUNY Statistics, 1994–2000," *Collection Building* 21, no. 3 (2002): 123–133.

27. See note 7; the Association of College and Research Libraries published annual statistical data from academic libraries in all Carnegie classifications. The most recent edition is Association of College and Research Libraries, *2005 Academic Library Trends and Statistics* (Chicago: Association of College and Research Libraries, 2007).

28. See note 18.

29. Barbara Hoffert, "Book Report, Part 2: What Academic Libraries Buy and How Much They Spend," *Library Journal* 123, no. 18 (September 1, 1998): 144–146.

30. Andrew Richard Albanese, "Moving from Books to Bytes," *Library Journal* 126, no. 14 (September 1, 2001): 52–54.

31. Fred W. Jenkins, "Benchmarking Library Budgets: Positioning the Library in a Competitive Environment," in *Advances in Library Administration and Organization*, vol. 16, ed. Delmus E. Williams and Edward D. Garten, 301–313 (Stamford, CT: JAI Press, 1999).

32. Frank R. Allen, "Materials Budgets in the Electronic Age: A Survey of Academic Libraries," *College and Research Libraries* 57, no. 2 (1996): 133–143

33. Peggy Johnson, *Materials Budgets in ARL Libraries: SPEC Kit 166* (Washington, DC: Association of Research Libraries, 1990).

34. Allen, "Materials Budgets in the Electronic Age."

35. John M. Budd, "Allocation Formulas in the Literature: A Review," *Library Acquisitions: Practice and Theory* 15, no. 1 (1991): 97.

36. Johnson, *Materials Budgets in ARL Libraries,* unnumbered introduction.

37. Jane H. Tuten and Beverly Jones, eds., *Allocation Formulas in Academic Libraries: CLIP Note 22* (Chicago: College Libraries Section, Association of College and Research Libraries, 1995).

38. Charles W. Brownson, "Modeling Library Materials Expenditure: Initial Experiments at Arizona State University," *Library Resources and Technical Services* 35, no. 1 (1991): 87–103.

39. William A. Britten, "A Use Statistic for Collection Management: The 80/20 Rule Revisited," *Library Acquisitions: Practice and Theory* 14, no. 2 (1990): 183–189.

40. Joseph Crotts, "Subject Usage and Funding of Library Monographs," *College and Research Libraries* 60, no. 3 (1999): 261–273.

41. Ian R. Young, "A Quantitative Comparison of Acquisitions Budget Allocation Formulas Using a Single Institutional Setting," *Library Acquisitions: Practice and Theory* 16, no. 3 (1992): 229–242.

42. Kenneth Wise and D. E. Perushek, "Linear Goal Programming for Academic Library Acquisitions Allocations," *Library Acquisitions: Practice and Theory* 20, no. 3 (1996): 311–327.

43. Kitti Canepi, "Fund Allocation Formula Analysis: Determining Elements for Best Practices in Libraries," *Library Collections, Acquisitions, and Technical Services* 31, no. 1(2007): 12–24.

44. Janis M. Bandelin and John K. Payne, "Collaboration and Reallocation: Implementing a New Collection Development Model," *Against the Grain* 12, no. 5 (2000): 40–45.

45. Lisa B. German and Karen A. Schmidt, "Finding the Right Balance: Campus Involvement in the Collections Allocation Process," *Library Collections,*

Acquisitions, and Technical Services 25, no. 4 (2001): 421–433.

46. Anish Arora and Diego Klabjan, "A Model for Budget Allocation in Multi-Unit Libraries," *Library Collections, Acquisitions, and Technical Services* 26, no. 4 (2002): 423–438.

47. Robert Sorgenfrei, "Slicing the Pie: Implementing and Living with a Journal Allocation Formula," *Library Collections, Acquisitions, and Technical Services* 23, no. 1 (1999): 39–45.

48. Charles B. Lowry, "Reconciling Pragmatism, Equity, and Need in the Formula Allocation of Books and Serials Funds," *College and Research Libraries* 53, no. 2 (1992): 121–137.

49. Susan Lafferty, Peter Warning, and Billie Vlies, "Foundation Resources: Formula-Based Allocation of an Acquisition Budget in a University Library," *Australian Academic and Research Libraries* 27, no. 4 (1996): 289–293.

50. Sulekha Kalyan, "Library Materials Budget Allocation Strategy for a Mid-Size Academic Library: A Case Study," *Acquisitions Librarian* 15, no. 29 (2003): 119–131; Claudia V. Weston, "Breaking with the Past: Formula Allocation at Portland State University," *Serials Librarian* 45, no. 4 (2004): 43–53; Merran Evans, "Library Acquisitions Formulae: The Monash Experience," *Australian Academic and Research Libraries* 27, no. 1 (1996): 47–57.

51. Timothy P. Bailey, Jeannette Barnes Lessels, and Rickey D. Best, "Using Universal Borrowing Data in the Library Book Fund Allocation Process," *Library Collections, Acquisitions, and Technical Services* 29, no. 1 (2005): 90–98.

52. Examples include Richard Snow, "Wasted Words: The Written Collection Development Policy and the Academic Library," *Journal of Academic Librarianship* 22, no. 3 (1996): 191–194; Dan C. Hazen, "Collection Development Policies in the Information Age," *College and Research Libraries* 56, no. 1 (1995): 29–31; G. Edward Evans, "Needs Analysis and Collection Development Policies for Culturally Diverse Populations," *Collection Building* 11, no. 4 (1992): 16–27; Glenn S. McGuigan and Gary W. White, "Subject-Specific Policy Statements: A Rationale and Framework for Collection Development," *Acquisitions Librarian* 15, no. 30 (2003): 15–32; Richard Fyffe, "Technological Change and the Scholarly Communications Reform Movement: Reflections on Castells and Giddens," *Library Resources and Technical Services* 46, no. 2 (2002): 50–61.

53. Examples include Joanne S. Anderson, ed., *Guide for Written Collection Policy Statements,* 2nd ed. (Chicago: American Library Association, 1996); Amanda Maple and Jean Morrow, *Guide to Writing Collection Development Policies for Music* (Lanham, MD: Scarecrow Press, 2001); Richard J. Wood and Frank Hoffman, *Library Collection Development Policies: A Reference and Writers' Handbook* (Lanham MD: Scarecrow Press, 1996).

54. Elizabeth Futas, ed., *Collection Development Policies and Procedures,* 3rd ed. (Phoenix, AZ: Oryx Press, 1995).

55. Barbara Susana Sanchez Vignau and Grizly Meneses, "Collection Development Policies in University Libraries: A Space for Reflection," *Collection Building* 24, no. 1 (2005): 35–43.

56. Kristine Brancolini, *Audiovisual Policies in College Libraries: CLIP Note 14.* (Chicago: Association of College and Research Libraries, 1991); Jennie S. Boyarkski and Kate Hickey, eds., *Collection Management in the Electronic Age: A Manual for Creating Community College Collection Development Policy Statements* (Chicago: Community and Junior College Libraries Section, Association of College and Research Libraries, 1994).

57. Jeremy Sayles, "The Textbooks-in-College-Libraries Mystery," *College and Undergraduate Libraries* 1, no. 1 (1994): 81–93.

58. Cynthia Hsieh and Rhonelle Runner, "Textbooks, Leisure Reading, and the Academic Library," *Library Collections, Acquisitions, and Technical Services* 29, no. 2 (2005): 192–204.

59. Elizabeth Parang and Laverna Saunders, eds., *Electronic Journals in ARL Libraries: Policies and Procedures: SPEC Kit 201* (Washington, DC: Association of Research Libraries, 1994); Joseph Straw, "Collection Management Statements on the World Wide Web," *Acquisitions Librarian* 15, no. 30 (2003): 77–86; Karla L. Hahn and Kari Schmidt, "Web Communications and Collections Outreach to Faculty," *College and Research Libraries* 66, no. 1 (2005): 28–37.

60. Lois Cherepon and Andrew Sankowski, "Collection Development at SJU Libraries: Compromises, Missions and Transitions, *Acquisitions Librarian* 15, no. 30, (2003): 63–76; Gary W. White and Gregory A. Crawford, "Developing an Electronic Information Resources Collection Development Policy," *Collection Building* 16, no. 2 (1997): 53–57; Ann T. Power and Jeanne Pavy, "Collection Development in the Field of Communication Studies," *Collection Building* 14, no. 2 (1995): 9–23; Ashley Robinson, "Acquisitions Policy for Contemporary Topics in an Academic Library: Managing the Ephemeral," *Acquisitions Librarian* 15, no. 30, (2003): 87–100.

61. Sheila S. Intner, "Using a Collection Development Curriculum as a Model for Developing Policy Documents in Practice," *Acquisitions Librarian* 15, no. 30 (2003): 49–62.

62. Kristine Brancolini and Rick E. Provine, *Video Collections and Multimedia in ARL Libraries: SPEC Kit 199* (Washington DC: Association of Research Libraries, 1993).

63. Kristine Brancolini, *Video Collections and Multimedia in ARL Libraries: Changing Technologies,* OMS Occasional Paper 19 (Washington DC: Association of Research Libraries, 1997).

64. Gregory A. Crawford and Matthew Harris, "Best Sellers in Academic Libraries," *College and Research Libraries* 62, no. 3 (2001): 216–225.

65. Matthew Harris and Gregory A. Crawford, "The Ownership of Religious Text by Academic Libraries," *College and Research Libraries* 63, no. 5 (2002): 450–458.

66. Michael T. Krieger, "The History and Collection of Popular American Catholic Periodicals," *Serials Librarian* 30, no. 2 (1996): 45–61; Charles A. Schwartz, "Empirical Analysis of Literature Loss," *Library Resources and Technical Services* 38, no. 2 (1994): 133–138.

67. Richard A. Stoddart and Teresa Kiser, "Zines and the Library," *Library Resources and Technical Services* 48, no. 3 (2004): 191–197.

68. Rita A. Marinko and Kristin H. Gerhard, "Representations of the Alternative Press in Academic Library Collections," *College and Research Libraries* 59, no. 4 (1998): 363–371.

69. Kevin P. Mulcahy, "Science Fiction Collections in ARL Academic Libraries," *College and Research Libraries* 67, no. 1 (2006): 15–34.

70. Lorraine J. Pellack, "Industry Standards in ARL Libraries: Electronic and On-Demand," *Collection Building* 24, no. 1 (2005): 20–28.

71. Joseph A. Salem, Jr., *Spatial Data Collections and Services: SPEC Kit 291* (Washington, DC: Association of Research Libraries, 2005).

72. Elizabeth Parang and Laverna Saunders, *Electronic Journals in ARL Libraries: Issues and Trends: SPEC Kit 202* (Washington, DC: Association of Research Libraries, 1994).

73. Parang and Saunders, *Electronic Journals: SPEC Kit 201.*

74. Linda Ashcroft and Colin Langdon, "Electronic Journals and University Library Collections," *Collection Building* 18, no. 3 (1999): 105–114.

75. Linda Ashcroft, "Issues in Developing, Managing and Marketing Electronic Journals Collections," *Collection Building* 21, no. 4 (2002): 147–154.

76. Mary M. Case, "A Snapshot in Time: ARL Libraries and Electronic Journal Resources," *ARL Bimonthly Report,* no. 235 (2004): 1–10.

77. Kristen DeVoe, "When Can Subscriptions Become Electronic-Only? Developing Guidelines for Decision Making," *Against the Grain* 17, no. 6 (2005/2006): 37–42.

78. Sarah Robbins, Cheryl McCain, and Laurie Scrivener, "The Changing Format of Reference Collections: Are Research Libraries Favoring Electronic Access over Print?" *Acquisitions Librarian* 18, no. 35/36 (2006): 75–95.

79. Michael Fosmire and Elizabeth Young, "Free Scholarly Electronic Journals: What Access Do College and University Libraries Provide?" *College and Research Libraries* 61, no. 6 (2000): 500–508.

80. Anna K. Hood. *Open Access Resources: SPEC Kit 300* (Washington, DC: Association of Research Libraries, 2007); Lavoie, Connaway, and O'Neill, "Mapping WorldCat's Digital Landscape."

81. Mary H. Munroe, John M. Haar, and Peggy Johnson, eds., *Guide to Collection Development and Management Administration, Organization, and Staffing* (Landam, MD: Scarecrow Press, 2001).

82. Gordon Rowley, *Organization of Collection Development: SPEC Kit 207* (Washington, DC: Association of Research Libraries, 1995).

83. Robert Kenselaar, "Collection Development Administration at Selected Major U.S. Research Libraries," *Collection Building* 15, no. 1 (1996): 4–9.

84. Bonita Bryant, "Staffing and Organization for Collection Development in a New Century," in *Collection Management for the 21st Century: A Handbook for Librarians*, ed. G. E. Gorman and Ruth H. Miller, 191–206. (Westport, CT: Greenwood Publishing, 1997).

85. William Fisher, "Impact of Organizational Structure on Acquisitions and Collection Development," *Library Collections, Acquisitions, and Technical Services* 25, no. 4 (2001): 409–419.

86. John Webb, "Collections and Systems: A New Organizational Paradigm for Collection Development," *Library Collections, Acquisitions, and Technical Services* 25, no. 4 (2001): 461–468.

87. Susan S. Biery, "Team Management of Collection Development from a Team Member's Perspective," *Collection Management* 25, no. 3 (2001): 11–22.

88. Gail Z. Eckwright and Mary K. Bolin, "The Hybrid Librarian: The Affinity of Collection Management with Technical Services and the Organizational Benefits of an Individualized Assignment," *Journal of Academic Librarianship* 27, no. 6 (2001): 452–456.

89. Chief among these were these articles describing the experience at Cornell's Mann Library: Samuel Demas, "Collection Development for the Electronic Library: A Conceptual and Organizational Model," *Library Hi Tech* 12, no. 3 (1994): 71–80; Samuel Demas, Peter McDonald, and Gregory Lawrence, "The Internet and Collection Development: Mainstreaming Selection of Internet Resources," *Library Resources and Technical Services* 39, no. 3 (1995): 275–290.

90. William C. Robinson, "Academic Library Collection Development and Management Positions: Announcements in *College and Research Libraries News* from 1980 through 1991," *Library Resources and Technical Services* 37, no. 2 (1993): 134–146

91. John Haar, "Scholar or Librarian? How Academic Libraries' Dualist Concept of the Bibliographer Affects Recruitment," *Collection Building* 12, no. 1/2 (1993): 18–23.

92. Gary W. White, "Academic Subject Specialist Positions in the United States: A Content Analysis of Announcements from 1990 through 1998," *Journal of Academic Librarianship* 25, no. 5 (1999): 372–382.

93. Sheila S. Intner, "Impact of the Internet on Collection Development: Where Are We Now? Where Are We Headed?: An Informal Study," *Library Collections, Acquisitions, and Technical Services* 25, no. 3 (2001):307–322.

94. Sonja L. McAbee and John-Bauer Graham, "Expectations, Realities, and Perceptions of Subject Specialist Librarians' Duties in Medium-Sized Academic Libraries," *Journal of Academic Librarianship* 31, no. 1 (2005): 19–28.

95. Myoung Chung Wilson and Hendrik Edelman, "Collection Development in an Interdisciplinary Context," *Journal of Academic Librarianship* 22, no. 3 (1996): 195–200.

96. Georgina Hardy and Sheila Corrall, "Revisiting the Subject Librarian: A Study of English, Law and Chemistry," *Journal of Librarianship and Information Science* 39, no. 2 (2007): 79–91.

97. Daniel G. Dorner, "The Impact of Digital Information Resources on the Roles of Collection Managers in Research Libraries," *Library Collections, Acquisitions, and Technical Services* 28, no. 3 (2004): 249–274.

98. Examples include Peggy Johnson, *Fundamentals of Collection Development and Management* (Chicago: American Library Association, 2004); G. Edward Evans and Margaret Z. Saponaro, *Developing Library and Information Center Collections,* 5th ed. (Westport CT: Libraries Unlimited, 2005); Peter Clayton and G. E. Gorman, *Managing Information Resources in Libraries: Collection Management in Theory and Practice* (London: Library Association Publishing, 2001); Clare Jenkins and Mary Morley, *Collection Management in Academic Libraries,* 2nd ed. (Aldershot, UK: Gower Publishing, 1999).

99. Haar, "Scholar or Librarian?"

100. John M. Budd and Patricia L. Brill, "Education for Collection Management: Results of a Survey of Educators and Practitioners," *Library Resources and Technical Services* 38, no. 4 (1994): 343–353.

101. Paul Metz, "Collection Development in the Library and Information Science Curriculum," in *Recruiting, Educating, and Training Librarians for Collection Development,* ed. Peggy Johnson and Sheila S. Intner, 87–97 (Westport CT: Greenwood Press, 1994).

102. Virgil L. P. Blake and Thomas T. Surprenant, "Navigating the Parallel Universe: Education for Collection Management in the Electronic Age," *Library Trends* 48, no. 4 (2000): 891–922.

103. Lewis-Guodo Liu and Bryce L. Allen, "Business Librarians: Their Education and Training," *College and Research Libraries* 62, no. 6 (2001): 555–563.

104. Examples include Vicki L. Gregory, *Selecting and Managing Electronic Resources: A How-to-Do-It Manual for Librarians 101* (New York: Neal-Schuman, 2000); Donnelyn Curtis, Virginia M. Scheschy, and Adolfo R. Tarango, *Developing and Managing Electronic Journal Collections: A How-to-Do-It Manual for Librarians 102* (New York: Neal-Schuman, 2000); Stuart Lee, *Building an Electronic Resource Collection: A Practical Guide* (London: Library Association Publishing, 2002); Susan L. Fales, ed., *Guide for Training Collection Development Librarians* (Chicago: American Library Association, 1996); Andrew White and Eric Djiva Kamal, *E-Metrics for Library and Information Professionals* (New York: Neal-Schuman, 2006).

105. Mary F. Casserly and Judith L. Hegg, "A Study of Collection Development Personnel Training and Evaluation in Academic Libraries," *Library Acquisitions: Practice and Theory* 17, no. 3 (1993): 249–262.

106. Eric Forte and others, "Developing a Training Program for Collection Managers," *Library Collections, Acquisitions, and Technical Services* 26, no. 3 (2002): 299–306.

107. Lucy Eleonore Lyons, "The Dilemma for Academic Librarians with Collection Development Responsibilities: A Comparison of the Value of Attending Library Conferences versus Academic Conferences," *Journal of Academic Librarianship* 33, no. 2 (2007): 180–189.

108. Juris Dilevko and others, "Investigating the Value of Scholarly Book Reviews for the Work of Academic Reference Librarians," *Journal of Academic Librarianship* 32, no. 5 (2006): 452–466.

109. Casserly and Hegg, "Study of Collection Development Personnel Training and Evaluation."

110. Jack Siggins, ed., *Performance Appraisal of Collection Development Librarians: SPEC Kit 181* (Washington, DC: Association of Research Libraries, 1992).

111. Kenselaar, "Collection Development Administration."

112. Russell F. Dennison, "Quality Assessment of Collection Development though Tiered Checklists: Can You Prove You Are a Good Collection Developer?" *Collection Building* 19, no. 1 (2000): 24–27

113. Diana Gonzalez-Kirby, "Case Studies in Collection Development: Setting an Agenda for Future Research," *Collection Building* 11, no. 2 (1991): 2–9.

114. Paul O. Jenkins, "Faculty Priorities: Where Does Material Selection Stand?" *Collection Building* 15, no. 1 (1996): 19–20.

115. Paul O. Jenkins, "Book Reviews and Faculty Book Selection," *Collection Building* 18, no. 1 (1999): 4–5.

116. Hui-Min Kuo, "Surveying Faculty Book Selection in a Comprehensive University Library," *Collection Building* 19, no. 1 (2000): 27–35.

117. Jeffrey D. Kushkowski, "A Method for Determining Faculty Preferences for Monographs," *Collection Building* 19, no. 1 (2000): 17–32.

118. Felix T. Chu, "Librarians-Faculty Relations in Collection Development," *Journal of Academic Librarianship* 23, no. 1 (1997): 15–20.

119. Robert Neville, James Williams III, and Caroline Hunt, "Faculty-Library Teamwork in Book Ordering," *College and Research Libraries* 59, no. 6 (1998): 524–533.

120. Gary W. White, "Collaborative Collection Building of Electronic Resources: A Business Faculty/Librarian Partnership," *Collection Building* 23, no. 4 (2004): 177–181.

121. Ada M. Ducas and Nicole Michaud-Oystryk, "Toward a New Venture: Building Partnerships with Faculty," *College and Research Libraries* 65, no. 4 (2004): 334–348.

122. James H. Walther, "Case Examination of Decision-Making Factors: Do Faculty and Librarians Agree on Criteria Upon Which to Cancel Journals?" in *Advances in Library Administration and Organization*, vol. 23, ed. Edward D. Garten, Delmus E. Williams, and James M. Nyce, 281–331 (Stamford, CT: JAI Press, 2006).

123. Hur-Li Lee, "Collection Development as a Social Process," *Journal of Academic*

Librarianship 29, no. 1 (2003): 23–31.

124. Jean Walstrom Haley and James Talaga, "Academic Library Responses to Journal Price Discrimination," *College and Research Libraries* 53, no.1 (1992): 61–70.

125. John S. Spencer and Christopher Millson-Martula, "Serials Cancellations in College and Small University Libraries: The National Scene," *Serials Librarian* 49, no. 4 (2006): 135–155.

126. Paul Metz and John Stemmer, "A Reputational Study of Academic Publishers," *College and Research Libraries* 57, no. 3 (1996): 234–247.

127. Janice Steed Lewis. "An Assessment of Publisher Quality by Political Science Librarians," *College and Research Libraries* 61, no. 4 (2000): 313–323.

128. James H. Sweetland and Peter G. Christensen, "Developing Language and Literature Collections in Academic Libraries: A Survey," *Journal of Academic Librarianship* 23, no. 2 (1997): 119–125.

129. Timothy D. Jewell, *Selection and Presentation of Commercially Available Electronic Resources: Issues and Practices* (Washington, DC: Digital Library Federation Council on Library and Information Resources, 2001).

130. Louis A. Pitschmann, *Building Sustainable Collections of Third-Party Web Resources* (Washington, DC: Digital Library Federation Council on Library and Information Resources, 2001).

131. Jean L. Loup and Helen Lloyd Snoke, "Analysis of Selection Activities to Supplement Approval Plans," *Library Resources and Technical Services* 35, no. 2 (1991): 202–216.

132. Susan Flood, *Evolution and Status of Approval Plans: SPEC Kit 221* (Washington, DC: Association of Research Libraries, 1997).

133. John C. Calhoun, James K. Bracken, and Kenneth L. Firestein, "Modeling an Academic Approval Program," *Library Resources and Technical Services* 34, no. 3 (1990): 367–379.

134. Keren Dali and Juris Dilevko, "Beyond Approval Plans: Methods of Selection and Acquisition of Books in Slavic and East European Languages in North American Libraries," *Library Collections, Acquisitions, and Technical Services* 29, no. 3 (2005): 238–269.

135. Joseph Kurien Pulikuthiel, "Book Procurement on Approval Basis in the Centre for Development Studies Library: A Micro Level Study," *Acquisitions Librarian* 15, no. 29 (2003): 133–148.

136. Betty Galbraith, "Evaluating Blackwell's Collection Manager as a Replacement for Approval Books," *Science and Technology Libraries* 20, no. 4 (2001): 5–12.

137. Pongracz Sennyey, "Assessing Blanket Order Effectiveness: A Neglected Task in Collection Development," *Library Acquisitions: Practice and Theory* 21, no. 4 (1997): 445–454.

138. John C. Calhoun, "Reviews, Holdings, and Presses and Publishers in Aca-

demic Library Books Acquisitions," *Library Resources and Technical Services* 45, no. 3 (2001): 127–177.

139. Denise Brush, "Circulation Analysis of an Engineering Monograph Approval Plan," *Collection Building* 26, no. 2 (2007): 59–62.

140. Judith Serebnick, "Selection and Holdings of Small Publishers' Books in OCLC Libraries: A Study of the Influence of Reviews, Publishers, and Vendors," *Library Quarterly* 62, no. 3 (1992): 259–294.

141. Juris Dilevko and Keren Dali, "Reviews of Independent Press Books in Counterpoise and Other Publications," *College and Research Libraries* 65, no. 1 (2004): 56–77.

142. Paula Wheeler Carlo and Allen Natowitz, "Choice Book Reviews in American History, Geography, and Area Studies: An Analysis for 1988–1993," *Library Acquisitions: Practice and Theory* 19, no. (1995): 153–165.

143. Matthew L. Jordy, Eileen L. McGrath, and John B. Rutledge, "Book Reviews as a Tool for Assessing Publisher Reputation," *College and Research Libraries* 60, no. 2 (1999): 132–142.

144. James H. Sweetland, "Reviewing the World Wide Web: Theory Versus Reality," *Library Trends* 48, no. 4 (2000): 748–768.

145. Karen Carter Williams and Rickey Best, "E-Book Usage and the Choice Outstanding Academic Book List: Is there a Correlation?" *Journal of Academic Librarianship* 32, no. 5 (2006): 474–478.

146. Dennis P. Carrigan, "Data Guided Collection Development: A Promise Unfulfilled," *College and Research Libraries* 57, no. 5 (1996): 429–437.

147. Mary F. Casserly and Anne C. Ciliberti, "Collection Management and Integrated Library Systems," in *Collection Management for the 21st Century: A Handbook for Librarians,* ed. G. E. Gorman and Ruth H. Miller, 58–80 (Westport, CT: Greenwood Publishing, 1997).

148. Alfred Kraemer and Michael Markwith, "Integrating Vendor Supplied Management Reports for Serials Evaluation: The Medical College of Wisconsin Experience," *Acquisitions Librarian* 12, no. 24 (2000): 65–74

149. Judy Luther, *White Paper on Electronic Journal Usage Statistics* (Washington, DC: Council on Library and Information Resources, 2000).

150. Alan Dawson, "Inferring User Behaviour from Journal Access Figures," *Serials Librarian* 35, no. 3 (1999): 31–41.

151. Deborah D. Blecic, Joan B. Fiscella, and Stephen E. Wiberley, Jr., "The Measurement of Use of Web-Based Information Resources: An Early Look at Vendor-Supplied Data," *College and Research Libraries* 62, no. 5 (2001): 434–453.

152. Wonsik Shim and Charles R. McClure, "Improving Database Vendors' Usage Statistics Reporting through Collaboration between Libraries and Vendors," *College and Research Libraries* 63, no. 6 (2002): 499–514.

153. Karla L. Hahn and Lila A. Faulkner, "Evaluative Usage-Based Metrics for

the Selection of E-Journals," *College and Research Libraries* 63, no. 3 (2002): 215–227.

154. Dennis P. Carrigan, "Collection Development: Evaluation," *Journal of Academic Librarianship* 22, no. 4 (1996): 274.

155. Dave Harmeyer, "Potential Collection Development Bias: Some Evidence on a Controversial Topic in California," *College and Research Libraries* 56, no. 2 (1995): 101–111.

156. John N. Ochola and Phillip J. Jones, "Assessment of the Liaison Program at Baylor University," *Collection Management* 26, no. 4 (2001): 29–41.

157. Freda Mozenter, Bridgette T. Sanders, and Jeanie M. Welch, "Restructuring a Liaison Program in an Academic Library," *College and Research Libraries* 61, no. 5 (2000): 432–440.

158. Zheng Ye (Lan) Yang, "University Faculty's Perception of a Library Liaison Program: A Case Study," *Journal of Academic Librarianship* 26, no. 2 (2000): 124–128.

159. Debbi Dinkins, "Circulation as Assessment: Collection Development Policies Evaluated in Terms of Circulation at a Small Academic Library," *College and Research Libraries* 64, no. 1 (2003): 46–53.

160. Scott Stebelman, "Using *Choice* as a Collection Assessment Tool," *Collection Building* 15, no. 2 (1996): 4–11.

161. Examples include Adrian W. Alexander, "Toward 'The Perfection of Work': Library Consortia in the Digital Age," *Journal of Library Administration* 28, no. 2 (1999): 1–14; Barbara McFadden Allen, "Consortia and Collections: Achieving a Balance between Local Action and Collaborative Interest," *Journal of Library Administration* 28, no. 4 (1999): 85–90; Ross Atkinson, "Uses and Abuses of Cooperation in a Digital Age," *Collection Management* 28, no. 1/2 (2003): 3–20; Bart Harloe, ed., *Guide to Cooperative Collection Development* (Chicago: American Library Association, 1994).

162. George Soete, *Collaborative Collections Management Programs in ARL Libraries: SPEC Kit 235* (Washington, DC: Association of Research Libraries, 1998).

163. John Haar, "Assessing the State of Cooperative Collection Development: Report of the Working Group to Map Current Cooperative Collection Development Projects," *Collection Management* 28, no. 3 (2003): 183–190.

164. Patricia Buck Dominguez and Luke Swindler, "Cooperative Collection Development at the Research Triangle University Libraries: A Model for the Nation," *College and Research Libraries* 54, no. 6 (1993): 470–496.

165. A. Hays Butler, "Cooperative Collection Development Programs in Law Libraries: Barriers and Benefits," *Legal Reference Services Quarterly* 20, no. 3 (2001): 13–25.

166. Christy Hightower and George Soete, "The Consortium as Learning Organization: Twelve Steps to Success in Collaborative Collections Projects," *Journal of Academic Librarianship* 21, no. 2 (1995): 87–91.

167. Gay N. Dannelly, "Cooperation Is the Future of Collection Management and Development: OhioLINK and CIC," in *Collection Management for the 21st Century: A Handbook for Librarians,* ed. G. E. Gorman and Ruth H. Miller, 249–262 (Westport, CT: Greenwood Press 1997).

168. Dan C. Hazen, "Cooperative Collection Development: Compelling Theory, Inconsequential Results?" in *Collection Management for the 21st Century: A Handbook for Librarians,* ed. G. E. Gorman and Ruth H. Miller, 263–283 (Westport, CT: Greenwood Press, 1997).

169. Cynthia Shelton, "Best Practices in Cooperative Collection Development: A Report Prepared by the Center for Research Libraries Working Group on Best Practices in Cooperative Collection Development," *Collection Management* 28, no. 3 (2003): 191–222.

170. Rodney Erickson, "Choice for Cooperative Collection Development," *Library Acquisitions: Practice and Theory* 16, no. 1 (1992): 43–49.

171. Marc Langston, "The California State University E-Book Pilot Project: Implications for Cooperative Collection Development," *Library Collections, Acquisitions, and Technical Services* 27, no. 1 (2003): 19–32.

172. Bruce R. Kingma, "Interlibrary Loan and Resource Sharing: The Economics of the SUNY Express Consortium," *Library Trends* 45, no. 3 (1997): 518–530.

173. Marisa Scigliano, "Consortium Purchases: Case Study for a Cost-Benefit Analysis," *Journal of Academic Librarianship* 28, no. 6 (2002): 393–399.

174. Stephen Bosch and others, "Measuring Success of Cooperative Collection Development: Report of the Center for Research Libraries / Greater Western Library Alliance Working Group for Quantitative Evaluation of Cooperative Collection Development Projects," *Collection Management* 28, no. 3 (2003): 223–239.

175. David F. Kohl and Tom Sanville, "More Bang for the Buck: Increasing the Effectiveness of Library Expenditures through Cooperation," *Library Trends* 54, no. 3 (2006): 394–410.

176. Julia A. Gammon and Michael Zeoli, "Practical Cooperative Collecting for Consortia: Books-Not-Bought in Ohio," *Collection Management* 28, no. 1/2 (2003): 77–105.

177. Margo Warner Curl and Michael Zeoli, "Developing a Consortial Shared Approval Plan for Monographs," *Collection Building* 23, no. 3 (2004): 122–128.

178. Terry Ann Rohe, Patrice O'Donovan, and Victoria Hanawalt, "Cooperative Collection Development in PORTALS," *Acquisitions Librarian* 12, no. 24 (2000): 89–101.

179. Wanda V. Dole and Sherry S. Chang, "Consortium Use of the OCLC / AMIGOS Collection Analysis CD: The SUNY Experience," *Library Resources and Technical Services* 41, no. 1 (1997): 50–57.

180. James R. Dwyer, "Consortial Review and Purchase of Networked Resources: The California State University Experience," *Bottom Line* 12, no. 1 (1999): 5–11.

181. Donnice Cochenour and Joel S. Rutstein, "A CARL Model for Cooperative Collection Development in a Regional Consortium," *Collection Building* 12, no. 1/2 (1993): 34–40.

182. Sue O. Medina and William C. Highfill, "Statewide Cooperation to Improve Academic Library Resources: The Alabama Experience," in *Advances in Collection Development and Resource Management,* vol. 1, ed. Thomas W. Leonhardt, 101–137 (Greenwich, CT: JAI Press, 1995).

183. Dennis Stephens, "Multi-Type Library Collection Planning in Alaska: A Conspectus-Based Approach," in *Collection Assessment: A Look at the RLG Conspectus,* ed. Richard J. Wood and Katina Strauch, 137–156 (New York: Haworth Press, 1991).

184. Examples of reviews include Bonnie MacEwan, "An Overview of Collection Assessment and Evaluation," in *Collection Management for the 1990s: Proceedings of the Midwest Collection Management and Development Institute, University of Illinois at Chicago, August 17–20, 1989,* ed. Joseph J. Branin, 95–104 (Chicago: American Library Association, 1992); Bonnie Strohl, *Collection Evaluation Techniques: A Short, Selective, Practical, Current, Annotated Bibliography, 1990–1998* (Chicago: American Library Association, 1999); G. E. Gorman and Ruth H. Miller, "Changing Collections, Changing Evaluation," in *International Yearbook of Library and Information Management 2000–2001: Collection Management,* ed. G. E. Gorman, 309–338 (London: Library Association Publishing, 2000); Kristine R. Brancolini, "Use and User Studies for Collection Evaluation," in *Collection Management for the 1990s: Proceedings of the Midwest Collection Management and Development Institute, University of Illinois at Chicago, August 17–20, 1989,* ed. Joseph J. Branin, 63–94 (Chicago: American Library Association, 1992); Nancy J. Butkovich, "Use Studies: A Selective Review," *Library Resources and Technical Services* 40, no. 4 (1996): 359–368; Thomas E. Nisonger, *Evaluation of Library Collections, Access and Electronic Resources: A Literature Guide and Annotated Bibliography* (Westport, CT: Libraries Unlimited, 2003); Thomas E. Nisonger, *Collection Evaluation in Academic Libraries: A Literature Guide and Annotated Bibliography* (Englewood, CO: Libraries Unlimited, 1992). Examples of guides and manuals include Dora Biblarz, Stephen Bosch, and Chris Sugnet, eds., *Guide to Library User Needs Assessment for Integrated information Resource Management and Collection Development* (Lanhan MD: Scarecrow Press, 2001); Danny P. Wallace and Connie Van Fleet, eds., *Library Evaluation: A Casebook and Can-Do Guide* (Englewood, CO: Libraries Unlimited, 2001).

185. Wanda V. Dole, "Myth and Reality: Using the OCLC/AMIGOS Collection Analysis CD to Measure Collections against Peer Collections and against Institutional Priorities," *Library Acquisitions: Practice and Theory* 18, no. 2 (1994): 179–192.

186. Anna H. Perrault and others, "The Effects of High Median Age on Currency of Resources in Community College Library Collections," *College and Research Libraries* 60, no. 4 (1999): 316–339.

187. Anna H. Perrault and others, "The Florida Community College Statewide Collection Assessment Project: Outcomes and Impact," *College and Research Libraries* 63, no. 3 (2002): 240–249.

188. Beth M. Paskoff and Anna H. Perrault, "A Tool for Comparative Collection Analysis: Conducting a Shelflist Sample to Construct a Collection Profile," *Library Resources and Technical Services* 34, no. 2 (1990): 199–215.

189. Paul Metz and Sharon Gasser, "Analyzing Current Serials in Virginia: An Application of the Ulrich's Serials Analysis System," *portal: Libraries and the Academy* 6, no. 1 (2006): 5–21.

190. Yelena Pancheshnikov, "Course-Centered Approach to Evaluating University Library Collections for Instructional Program Reviews," *Collection Building* 22, no. 4 (2003): 177–185.

191. Michael G. Webster, "Using the AMIGOS/OCLC Collection Analysis CD and Student Credit Hour Statistics to Evaluate Collection Growth Patterns and Potential Demand," *Library Acquisitions: Practice and Theory* 19, no. 2 (1995): 197–210.

192. Jane A. Dodd and Suzanne D. Gyeszly, "Automated Collection Analysis and Development: Business Collection," in *Advances in Library Administration and Organization,* vol. 11, ed. Gerald B. McCabe and Bernard Kreissman, 201–215 (Greenwood, CT: JAI Press, 1993).

193. Mark Grover, "Large Scale Collection Assessment," *Collection Building* 18, no. 2 (1999): 58–66.

194. Anne C. Ciliberti, "Collection Evaluation and Academic Review: A Pilot Study Using the OCLC/AMIGOS Collection Analysis CD," *Library Acquisitions: Practice and Theory* 18, no. 4 (1994): 431–445.

195. Sarojini D. Lotlikar, "Collection Assessment at the Ganser Library: A Case Study," *Collection Building* 16, no. 1 (1997): 24–29.

196. Paul Robert Green, "Monitoring the Usage of Science and Engineering Journals at the Edward Boyle Library, University of Leeds," *Serials Librarian* 25, no. 1/2 (1994): 169–180.

197. Tina E. Chrzastowski and Brian M. Olesko, "Chemistry Journal Use and Cost: Results of a Longitudinal Study," *Library Resources and Technical Services* 41, no. 2 (1997): 101–111.

198. Regina C. McBride and Kathlyn Behm, "A Journal Usage Study in an Academic Library: Evaluation of Selected Criteria," *Serials Librarian* 45, no. 3 (2003): 23–37.

199. Wanda V. Dole and Sherry S. Chang, "Survey and Analysis of Demand for Journals at the State University of New York at Stony Brook," *Library Acquisitions: Practice and Theory* 20, no. 1(1996): 23–38.

200. Margie Ruppel, "Tying Collection Development's Loose Ends with Interlibrary Loan," *Collection Building* 25, no. 3 (2006): 72–77.

201. Robin Lent, "Women's Studies Journals: Getting the Collection Right!" *Seri-*

als Librarian 35, no. 1/2 (1998): 45–58.

202. Marifran Bustion and John L. Eltinge, "Relationships among Faculty Ratings, Academic Area, and Price for Current Periodicals in a Large Land-Grant University Library," *Library Acquisitions: Practice and Theory* 18, no. 3 (1994): 265–276.

203. Betty E. Tucker, "The Journal Deselection Project: The LSUMC-S Experience," *Library Acquisitions: Practice and Theory* 19, no. 3 (1995): 313–320.

204. Jennifer Knievel, Heather Wicht, and Lynn Silipigni Connaway, "Collection Analysis Using Circulation, ILL, and Collection Data," *Against the Grain* 16, no. 6 (2004/2005): 24–26.

205. John N. Ochola, "Use of Circulation Statistics and Interlibrary Loan Data in Collection Management," *Collection Management* 27, no. 1 (2002): 1–13.

206. Justin Littman and Lynn Silipigni Connaway, "A Circulation Analysis of Print Books and E-Books in an Academic Research Library," *Library Resources and Technical Services* 48, no. 4 (2004): 256–262.

207. Timothy P. Bailey, "Electronic Book Usage at a Master's Level 1 University: A Longitudinal Study," *Journal of Academic Librarianship* 32, no. 1 (2006): 52–59.

208. Tina E. Chrzastowski, Paul M. Blobaum, and Margaret A. Welshmer, "A Cost/Use Analysis of Beilstein's *Handbuch der Organischen Chemie* at Two Academic Chemistry Libraries," *Serials Librarian* 20, no. 4 (1991): 73–84.

209. Steve Black, "Journal Collection Analysis at a Liberal Arts College," *Library Resources and Technical Services* 41, no. 4 (1997): 283–294.

210. Sue Samson, Sebastian Derry, and Holly Eggleston, "Networked Resources, Assessment and Collection Development," *Journal of Academic Librarianship* 30, no. 6 (2004): 476–481.

211. Jean-Pierre V. M. Herubel, "Philosophy Dissertation Bibliographies and Citations in Serials Evaluation," *Serials Librarian* 20, no. 2/3 (1991): 65–73.

212. Margaret Sylvia and Marcella Lesher, "What Journals Do Psychology Graduate Students Need? A Citation Analysis of Thesis References," *College and Research Libraries* 56, no. 4 (1995): 313–318.

213. Erin T. Smith, "Assessing Collection Usefulness: An Investigation of Library Ownership of the Resources Graduate Students Use," *College and Research Libraries* 64, no. 5 (2003): 344–355.

214. Laurel A. Haycock, "Citation Analysis of Education Dissertations for Collection Development," *Library Resources and Technical Services* 48, no. 2 (2004): 102–106.

215. C. Keith Waugh and Margie Ruppel, "Citation Analysis of Dissertation, Thesis, and Research Paper References in Workforce Education and Development," *Journal of Academic Librarianship* 30, no. 4 (2004): 276–284.

216. Margaret J. Sylvia, "Citation Analysis as an Unobtrusive Method for Journal Collection Evaluation Using Psychology Student Research Bibliographies,"

Collection Building 17, no. 1 (1998): 20–28.

217. Reba Leiding, "Using Citation Checking of Undergraduate Honors Thesis Bibliographies to Evaluate Library Collections," *College and Research Libraries* 66, no. 5 (2005): 417–429.

218. Gloriana St. Clair and Rose Mary Magrill, "Undergraduate Use of Four Library Collections: Format and Age of Materials," *Collection Building* 11, no. 4 (1992): 2–15.

219. Janet Hughes, "Use of Faculty Publication Lists and ISI Citation Data to Identify a Core List of Journals with Local Importance," *Library Acquisitions: Practice and Theory* 19, no. 4 (1995): 403–413.

220. Claudia Lascar and Loren D. Mendelsohn, "An Analysis of Journal Use by Structural Biologists with Applications for Journal Collection Development Decisions," *College and Research Libraries* 62, no. 5 (2001): 422–433.

221. Mark Crotteau, "Support for Biological Research by an Academic Library: A Journal Citation Study," *Science and Technology Libraries* 17, no. 1 (1997): 67–83.

222. Stephanie C. Haas and Kate Lee, "Research Journal Usage by the Forestry Faculty at the University of Florida Gainesville," *Collection Building* 11, no. 2 (1991): 23–25.

223. Harriet Lightman with Sabina Manilov, "A Simple Method for Evaluating a Journal Collection: A Case Study of Northwestern University Library's Economics Collection," *Journal of Academic Librarianship* 26, no. 3 (2000): 183–190.

224. Amy Dykeman, "Faculty Citations: An Approach to Assessing the Impact of Diminishing Resources on Scientific Research," *Library Acquisitions: Practice and Theory* 18, no. 2 (1994): 137–146; Thomas Schaffer, "Psychology Citations Revisited: Behavioral Research in the Age of Electronic Resources," *Journal of Academic Librarianship* 30, no. 5 (2004): 354–360.

225. Shi Jian Gao and Wang Zhi Yu, "A Local Citation Analysis in China: From Wuhan University Faculty in Surveying and Mapping," *Journal of Academic Librarianship* 31, no. 5 (2005): 449–455.

226. Roger Edward Stelk and F. Wilfrid Lancaster, "The Use of Textbooks in Evaluating the Collection of an Undergraduate Library," *Library Acquisitions: Practice and Theory* 14, no. 2 (1990): 191–193.

227. Karen Rupp-Serrano, "Putting Theory into Practice: Social Sciences Needs Analysis," *Library Collections, Acquisitions, and Technical Services* 25, no. 4 (2001): 435–447.

228. Patricia Weaver, "A Student-Centered, Classroom-Based Approach to Collection Building," *Journal of Academic Librarianship* 25, no. 3 (1999): 202–210.

229. Kristine Condic, "Student Preferences for Purchase Given Limited Library Budgets," *Collection Building* 23, no. 1 (2004): 5–12.

230. Bette Rathe and Lisa Blankenship, "Recreational Reading Collections in

Academic Libraries," *Collection Management* 30, no. 2 (2005): 73–85.

231. Larry Hardesty and Collette Mak, "Searching for the Holy Grail: A Core Collection for Undergraduate Libraries," *Journal of Academic Librarianship* 19, no. 6 (1994): 362– 371.

232. Scott E. Siverson, "Bibliographic Checking and Qualitative Assessment; A Modified Approach," in *Acquisitions '91: Conference on Acquisitions, Budgets, and Collections, April 10 and 11, 1991, Minneapolis, Minnesota: Proceedings,* ed. David C. Genaway, 279–290 (Canfield, OH: Genaway & Associates, 1991).

233. William E. McGrath and Nancy B. Nuzzo, "'Existing Collection Strength' and Shelflist Count Correlations in RLG's *Conspectus for Music*," *College and Research Libraries* 52, no. 2 (1991): 194–203.

234. Howard D. White, *Brief Tests of Collection Strength* (Westport, CT: Greenwood, 1995).

235. Thomas M. Twiss, "A Validation of Brief Tests of Collection Strength," *Collection Management* 25, no. 3 (2001): 23–37.

236. Jennifer Benedetto Beals and Ron Gilmour, "Assessing Collections Using Brief Tests and WorldCat Collection Analysis," *Collection Building* 26, no. 4 (2007): 104–107.

237. Jay H. Bernstein, "From the Ubiquitous to the Nonexistent: A Demographic Study of OCLC WorldCat," *Library Resources and Technical Services* 50, no. 2 (2006): 79–90.

238. William A. Britten and Judith D. Webster, "Comparing Characteristics of Highly Circulated Titles for Demand-Driven Collection Development," *College and Research Libraries* 53, no. 3 (1992): 239–248.

239. Julie Banks, "Weeding Book Collections in the Age of the Internet," *Collection Building* 21, no. 3 (2002): 113–119.

240. Jefferson P. Selth, Nancy Koller, and Peter M. Briscoe, "The Use of Books within the Library," *College and Research Libraries* 53, no. 3 (1992): 197–205.

241. Dennis R. Ridley and Joseph E. Weber, "Toward Assessing In-House Use of Print Resources in the Undergraduate Academic Library: An Inter-Institutional Study," *Library Collections, Acquisitions, and Technical Services* 24, no. 1 (2000): 89–103.

242. Lynn Silipigni Connaway and Clifton Snyder, "Transaction Log Analyses of Electronic Book (eBook) Usage," *Against the Grain* 17, no. 1 (2005): 85–89.

243. Jean S. Sauer, "Unused Current Issues: A Predictor of Unused Bound Volumes?" *Serials Librarian* 18, no. 1/2 (1990): 97–107.

244. Maiken Naylor, "Comparative Results of Two Current Periodical Use Studies," *Library Resources and Technical Services* 38, no. 4 (1994): 373–388.

245. Philip M. Davis, "For Electronic Journals, Total Downloads Can Predict Number of Users," *portal: Libraries and the Academy* 4, no. 3 (2004): 379–392.

246. Jetta Carol Culpepper, "Watch Out and Listen: Faculty Assess Electronic

Resources," *Acquisitions Librarian* 12, no. 24 (2000): 29–40.

247. Kathleen Bauer, "Indexes as Tools for Measuring Usage of Print and Electronic Resources," *College and Research Libraries* 62, no. 1 (2001): 36–42.

248. Joanna Duy and Liwen Vaughan, "Usage Data for Electronic Resources: A Comparison Between Locally Collected and Vendor-Provided Statistics," *Journal of Academic Librarianship* 29, no. 1 (2003): 16–22.

249. Joanna Duy and Liwen Vaughan, "Can Electronic Journal Usage Data Replace Citation Data as a Measure of Journal Use? An Empirical Examination." *Journal of Academic Librarianship* 32, no. 5 (2006): 512–517.

250. Nicola McDowell and G. E. Gorman, "The Relevance of Vendors' Usage Statistics in Academic Library E-Resource Management: A New Zealand Study," *Australian Academic and Research Libraries* 35, no. 4 (2004): 322–343.

251. Penny M. Beile, David N. Botte, and Elizabeth K. Killingsworth, "A Microscope or a Mirror?: A Question of Study Validity Regarding the Use of Dissertation Citation Analysis for Evaluating Research Collections," *Journal of Academic Librarianship* 30, no. 5 (2004): 347–353.

252. Louise S. Zipp, "Thesis and Dissertation Citations as Indicators of Faculty Research Use of University Library Journal Collections," *Library Resources and Technical Services* 40, no. 4 (1996): 335–342.

253. Christopher Millson-Martula and Mary Frances Watson, "Evaluating Students' Serials Needs: Effective Methodologies for College Libraries," *College and Undergraduate Libraries* 3, no. 2 (1996): 75–89.

254. Thomas E. Nisonger, "A Methodological Issue Concerning the Use of Social Sciences Citation Index Journal Citation Reports Impact Factor Data for Journal Ranking," *Library Acquisitions: Practice and Theory* 18, no. 4 (1994): 447–458.

255. Thomas E. Nisonger, "Use of the *Journal of Citation Reports* for Serials Management in Research Libraries: An Investigation of the Effect of Self-Citation on Journal Rankings in Library and Information Sciences and Genetics," *College and Research Libraries* 61, no. 3 (2000): 262–275.

256. Klaus G. Altmann and G. E. Gorman, "Can Impact Factors Substitute for the Results of Local Use Studies? Findings from an Australian Case Study," *Collection Building* 18, no. 2 (1999): 90–94.

257. Hye-Kyung Chung, "Evaluating Academic Journals Using Impact Factor and Local Citation Score," *Journal of Academic Librarianship* 33, no. 3 (2007): 393–402.

258. Sandra R. Moline, "Mathematics Journals: Impact Factors and Cents per Thousand Characters," *Serials Librarian* 20, no. 4 (1991): 65–71.

259. Juris Dilevko and Esther Atkinson, "Evaluating Academic Journals without Impact Factors for Collection Management Decisions," *College and Research Libraries* 63, no. 6 (2002): 562–577.

260. Janice Kreider, "The Correlation of Local Citation Data with Citation Data

from Journal Citation Reports," *Library Resources and Technical Services* 43, no. 2 (1999): 67–77.

261. Sandra E. Goldstein, "The Role of Citation Analysis in Evaluating Chemistry Journals: A Pilot Study," in *Advances in Library Administration and Organization,* vol. 10, ed. Gerald B. McCabe and Bernard Kreissman, 97–112 (Greenwood, CT: JAI Press, 1992).

262. Anita Coleman, "Assessing the Value of a Journal Beyond the Impact Factor," *Journal of the American Society for Information Science and Technology* 58, no. 8 (2007): 1148–1161.

263 Lu An and Junping Qiu, "Research on the Relationships between Chinese Journal Impact Factors and External Web Link Counts and Web Impact Factors," *Journal of Academic Librarianship* 30, no. 3 (2004): 199–204.

264. F. W. Lancaster and others, "The Relationship between Literature Scatter and Journal Accessibility in an Academic Special Library," *Collection Building* 11, no. 1 (1991): 19–22.

265. John C. Calhoun, "Serials Citations and Holdings Correlation," *Library Resources and Technical Services* 39, no. 1 (1995): 53–77.

266. Peter Hernon, "Going Beyond 'Same Old, Same Old,'" *Journal of Academic Librarianship* 23, no. 3 (1997): 169.

4 Knowledge Organization

Sherry L. Vellucci

Since Svenonius analyzed the research base in bibliographic control in 1990, the intervening years have seen major shifts in the focus of information organization in academic libraries. New technologies continue to reshape the nature and content of catalogs, stretch the boundaries of classification research, and provide new alternatives for the organization of information. Research studies have rigorously analyzed the structure of the Anglo-American Cataloguing Rules using entity-relationship modeling and expanded on the bibliographic and authority relationship research to develop new data models (Functional Requirements for Bibliographic Records [FRBR] and Functional Requirements and Numbering of Authority Records [FRANAR]). Applied research into the information organization process has led to the development of cataloguing tools and harvesting applications for bibliographic data collection and automatic record creation. A growing international perspective focused research on multilingual subject access, transliteration problems in surrogate records, and user studies to improve Online Public Access Catalog (OPAC) displays for large retrieval sets resulting from federated searches. The need to organize local and remote electronic resources led to metadata research that developed general and domain-specific metadata schemes. Ongoing research in this area focuses on record structures and architectural models to enable interoperability among the various schemes and differing application platforms. Research in the area of subject access and classification is strong, covering areas such as vocabulary mapping, automatic facet construction and deconstruction for Web resources, development of expert systems for automatic classification, dynamically altered classificatory structures linked to domain-specific thesauri, crosscultural conceptual structures in classification, identification of semantic relationships for vocabulary mapped to classification systems, and the expanded use of traditional classification systems as switching languages in the global Web environment. Finally, descriptive research into library and information science (LIS) education and curricula for knowledge organization continues. All of this research is applicable to knowledge organization in academic and research libraries. This chapter examines this body of research in depth, describes the research methodologies employed, and identifies areas of lacunae in need of further research.

Introduction

In the years since Svenonius analyzed the research base in bibliographic control,[1] there have been rapid and dramatic changes in academic libraries. The resources acquired and made accessible to users appear in many different formats, but increasingly they are digital objects. The term *bibliographic control*, which referred to the traditional organizational functions of descriptive cataloging, subject cataloging, and classification, is principally associated with physical items and is now considered by some to be an inadequate term to describe the range of organizing functions in an increasingly digital networked environment. The terms *information organization* and *knowledge organization* have largely replaced it. While many of the processes remain similar or identical to those which fell under the rubric of bibliographic control, new processes and systems of organization are emerging rapidly.

In this chapter the term *knowledge organization* will be used to include descriptive cataloging, subject cataloging, classification, metadata creation, and the activities of each process that contribute to the making of a catalog or database for the purpose of information retrieval. The term should not be confused with the term *knowledge management*, which has a much broader scope and is primarily found in the context of business environments. The terms *bibliographic data* and *metadata* are often used interchangeably to describe the attributes of a given work; however, the term *metadata* is usually applied in the context of newer organizational systems associated with digital resources. As federated searching becomes more prevalent and metadata creation merges with cataloging functions, the boundaries between the old and new are becoming less clear. These terms, therefore, should not be considered mutually exclusive, as their definitions will no doubt continue to shift with the inevitable evolution of the field of knowledge organization.

In addition to a change in terminology, two noticeable trends have influenced the research and literature of knowledge organization: the continuous development of new technologies and the increasing globalization of information. New technologies continue to reshape the nature, content, and boundaries of library catalogs, the tools we use for information organization, and the work-flow processes. Applied research has enabled the development of computer applications that further automate and assist the information organization processes, in both the library and commercial outsourced settings. The Internet has allowed the cataloging community to focus on information organization beyond the local and national levels. Thanks to the conceptual, empirical, and applied research in knowledge organization, catalog records can be shared internationally, and global access to digital libraries can be provided. Globalization of information has influenced views on authority control as well and enabled the creation of a Virtual International Authority File. Economies of cooperation and scale necessitate that national libraries, bibliographic utilities, and academic and research libraries collaborate and lead the way in research, development, and implementation of more effective systems of organization.

Another area of internationalization that depends heavily on conceptual research is the ongoing development of international standards. Knowledge organization is inextricably entwined with standards development. Thus, knowledge organization research informs the development of standards, as well as innovations in the processes and systems of organizing information. Cataloging codes and other standards for description and access of all types of resources are now developed in an international context. Currently there are international committees that are helping to redesign the *Anglo-American Cataloguing Rules (AACR2);* the product of their redesign efforts will be called *Resource Description and Access* (RDA). Groups of international cataloging experts are developing a new set of principles and creating and revising new metadata schemas and new ways to structure the data in the catalog. A critical mass of research has been conducted in this area over the past 15 years and has become an important part of the research literature.

Several journals that are specific to knowledge organization publish detailed articles that report on research projects, including *Cataloging and Classification Quarterly, Serials Librarian,* and *Library Resources and Technical Services.* The relatively new publication *The Journal of Internet Cataloging* is devoted exclusively to the organization of digital resources. Other journals that are broader in scope but often include articles on information organization research are *College and Research Libraries; Information Technology and Libraries; Journal of Academic Librarianship; Library Collections, Acquisitions, and Technical Services; OCLC Systems and Services;* and *Technical Services Quarterly.* Shorter articles that discuss research can be found in *International Cataloguing and Bibliographic Control, Electronic*

Library, and *Library Hi Tech.* As the boundaries blur between cataloging and metadata, overlap with research in the field of information retrieval (IR) also increases. Because of the vast amount of published research in the area of IR, this chapter will address the IR literature only as it directly relates to library catalogs and related systems of knowledge organization. *Journal of the American Society for Information Science and Technology, Journal of Documentation,* and *Information Processing and Management* are IR journals that often include research articles on knowledge organization, especially in the areas of classification, taxonomies, ontologies, and the semantic web. The extensive amount of research literature in the broad field of knowledge organization necessitates selectivity in the research discussed in this chapter. The author selected the studies discussed here based on the impact of the research on the working academic library environment and the desire to provide an overview of the research areas important to the academic cataloging community.

Academic and research libraries play a vital role in defining the research agenda of knowledge organization, along with the Library of Congress, other national libraries, OCLC, and the Research Libraries Group (RLG). Since academic libraries are often the first organizations to help develop, test, and implement new computer applications and systems, many of these systems have become the de facto standard. The key areas of knowledge organization that will be addressed here include descriptive cataloging, authority control, metadata issues, subject access, and the Online Public Access Catalog (OPAC). Standards are integral to every aspect of knowledge organization, and standards research and development are addressed throughout the text. Although academic libraries are not specifically mentioned in all discussions of the research literature, all of the research examined here has a bearing on academic libraries.

Descriptive Cataloging

Traditionally, the cataloging process is divided into descriptive cataloging and subject cataloging. Descriptive cataloging involves identifying the important characteristics of both the content of a work and the carrier of that content. Another part of the descriptive cataloging process is creating access points for names and titles associated with the work. The creation of access points involves authority control, a process that brings consistency and uniqueness to the access points in a catalog. The second part of the cataloging process—subject cataloging—involves using controlled vocabularies to assign subject terms and classification notation to describe what the work is about. Both parts of the process should focus on providing an efficient system for users of the catalog to retrieve information. Subject access is discussed later in this chapter.

In the 1990s, several descriptive cataloging issues converged and led to a fundamental rethinking of the conceptual model upon which the *AACR2* were based. These factors included the description of electronic resources with the attendant "content vs. carrier" issue, the growing importance of identifying relationships between works, the ubiquitous access to library catalogs via the Internet, and the desire to share bibliographic and authority data on an international scale. Conceptual research, defined by Svenonius as being "characterized by asking questions, defining terms, imagining possibilities, and analyzing concepts,"[2] was the methodology of choice that enabled experts in the field to rethink and restructure the fundamental concepts of knowledge organization.

Conceptual Models, Theories, and Principles

The most important conceptual research to date has been the development of new conceptual models of the bibliographic universe and the ongoing review and development of cataloging principles better suited to the digital environment. Researchers are examining such questions as "What is a work? How is a work expressed? What kinds of relationships exist among different entities? And given this information, how can we improve catalog functionality for users?"

The Functional Requirements for Bibliographic Records (FRBR)

The IFLA (International Federation of Library Associations and Institutions) Study Group on the *Functional Requirements for Bibliographic Records*[3] (FRBR) began its work with the following objectives:

- to provide a clearly structured framework for relating the data recorded in bibliographic records to the user's needs;
- to create conceptual models for national database systems; and
- to recommend a basic level for national bibliographic records.[4]

In addition, the new conceptual model would be a framework to assist in the development of catalog system designs, in order to take advantage of the computer's ability to link related works in the catalog and to present a more meaningful OPAC display of the different versions of a work to the user.

An entity-relationship modeling technique was used to develop the new conceptual model. The study group's analysis identified tasks that users might want to perform using a catalog and entities that represent key objects of interest to users of bibliographic databases. The new model represents a shift from a system-centered focus on the functions of the catalog to a user-centered focus on the tasks that catalog users wish to accomplish. The user tasks are to find, to identify, to select, and to obtain. The FRBR conceptual model is composed of three groups of entities. The entities identified in group one are the products of intellectual or artistic endeavor and include the work, the expression, the manifestation, and the item—i.e., the things we catalog. The group two entities are those responsible for the intellectual and artistic content, physical production or custodianship of group one entities, and include persons, corporate bodies, and the recently added entity families. The group three entities serve as the subjects of works and include concepts, objects, events, and places. The links between the entities in all three groups identify the types of relationships that exist between them. The model also identifies the attributes of each entity and maps them to the user tasks served by that attribute.

The FRBR model opened new avenues of research in many aspects of knowledge organization. Some system vendors[5] and bibliographic utilities[6] conducted studies to determine the proportion of works in a particular database that would benefit from application of the FRBR model and to test the viability of applying the model to existing records.[7] Applied research led to the development of new database and record structures,[8] to the creation of record-conversion algorithms to accommodate the model,[9] and to the construction of new interface design tools.[10] Expanding the use of the FRBR model, Naun developed an online journal-finding aid using the FRBR principles to determine the user tasks to be served by the system, the appropriate data structure for the system, and the feasibility of mapping the required data from existing sources.[11] Some researchers are enhancing and extending the model,[12] while others are applying the FRBR model to particular subject domains[13] or reconceptualizing portions of the model.[14] Taniguchi developed a different conceptual model that gives primacy to the expression-level entity rather than the work-level. He viewed his new construct as a means of dealing with the issue of multiple versions while retaining consistency in the model.[15] In a follow-up study, Taniguchi focused on the whole-part relationship and compared component parts of bibliographic resources using both the FRBR model and his expression-prioritized model.[16] He identified two types of component parts, a "content part" that is contained within the physical structure of the host resource and a "document part" that is physically separate. He concluded that in the FRBR model, the "whole" and the component part are modeled in the same way, but a different model is used for the content part. In Taniguchi's model, all three are modeled in the same way (the whole resource, the component part, and the content part), thus, in his opinion, making the model more consistent than FRBR. Considering the problems that the FRBR model now has with aggregated works, it is possible that by giving primacy to the expression level, Taniguchi's model would solve this problem.

The FRBR model has had an impact on the cataloging rules used in the United States and abroad. A study by Delsey and others rigorously analyzed the structure of the *AACR2* using the entity-relationship modeling technique. "The principal objective of this study [was] to develop a formalized schema to reflect the internal logic of the *Anglo-American Cataloguing Rules*, [which in turn would] serve as a tool to assist in the re-examination of the principles underlying the code and in setting directions for its future development."[17] This analysis was the preliminary step in what is to be a new content standard for bibliographic records. Envisioned for use beyond the cataloging community, the new cataloging standard, the RDA, will be independent of record structures (e.g., MARC 21) and will integrate the FRBR conceptual model and its terminology.[18] Major criticisms from important constituent groups regarding, among other issues, the lack of FRBR integration have compelled the developers to abandon the first two drafts of RDA. The RDA standard is scheduled for completion in 2009; however, many believe the reconceptualization of the standard will meet the needs of neither 21st century catalog users nor the broader metadata communities as was hoped.

While it is too early for a substantive body of RDA research to appear, Dunsire explored the basic concept of separating content description from carrier description in order to develop the RDA/ONIX Framework for resource categorization.[19] The framework, which is designed to improve metadata interoperability between libraries and publishers, identifies and defines two distinct sets of attributes: (1) the intellectual or artistic content of an information resource and (2) the type of carrier for such content. The framework provides for constructing higher-level categories of resource content and carrier from the attribute and value sets and includes recommendations on applying such categories to resource descriptions.

Several research projects have focused on mapping the FRBR entities and attributes to other standards. Delsey produced a research report for the IFLA International Standard Bibliographic Description Review Group (ISBD) that analyzed and mapped "each of the elements specified in the ISBDs to its corresponding entity attribute or relationship as defined in the FRBR model."[20] LeBoeuf examined the impact that the FRBR model would have on future revisions of the ISBD standards.[21] Delsey also conducted a conceptual analysis of the MARC21 (Machine-Readable Cataloging) communications format and mapped the FRBR data elements to the MARC 21 data elements.[22] The mapping was updated and revised in 2004 by the Network Development and MARC Standards Office at the Library of Congress (LC).[23] All of these critical analyses and mappings help to clarify the FRBR entities and data elements by placing them within the context of standards that are already familiar to catalogers.

Works and Relationships

Empirical research uses quantitative and qualitative methods to measure and analyze existing phenomena and is dependent on appropriate constructs and interpretation of the data to inform future research and decision making. The FRBR conceptual model draws on a body of empirical research that examined the nature of a work and the concepts of bibliographic families and bibliographic relationships. The identification and referencing of bibliographic and authority relationships is a formal way to create the syndetic structure of the catalog. Research in this area is ultimately focused on finding better ways to exploit the capabilities of computers to provide a more meaningful grouping for a clearer presentation of related entities described in a catalog. The seminal research conducted by Tillett used both analytic and empirical methodologies to examine bibliographic relationships in depth.[24] Her study began with the creation of a taxonomy of bibliographic relationships that she discovered by examining 24 different cataloging codes from Panizzi's 1841 *Rules* to the

1978 edition of *AACR2*. The results of her analysis identified seven types of bibliographic relationships, which consist of equivalent, derivative, whole-part, accompanying, sequential, descriptive, and shared characteristics. Tillett also examined the cataloging codes to identify the various types of linking devices used to establish each type of relationship on the bibliographic record. The second part of Tillett's work included an empirical study designed to examine the extent of bibliographic relationships as reflected in their frequencies of occurrence in MARC records entered in the LC machine-readable database between 1968 and 1986. Although there were problems with the sampling frame due to the types of materials cataloged by LC in the MARC format at that time, one important finding of this portion of the study indicated that bibliographic relationships were widespread throughout the bibliographic universe, i.e., Tillett found that almost 75% of the records in the database contained some type of relationship information.[25]

Tillett's landmark study became the starting point for two further investigations that focused on the bibliographic universe represented in library catalogs, both of which were narrower in scope. Smiraglia conducted an empirical study of works that focused on the derivative relationship, one of the most frequently found relationships in the catalogs of large academic libraries.[26] His analysis identified seven types of derivative relationships found in 49.9% of works in his sample. The derivative types identified by Smiraglia include simultaneous derivations, successive derivations, translations, amplifications, extractions, adaptations, and performances. Smiraglia's research findings indicate the importance of identifying and linking surrogate records for members of bibliographic families in academic library catalogs. Further research by Vellucci examined the bibliographic universe of musical entities to identify bibliographic relationships found in catalogs representing large collections of music.[27] Vellucci's sampling frame used the musical scores catalog of Sibley Library at the Eastman School of Music. She then searched the OCLC and RLIN (Research Library Information Network) databases to identify bibliographic entities related to each member of the sample, then analyzed and categorized the types of relationships found to exist for musical works. Her findings indicated that 97% of the music scores in the sample exhibited at least one relationship, a considerably higher figure than that discovered by Tillett in the general bibliographic universe. Vellucci's research findings suggest that the overall proportion of relationships found among entities in a catalog may differ by discipline and format of the entity. This research has direct implications for OPAC transition to a new FRBR-based system design, for the results indicate that a large portion of works represented in a music catalog would benefit from use of the FRBR model.

In addition to identifying types and degrees of relatedness, all three studies examined the methods by which relationships were identified and represented in library catalogs at the time of the respective studies. Each study concluded that new OPAC and surrogate record designs were necessary to enable better exploitation of the computer's capability to link and display related entities in library catalogs. A thorough analysis of the history, research, issues, and contexts of bibliographic relationships was presented by Vellucci at the Toronto Conference on the Principles and Future of AACR.[28] The paper concludes with her identification of four fundamental principles for the treatment of bibliographic relationships that should guide the development of cataloging codes and system design. These are the principles of relationship identification, enabled linkage, multilevel description, and consistency.

Yee focused her research specifically on the concept of the work.[29] Drawing on her doctoral research, she showed the lack of a formal definition of a work throughout the history of the *AACR2* codes and concluded with an extensive definition of a "work," which evolved from her research. Included in her definition are the separate concepts of expression and publication, which are later used in the IFLA FRBR model as the expression and manifestation entities. Carlyle's dissertation research examined how works were collocated in OPAC displays and suggested ways to improve the grouping of bibliographic families.[30] Her later research continued to focus on improving catalog displays through grouping related resources by investigating how users categorize works.[31] In another study, Carlyle conducted a survey of 18 online catalogs to compare the displays resulting from five author and five work queries.[32] A more recent article by Carlyle and Summerlin discussed their research on record clustering of works of fiction to improve catalog displays.[33]

Continuing his earlier research, Smiraglia examined the work entity in greater depth.[34] His theoretical analysis drew on linguistic and semiotic theories to develop a new "theory of the work." Smiraglia's concept of the work has greatly influenced the ongoing refinement of the FRBR model and conceptual models developed in other communities.[35] In order to estimate the number of works in OCLC's WorldCat database, Bennett, Lavoie, and O'Neill constructed a sample of works by applying the FRBR model to randomly selected WorldCat records.[36] This sample was used to describe the key characteristics of works. Results suggest that the majority of benefits associated with applying FRBR to WorldCat could be obtained by concentrating on a relatively small number of complex works. Finally, a special issue of *Cataloging and Classification Quarterly*, edited by Smiraglia, was devoted to modeling a wide variety of works, including fiction, television series, videos, digital resources, and cartographic resources, as well as scientific, multimedia, collected, and theological works.[37]

The generalized nature of the FRBR model is both a strength and a weakness. Its strength is as a logical framework that provides common ground for further discussion and research on bibliographic data and the entities that these data describe. Another strength of the model "lies in its separation of the logic and principles of description from display issues."[38] Problems with the FRBR conceptual model arise with its implementation, for the generalized entities, attributes, and relationships do not provide enough detail on which to develop a database. Another weakness of the model lies in the method used for identifying user tasks and mapping entity attributes to specific user tasks, i.e. critical analysis at a high level. This research calls into question the validity of the user tasks identified and used in the model. User studies are needed to confirm the validity of these user tasks and to test the accuracy of the data mapping by comparing both to the real world within the context of the catalog and the bibliographic record data elements that satisfy specific user information needs. As the IFLA Study Group on FRBR identified a wide range of catalog users both within and outside the library environment, the user studies must be conducted with similarly wide user groups. In addition, the report gives no evidence that the body of research on information-seeking behavior was consulted, much of which would be useful in confirming the validity of the users' needs.

Problematic issues with the FRBR model continue to be examined.[39] One such problem is that of aggregate entities, which becomes particularly fuzzy when dealing with serial works. Antelman's analytical research examined serial work identifiers used by the rights-holder community (e.g., International Standard Serial Number [ISSN], Digital Object Identifier [DOI], etc.) and dismissed their usefulness as work identifiers in the library community. She notes that "there is a practical need in bibliographic control for a level of abstraction that brings together related items that do not exhibit textual identity,"[40] citing other terms such as *superwork, superwork record set, super records,* or *package content* that have been used by other researchers. Antelman then developed a conceptual model of a serial work based on the FRBR model, giving primacy to an abstract work level that collocates the bibliographic family, followed by her concept of different expressions of the work. Her manifestation level contains the published versions of the expressions. Included at the manifestation level are different aggregator versions of selected articles. The model is not logically consistent, as it conflates the manifestation and item levels for nondigital versions of the serial (paper, microfilm, etc.) and separates the digital versions into a manifestation level consisting of aggregator versions of separate articles and an item level comprised of the different file formats (HTML, PDF, ASCII, etc.). Nor does the model consider the possibility of a serial as a "work of works," with an issue or article as a work in its own right. Antelman's research is useful, however, because it brings a new perspective to modeling serial works, but the question "What is the work?" is still not resolved for serials. Flexibility seems to be the answer at this point, but further research that includes different serial models is needed in order to determine how to handle aggregates and identify the problems that would arise when trying to accommodate this flexibility in a catalog.

Hirons and Graham developed a conceptual model for seriality that strongly influenced the revision of the *AACR2*.[41] Their model created a three-dimensional approach to cataloging serials that is based on the attributes of the content, the carrier, and the publication status of the work. Static materials are those that are complete when issued. Ongoing or continuing resources are those that are not complete when first issued; these can be either indeterminate or determinate. Determinate publications are continuing resources that are intended to be complete in a finite number of parts or over a finite period of time. Indeterminate publications are continuing resources that are intended to continue indefinitely.[42] Resources in both of these categories can be multipart or single-part updating. Another layer is added to the multipart indeterminate resources, which can be either numbered or unnumbered. This model is especially useful when dealing with looseleaf materials and electronic serials.

Finally, an important new publication edited by Taylor provides a general overview of FRBR and offers chapters by experts in the field that examine the FRBR model in relation to a wide variety of topics, including the Functional Requirements of Authority Data (FRAD), the history of cataloging, research, bibliographic families, RDA, archival materials, moving image materials, music, and serials.[43]

Another important conceptual research project being conducted by IFLA is the creation of a new set of principles for the development of international cataloging codes.[44] Building on the conceptual model for the FRBR and the draft of the FRANAR (see below), IFLA has conducted several International Meetings of Experts (IME) for input into the process. "These new principles replace and broaden the Paris Principles [of 1961] from just textual works to all types of materials and from just the choice and form of entry to all aspects of the bibliographic and authority records used in library catalogs."[45] IFLA intends for these principles to be applicable to online library catalogs and other appropriate databases. Also included in the new statement are objectives for the construction of cataloging codes.

Electronic Resources

Many studies have focused on the description and access of special types and formats of materials. The largest body of research in this area over the last decade concentrated on the newly emerging electronic resources.

In the 1990s, the need to describe digital objects challenged the adequacy of *AACR2*'s cardinal principle—to describe the item in hand. This tradition of description based on physical format created obstacles for dealing with issues such as multiple versions and electronic resources. The increasing complexity of the bibliographic universe called into question the role of the catalog and the ability of the current cataloging code to describe electronic resources in a networked environment. In 1998, OCLC began development of the Cooperative Online Resource Catalog (CORC), a major research project to test the process of cataloging electronic resources using traditional library standards and newly developed software applications.[46] When the prototype system went online in 1999, academic and research libraries were major participants in beta testing the system, eager to try new methods of providing access to electronic resources. The CORC prototype incorporated several software applications developed by

OCLC, including Mantis, Kilroy, Scorpion, and Wordsmith.[47] Traditional cataloging standards were used, including *AACR2*, the MARC format, *Library of Congress Subject Headings (LCSH)*, *Library of Congress Classification (LCC)* and the *Dewey Decimal Classification (DDC)*. The research project also included experiments with reciprocal conversion of MARC records and Dublin Core metadata records, automatic assignment of subject headings, automatic assignment of *DDC* numbers, and automatic creation of metadata extracted from the Web site.[48] During the beta-testing period, research by Hsieh-Yee and Smith indicated that while overall the participants considered the experience positive, there was need to improve the speed of the system to make it a viable working tool.[49]

At the end of the CORC experimental stage, Connell and Prabha conducted a study using a proportional sample of member-created records in the CORC database to examine characteristics of the resources represented.[50] The results indicated that academic libraries were the largest contributors to the database, adding 67% of all records. This finding supports the notion that academic libraries have a high level of concern about providing access to electronic resources for their users. One unexpected result from this study showed that only 21% of the CORC records were for resources held locally by the contributing library, with 78% being external to the institution. Although the researchers expected libraries to be more concerned with making their own unique resources available on the Web, upon consideration, they decided that the likely explanation for this outside focus was that the time and expense to create digital versions of their unique materials would be much greater than adding records for existing Web resources. This hypothesis needs to be verified by further research. The researchers also categorized the Web resources by discipline, publication pattern, and the unit being cataloged. It was noted that current definitions for Web units were inadequate for categorizing the level of granularity for a Web site and further research was needed to develop definitions that would be meaningful to users.

Additional research conducted during the CORC Project studied the potential for automatic classification and description of Internet resources and examined options for catalog interface displays.[51] OCLC developed the Persistent URL (PURL) for the CORC project to alleviate a library's burden of periodically checking each record to ensure that the URL links were active.[52] Another tangible result of this research project was the revision of the MARC 856 field to accommodate more electronic resources information and the revision of the MARC 856 subfield u to end repeatability of the URL and require each location of an electronic resource to be entered in a new 856 field. Records created in this research project have been added to the WorldCat database and contributed a substantial group of records for Internet resources.

During and following the CORC project, academic librarians began to experiment with different methods of describing and accessing the different types of electronic resources identified above by Hirons and Graham. The following studies were selected from a large body of literature in this area.[53] At Cornell, Calhoun explored a new team-based model that required crossfunctional collaboration. In this model, data for description and access could be gathered from selectors, public service librarians, information technology staff, authors, vendors, publishers, and catalogers.[54] Because cataloging electronic resources was a new issue for most libraries, several studies applied survey research to gather descriptive information about local practices. Chen and others surveyed academic libraries to discover their cataloging practices for electronic resources.[55] Their findings show that the task of organizing electronic resources presented librarians with a host of new and complex challenges. "This volatile set of unstable resources ... change names, contents, providers and URLs with alarming frequency ... [requiring] repeated revisions to their surrogate records."[56] This was complicated by the lack of comprehensive standards for cataloging electronic resources. Chen and others made several other discoveries, including the fact that all libraries were presenting holdings information on Web lists instead of, or in addition to, the OPAC; there was no consistency on whether to catalog different formats on individual records or one integrated record; there was no consistency on which part of the resource a URL linked to; and volatile URLs were difficult to cope with. Trends in cataloging electronic resources were also identified. Martin and Hoffman conducted a similar study that focused on cataloging journal titles in aggregator databases.[57] Li and Leung discussed the development of a software program to automatically integrate full-text electronic journal titles in unstable aggregator databases into a library's OPAC.[58] Banush, Kurth, and Pajerek developed an automated system for controlling serial titles in the catalog.[59] A large portion of the literature on organizing electronic serials is case studies and descriptive analyses of problems and solutions representing practice and opinion. Copeland provided a review that discusses much of this literature in detail.[60]

Authority Control

The FRANAR IFLA Working Group was charged with developing a conceptual model for authority records and studying the feasibility of an International Standard Authority Data Number (ISADN). Continuing on the work initiated by the FRBR Study Group, the FRANAR Study Group's research and analysis identified five functions of an authority file (document decisions, serve as reference tool, control forms of access points, support access to bibliographic records, and link bibliographic and authority files) and four tasks important to users of authority records (find, identify, contextualize, and justify). The initial draft reports containing the conceptual model were released for worldwide comment under the title *Functional Requirements for Authority Records (FRAR)*; the latest draft has been retitled *Functional Requirements for Authority Data (FRAD)*[61]. The FRAD conceptual model expands on the FRBR Group Two entities (person and corporate body) to include the new entity *family*. The model then identifies attributes and relationships of the three FRAD entities and the FRBR Group One entities (work, expression, manifestation, and item) within an authority record context and maps each attribute to a specific user task. A new IFLA Working Group will analyze the "entities that are the centre of focus for subject authorities, thesauri, and classification schemes, and of the relationships between those entities," and develop a conceptual model of "Group 3 entities within the FRBR framework as they relate to the aboutness of works."[62] On a final note, all of these IFLA reports thus far claim to be user-centered, yet no research was conducted involving users, and the user tasks were based on educated assumptions, thus resulting in a lack of validity and generalizability for those aspects of the reports. This lack of user research does not, however, detract from the importance of the conceptual models in clarifying and mapping the complex bibliographic universe.

In addition to these major IFLA research projects, other authority control research in descriptive cataloging continued to examine more specific segments of the topic. Much of this research falls into the categories of retrievability, including international issues, and process and cost issues. The measure of success and the ultimate goal for authority control research is retrievability. Studies in this category examined data quality, automation, foreign and nonroman languages, and internationalization. Using a transaction log analysis methodology, Taylor's research examined variations appearing in name access points found in OCLC bibliographic records.[63] In a similar study, Weintraub examined the effects of personal name variations on authority control and data retrieval in computerized catalogs.[64] Bowman examined 38 OPACs available on the Internet in order to identify retrieval problems resulting from lack of crossreferences and variant author names.[65] Jin compared forms of corporate names found in the Library of Congress Name Authority File with the forms found on corporate Web sites.[66] Calhoun and Oskins used several different variables to investigate the types of changes made to LC authority records over time.[67]

Several studies addressed the authority control problems dealing with foreign and nonroman names. Ruiz-Pérez and others investigated how Spanish names were handled in three different databases and identified mistakes that would have a negative impact on locating and retrieving works by Spanish authors.[68] Hu used a transactional analysis method to examine problems in cataloging Chinese names, including transliterating Chinese characters and establishing entries for personal names.[69] Bolick also studied Chinese names, examining the reasons why vendor software produced negative results for nonunique Chinese names.[70] Wang examined the problems of Chinese names in different languages, i.e., English transliteration, transliterated name from spoken Chinese dialect, westernized Chinese, and pure Chinese.[71] Influenced by a Machine-Readable Bibliographic Information (MARBI) discussion paper on multilingual authority records,[72] Plettner developed three models for entry of Arabic names.[73]

Authority control has always been the most time consuming and expensive part of the cataloging process, so improving the quality of the data for retrievability, while reducing the time and labor costs involved with the process, is an ongoing area for research. Research in the process and costs category included quality control and evaluation research, workflow studies, and cost-benefit analysis. Kulczak used the OCLC database to evaluate the quality of front-end authority work for monographs in order to determine whether authority work was necessary at the copy cataloging stage.[74] Pappas conducted a similar study using records from the RLIN database.[75] Beall investigated the impact of typographical errors in authority records.[76] Ellero investigated the use of the Web as a source of information for authority records.[77] Jin adopted a narrower research focus and examined the process of constructing corporate name headings using data from the corporate body's home page.[78] Wolverton surveyed the authority control practices and staffing and training issues related to authority control in large academic research libraries.[79] Bangalore and Prabha investigated the copy cataloging process by measuring the time and effort expended.[80] Santizo and Rezabek surveyed academic libraries to find information about the type of decisions and level of responsibility of authority control required of copy catalogers.[81] Tsui and Hinders conducted a cost-benefit analysis for outsourcing the authority control process.[82]

Technology and automation were important catalysts for authority control research, much of which used applied and experimental research to develop new software tools and systems and to integrate authority records with bibliographic records in databases. The primary goal of this type of research is to reduce the amount of human intervention needed to create authority records. One method of evaluating these automated systems is to measure the accuracy of the system in terms of its ability to disambiguate like names and titles. As development of the Virtual International Authority File (VIAF) progresses, this research is particularly concerned with merging large data files. Merged records in the VIAF contain the form of name or title used in different countries. Local libraries will have options when deciding which form or forms to display. Another evaluation method is to test how well an automated system performs when its accuracy is compared to a human-created authority record. DiLauro and others presented a detailed report of the process used to create an automated authority record for the Lester S. Levy Collection of Sheet Music.[83] Patton and others developed and tested an automated name authority control (ANAC) tool as part of the Lester S. Levy Sheet Music digitization project.[84] The goal of their research was to reduce the costs associated with applying authority control to the metadata for the collection, and "the development of tools that combine automated processes and human intervention, with the overall goal of involving humans at higher levels of analysis and decision making."[85] The researchers extracted names from the statements of responsibility in their metadata records using a rule-based name extraction algorithm developed for the project.

The resulting name records were automatically compared to the records in the LC Name Authority File, using probability theory to determine a match. "Overall, ANAC was successful 58% of the time. When a name had an LC record, ANAC was successful 77% of the time, but when an LC record did not exist for a name ANAC was successful only 12% of the time."[86] These results confirm that the ANAC system would not function well without human intervention in some cases. The researchers emphasized that their intention was not to eliminate human intervention completely from the process, but to be able to predict the amount and type of intervention that would be needed.

In order to test the dependability of a new authority control module in the library's automated system, Greever compared the module's effectiveness to the currently used manual procedures for authority control.[87] Running the two systems simultaneously, Greever compared the number and type of established headings for which authority records would be added to the local system using the precataloging procedures to the number and type of established headings for which local authority records would be added by the automated system. Her results showed that the new automated module was in fact equal to or more effective in establishing headings and the new system reduced redundancy and generated fewer errors. French and Powell investigated approximate string-matching techniques and introduced the concept of approximate word matching to improve detection and categorization of variant forms of names.[88] Miller discussed the development of XOBIS, an XML schema that reorganizes bibliographic and authority data elements into a single integrated structure.[89] The LEAF (Linking and Exploring Authority Files) research project is developing a model architecture for collecting, harvesting, linking, and providing access to existing local or national name authority data.[90] The architecture will provide a mechanism to search the authority records of individual data providers and merge the information into one LEAF authority record containing international name data that will be stored in a "Central Name Authority File."

In addition to these experimental and developmental studies, the literature contains examples of local implementation reports on the topic of outsourcing authority control work. Lam described the outsourcing experience of the University of Saskatchewan.[91] This experiential report included statistical information on each phase of the process and cost information for an initial database clean-up, an annual authority database updating, and a weekly service for current authority work. The university was satisfied with the vendor's overall linking rate of 85.9% for headings. An analytical study conducted by Vellucci describes the outsourcing process in detail and speculates on the future problems of outsourcing authority control on an international scale.[92] All of this research provides useful information for practical decision making. It is important, however, to weigh the results of any given study against a comparable situation in terms of the type of library, how a system functions, the nature of the records being processed, and the participants in the research before generalizations can be made.

Finally, a major international conference on authority control was held in Florence, Italy, in 2003, and proceedings were published.[93] Forty-eight papers were presented, organized into the following categories: state of the art and new theoretical perspectives; standards, exchange formats, metadata; authority control for names and works; authority control for subjects; and authority control experiences and projects. The proceedings provide a wealth of information on every aspect of the topic, including research using a variety of methodologies.

Metadata

Metadata is structured data that describes a resource, identifies its relationships to other resources, and facilitates the discovery, management, and use of a resource. Although traditional cataloging information can accurately be described as metadata, most people use the term in the context of digital resources. A major paradigm shift occurred in knowledge organization with the development of metadata schemas and markup languages that could serve as alternatives to the *AACR2* and the *MARC Bibliographic Format* for catalog records. Both cataloging and metadata require the same conceptual knowledge; it is the application and management of the metadata that differs. The processes of creating metadata and cataloging are so closely linked that in many academic libraries the boundaries between the two are obscured and the two units are often merged into one department. This merger opens new opportunities for academic library catalogers to expand their expertise. The research conducted in the area of knowledge organization is also becoming more integrated, and the work that is done in one community often has an impact on the other. Due to the large number of studies conducted in the area of metadata, the research discussed in this section is selective and will provide only a general overview of the directions in which metadata research is progressing.

Several general metadata schemas exist such, as the simple and popular Dublin Core Metadata Element Set (DCMES) and the more complex Encoded Archival Description (EAD) and Text Encoding Initiative (TEI). In addition to these general schemas, many subject-specific metadata schemas have been developed since the mid-1990s; however, discussion of each metadata set is beyond the scope of this chapter.[94] A great deal of conceptual research was invested in developing these schemas; those efforts are reflected in the descriptive nature of the research that was initially published. As the field of metadata matured, researchers looked beyond metadata schema description and began to examine a wide range of metadata related issues. These ongoing research initiatives fall into several categories that are not mutually exclusive, including options for metadata creation, development of tools to aid metadata creation, expanding metadata interoperability, developing vocabularies to support the semantic web, and developing ways to evaluate the quality and usability of metadata.

Metadata Creation

Because of the substantial number of digital resources requiring metadata for description and retrieval and the high cost and subjectivity of human-created metadata, several researchers explored alternative methods for the metadata creation process. One option is to have author-generated metadata. Since the Dublin Core was originally designed for resource authors to create their own metadata, in a baseline study using a mixed-mode methodology, Greenberg and others examined the ability of authors to generate acceptable Dublin Core metadata for their own resources.[95] The study involved a training session for the authors prior to metadata creation, author creation of metadata using a template designed for the project, analysis of the newly created metadata by a research team of experts, and a survey questionnaire to ascertain the authors' perspective on the project. The results of the study indicated that 64% of the metadata records were either good or excellent and 36% needed major revision. All records were considered acceptable for resource description and retrieval by the research analysis team. From author questionnaire feedback, the researchers realized that a redesign of the input template was necessary. After the redesign, the study was conducted again with 29 participants, and the authors were asked to answer additional questions about their metadata experience.[96] These findings showed serious problems with author motivation for creating metadata themselves. Several authors believed that it was not their job or interest to create metadata, and others questioned the benefits of metadata. The study concluded that it is imperative to create metadata input tools where the interface template is clear, is easy to use, and provides a comprehensive explanation of the metadata process. Taking into consideration the small sample size of both studies and the fact that the studies were conducted in an organizational environment, the results are not generalizable to the academic setting. Academic libraries, however, might wish to replicate this study with faculty and noncataloging staff to determine if the results are comparable, if the quality success rate is acceptable in academe, and if there are institutional factors that might influence metadata creation.

Wilson conducted a recent study of contributor-supplied metadata[97] using the RILM Abstracts of Music Literature (RILM), an international database of scholarly works about music.[98] The RILM database relies on authors and subject-expert volunteers to provide the basic metadata records and abstracts that describe the literature. Metadata records submitted through a Web form were compared to the final published version of the record that had been reviewed and enhanced by a metadata professional. A sample of English-language records were examined for quality based on the completeness of each record; the types of errors (typographical/grammatical or semantic), if any, in each record; and the appearance and type of "value-added" or additional metadata supplied by the contributor in each record. Structural and semantic errors were noted throughout the records evaluated. Results of the study showed that overall, the semantic quality was very high, reflecting the subject expertise of the contributors. The appearance and type of structural errors suggested that improvements to the interface of the Web form, such as drop-down lists, could reduce structural errors to create high-quality contributor-supplied metadata records.

Another option for metadata creation is to develop applications that can automatically extract data from the document and generate metadata.

Earlier reference was made to the Johns Hopkins University's Levy Digital Sheet Music Project experience with automatically generated authority records.[99] A sample of other research work will be mentioned here. Yilmazel, Finneran, and Liddy developed a natural language processing system to automatically assign metadata.[100] A collection of educational documents was used, and three distinct extraction modules were designed to compile the data, along with constant data extracted from the collection level file. The results of the data extraction from all modules were then collocated, prioritized, and output as a single metadata record. The generated and manual metadata records were then evaluated by teachers for how well the metadata represented the lesson plans. The results indicated that in most data elements there was no significant difference between the manual and generated metadata. The only elements where the manual metadata were significantly better were title and keyword.

Paynter described a large ongoing project to develop automatic metadata assignment and evaluation tools for the INFOMINE Project.[101] "The assignment tools that resulted from this research range in complexity from simple rules for assigning Title and Creator metadata by harvesting the text of HTML tags, to Keyphrase and Description extraction algorithms based on syntactic processing of Metatags and to complex Library of Congress Classification (LCC) and Library of Congress Subject Heading (LCSH) classifiers based on algorithms."[102] Manually assigned metadata was used to train the machine learning tool for assigning both LCC and LCSH metadata, and an automatic evaluation tool was used to determine the metadata quality. Paynter included extensive discussions of the extracting and assigning processes for each data element and a useful survey of the research previously conducted for each method used.

All of these studies indicate that automatically generated metadata, combined with manually created metadata for specific elements, can optimize the quality of the metadata while reducing the time and cost of having experts create the entire metadata record. Academic libraries could use this information to create a new metadata creation model that would be especially useful for supporting digital library collections and metadata repositories.

Common Research Goals

As mentioned earlier in this chapter, the overlap between cataloging and metadata has blurred to the extent that the boundaries are often artificial. The research discussed in this section is of mutual concern to the cataloging and metadata communities. Globalization, economies of scale and cooperation, the plethora of knowledge organization systems (KOS), and the advancement of technology are all factors leading to a confluence of research among the cataloging, metadata, and information-retrieval domains. Key problems common to all include interoperability and automatically generated subject terms and classification.

Interoperability

The American Library Association has defined interoperability as the ability of two or more systems or components to exchange information and use the exchanged information without special effort on the part of either system.[103] Interoperability research extends to developing crosswalks between different KOS, searching and retrieving data from multiple repository databases, simplifying subject access, mapping subject terms among different vocabularies and languages, using classification as a switching language, and developing taxonomies and ontologies for specific subject domains. This last area of taxonomies and ontologies will not be covered in this chapter.

Technical Interoperability

Interoperability is an important issue for academic libraries that participate in distributed networked environments where cross-domain, cross-repository, and cross-language searching are increasingly important. Interoperability research can be viewed from two perspectives: technical data transfer and/or conversion and content compatibility. The research on the technical transfer and conversion of metadata focuses on system architecture, record structure, syntax, and types of data elements. Content interoperability research is concerned with standards for description, such as *AACR2R* or the *International Standards for Archival Description* (ISAD), authority control for names, identifiers, controlled vocabularies, natural language processing and classification. Both aspects of interoperability are critical for the efficient exchange of high-quality metadata with or without human intervention.

Crosswalks are used to facilitate machine processing and data transfer. "A crosswalk is a mapping of the elements, semantics, and syntax from one metadata schema to those of another."[104] The elements (or fields) in one metadata set are correlated with the elements of another metadata set that have the same or similar meanings. Many metadata schemas are mapped to the MARC format, using crosswalks to exchange and convert data to and from MARC. Conceptual research is used to develop a single file table of equivalency, while applied research is the basis for crosswalk implementation. Problems arise when metadata records with incompatible data elements in the two schemas are mapped to each other. It is often the case that there is not a one-to-one match between all data elements in the two schemas and data from the richer schema is lost during the transformation process. In addition, as these single files contain all information in one equivalency table, each crosswalk is limited in its use and usually applies only to a single digital project.

A research project conducted at OCLC by Godby, Young, and Childress addressed this problem by developing a repository of metadata crosswalks.[105] The project goes beyond the standard single file mapping table and uses the Metadata Encoding and Transmission Standard (METS), a structural framework, to define a complex data model that brings together three separate files: one for the table of equivalence, one for the source metadata standard, and one for the target metadata standard. These data are then processed to create XML-encoded METS records for each crosswalk and are available for processing by "search engines, OAI (Open Archives Initiative) harvesters, and custom-designed web services."[106] By using separate files to maintain the element sets of each metadata schema and each equivalency table, one can create a customized crosswalk by selecting the metadata and table of choice. This prototype is an important step forward to improve and standardize crosswalk formats; however, the authors note that this area of research must continue in order to develop "robust systems that handle validation, enhancement, and multiple character encodings and allow human guidance of the translation process."[107]

The OAI-PMH (Open Archives Initiative-Protocol for Metadata Harvesting) is an applied research project that seeks to develop an efficient system to search and retrieve metadata simultaneously from multiple database repositories. Several years of conceptual and applied research went into "drafting and designing a useful and useable technical specification" that is now in use by many academic libraries.[108] Differing from other protocols, the OAI model was designed to collect metadata by harvesting (i.e., "pull") rather than contribution (i.e., "push") to one central repository. After the initial implementation, the model was refined to extend its capacity to identify and harvest a variety of metadata schemas using the Dublin Core as the mandatory standard. An additional refinement of the protocol model allowed for discovery and retrieval of data in repositories of nondigital objects.

Van de Sompel and others identified several limitations with the OAI-PMH protocol.[109] The Dublin Core element "dc.identifier" was not expressive enough to distinguish among the variety of identifiers permissible in the Dublin Core and therefore could not accurately harvest the actual digital resources. The inability to harvest the resources described by the metadata was also a problem for their preservation, which requires archiving a large, synchronized repository. Van de Sompel and others designed a new model to extend the capabilities of the OAI-PMH to include harvesting resources as well as metadata. The model represents increasingly expressive metadata formats contained in a XML document wrapper. The first level below the actual resource is the OAI-PMH identifier, which acts as the entry point to all of the metadata formats. These formats include the minimalist Dublin Core Metadata format, the richer and more expressive MARCXML metadata format, and the METS XML complex object metadata format, which is the most complex and accurate description of the resource. This combination of formats allows for greater depth of expressiveness and provides secondary information that was not accessible in the original OAI-PMH model, including rights management and technical, structural, and provenance metadata. The new model also provides access to the resource, thus solving the problems of unambiguous resource discovery and harvesting of resources for preservation.

The importance of the new model becomes evident in a federated search environment. The model allows academic libraries to reuse their MARC metadata and thus provides integrated access to metadata for nondigital objects and allows harvesting of digital resources for access or preservation purposes.

Subject Access

As the need for internationalization and the volume of Web resources grew, there was heightened interest in improving the interoperability of KOS and making these systems easier to use. Solutions to these goals are not limited to any one domain, and the literature of cataloging, classification, metadata, and information retrieval all provide examples of research in this area. The overlap of research interests has created a vast body of literature, and of necessity the studies discussed here are selective examples to provide some understanding of the breadth of research. Researchers are investigating the development of less complex subject systems, automatic generation of subject headings and classification, multilingual subject access, and tools that will aid the user in subject searching.

In response to the trend to simplify cataloging and reduce costs by eliminating controlled vocabulary terms from catalog records, Gross and Taylor conducted research to identify the proportion of OPAC records retrieved by a keyword search that had the "keyword only in a subject heading field and thus would not be retrieved if there were no subject headings."[110] The authors used a transaction log analysis methodology to sample keyword searches in an academic library catalog and then performed keyword searches in an OPAC using those terms. Gross and Taylor found that an average of 35.9% of records retrieved by successful keyword searches would not be retrieved if subject headings were not included in the record. Their research also discovered many individual cases in which 80, 90, and even 100 percent of the retrieved records would not be retrieved in the absence of subject headings.[111]

Zeng and Chan reviewed the research methodologies used in projects to establish content interoperability among KOS that focused on subject terms and classification schemes.[112] The authors identified several problematic issues for subject interoperability, including mapping systems with different structures and characteristics (e.g., controlled word-based vocabularies to classification systems), mapping similarly structured schemes (e.g., word-based vocabularies to other word-based vocabularies, or classification schemes to other classification schemes), mapping vocabularies in different languages, and integrating the views of different cultures. Zeng and Chan identified several mapping methodologies, among which are derivative modeling (creating a simpler KOS based on a more comprehensive system), direct mapping (equivalence matching term to term or term to classification), translation and adaptation, and using a switching language to mediate between languages. The authors report on research projects dealing with each of these issues and methodologies.

The exponential growth of electronic resources led researchers at OCLC to seek ways to provide subject access to large volumes of resources, yet make it easier and less costly to use than the complex syntax of the LCSH.[113] Implementations of the minimalist Dublin Core metadata schema created the impetus to develop a subject vocabulary that was simple in structure, provided optimal access points, and was flexible and interoperable across a variety of KOS, including OPACs. Deriving their new vocabulary from the LCSH and simplifying the syntax, the researchers created the Faceted Application of Subject Terminology (FAST) as a postcoordinate approach. Literary warrant was used to determine which headings would be established, based on the frequency with which a heading appeared in the OCLC WorldCat database. FAST headings were established by deconstructing the LCSH headings into facets, which enabled the vocabulary to remain compatible with LCSH, thus improving subject interoperability between Dublin Core and MARC metadata.

Multilingual linking and mapping are used to provide access to multiple languages across systems. The MACS (Multilingual Access to Subjects) research project uses a linking method approach.[114] Three vocabularies (LCSH, RAMEAU,[115] and SWD[116]) are manually matched and linked to each other by using conceptual clusters, thus allowing each subject heading list to remain autonomous. The research team also developed, tested, and refined a Linked Management Interface (LMI) that assists in link creation. Landry notes, however, that since the matching process is done manually, "the basic task of establishing links will remain very time-consuming."[117]

Classification systems are often used as an intermediary or switching language between different languages and different KOS because they are perceived as being language independent. Kwasnik and Rubin studied the impact of the differences in knowledge structures from language to language and culture to culture by examining a set of terms related to the concepts of family, which are universal yet culturally bound.[118] The purpose of the study was to identify problems surfacing from the extension of a source classification system to accommodate another language and culture and to suggest methods to deal with the problem. Their research first explored the differences in kinship terms and relationships through interviews with 14 informants of diverse language and cultural backgrounds, using ethnographic interview techniques that included creating a visual display of the family relationships. Kwasnik and Rubin then compared the resultant terms to the way in which the *Dewey Decimal Classification* (DDC) and the *Library of Congress Classification* (LCC) expressed kinship terms and relationships. This study revealed seven problematic patterns, and the researchers suggested ways to deal with some of the problems. The area of language and culture is an important one for academic libraries with diverse user populations. This significant study needs replication with multiple informants for each language/culture and a more comprehensive range of languages.

The OCLC Research Office has a strong research agenda for vocabulary mapping, automatic classification, and automatic term assignment. In the late 1990s, OCLC launched the Scorpion project to explore the automatic classification of electronic resources by creating clusters of terms based on statistical and linguistic methodologies.[119] Scorpion software used the DDC data files "to create a searchable database of subject terminology used to describe each Dewey number in the Dewey schedules."[120] Classification categories are mapped to DDC and create predefined subject clusters. The document is then filtered through the predefined clusters as a query and Dewey classes are assigned in ranked order. Scorpion software was integrated into the OCLC CORC project to automatically class internet resources using terms extracted from the document. The researchers view the use of a language-independent notation scheme as a way to enable different language translations of DDC vocabulary and captions to link to a Dewey class number and allow the user to select the appropriate language view.[121] Other research undertaken by the OCLC team includes development of the DeweyBrowser for library collections, mapping different vocabularies to each other to create a linked semantic system that will accommodate cross-domain searching, and the WordSmith Toolkit, which extracts words and phrases from full-text documents.[122] In addition, information about many other current research projects can be found at the OCLC Research-Works site (http://www.oclc.org/research/researchworks/) and in the journals *Knowledge Organization*, *Journal of Documentation*, and *Journal of the American Society for Information Science and Technology*.

The Library OPAC

The library OPAC is the focus of the final section of research discussed in this chapter. When all is said and done, the goal of research in knowledge organization is to improve the quality, functionality and usability of library catalogs and databases for information retrieval. OPAC research consists of two primary areas. One sphere of research is quality assessment and evaluation of existing knowledge organization systems, including data content, record syntax, and system performance. The other sphere is applied research to enhance the functionality and usability of existing systems and to develop new systems. Of necessity the research discussed here is selective and limited to those projects that specifically address library catalogs. For a broader discussion of system evaluation, one should refer to the information science literature.

Many different research methodologies are used in evaluative research, often in combination with one another. Common methods include transaction log and content analysis, grounded theory, survey questionnaires, focus groups and interviews, think-aloud protocols, and observation. Two articles in the 1990s by Seymour[123] and Large and Beheshti[124] provided in-depth reviews of the OPAC research conducted from the mid-1980s to the mid-1990s. Much of the research discussed in these two reviews involves evaluation and quality assessment.

A 1996 special issue of *JASIS* was devoted to OPAC research and contained several articles that focus on various aspects of research on this topic.[125] Following up on an earlier article, Borgman asks the question "Why are Online Catalogs *Still* So Hard to Use?"[126] In her theoretical analysis, the author cites two underlying causes for the problem: the lack of focus on user information-seeking behavior to inform OPAC design and ongoing emulation of the card catalog search process. Hert examined the goals of users searching an OPAC (and other multifile systems) as part of a larger project that focused on users' interactions with the OPAC.[127] Using a grounded theory methodology where the data analysis was iterative and generalizations were formed from the data itself, Hert found that although the users expressed their goals to some extent, it was necessary to identify the critical incidents (i.e., when the user became aware of a gap in knowledge, thus creating an information need) that had shaped the goal to gain a fuller understanding of the search. Hert's research also showed that the goals of the search were not greatly modified during the search process. The findings of this study suggest that OPAC design may be improved "by providing detailed information on the situational elements which influence goals and on the potential constancy of goals on such systems."[128]

For several decades, user studies have documented problems with subject searching in OPACs.[129] Larson conducted a longitudinal study of the University of California's MELVYL online catalog over a six-year period, using a transaction log analysis methodology.[130] His results showed that only 12% of subject searches recovered between 1 and 20 items, thus signifying that subject searches were more likely to fail (no hits or too many hits) than to succeed in a very large university library. Larson's findings also indicated a persistent decline in the percentage of subject searches over the data collection period and a corresponding increase in the percentage of known item, especially title keyword, searches. These results suggest that over time users learned to substitute various forms of known item searches for subject searches in response to the frequent failure of subject searches.

Drabenstott and Weller created an experimental OPAC (ASTUTE) that contained two separate catalogs.[131] Both catalogs used extended subject searching functionality, but only one catalog also used subject search trees to direct the system's selection of searching techniques in response to user queries. The study was conducted in two academic libraries, using both quantitative and qualitative methodologies. While the quantitative analysis based on retrieval precision yielded mixed results, the qualitative data gathered from the users was more conclusive. The overall research results showed that the "subject-access design that featured search trees was more effective in selecting a subject-searching approach that would produce useful information for the subjects users seek than users would select on their own."[132]

Another more recent study by Yu and Young used a transaction log analysis (TLA) methodology in a longitudinal study over a two-year period to identify and define unsuccessful OPAC subject searches.[133] The TLA indicated that a major portion of subject searches would have been more successful if the search had been conducted using other bibliographic tools. The authors suggested that this problem is attributed to the ubiquitous use and familiarity with Web search engines and online bookstores and the subsequent mental models that users bring to OPAC searching. Several suggestions were made to improve OPAC searching based on the functionality of Web-based search applications. Graham used TLA to identify and analyze no-hit subject searches in the college OPAC.[134] After noting specific subject searches for which no records were retrieved but for which appropriate information resources actually were represented in the catalog, Graham explored two potential methods to ameliorate the problem through the use of authority record cross-references and "pathfinder" records providing brief instructions on search refinement. The author also outlines additional steps needed to determine whether the potential ameliorations make a difference to users' subject searching experiences.

Content-focused research looks at the quality and accuracy of the data in catalog/metadata records in order to reduce errors and improve retrieval. An early study by Ballard described a systematic method for finding and eliminating typographical errors in catalogs and listed the most commonly found misspellings.[135] Another study by Ballard and Lifshin analyzed the misspellings and discovered that repeated misspellings tended to have eight or more letters, at least three syllables, and be more common words rather than esoteric technical terms.[136] Ballard and Grimaldi examined errors in MARC tagging to improve OPAC searching.[137] Bowman conducted several studies that examined data content problems that acted as barriers to retrieval.[138] Beall and Kafadar studied the typographical errors in shared bibliographic records to determine whether corrections were made during the copy cataloging process.[139]

MacEwan and Young developed another method for measuring the quality of both the data content and the overall catalog record.[140] These researchers employed the FRBR mapping of user tasks to data attributes and relationships to measure the quality of catalog records in the British Library. Using the data element weighting method developed for FRBR and a sophisticated statistical process, the authors were able to assign an overall quality score to each catalog record examined.

Improving accessibility to networked digital information and resources is another concern of the OPAC research community. Burke, Germain, and Van Ullen conducted survey research to study the effect that adding surrogates for free Web resources would have on the integrity of the catalog.[141] By examining 567 URLs in the OPACs of 24 Association of Research Libraries (ARL) member libraries, they discovered that the percentage of total catalog and maintenance errors varied from 0.0% in three OPACs to a high of 58.32% in one catalog. The authors also found that these libraries did not commonly use persistent URLs, perhaps contributing to the problem. Other OPAC accessibility research examined the effects of OPAC screen changes on search behavior and success.[142]

The metadata community has now matured to the point where studies of evaluation and quality assessment have entered the literature. Initially, research in metadata evaluation was conceptual and addressed the issues of "What is quality?" and "How do we measure it?" Barton, Currier, and Hey studied metadata projects in two communities of practice: learning object repositories and e-print archives.[143] In each project, the researchers analyzed the metadata to identify defects that demonstrated a need for quality assurance in the assignment of metadata. Bruce and Hillman adopted a different approach to defining metadata quality and used a systematic, domain- and method-independent way to identify metadata quality indicators.[144] Kelly, Closier, and Hiom used theoretical and applied research to develop a quality assessment framework for metadata and a self-assessment tool kit.[145] Moen, Stewart, and McClure identified a list of assessment criteria drawn from the literature and applied qualitative and quantitative content analysis techniques to assess the quality of metadata records in the Government Information Locator Service (GILS).[146]

The research on evaluation and quality assessment of catalogs, cataloging, and metadata is immensely important in academic libraries in light of the rapid growth of digital libraries and metadata use. As academic libraries seek and develop new methods for generating automated and partially automated metadata, the importance of quality assessment and evaluation increases significantly. Many digital library projects allow the object creators or curators to assign metadata to their own objects. This type of distributed metadata creation will need quality assurance measures embedded in the process design.[147]

Library 2.0 and OPAC Design Enhancements

The Library 2.0 movement, with its emphasis on service, interactivity, and personalization, calls into question the limited functionality of library OPACs in terms of capitalizing on recent developments in Web service-oriented applications and architecture. In order to plan for the future, several recent studies have analyzed the technological and social trends that could impact major academic and research libraries. In one study commissioned by the LC, Calhoun explored the future of research library catalogs in the context of today's Web search engines, online bookstores, user expectations, and economic considerations.[148] She derived her research questions from an extensive multidisciplinary literature review, which included marketing and business perspectives along with those of the library science and information retrieval communities. Calhoun then developed a set of structured interview questions from the literature search and identified interviewees from among library and information science leaders, scholars, technologists, systems developers and implementers, vendors, and library practitioners in order to collect different points of view on the future of catalogs. Her purposive sample consisted of 23 experts in the field.[149] After data analysis was completed, Calhoun made 32 recommendations to LC based on the literature review and expert interviews. Recommendations centered on revitalizing catalogs for internal operations as well as the communities they serve and integrating catalogs with other discovery tools. High on the list of recommendations was rethinking catalog content and services to significantly enhance functionality by using many of the features found in popular Web search engines. This report helps set the research agenda for online catalogs for the short-term future, as many areas of the recommendations will require further investigation before they can be implemented. Some members of the library community took issue with Calhoun's marketing framework and realistic assessment of user expectations;[150] however, two other studies, one by the University of California[151] and another by Indiana University[152] support many of Calhoun's findings and suggestions.

Most college students today are technologically savvy and, as Calhoun pointed out, the mental models that they bring to library Web-based catalogs, databases, and portals are often based on their experiences with Web resources such as Amazon.com, Google, MySpace, or the Internet Movie Database. Influenced by Web sites that provide seamless interactive functionality and access to different databases, both commercial vendors and open-source application developers are rapidly designing new interfaces for library catalogs and portals. Many new products incorporate relevance ranking, faceted navigation, meaningful result clustering, visual representation of results, breadcrumb trails, and federated search tools.[153] Some of these applications include Endeca,[154] AquaBrowser,[155] Evergreen,[156] Encore,[157] and Primo.[158] To date, the body of research is small and consists primarily of case studies and anecdotal articles on implementation; however, as these features become more commonplace, the usability and evaluative research no doubt will grow.

Other Library 2.0 concepts of personalization and interactivity (social tagging, adding reviews, blogging comments, etc.) are beginning to influence library catalog and portal design. The scarce research that exists tends to focus on public libraries or social tagging Web sites. One usability study, however, did examine an academic portal customization software application, *MyLibrary*. Brantley, Armstrong, and Lewis used categories of common tasks to test "the participants' abilities to customize a personal library web page, understand the resource categories as defined by librarians, and manage the discipline-specific content available in the portal."[159] The results of the study indicated that even experienced computer users struggled with customizing the library portal; however, when users overcame the learning curve, they appreciated the shortcuts offered by the portal. This study also revealed that user misunderstanding of librarian-defined resource categories remains a serious stumbling block to library Web site usability.

One way to help overcome the disconnect between user and library vocabularies brings us to another Library 2.0 concept: user interaction with the catalog through social tagging, reviews, and comments. Again it is public libraries that have taken the lead in implementing these features,[160] but academic institutions are not far behind. Plymouth State University developed a prototype open-source OPAC called Scriblio.[161] Based on the WordPress blog software platform, Scriblio has many Library 2.0 features, including a "recent searches" sidebar; book jacket displays; reviews; holdings data; automatic identification of related items based on author and subject data; and a box to "search inside the book" that uses Amazon's Application Programming Interface (API). In addition, each catalog record allows comments, trackbacks, and tagging. Although these front-end OPAC applications are too new to have generated a body of research, it is expected that this area of investigation will grow rapidly in the near future.

Conclusions

For the past 15 years, researchers have sought to develop ways to automate the systems and processes of knowledge organization. The digital environment presented opportunities for academic libraries to explore alternative methods for organizing digital resources, as seen by the many new metadata schemas that have been developed and the application of XML markup to provide more flexibility in these systems. Another research trend shows a move toward developing systems of organization that are simpler and easier to apply than the currently used rules, tools, and processes. The approaches of the Dublin Core Metadata Initiative (DCMI) and the FAST project indicate not only a need for simplicity, but also an attempt to extend the use of library organizational practices outside the library community, and in turn to use metadata created by these other communities. The distributed networked environment, coupled with a growing emphasis on global cooperation, is the catalyst for interoperability research that is key to both cataloging and metadata knowledge organization systems.

When the research conducted in the field of knowledge organization and its impact on academic libraries are examined, other trends prevail that represent major paradigm shifts in the approach to organizing information. The reconceptualization of the fundamental principles and structures undergirding the view of the bibliographic universe and the organizational process has led to the adaptation of catalog and record structures that will allow more meaningful displays of multiple versions of a work and will express the relationships among works more clearly; both issues must be dealt with on a daily basis by catalogers in academic libraries with collection depth. This reconceptualization was the catalyst for the ongoing revision and restructuring of the *AACR2* cataloging code that is used by academic libraries. The question remains as to whether the final version of the RDA code will be a contemporary set of rules that is based on the research and trends discussed in this chapter and will appeal to the broadening knowledge organization community, or an outdated rehash of the current system with only a passing nod to the dramatic changes facing academic libraries today.

None of the research projects discussed here exists in a vacuum. They were undertaken to solve problems of a practical nature or refute incorrect assumptions. Many of the projects were carried out in academic environments or with academic library needs as the focal point, since academic and research libraries have the most to gain from automation and applications that can facilitate multilingual subject access and streamline the cataloging, classification, and metadata creation processes. It is appropriate therefore, that academic libraries serve as test beds for research that will ultimately be used or implemented to assist in the task of knowledge organization.

The integration of cataloging and metadata creation is fast becoming the norm in academic libraries and will require an expanded view of data curation.[162] Knowledge organization specialists will be called upon to work collaboratively with systems and information technology personnel to develop the means of discovery and access for information distributed throughout the university. Catalogers will be increasingly involved in research projects to develop and evaluate digital libraries, electronic dissertations and theses, institutional repositories, and large research data sets.

This research review indicates that the knowledge organization research community is thriving and is responsible for many of the rapid changes taking place in libraries today. In order to remain at the cutting edge of this field, however, more extensive research studies are needed. The expanding diversity of our academic communities demands better search and display capabilities for nonroman script materials. We must identify and develop alternative actions for failed searches and better navigation of large retrieval sets. We have only just begun to investigate the effects of Library 2.0 concepts such as expanded record content (e.g., tables of contents, images, music snippets, etc.) and user interactivity (e.g., assigning tags and adding reviews and comments) on catalog usage and library resources. Additional services such as those provided by online bookstores that use active agents for recommendations, relevance ranking, and improved precision and recall need to be studied. More research is required for catalog-based alert services and customization of the library catalog and portal. There is much to be learned from Internet services, but in order to move forward we must explore the possibility of successful implementation of such services and their impact on the academic community. It is unfortunate that in today's economic climate most research is funded by agencies for short-term projects (one to three years), rather than supporting researchers to develop and implement long-term research agendas. Researchers dedicated to the improvement of knowledge organization and retrieval should not be content with reaching Google or Amazon.com benchmark functionalities, but should look beyond these popular services and begin to identify new avenues of research for the knowledge organization community of the future.

References

1. Elaine Svenonius, "Bibliographic Control," in *Academic Libraries: Research Perspectives,* ed. Mary Jo Lynch and Arthur P. Young, 38–66 (Chicago: American Library Association, 1990).

2. Ibid., 42–43.

3. IFLA UBCIM Study Group on the Functional Requirements for Bibliographic Records, *Functional Requirements for Bibliographic Records: Final Report* (Munich: K.G. Saur, 1998).

4. Eeva Murtomaa,"The Impact of the Functional Requirements for Bibliographic Records Recommendations on the ISBD(ER)" *Cataloging and Classification Quarterly* 28, no. 1 (1999): 34.

5. VTLS was the first vendor to experiment with developing a FRBR structured catalog. Some issues and options for developing the system are presented in a PowerPoint presentation by Vinod Chachra and John Espley, "Differentiating Libraries through Enriched User Searching: FRBR as the Next Dimension in Meaningful Information Retrieval," www.ala.org/ala/alcts/education/presentations/ac04/ac04presentations.cfm (accessed March 30, 2008).

6. Rick Bennett, Brian F. Lavoie, and Edward T. O'Neill, "The Concept of a Work in WorldCat: An Application of FRBR," *Library Collections, Acquisitions, and Technical Services* 27, no. 1 (2003): 45–59.

7. Edward T. O'Neill, "FRBR: Functional Requirements for Bibliographic Records: Application of the Entity-Relationship Model to Humphry Clinker," *Library Resources and Technical Services* 46, no. 4 (2002): 150–159.

8. Roberto Sturman, "Implementing the FRBR Conceptual Approach in the ISIS Software Environment: IFPA (ISIS FRBR Prototype Application)," *Cataloging and Classification Quarterly* 39, no. 3/4 (2005): 253–70; Stefan Gradmann, "RDFS:FRBR : Towards an Implementation Model for Library Catalogs Using Semantic Web Technology," *Cataloging and Classification Quarterly* 39, no. 3/4 (2005): 63–75.

9. Thomas B. Hickey, Edward T. O'Neill, and Jenny Toves, "Experiments with the IFLA Functional Requirements for Bibliographic Records (FRBR)," *D-Lib Magazine* 8, no. 9 (2002), http://www.dlib.org/dlib/september02/hickey/09hickey.html (accessed March 31, 2008); Thomas B. Hickey and Edward T. O'Neill, "FRBRizing OCLC's Worldcat," *Cataloging and Classification Quarterly* 39, no. 3/4 (2005): 239–251.

10. Jackie Radebaugh and Corey Keith, "FRBR Display Tool," *Cataloging and Classification Quarterly* 39, no. 3/4 (2005): 253–270.

11. Chew Chiat Naun, "FRBR Principles Applied to a Local Online Journal Finding Aid," *Library Resources and Technical Services* 51, no. 2 (2007): 134–145.

12. Ketil Albertsen and Carol van Nuys, "Paradigma: FRBR and Digital Documents," *Cataloging and Classification Quarterly* 39, no. 3/4 (2005): 125–149; Tom Delsey, "Modeling Subject Access: Extending the FRBR and FRANAR Conceptual Models," *Cataloging and Classification Quarterly* 39, no. 3/4 (2005): 49–61; Kerry Kilner, "The AustLit Gateway and Scholarly Bibliography: A Specialist Implementation of the FRBR," *Cataloging and Classification* 39, no. 3/4 (2005): 87–102.

13. Robyn Holmes and Marie-Louise Ayres, "MusicAustralia: Towards a National Music Information Infrastructure" (paper presented at the International Symposium for Music Information Retrieval [ISMIR] Conference, Barcelona, Spain, October 10–14, 2004), online at http://www.nla.gov.au/nla/staffpaper/2004/ayres2.html (accessed March 30, 2008); Gunilla Jonsson. "Cataloguing of Hand Press Materials and the Concept of Expression in FRBR." *Cataloging and Classification Quarterly* 39, no. 3/4 (2005): 77–86; Patrick LeBoeuf., "Musical Works in the FRBR Model or 'Quasi La Stessa Cosa': Variations on a Theme by Umberto Eco," *Cataloging and Classification Quarterly* 39, no. 3/4 (2005): 103–124; Simon C. Lin and others, "A Metadata Case Study for the FRBR Model Based on Chinese Painting and Calligraphy at the National Palace Museum in Taipei"(paper presented at the International Conference on Dublin Core and Metadata Applications, Tokyo, October 24–26, 2001), online at http://www.nii.ac.jp/dc2001/proceedings/product/paper-08.pdf (accessed March 30, 2008); David Miller and Patrick LeBoeuf, "'Such Stuff as Dreams Are Made On': How Does FRBR Fit Performing Arts?" *Cataloging and Classification Quarterly* 39, no. 3/4 (2005): 151–178; Yann Nicolas, "Folklore Requirements for Bibliographic Records: Oral Traditions and FRBR," *Cataloging and Classification Quarterly* 39, no. 3/4 (2005): 179–195.

14. Glenn Patton, "Extending FRBR to Authorities," Cataloging and Classification Quarterly 39, no. 3/4 (2005): 39–48.

15. Shoichi Taniguchi, "Expression-Level Bibliographic Entity Records: A Trial on Creation from Pre-Existing MARC Records," *Cataloging and Classification Quarterly* 38, no. 2 (2004): 33–59.

16. Shoichi Taniguchi, "Conceptual Modelling of Component Parts of Bibliographic Resources in Cataloguing," *Journal of Documentation* 59, no. 6 (2003): 692–708.

17. Tom Delsey and others, *The Logical Structure of the Anglo-American Cataloguing Rules, Part I* (Joint Steering Committee for Revision of AACR, August 1998): 1, http://www.collectionscanada.ca/jsc/docs/aacr.pdf (accessed March 30, 2008); see also Tom Delsey with Beth Dulabahn and Michael Heaney, *The Logical Structure of the Anglo-American Cataloguing Rules. Part II* (Joint Steering Committee for Revision of AACR, January 1999), http://www.collectionscanada.ca/jsc/docs/aacr2.pdf (accessed March 30, 2008).

18. Barbara B. Tillett, "RDA: Resource Description and Access: Background and Context" (paper presented at the ALA Annual Conference. Chicago, IL, June 6, 2005), http://www.ala.org/ala/alcts/alctsconted/alctsceevents/alctsannual/AACR3_Tillett.pdf (accessed March 30, 2008).

19. Gordon Dunsire, "Distinguishing Content from Carrier: The RDA/ONIX Framework for Resource Categorization," *D-Lib Magazine* 13, no. 1/2 (2007), http://www.dlib.org/dlib/january07/dunsire/01dunsire.html (accessed March 30, 2008).

20. Tom Delsey, *Mapping ISBD Elements to FRBR Entity Attributes and Relationships:*

A Report (Den Haag, Netherlands: International Federation for Library Associations, 2004), 1, http://www.ifla.org/VII/s13/pubs/ISBD-FRBR-mappingFinal.pdf (accessed March 30, 2008).

21. Patrick Le Boeuf, "The Impact of the FRBR Model on the Future Revisions of the ISBDs: A Challenge for the IFLA Section on Cataloguing," *International Cataloguing and Bibliographic Control* 31, no. 1 (2002): 3–6.

22. Tom Delsey, "Functional Analysis of the MARC 21 Bibliographic and Holdings Formats," 2002, http://www.loc.gov/marc/marc-functional-analysis/original_frbr.html (accessed March 30, 2008).

23. Library of Congress, Network Development and MARC Standards Office, "Functional Analysis of the MARC 21 Bibliographic and Holdings Formats," 2006, Library of Congress, http://www.loc.gov/marc/marc-functional-analysis/functional-analysis.html (accessed March 30, 2008).

24. Barbara B. Tillett, "Bibliographic Relationships: Toward a Conceptual Structure of Bibliographic Information Used in Cataloging" (PhD diss., University of California, Los Angeles, 1987).

25. Tillett, "Bibliographic Relationships," 190.

26. Richard P. Smiraglia, "Authority Control and the Extent of Bibliographic Relationships" (PhD diss, University of Chicago, 1992).

27. Sherry L. Vellucci, "Bibliographic Relationships Among Musical Bibliographic Entities: A Conceptual Analysis of Music Represented in a Library Catalog with a Taxonomy of the Relationships Discovered" (DLS diss., School of Library Service, Columbia University, 1995); Sherry L. Vellucci, *Bibliographic Relationships in Music Catalogs* (Lanham, MD: Scarecrow Press, 1997).

28. Sherry L. Vellucci," Bibliographic Relationships," in *The Principles and Future of AACR: Proceedings of the International Conference on the Principles and Future Development of AACR Toronto, Canada, October 23–25, 1997,* ed. Jean Weihs, 105–146 (Toronto: Canadian Library Association; Chicago: American Library Association, 1998).

29. Martha M. Yee, "What Is a Work? Part 1: The User and the Objects of the Catalog," *Cataloging and Classification Quarterly* 19, no. 1 (1994): 33–40; Martha M. Yee, "What Is a Work? Part 2: The Anglo-American Cataloging Codes," *Cataloging and Classification Quarterly* 19, no. 2 (1994): 5–22; Martha M. Yee, "What Is a Work? Part 3: The Anglo-American Cataloging Codes," *Cataloging and Classification Quarterly* 20, no. 1 (1995): 25–46; Martha M. Yee, "What Is a Work? Part 4: Cataloging Theorists and a Definition," *Cataloging and Classification Quarterly* 20, no. 2 (1995): 3–24.

30. Allyson Carlyle, "The Second Objective of the Catalog: An Evaluation of Collocation in Online Catalog Displays" (PhD diss, University of California, Los Angeles, 1994).

31. Allyson Carlyle, "User Categorisation of Works: Toward Improved Organisa-

tion of Online Catalog Displays," *Journal of Documentation* 55, no. 2 (1999): 184–208.

32. Allyson Carlyle, "Ordering Author and Work Records: An Evaluation of Collocation in Online Catalog Displays," *Journal of the American Society for Information Science* 47, no. 7 (1996): 538–554.

33. Allyson Carlyle and Joel Summerlin, "Transforming Catalog Displays: Record Clustering for Works of Fiction," *Cataloging and Classification Quarterly* 33, no. 3/4 (2002): 13–25.

34. Richard P. Smiraglia, *The Nature of "a Work": Implications for the Organization of Knowledge.* (Lanham, MD: Scarecrow Press, 2001).

35. Patrick Le Boeuf, "'Convergence Is the Goal': Activity Report of the IFLA/FRBR/CIDOC CRM Harmonization Group" (PowerPoint presentation made at FRBR in 21st Century Catalogs: An Invitational Workshop, Dublin, OH, May 2–4, 2005), http://www.oclc.org/research/events/FRBR-workshop/presentations/leboeuf/FRBR_CRM_Harmonization.ppt (accessed March 30, 2008).

36. Bennett, Lavoie, and O'Neill, "The Concept of a Work."

37. Richard P. Smiraglia, ed., "Works as Entities for Information Retrieval," special issue, *Cataloging and Classification Quarterly* 33, no. 3/4 (2002).

38. Kristin Antelman, "Identifying the Serial Work as a Bibliographic Entity," *Library Resources and Technical Services* 48, no. 4 (2004): 250.

39. See the discussion papers presented at FRBR in 21st Century Catalogs: An Invitational Workshop, Dublin, OH, May 2–4, 2005, http://www.oclc.org/research/events/FRBR-workshop/program.htm (accessed March 30, 2008).

40. Antelman, "Identifying the Serial Work as a Bibliographic Entity," 240.

41. Jean Hirons and Crystal Graham, "Issues Related to Seriality," in *The Principles and Future Development of AACR: Proceedings of the International Conference on the Principles and Future Development of AACR: Toronto, Ontario, Canada, October 23–25, 1997,* ed. Jean Weihs, 180–212 (Chicago: American Library Association, 1998).

42. Ibid., 183.

43. Arlene G. Taylor, ed., *Understanding FRBR: What It Is and How It Will Affect Our Retrieval Tools* (Westport, CT: Libraries Unlimited, 2007). This collection of essays includes the following chapters: Arlene G. Taylor, "An Introduction to Functional Requirements for Bibliographic Records (FRBR)," 1–21; Glenn E. Patton, "An Introduction to Functional Requirements for Authority Data (FRAD)," 21–28; Glenn E. Patton. "Understanding the Relationship between FRBR and FRAD," 29–34; William Dent, "FRBR and the History of Cataloging," 35–58; Edward T. O'Neill, "The Impact of Research on the Development of FRBR," 59–72; Richard P. Smiraglia. "Bibliographic Families and Superworks," 73–86; Barbara B. Tillett.. "FRBR and RDA (Resource Description and Access)," 87–96; Alexander C. Thurman. "FRBR and Archival

Materials," 97–102; Murtha Baca and Sherman Clarke, "FRBR and Works of Art, Architecture, and Material Culture," 103–110; Mary Lynette Larsgaard, "FRBR and Cartographic Materials," 111–116; Martha M. Yee, "FRBR and Moving Image Materials," 117–130; Sherry L. Vellucci, "FRBR and Music," 131–152; and Steven C. Shadle, "FRBR and Serials," 153–174.

44. IFLA Meeting of Experts on an International Cataloguing Code, "Statement of International Cataloguing Principles" (April 2006 draft), International Federation of Library Associations and Institutions, http://www.loc.gov/loc/ifla/imeicc/pdf/statement-draft3_apr06cleancopy.pdf (accessed March 30, 2008).

45. IFLA Meeting of Experts on an International Cataloguing Code, "Statement of International Cataloguing Principles," 1.

46. Two entire issues of the *Journal of Internet Cataloging* (vol. 4, nos. 1 and 2, 2001) are devoted to the CORC project.

47. Keith E. Shafer, "Mantis Project: A Toolkit for Cataloging," in *Annual Review of OCLC Research 1998* (published online by OCLC in 1999), archived at http://digitalarchive.oclc.org/da/ViewObject.jsp?objid=0000003483 (accessed March 30, 2008); Keith E. Shafer, "Kilroy: An Internet Research Project," in *Annual Review of OCLC Research 1996* (published online by OCLC in 1997), archived at http://digitalarchive.oclc.org/da/ViewObject.jsp?objid=0000003364 (accessed March 30, 2008); Keith E. Shafer, "Scorpion Helps Catalog the Web," *Bulletin of the American Society for Information Science and Technology* 24, no. 1 (1997): 28–29.

48. Eric Childress, "Crosswalking Metadata in the OCLC CORC Service," 81–88; Carol Jean Godby and Ray Reighart, "Terminology Identification in a Collection of Web Resources," 49–66; Vizine-Goetz, Diane. "Dewey in CORC: Classification in Metadata and Pathfinders," 67–80; Thomas B. Hickey, "Collaboration in CORC," 5–16; all in *Journal of Internet Cataloging* 4, no. 1/2 (2001).

49. Ingrid Hsieh-Yee and Michael Smith, "The CORC Experience: Survey of Founding Libraries, Part 1," *OCLC Systems and Services* 17, no. 3 (2001):133–140; Ingrid Hsieh-Yee and Michael Smith, "The CORC Experience: Survey of Founding Libraries, Part 2," *OCLC Systems and Services* 17, no. 4 (2001):166–177.

50. Tschera Harkness Connell and Chandra Prabha, "Characteristics of Resources Represented in the OCLC CORC Database," *Library Resources and Technical Services* 46, no. 2 (2002): 39–49.

51. Diane Vizine-Goetz, "Dewey in CORC: Classification in Metadata and Pathfinders," *Journal of Internet Cataloging* 4, no. 1/2 (2001): 67–80; Edward T. O'Neill and Brian F. Lavoie, "Bibliographic Control for the Web," *Serials Librarian* 37, no. 3 (2000): 53–69; Lorraine Normore, "CORC Interface Designed for Experienced Catalogers as Well as Other Users," *OCLC Newsletter,* no. 239 (1999): 35.

52. Keith Shafer and others, "Introduction to Persistent Uniform Resource Locators," (paper presented at INET96, Montreal, Quebec, Canada, June 24–28, 1996), http://www.isoc.org/inet96/proceedings/a4/a4%5F1.htm (accessed March 30, 2008).

53. Two journals in particular cover the organization of electronic resources. *Serials Librarian* includes articles on all types of seriality, much of which includes electronic resources, and *The Journal of Internet Cataloging* is devoted exclusively to the organization of all types of electronic resources.

54. Karen S. Calhoun, "Redesign of Library Workflows: Experimental Models for Electronic Resource Description," in *Bicentennial Conference on Bibliographic Control for the New Millennium: Conference Proceedings,* ed. Ann M. Sandberg-Fox, 357–376 (Washington, DC: Library of Congress, Catalog Distribution Center, 2001).

55. Xiaotian Chen and others, "E-Resource Cataloging Practices: A Survey of Academic Libraries and Consortia." *Serials Librarian* 47, no. 1/2 (2004): 153–179.

56. Ibid., 174.

57. Charity K. Martin and Paul S. Hoffman, "Do We Catalog or Not? How Research Libraries Provide Bibliographic Access to Electronic Journals in Aggregated Databases," *Serials Librarian* 43, no. 1 (2002): 61–77.

58. Yiu-On Li and Shirley W. Leung, "Computer Cataloging of Electronic Journals in Unstable Aggregator Databases: The Hong Kong Baptist University Library Experience," *Library Resources and Technical Services* 45, no. 4 (2001): 198–211.

59. David Banush, Martin Kurth, and Jean Pajerek, "Rehabilitating Killer Serials: An Automated Strategy for Maintaining E-Journal Metadata," *Library Resources and Technical Services* 49 no. 3 (July 2005): 190–203.

60. Ann Copeland, "E-Serials Cataloging in the 1990s: A Review of the Literature," *Serials Librarian* 41, no. 3/4 (2002): 7–29.

61. IFLA Working Group on Functional Requirements and Numbering of Authority Records (FRANAR), "Functional Requirements for Authority Data: A Conceptual Model" (April 1, 2007 draft), International Federation of Library Associations and Institutions, http://www.ifla.org/VII/d4/FRANAR-ConceptualModel-2ndReview.pdf (accessed March 30, 2008).

62. IFLA Working Group on the Functional Requirements for Subject Authority Records, "Terms of Reference," IFLANET, http://www.ifla.org/VII/s29/wgfrsar.htm (accessed March 30, 2008).

63. Arlene G. Taylor, "Variations in Personal Name Access Points in OCLC Bibliographic Records," *Library Resources and Technical Services* 36, no. 2 (1992): 224–241.

64. Tamara S. Weintraub, "Personal Name Variations: Implications for Authority Control in Computerized Catalogs," *Library Resources and Technical Services* 35, no. 2 (1991): 217–228.

65. J. H. Bowman, "The Catalog as Barrier to Retrieval, Part 2: Forms of Names," *Cataloging and Classification Quarterly* 30, no. 4 (2000): 51–73.

66. Qiang Jin, "Comparing and Evaluating Corporate Names in the National Authority File (LCNAF) on OCLC and on the Web," *Cataloging and Classification Quarterly* 36, no. 2 (2003): 21–30.

67. Karen S Calhoun and W. Michael Oskins, "Rates and Types of Changes to LC Authority Files," *Information Technology and Libraries* 1, no. 2 (1992): 132–136.

68. R. Ruiz-Pérez, E. Delgado López-Cózar, and E. Jiménez-Contreras, "Spanish Personal Name Variations in National and International Biomedical Databases: Implications for Information Retrieval and Bibliometric Studies," *Journal of the Medical Library Association (JMLA)* 90, no. 4 (2002): 411–430.

69. Jiajian Hu, "Transactional Analysis: Problems in Cataloging Chinese Names," *Illinois Libraries* 82, no. 4 (2000): 251–260.

70. H.-C. Bolick, "Problems in the Establishment of Nonunique Chinese Personal Headings with Special Reference to NACO Guidelines and Vendor-Supplied Authority Control," *Library Resources and Technical Services* 43, no. 2 (1999): 95–105.

71. Yewang Wang, "A Look into Chinese Persons' Names in Bibliography Practice," *Cataloging and Classification Quarterly* 31, no. 1 (2000): 51–81.

72. MARBI Multilingual Record Task Force, "Multilingual Authority Records in the MARC 21 Authority Format," Discussion Paper 2001-DP05 (2001), Library of Congress, http://www.loc.gov/marc/marbi/2001/2001-dp05.html (accessed March 31, 2008).

73. Martha Speirs Plettner, "Arabic Name Authority in the Online Environment: Options and Implications," *International Cataloguing and Bibliographic Control* 32, no. 2 (2003): 23–26.

74. Deborah E. Kulczak, "Name Authority Work for OCLC Copy Cataloging: Is It Worth the Effort?" *Cataloging and Classification Quarterly* 28, no. 1 (1999): 69–81.

75. Evan Pappas, "An Analysis of Eight RLIN-Members' Authority-Controlled Access Points for Purposes of Speeding Copy Cataloging Work Flow," *Cataloging and Classification Quarterly* 22, no. 1 (1996): 29–47.

76. Jeffrey Beall. "Using OCLC Connexion to Find Typographical Errors in Authority Records," *OCLC Systems and Services* 20, no. 2 (2004): 71–75.

77. Nadine P. Ellero, "Panning for Gold: Utility of the World Wide Web for Metadata and Authority Control in Special Collections," *Library Resources and Technical Services* 46, no. 3 (2002): 79–84, 87–91.

78. Qiang Jin, "Creating Up-to-Date Corporate Name Authority Records by Using Official Corporate Home Web Pages," *Cataloging and Classification Quarterly* 38, no. 3/4 (2004): 281–290; Qiang Jin, "Is the Current Way of Constructing Corporate Authority Records Still Useful?" *Information Technology and Libraries* 24, no. 2 (2005): 68–76.

79. Robert E. Wolverton. "Authority Control in Academic Libraries in the United States: A Survey," *Cataloging and Classification Quarterly* 41, no. 1 (2005): 111–131.

80. N. S. Bangalore and Chandra G. Prabha, "Authority Work in Copy (Derived) Cataloging: A Case Study," *Technical Services Quarterly* 15, no. 4 (1998): 39–56.

81. Nedria A. Santizo and Charlene S. Rezabek, "Series Authority Control: Report of a Survey," *Cataloging and Classification Quarterly* 15, no. 1 (1992): 75–81.

82. Susan Lee Tsui, and Carole F. Hinders, "Cost-Effectiveness and Benefits of Outsourcing Authority Control," *Cataloging and Classification Quarterly* 26, no. 4 (1999): 43–61.

83. Tim DiLauro and others, "Automated Name Authority Control and Enhanced Searching in the Levy Collection {Computer File}," *D-Lib Magazine* 7, no. 4 (2001), http://www.dlib.org/dlib/april01/dilauro/04dilauro.html (accessed March 30, 2008).

84. Mark Patton and others, "Toward a Metadata Generation Framework: A Case Study at Johns Hopkins University," *D-Lib Magazine* 10, no. 11 (2004), http://www.dlib.org/dlib/november04/choudhury/11choudhury.html (accessed March 30, 2008).

85. Ibid.

86. Ibid.

87. Karen E. Greever, "A Comparison of Pre- and Post-Cataloging Authority Control," *Library Resources and Technical Services* 41, no. 1 (1997): 39–49.

88. James C. French and Allison L. Powell, "Using Clustering Strategies for Creating Authority Files," *Journal of the American Society for Information Science* 51, no. 8 (2000): 774–786.

89. David Miller, "XOBIS: An Experimental Schema for Unifying Bibliographic and Authority Records," *Cataloging and Classification Quarterly* 39, no. 3/4 (2005): 285–303.

90. Jutta Weber, "LEAF: Linking and Exploring Authority Files," *Cataloging and Classification Quarterly* 38, no. 3/4 (2004): 227–236.

91. Vinh-The Lam, "Outsourcing Authority Control: Experience of the University of Saskatchewan Libraries," *Cataloging and Classification Quarterly* 32, no. 4 (2001): 53–69.

92. Sherry L. Vellucci, "Commercial Services for Providing Authority Control: Outsourcing the Process," *Cataloging and Classification Quarterly* 39, no. 1/2 (2004): 443–456.

93. Arlene G. Taylor, and others, eds., *Authority Control in Organizing and Accessing Information: Definition and International Experience* (Binghamton, NY: Haworth Information Press, 2004).

94. For an early overview of metadata development see Sherry L. Vellucci, "Metadata," in *Annual Review of Information Science and Technology 33*, ed. Martha

E. Williams 187–222 (Medford, NJ: Information Today for the American Society for Information Science, 1998).

95. Jane Greenberg and others, "Author-Generated Dublin Core Metadata for Web Resources: A Baseline Study in an Organization," *Journal of Digital Information* 2, no. 2 (2002).

96. Jane Greenberg and others, "Iterative Design of Metadata Creation Tools for Resource Authors" (paper presented at 2003 Dublin Core Conference: Supporting Communities of Discourse and Practice—Metadata Research & Applications, Seattle, WA, September 28–October 2, 2003), http://www.siderean.com/dc2003/202_Paper82-color-NEW.pdf (accessed March 31, 2008).

97. Amanda J. Wilson, "Toward Releasing the Metadata Bottleneck: A Baseline Evaluation of Contributor-Supplied Metadata," *Library Resources and Technical Services* 51, no. 1 (2007): 16–28.

98. "Répertoire International de Littérature Musicale," http://www.rilm.org/ (accessed March 30, 2008).

99. DiLauro and others, "Automatic Name Authority Control"; Patton and others, "Toward a Metadata Generation Framework."

100. Ozgur Yilmazel, Christina M. Finneran, and Elizabeth D. Liddy, "MetaExtract: An NLP System to Automatically Assign Metadata," in *ACM/IEEE Joint Conference on Digital Libraries, JCDL 2004, Tucson, AZ, USA, June 7–11, 2004, Proceedings,* ed. Hsinchun Chen and others, 241–242 (ACM, 2004).

101. Gordon W. Paynter, "Developing Practical Automatic Metadata Assignment and Evaluation Tools for Internet Resources," in *ACM/IEEE Joint Conference on Digital Libraries, JCDL 2005, Denver, CO, USA, June 7–11, 2005, Proceedings,* ed. Mary Marlino, Tamara Sumner, and Frank M. Shipman III, 291–300 (ACM, 2005).

102. Ibid., 291.

103. American Library Association, Committee on Cataloging: Description and Access (CC:DA), "Task Force on Metadata: Final Report," American Library Association (2002), http://www.libraries.psu.edu/tas/jca/ccda/tf-meta6.html (accessed March 31, 2008).

104. National Information Standards Organization, *Understanding Metadata* (Bethesda, MD: NISO Press, 2004), 13, http://www.niso.org/publications/press/UnderstandingMetadata.pdf (accessed March 31, 2008).

105. Carol Jean Godby, Jeffrey Young, and Eric Childress, "A Repository of Metadata Crosswalks," *D-Lib Magazine* 10, no. 12 (2004), http://www.dlib.org/dlib/december04/godby/12godby.html (accessed March 31, 2008).

106. Ibid.

107. Ibid.

108. Carl Lagoze and Herbert Van de Sompel, "The Making of the Open Archives Initiative Protocol for Metadata Harvesting," *Library Hi-Tech* 21, no. 2 (2003):

118–128.

109. Herbert Van de Sompel and others, "Resource Harvesting within the OAI-PMH Framework," *D-Lib Magazine* 10, no. 12 (2004), http://www.dlib.org/dlib/december04/vandesompel/12vandesompel.html (accessed March 31, 2008).

110. Tina Gross and Arlene G. Taylor, "What Have We Got to Lose? The Effect of Controlled Vocabulary on Keyword Searching Results," *College and Research Libraries* 66, no. 3 (2005): 215.

111. Ibid.

112. Marcia Zeng and Lois Mai Chan, "Trends and Issues in Establishing Interoperability Among Knowledge Organization Systems," *Journal of the American Society of Information Science and Technology* 55, no. 5 (2003): 377–395.

113. Lois Mai Chan and Edward T. O'Neill, "FAST (Faceted Application of Subject Terminology): A Simplified Vocabulary Based on the Library of Congress Subject Headings," *IFLA Journal* 29, no. 4 (2003): 336–342.

114. Patrice Landry, "Multilingual Subject Access: The Linking Approach of MACS," *Cataloging and Classification Quarterly* 37, no. 3/4 (2004): 177–191.

115. "Recherche Autorités RAMEAU," Catalogue Bn-Opale Plus, http://catalogue.bnf.fr/jsp/recherche_autorites_rameau.jsp?host=catalogue (accessed March 31, 2008)

116. *SWD (Schlagwortnormdatei)* refers to the subject heading list. *RSWK (die Regeln für den Schlagwortkatalog)* refers to the rules for creating a subject heading list. Both are discussed in detail in Konrad Umlauf, *Einführung in die Regeln für den Schlagwortkatalog RSWK,* Berliner Handreichungen zur Bibliothekswissenschaft., v. 66 (Berlin: Institut für Bibliothekswissenschaft der Humboldt-Universität zu Berlin, 1999), http://www.ib.hu-berlin.de/~kumlau/handreichungen/h66/ (accessed March 31, 2008)

117. Landry, "Multilingual Subject Access," 187.

118. Barbara H. Kwasnik and Victoria L. Rubin, "Stretching Conceptual Structures in Classifications across Languages and Cultures," *Cataloging and Classification Quarterly* 37, no. 1/2 (2004): 33–47.

119. Srividhya Subramanian and Keith Shafer, "Clustering," *Journal of Library Administration* 34, no. 3/4 (2001): 221–228.

120. Thomas B. Hickey and Diane Vizine-Goetz, "The Role of Classification in CORC," *Journal of Library Administration* 34, no. 3/4 (2001): 425.

121. Ibid., 424–425.

122. Online Computer Library Center, "Learn More about the DeweyBrowser," OCLC, http://www.oclc.org/research/researchworks/ddc/browser.htm (accessed March 31, 2008); Diane Vizine-Goetz and others, "Vocabulary Mapping for Terminology Services," *Journal of Digital Information* 4, no. 4 (2004), http://journals.tdl.org/jodi/article/view/jodi-128/113 (accessed March 31, 2008); C. Jean Godby and Ray R. Reighart, "The WordSmith

Toolkit," *Journal of Library Administration* 34, 3/4 (2001): 307–316.

123. Sharon Seymour, "Online Public-Access Catalog User Studies: A Review of Research Methodologies, March 1986–November 1989," *Library and Information Science Research* 13, no. 2 (1991): 89–102.

124. Andrew Large and Jamshid Beheshti, "OPACs: A Research Review," *Library and Information Science Research* 19, no. 2 (1997): 2, 111–133.

125. Micheline Beaulieu and Christine L. Borgman, eds., "Current Research in Online Public Access Systems," special issue, *Journal of the American Society for Information Science* 47, no. 7 (1996).

126. Christine L. Borgman, "Why Are Online Catalogs Still Hard to Use?" *Journal of the American Society of Information Science* 47, no. 7 (1996): 493–503.

127. Carol A. Hert, "User Goals on an Online Public Access Catalog," *Journal of the American Society for Information Science* 47, no. 7 (1996): 504–518.

128. Ibid., 516.

129. Seymour, "Online Public Access Catalog User Studies"; Jon R. Hufford, "Use Studies and OPACS," *Technical Services Quarterly* 9, no. 1 (1991): 57–70.

130. Ray Larson, "The Decline of Subject Searching: Long-Term Trends and Patterns of Index Use in an Online Catalog," *Journal of the American Society for Information Science* 42, no. 3 (1991): 197–215.

131. Karen M. Drabenstott and Marjorie S. Weller, "Failure Analysis of Subject Searches in a Test of a New Design for Subject Access to Online Catalogs," *Journal of the American Society for Information Science* 47, no. 7 (1996): 519–537.

132. Ibid., 519.

133. Holly Yu and Margo Young, "The Impact of Web Search Engines on Subject Searching in OPAC," *Information Technology and Libraries* 23, no. 4 (2004):168–180.

134. Rumi Y. Graham, "Subject No-Hits Searches in an Academic Library Online Catalog: An Exploration of Two Potential Ameliorations," *College and Research Libraries* 65, no. 1 (2004): 36–54.

135. Terry Ballard, "Spelling and Typographical Errors in Library Databases," *Computers in Libraries* 12, no. 6 (1992): 14–17.

136. Terry Ballard and Arthur Lifshin, "Prediction of OPAC Spelling Errors through a Keyword Inventory," *Information Technology and Libraries* 11, no. 2 (1992): 139–145.

137. Terry Ballard and Anthony Grimaldi, "Improve OPAC Searching by Reducing Tagging Errors in MARC Records," *Library Software Review* 16, no. 3 (1997): 152–155.

138. J. H. Bowman, "The Catalog as Barrier to Retrieval, Part 1: Hyphens and Ampersands in Titles," *Cataloging and Classification Quarterly* 29, no. 4 (2000): 39–60; Bowman, "The Catalog as Barrier, Part 2"; J. H. Bowman, "Sic Catalog Syndrome: Title Page Transcription as a Barrier to Retrieval," *Cataloging and*

Classification Quarterly 32, no. 1 (2001): 39–54.

139. Jeffrey Beall and Karen Kafadar, "The Effectiveness of Copy Cataloging at Eliminating Typographical Errors in Shared Bibliographic Records," *Library Resources and Technical Services* 48, no. 2 (2004): 92–101.

140. Andrew MacEwan and Thurstan Young, "Quality vs. Quantity: Developing a Systematic Approach to a Perennial Problem," *Catalogue and Index,* no. 152 (2004): 1–7.

141. Gerald Burke, Carol Anne Germain, and Mary K. Van Ullen, "URLs in the OPAC: Integrating or Disintegrating Research Libraries Catalogs," *Journal of Academic Librarianship* 29, no. 5 (2003): 290–297.

142. Deborah D. Blecic, Josephine Dorsch, and Melissa Koenig, "A Longitudinal Study of the Effects of OPAC Screen Changes on Searching Behavior and Searcher Success," *College and Research Libraries* 60, no. 6 (1999): 515–530.

143. Deborah D Barton, Sarah Currier, and Jessie M. N. Hey, "Building Quality Assurance into Metadata Creation: An Analysis Based on the Learning Objects and E-Prints Communities of Practice" (paper presented at 2003 Dublin Core Conference: Supporting Communities of Discourse and Practice—Metadata Research & Applications, Seattle, WA, September28–October 2, 2003), http://www.siderean.com/dc2003/201_paper60.pdf (accessed March 31, 2008).

144. Thomas R. Bruce and Diane I. Hillman, "The Continuum of Metadata Quality: Defining, Expressing, Exploiting," in *Metadata in Practice,* ed. Diane I. Hillman and Elaine L. Westbrooks, 238–256 (Chicago: American Library Association, 2004).

145. Brian Kelly, Amanda Closier, and Debra Hiom, "Gateway Standardization: A Quality Assurance Framework for Metadata," *Library Trends* 53, no. 4 (2005): 637–650.

146. William E Moen, Erin L. Stewart, and Charles R. McClure, "The Role of Content Analysis in Evaluating Metadata for the U.S. Government Information Locator Service (GILS): Results from an Exploratory Study" (paper presented at Second IEEE Metadata Conference, Washington, DC, September 15–16 1997, http://www.unt.edu/wmoen/publications/GILSMDContentAnalysis.htm. (accessed March 31, 2008).

147. See the New Jersey Digital Highway, a new project to digitize special collections related to New Jersey, which requires librarians and curators to create the metadata for their collection: http://www.njdigitalhighway.org/librarians.php (accessed March 31, 2008).

148. Karen Calhoun, "The Changing Nature of the Catalog and its Integration with Other Discovery Tools: A Report Prepared for the Library of Congress," Cornell University, February 2006, http://www.loc.gov/catdir/calhoun-report-final.pdf (accessed March 31, 2008).

149. Ibid., Appendix A, 23–27.

150. Thomas Mann, "'The Changing Nature of the Catalog and Its Integration

with Other Discovery Tools. Final Report. March 17, 2006. Prepared for the Library of Congress by Karen Calhoun': A Critical Review," Library of Congress Professional Guild, AFSME Local 2910 (April 3, 2006), http://www.guild2910.org/AFSCMECalhounReviewREV.pdf (accessed March 31, 2008).

151. University of California, Bibliographic Services Task Force, "Rethinking How We Provide Bibliographic Services for the University of California," final report (December 2005), University of California Libraries, http://libraries.universityofcalifornia.edu/sopag/BSTF/Final.pdf (accessed March 31, 2008).

152. Jackie Byrd and others, "A White Paper on the Future of Cataloging at Indiana University," (January 15, 2006), Indiana University, http://www.iub.edu/~libtserv/pub/Future_of_Cataloging_White_Paper.doc (accessed March 31, 2008).

153. Marshall Breeding, "Thinking About Your Next OPAC," *Computers in Libraries* 27, no 4 (2007): 28–30.

154. The Endeca Web site is at http://endeca.com/ (accessed March 31, 2008). To view an academic library's implementation of Endeca, see the catalog of North Carolina State University at http://www.lib.ncsu.edu/catalog/ (accessed March 31, 2008).

155. The AquaBrowser Web site is at http://www.aquabrowser.com/. To view an academic library's implementation of AquaBrowser, see Trinity College, Dublin's Stella Catalogue at http://stella.tcd.ie/ (accessed March 31, 2008).

156. The Evergreen ILS Web site is at http://gapines.org/opac/en-US/skin/default/xml/index.xml (accessed March 31, 2008).

157. Information on Encore is on the Innovative Interfaces Web site at http://www.iii.com/products/encore.shtml. To view an academic library's implementation of Encore, see Yale Law Library at http://morris.law.yale.edu/ (accessed March 31, 2008).

158. Information on Primo is on the ExLibris Web site at http://exlibrisgroup.com/category/PrimoOverview. To view an academic library's implementation of Primo, see Vanderbilt University's Acorn Catalog at https://acorn.library.vanderbilt.edu/ (accessed March 31, 2008).

159. Steve Brantley, Annie Armstrong, and Krystal M. Lewis, "Usability Testing of a Customizable Library Web Portal," *College and Research Libraries* 67, no. 2 (2006): 146.

160. See the Ann Arbor District Library catalog for an example of user-added tags: http://www.aadl.org/catalog (accessed March 31, 2008).

161. The Scriblio Web site it at. http://about.scriblio.net/about. See the Lamson Library implementation of Scriblio at http://library.plymouth.edu/read/223702. (accessed March 31, 2008).

162. Andrew Treloar, David Groenwegen, and Catherine Harboe-Ree, "The Data

Curation Continuum: Managing Data Objects in Institutional Repositories," *D-Lib Magazine* 13, no. 9/10 (2007), http://www.dlib.org/dlib/september07/treloar/09treloar.html (accessed March 31, 2008).

5

Leadership Research in Library and Information Science

Mark Winston

In 2004, the first Encyclopedia of Leadership, edited by researcher and theorist James MacGregor Burns, was published.[1] The introduction of such a publication indicates the growing body of theory, research, and scholarly and professional discussion of this topic. It is important to note that the Encyclopedia includes a section on library leadership, which indicates its emerging importance as a part of a broader conversation. However, while there is professional discussion of the issue of leadership, particularly with regard to academic libraries, and substantial indications of the increasing importance of this topic in library and information service organizations and in the profession overall, there is some question regarding the extent to which that discussion is informed by and reflective of original research and best practices or supported by theory. In fact, one of the challenges associated with leadership research and theory development in library and information science (LIS) is the fact that they are based primarily on work done in the private sector and published in the general leadership and organizational behavior and management literature. Thus, the limited body of leadership literature in LIS is referred to in relation to the substantive research published in the general literature, acknowledging the differences in context between libraries and private sector organizations. In addition to providing an analysis of recent leadership research and discussion in LIS, this chapter addresses its implications, as well as the gaps in the literature in relation to practice in the profession and in individual libraries.

Introduction

Library and information science (LIS) literature from 1990 to present has addressed the need for leadership in the profession, particularly in light of anticipated retirements and the apprehension that many feel about pursuing more responsible roles, and the related issue of the need for fostering leadership at all levels, particularly in academic libraries. The literature has also addressed these roles in various types of institutions, particularly academic and public libraries, and presented training program reports and very limited discussion of shared leadership and followership, diversity and/or gender issues, and evaluation.

The LIS literature, which is based on original research, has addressed related topics including competencies, education and training, and diversity, which relates for the most part to the documented connection between investment in diversity and organizational performance and success. Sharon Gray Weiner published an analysis of "what is known about the characteristics and leadership style of university librarians and academic library directors" in 2003.[2] She noted that "it is clear that many aspects have not been addressed and that a comprehensive body of cohesive, evidence-based research is needed. There is a dearth of published studies or dissertations that relate leadership to effectiveness of library directors, their organizations, or outcomes."[3]

In addition to providing an indication of the context in which leadership developments and discussion have taken place in the profession, this chapter addresses a number of aspects of the complexities of the issue, including the distinction between management and leadership, the evolution of leadership in the profession, and an analysis of the scholarly and professional discussion of its key aspects.

It is clear in surveying the post-1990 literature that additional research is critically needed to address present and future challenges. A number of developments and research findings indicate the need for an enhanced focus on issues of management and leadership in general, and in LIS organizations in particular. For example, a range of organizational, economic, technological, and societal issues have placed greater demands on managers and highlighted the need for effective practice in a variety of organizations. Issues including increased competitiveness, limited resources, the call for greater accountability from various stakeholders, and the technologically savvy and increasingly demanding user population have indicated the need for effective and informed managerial decision making and forward-thinking leadership. Organizational changes, such as greater use of team-based decision making and matrix organizational structures that combine the functional departments of the hierarchical (vertical) organizational structure and project management that cuts across functional areas horizontally in the organizational chart, provide additional challenges to those in positions of authority.

The extent to which such professional developments and research findings, including the advent of the learning-organization model, have all led to greater research and practical interest in the study and application of effective leadership strategies will be addressed. In addition, there is enhanced focus on the evaluation of operations and services, including their evaluation in terms of social good, in contributing to student learning, and in the development of skills valued by employers, in academic and school settings. There is increased attention on managing diversity in library organizations, and on successful development and fundraising as a part of securing and managing financial resources. In addition, the use of team-based decision making and matrix organizational structures has reinforced the need for fostering leadership at all levels in organizations.

The Distinction between Management and Leadership

One key aspect of an informed discussion of the complexity of the concept of leadership relates to clarifying the distinction between it and management. Although the terms are inextricably linked but not interchangeable, they are often used interchangeably. In fact, there is a significant distinction between the two terms. From an organizational perspective, a traditional definition of management is reflected in the statement "doing things right," which is a necessary consideration in organizations, with regard to fulfilling organizational goals and making effective use of resources, for example. Similarly, a traditional definition of leadership refers to "doing the right things." Such a definition refers to a view of the big picture in planning, decision making, and defining what the organization exists to accomplish, but it also relates to the ethical questions facing leaders and institutions.

Going beyond these traditional definitions, management is position-specific and related to specific titles and roles within organizational hierarchies, flattened or otherwise. Leadership also encompasses the issue of influence, presumably from those at all levels in organizations. Also, management focuses on fulfilling the organization's mission and vision and achieving its goals. Inversely, leadership centers on conceptualizing the organizational mission and vision. Certainly, the recent discussion of management and organizational behavior has been expanded to include views of the larger picture,[4] particularly for stimulating supervisors and managers to think in terms of the entire organization and not simply their individual units. In contrast, leadership has always paid attention on this issue of the entire organizational system. Thus, although there is some overlap, leadership is broader than management, both conceptually and with regard to the inclusion of those who are in managerial positions and those at other levels.

History of Leadership and Leadership Theory

As indicated, LIS leadership research and theory are based primarily on work done in the private sector and published in the general organizational behavior and management literature. Thus, the history of the study of leadership is a relevant component of the discussion of context with regard to leadership in LIS.

To a large extent, though not exclusively, the study of organizational leadership emerged from the study of management. With the advent of the industrial revolution and the move from one-person or other small businesses, large and complex organizations began to emerge. Researchers began to study the way in which the organizations operated, with a particular focus on factors that contribute to bottom-line performance and success. In addition to businesses, the organizations studied included the Catholic Church as a large, complex, and successful institution, and political and governmental structures as well.[5] The major developments in the study of organizations have related primarily to the view of the employee—moving from that of being an input in the process to that of being a contributor in decision making and having a more substantive influence on organizational outcomes. Thus, the study of leadership has emerged from the study of organizations as well, with a focus on how leaders—charismatic leaders, powerful leaders, brilliant leaders, for example—contribute to organizational success. There has been some evolution, from the idea that the leadership qualities of individuals (typically, thought of as a small number of individuals with superior qualities) are the basis for having others follow and for success to the idea that context is a factor and that these qualities may be the purview of the many.

According to Jonathan Doh, "Historically, there has been debate over whether leadership is a skill, trait, or innate behavior. Although most management educators now agree that leadership is both a skill and a behavior that exhibits that skill, this dual definition has generated additional disagreement over whether leadership can be taught."[6] Not only does this quote from the highly respected journal *Academy of Management Learning and Education* indicate the complexity of the question of whether leaders are born or made (including development via education programs), but it also highlights the fact that management educators are central to the resolution of major questions related to this topic.

The complexity of the definition and presence of leadership qualities in individuals highlights the importance of the literature in informing this conversation and in supporting education and instruction, which are based on scholarship as well as on professional discussion. The literature has addressed the long history and recent advancement of leadership education by referring to the "marked increase in leadership programs."[7] In contrast, only 10% of the ALA-accredited master's programs offer coursework in leadership as further described below.[8]

Another subset of this literature relates to leadership theory. Assuming that it is based on the study of the ways in which individuals can influence the success of organizations through their efforts and those of others, the body of leadership theory can be characterized in more than one way. For example, there are considerations of "the trait approach, which seeks to discover what leadership traits make people great leaders; the skills approach, which focuses on skills and abilities that can be learned; and the style approach, which emphasizes leader behavior and [to a certain extent] people relationships."[9]

Leadership theory relates to several dimensions, including the study of the leader, the study of the followers, and the consideration of the context. A significant body of the scholarship focuses on the extent to which the leader's personal qualities, such as intellectual ability, power, charisma, and virtue, and the leader's ability to influence followers as a result of his or her values, for example, form the basis for effective leadership.[10] For example, contingency theory, "also called pragmatism, realism, and Realpolitik"[11] is based on the concept that the achievement of leaders' goals requires varying "styles and approaches depending of what will most effectively allow them to achieve" those goals.[12] In terms of the relationship with followers, according to Burns and Otte, leader-member exchange theory "holds that the manager's efficiency and effectiveness are affected by the quality of the relationship he or she has with each subordinate."[13] The issue of context beyond the followers is considered in relation to aspects of leadership theory, as well.[14] Historical determinism, for example, suggests that it is the temporal context or the needs of the time that "create the leader."[15] In addition, the issue of context, particularly in relation to the environment, is considered in theories such as transformational leadership, administrative conservatorship, and ecovision, as well.[16] Ecovision is based on the premise that an organization's success in a dynamic and changing environment is based largely on the organization's ability to define and articulate its identity in relation to the environment of which it is a part and to function innovatively in that context.

It is important to note that there has been increased emphasis on the importance of theory in supporting organizational decision making overall, including providing managers with well-articulated theories, supported by research and presented in the literature, indicating the patterns in data and the context in which the specific theory is likely to be relevant.[17] While most of the thought and discussion of leadership that are based on original research are focused on private-sector organizations, much of this scholarship and theory development are not only substantive, but validated over time—an important consideration in light of the limited original or theory-supported research in the LIS literature.

Leadership in Library and Information Sciences

The focus on leadership in the profession is a relatively recent phenomenon, as evidenced by a number of manifestations, such as the move from a small number of leadership development programs before 1990 to quite a number of such programs now. This growth is coupled with the development of statements of leadership competencies (and core competencies that include leadership) for LIS professionals in a range of specialties and types of library services organizations. While the mission statements of nearly all of the ALA-accredited LIS programs emphasize the importance of the development of future leaders for the profession, the academic curricula reflect a lack of attention to leadership education.

The Leadership Crisis in Library and Information Sciences

Donald Riggs suggested that the limited focus on leadership in the profession is evidence of an impending crisis. Riggs published the first book on library leadership in the early 1980s[18] and many subsequent books, articles, and chapters, including the section on libraries in the first *Encyclopedia of Leadership*.[19] He noted that "now is the time to better understand leadership; take it seriously as part of our daily working lives, and become more conscious of the potential for a leadership crisis."[20] He indicated both the paucity of LIS literature on the topic and the need for "strong, dynamic, and transformative leadership" in the profession.[21] Similarly, in their research related to the need for leadership in academic libraries, Renaud and Murray have indicated the lack of a cadre of leaders for the profession in the future.[22]

This issue of the potential crisis that Donald Riggs suggested is evidenced by a number of factors. These factors include a historical reluctance in the profession to embrace leadership, the steadily increasing number of pending retirements in the field, the fact that many of the retirements have been and will continue to be among those in clearly defined leadership roles, and the fact that some challenges are already becoming evident in the recruitment for these positions. An understanding of the hesitation of the profession to embrace leadership can be informed by consideration of this reluctance on the part of individuals to take on authoritative roles.

One aspect of this reluctance appears to be related to how leadership is defined. As indicated, leadership and management are considered to be synonymous, and management positions are unattractive to many in the profession. Anecdotally, many LIS educators have noted the large number of students who have indicated, prior to their first professional positions, that they are not interested in management and, of more concern, that they do not see themselves as leaders. With regard to those with substantial experience in the field, there are data and predictions regarding the current and increasing rate of pending retirements in the LIS discipline among teaching faculty as well as among members of the profession[23] who are older than the average for all professions.[24] The research associated with the retirements indicates that the concern is particularly acute with regard to the leadership vacuum that is anticipated, both in terms of those who are currently in managerial and administrative positions in libraries, as well as in growing recruitment concerns. In addition to a potential shortage of those who are prepared for these positions, there is a specific concern related to the apprehension of those at the assistant and associate director levels at the though of pursuing director positions and of "line" librarians to seriously consider management opportunities at all.[25]

One of the challenges, supported by the anecdotal information and by slowly emerging data, relates to an apprehension among those who might be poised for senior leadership responsibilities at considering such professional opportunities for a number of reasons, such as quality-of-life concerns, a sense of limited preparation for leadership roles, lack of desire to undertake fundraising and development activities, and further removal from the work that led to their interest in entering the profession.[26] It might also be suggested that there continues to be the perception that leadership is the purview of the charismatic few and that the constant stress, scrutiny, and criticism associated with certain leadership roles are pervasive and completely unattractive.

Leadership at All Levels in Organizations

As suggested in the analysis of the distinction between management and leadership, defining leadership is a necessary component of an informed discussion of the topic. One major consideration in the profession has related to the idea of fostering leadership at all levels in organizations. This focus has emerged in relation to the discussion of team-based decision making, flattened hierarchies, matrix organizational structures, participative management, shared leadership, and followership.

Ensuring effective, informed, forward-thinking, and innovative leadership in libraries represents an organizational challenge with regard to those at various levels, based on the availability of information to support decision making and the opportunity to address issues that relate to the big picture. Thus, there is the need to ensure that those who are not in senior management have the information, preparation, and appropriate authority to exhibit leadership—that is, to have influence in their organizations.

In this regard, one particular aspect of leadership, which has received limited coverage in the discussion in the general management literature and almost no coverage in LIS, is the issue of followership. The topic of followership represents "loaded" terminology, in that the connotations associated with the word *follower* suggest that followers are sheep and are following blindly. However, the term should refer to supporting the established leader and organizational mission and vision. Ideally, the concept of followership is defined as a type of leadership—the focus being that of influence. The key point is that there is more than one type of leadership that can take place within organizations. Presumably, the idea of supporting the established leader in making substantive contributions to the organization as a type of leadership should allow defining leadership more broadly and provide more opportunities at all levels. Thus, followership should provide the opportunity for participation, for input, and for support.[27]

It is necessary that the person in this followership role fulfills his or her responsibilities in contributing to the organizational success as an individual performer and assists in promoting the success of others in the organization—an important support role in the organization. A quote from the *Harvard Business Review* regarding the effective follower indicates that "What distinguishes an effective follower from an ineffective follower is enthusiastic, intelligent, and self-reliant participation without star billing in the pursuit of an organizational goal."[28] However, this idea of subordination of self-interest may be contrary to the way in which leadership within organizations is conceptualized in most instances.

Similarly, while leadership focuses on influence within the organization, there is the consideration of exerting influence beyond the organization, as well. In particular, the LIS literature has addressed the "opportunity for academic librarians to take a leadership role in our institutions for leveraging opportunities to reach students during significant learning moments outside the classroom."[29] For example, in her dissertation research, Debra Gilchrist studied the role of librarians in exhibiting leadership in fostering instructional change. Her 2007 dissertation entitled "Academic Libraries at the Center of Instructional Change: Faculty and Librarian Experience of Library Leadership in the Transformation of Teaching and Learning," is based on interviews with librarians and faculty involved in the development of a new instructional program for undergraduate students.[30] The academic librarians at the university studied were seen as having a leadership role in working with faculty in influencing change in the instructional process. In this regard, the study considered the need for librarians to lead in direct and indirect ways and to take advantage of the library's unique role in the university in influencing the change process. In addition, the study addressed the need to change the culture and to foster collaboration with teaching faculty in facilitating changes in instruction.

Leadership Competencies

One particular area of consideration in the general and LIS literature has related to defining the nature of successful leadership in organizations. Private-sector research has focused on the issue of leadership competencies for some time, representing a clear indication of the relevance of the general leadership literature in informing the discussion in LIS.

The research associated with leadership competencies has been designed to "identify a small set of attributes that successful leaders possess, articulate them in ways that could be transferred across all leaders, and create developmental experiences to ensure that future leaders possess these attributes."[31] Thus, this discussion helps to define the nature of effective leadership, to identify "leadership competency gaps for the … leadership team"[32] in an organization, and to identify components of leadership education and development that are relevant to the needs of organizations. Leadership competencies that are generally considered to be of importance include "adaptability, effective interpersonal communication, and good decision making."[33] Other competencies, which have been identified as important but which have been described as potentially too general by some researchers, include the ability "to act with integrity, set a vision, have energy, execute strategy, and energize others."[34] Recent literature has focused on the need to expand the focus to include global leadership competencies,[35] such as renewed attention to understanding and valuing diversity and developing a better understanding of and "knowing customers."[36] In addition, there is particular attention being paid to the development of leadership competency models that are organization-specific,[37] including the unique organizational requirements and strategies that have an impact on the leadership needs for the company in question.[38]

The initial development of a statement of competencies for library administrators has been based on statements of managerial competencies, such as budget management, personnel management, and planning,[39] as well as leadership competencies, such as realizing the organizational vision, modeling valued behaviors, and achieving effective interpersonal communication.[40] In addition, the learning-organization model in libraries has been associated with "the identification of core competencies involving the evaluation of success in terms of analytical skills and decision making, as well as communication skills, budget management, and leadership."[41] The issue of analytical abilities has also been defined in relation to the competency associated with "the ability to synthesize all the information that is available and can be gathered to help resolve a question, provide a direction, or to solve a problem."[42] This competency has been defined in terms of the decision making of the information professional and of influencing the decision making of other organizational leaders.

Along with the statements of professional competencies of a number of professional organizations in LIS, which have addressed the importance of leadership in an array of professional settings,[43] the most recent and comprehensive look at managerial and leadership competencies in library and information services appears to be the research done by Hernon, Powell, and Young.[44] Using a combination of content analysis, interviews, and Delphi studies, these scholars surveyed directors and later assistant and associate directors in Association of Research Library (ARL) member institutions. They identified attributes of library leaders in areas such as planning and management and also in terms of personal attributes, such as working with other people and influencing others.[45] Hernon, Powell, and Young's research also addressed competencies associated with effective organizational decision making. Similarly, they have studied "the perceptions of Gen-X librarians about the attributes essential for library leaders."[46] They identified what appear to be "significant differences between the attributes most highly valued by a number of academic library directors and by the Gen-X librarians. The latter appear to place more value on maintaining a balance between one's job and personal life, and they frequently stress the importance of person- or employee-oriented workplace that values teamwork, fairness, and loyalty."[47] This recent research appears to build upon the general focus of Patha Suwannarat's 1994 dissertation, which considered the broader question of the leadership styles of research library directors and the extent to which they were more likely to exhibit transformational or transactional leadership.[48]

Research has also been conducted in relation to defining the leadership competencies in terms of emotional intelligence,[49] "cultural intelligence,"[50] and "intercultural leadership,"[51] and considering the leadership competencies associated with specific professional responsibilities, including those with both an internal and an external focus. In general, competencies identified by professional associations and articulated in job announcements for leadership positions highlight the importance of roles related to marketing, fundraising, and development, for example. However, the research results indicate that the curricula of LIS education programs and the nature of professional positions preceding that of library director or dean do not provide adequate preparation for development of such competencies.[52] Thus, defining the nature of leadership competencies associated with organizational roles necessarily requires ensuring appropriate educational preparation to support the individual's development.

Leadership Education and Training

As indicated, both the enhanced focus on leadership, including leadership at all levels in organizations, and the complexity of the issues associated with leadership, as well as the focus on leadership competencies, highlight the importance of preparing future graduates to be managers and leaders. More immediately, it is critically important for graduates to understand the needs of and to support established leaders (including managers) in library and information services organizations of which they are a part.

In terms of LIS education, despite the articulated goal of preparing graduates for leadership roles in the profession, studies of leadership coursework in the curricula indicate that the number of ALA-accredited programs offering coursework in leadership ranged from a high of 10.4% in the ALA-accredited programs in the United States[53] to 5.6% for all of the ALA-accredited programs.[54] None of the programs indicate that leadership is a required course.[55]

It is certainly the case that the curricula of the programs must address a range of other content areas, such as information technology, including searching and retrieval, knowledge organization, cataloging and classification, and reference and information services, among others. Thus, despite the indication that leadership is a central component of the purpose of LIS education, it may be unlikely that such coursework will be required or offered in all degree programs. It is certainly the case that leadership issues may be addressed to a limited extent in management courses. The research related to management offerings indicates that general "coursework in management is offered in all of the programs."[56] "Such coursework is required of all students in more than two-thirds (69.1%) of the programs, with the course being either an elective or required of those in certain areas of concentration in the remaining 30.9%."[57] However, research based on surveys of new graduates shows that two of the most frequently cited areas for which new LIS professionals indicate the need for greater academic preparation are management and, more specifically, budget management.[58]

The concern related to the future leadership of the profession has led to the development of quite a number of new leadership development programs—both at the state and national levels and in other countries, including Canada and Australia. These programs focus on librarians at various stages in their careers—not only those who are already, or are poised to be, directors. The programs address various content areas, using various formats and approaches to learning and interaction. One of the most recently implemented programs is the Association of Research Libraries' Library Leadership Fellows Program, developed in response to the desire to foster the leadership potential of those who are ready to try roles of greater responsibility.[59] While the introduction of new leadership training programs has been ongoing for the last 15 years or so, the specific concern of fostering interest in senior positions has been an articulated consideration most recently. Other programs introduced in the last 15 years have included the ACRL/Harvard Leadership Institute, the Frye Institute, and statewide programs implemented in Illinois, New Jersey, and California, among others, as well as longstanding programs in Ohio and Texas. Published reports by participants, organizers, and facilitators in the programs address issues of program content and structure, the nature of the groups of program participants, and evaluative comments.[60] There has been limited original research measuring the performance and success of such programs in fulfilling their goals. Most notably, research regarding the UCLA Senior Fellows Program, implemented in 1982, has addressed the importance of leadership training and the nature of the curricular content of programs geared toward those who are academic library directors or likely to be in such positions in the very near future.[61] Research regarding the Library Leadership Institute at Snowbird has reflected the impact of participation in such training in relation to both career progression and increased involvement in leadership activities, based on the perceptions of the librarians who have completed the program.[62] Similarly, research regarding the Pacific Northwest Library Association's Leads Leadership Institute has shown that former "participants become more involved in leadership activities in professional associations and in their workplace."[63] The evaluation of the University of Hong Kong Libraries' Leadership Institute was based on the analysis of the extent to which former participants believed the institute prepared them for the "challenges faced by academic library leaders."[64]

In considering the different roles and potential impact of LIS education and leadership development programs, it is important to note that while a relatively small number of individuals will participate in the leadership training programs and many of them will self-select to pursue involvement, graduate education reaches a larger base of students. In addition, graduate education offers the opportunity to present the theory underlying management principles and leadership questions, to address issues in the context of other substantive aspects of the curricula, such as decision making associated with intellectual freedom and financial considerations associated with outsourcing concerns, as well as to provide the safe environment for students to develop and present opinions and formulate a well-informed frame of reference that is supported by the literature. Of course, graduate education that includes leadership preparation and training programs are supplemented by other methods of preparing individuals to exert influence within organizations. In particular, it appears that mentoring programs have expanded, with the focus being leadership preparation in only some instances, and professional success, more broadly, in others. In this regard, the LIS literature has focused primarily on mentoring programs in individual academic libraries, with discussion of the rationale, implementation, and results associated with programs, which have been associated primarily with the development and retention of tenure-track librarians.[65]

Leadership Diversity

Leadership diversity is based upon organizational behavior research in the private sector, as well as the academic environment, which has documented the connection between investment in diversity and overall organizational performance and success. Fostering diversity in organizations is generally considered to be a priority in relation to the need to provide services for and recruit from the increasingly diverse population, as well as addressing past inequities and current unfairness and eliminating underrepresentation. However, recent research in the study of diversity in the private sector and, to a limited extent, in the academic environment, has also highlighted a connection between investment in diversity and overall organizational performance and success.[66] Among managers and researchers, there is the realization that the reasons for promoting and fostering diversity within organizations go beyond the fact that it is a good thing to do. According to Koonce, "Now, companies are embracing diversity as a business focus and corporate value. Embracing diversity isn't just the right thing to do; there's a strong business case for it."[67]

Researchers in organizational theory have documented the fact that the companies that are the most diverse, as measured by factors such as minority employment at all levels, spending with minority suppliers, and underwriting business that goes to minority-owned investment banks, have also been identified as more successful companies overall.[68] Stock performance has generally been used as the measure of organizational success in such research. Stock performance represents a measure of factors, such as organizational performance, customer satisfaction, the strength of the company, and investor confidence, among other considerations. In the 1999 *Fortune* magazine article identifying "America's Best Companies for Minorities," the researcher reports rankings that indicate that the "companies that pursue diversity outperform the S&P 500."[69] Kuczynski reports similar results in her research, addressing what she has described as "a direct link between a company's leadership diversity [in particular, diverse representation among company leaders] and its stock market performance."[70]

In providing an initial explanation for this relationship between diversity and organizational performance, Kuczynski notes that "Diverse leadership suggests that a company has drawn a wide pool of talent up through its ranks and is opening itself up to a variety of different views and ideas."[71] This representation of diverse leadership includes the composition of the company's board and senior management, among other positions. Dean has shown similar results in relation to financial indicators of success being linked to having women in leadership roles specifically, and greater diversity of perspectives in general.[72] The research indicates that diversity-related goals, diversity programs and initiatives are the norm in many companies, as reflected in financial decisions.[73]

However, the relationship between diversity and organizational success is complex. Some studies have found a negative correlation between leadership diversity and organizational performance in the short term. The reasons for such changes in performance have included the difficulties associated with building consensus.[74] The research reflects the fact that differences in perspective create challenges associated with reaching consensus, overcoming traditional organizational cultures reflective of less diverse organizations, and the hindering of organizational performance, as organizational cultures change. Indeed, among the companies that have made substantial efforts in relation to fostering diversity and that have been the most successful companies overall, often the prevailing organizational culture had to be dismantled, with "a more inclusive one in its place."[75]

The limited study of leadership diversity in the academic environment has focused on women and racial minorities, with specific consideration of student populations. The research results have indicated that the colleges that are the most diverse are also the most highly rated, based on established rankings of academic and financial performance.[76] In addition, many university presidents have articulated the importance of fostering diversity in order to enhance the learning environment.[77]

As leadership theory is based on the study of the ways in which individuals can influence the success of organizations through their efforts and those of others, leadership theory has provided the basis for the consideration of issues of diversity as related to organizational success in leadership diversity theory. Leadership theory is relevant in regard to the ways in which organizational leaders exhibit influence in fostering diversity and in contributing to overall organizational success and user satisfaction.

With regard to the complex relationship between diversity and organizational success, the results of one study were widely reported to prove that "Diversity's Business Case Doesn't Add Up."[78] The results were purported to show that "racial and gender diversity has virtually no impact on bottom-line performance."[79] However, the research, which was based on the study of only four companies and initial conversations with 20 or so companies, showed that few companies have "ever conducted a systematic examination of the effects of diversity efforts on bottom-line performance."[80] Thus, the results reflect not a contradiction of the earlier research findings but an overall lack of research regarding the correlation between diversity and organizational performance in individual companies.

The research and discussions related to diversity in libraries focus on issues of staffing, collections, services, and organizational climate.[81] However, there has been limited diversity-related research in library and information services that focuses on services and organizational changes that are substantive in nature.

The literature includes opinion pieces,[82] or a focus on service to specific populations, such as individual ethnic groups[83] or the homeless,[84] for example. There is limited research-supported discussion related to issues of recruitment,[85] as well as minimal discussion of issues of assessment of the library's diversity climate[86] and organizational design and collaboration with other agencies.[87] Winston's research on leadership diversity has considered the relationship between investment in diversity and organizational success in the academic environment (i.e., the college or university level and in the academic library). The research results indicate that the most successful colleges are also those which are the most diverse. Winston and Li's research has addressed the comprehensive role of leadership in the library and at the level of the vice president for academic affairs in fostering diversity in the academic environment.[88]

While there has been research related to the representation of women in senior management roles in the profession,[89] Betty Turock's article on "Women and Leadership" is likely the most comprehensive analysis of the evolution and applicability of feminist theory and discussion, addressed in relation to the development of programs to foster equity in the profession at the national level.[90]

Values-Based Leadership

The need for leaders to exhibit integrity, particularly with regard to ethical decision making, has been highlighted in the general leadership literature and in the literature of specific disciplines and professions, including LIS. With regard to the issue of context:

> In general, a range of professional challenges necessitate effective and informed leadership in organizations: increased accountability and enhanced scrutiny of leaders and organizations of all types (required by funding agencies and other stakeholders), limited financial resources, enhanced competition ... as well as greater opportunities for ethical abuses and the overall importance of effective decision making to ensure organizational performance and success.[91]

In the private-sector research, the study of leadership competencies—the qualities, areas of knowledge, and abilities possessed by successful leaders—has focused on issues such as effective decision making and communication skills, among others. Integrity has also been identified as important, but as a competency that is difficult to measure.[92] There is limited discussion of ethical leadership and ethical decision making in the LIS literature. Of the "attributes" needed by academic library leaders, Hernon, Powell, and Young addressed the importance of effective decision making, such as the ability to "think 'outside the box' (in new and creative ways applicable to the problem)," exhibit "good judgment," make "tough decisions," and exhibit integrity.[93]

There has been discussion of the professional values that are intended to guide decision making in the profession. Researchers such as Koehler have addressed the importance of ensuring that professional values are an integral part of LIS education.[94] Koehler defines the distinction between ethics and professional values: "Ethics are generally perceived to derive from and serve as the application of moral principles. Morals represent a set of mores, customs and traditions that may have been derived from social practice or from religious guidance."[95] Professional values, on the other hand, may be supported by ethical principles, are intended to guide the work and decision making of professionals, and are often codified by professional and scholarly associations, with the understanding that codes of ethics vary somewhat by profession. In library and information services, professional values include: privacy, intellectual freedom, valuing intellectual property, and equity of access.[96]

Conclusion and Implications

While the substantive components of the leadership discussion have been evident in the private sector and the general literature for some time, the focus on leadership has been a more recent phenomenon in library and information services. Certainly, a range of societal, organizational, economic, and technological issues indicate the need for sound leadership, particularly in light of the predicted leadership vacuum in the profession.

The growing but still small body of library literature on leadership reflects limited discussion and, more so, limited research in the profession and the discipline. However, the evidence of both increased research and practical interest in the profession and attempts to foster such leadership, including the introduction of more leadership training programs, is substantial. The increasingly sophisticated statements of leadership competencies that address issues such as communication skills and acting with integrity, as well as the need for understanding the diverse nature of user populations and the importance of understanding customers of all types, further support the notion of leadership preparation that is substantive.

However, the limited body of literature related to leadership in LIS indicates the need to rely on the substantive research published in the general leadership literature, acknowledging the differences in context between libraries and other types of organizations and focusing greater effort on leadership research that considers the leadership issues and concerns in libraries. It is necessarily the case that the leadership education and training should be supported and informed by research, including practice-based research. In addition, the decision making in libraries should be informed by research that reflects a broad understanding of best practices and a thorough analysis of the issues. An agenda for research associated with leadership in LIS should be informed by the gathering and analysis of original data and reflect best practices and the application of leadership theory in the following areas:

- the nature of leadership needed for the 21st century academic library and the associated recruitment challenges;
- the leadership competencies associated with organizational success;
- the leadership challenges associated with team-based organizations and matrix organizational structures;
- measurement of the impact of leadership education in LIS degree programs and leadership training programs in the development of leadership in the profession;
- the expanding importance and role of leadership at all levels in academic libraries, including the opportunities for shared leadership and the role of followership;
- enhanced understanding of leadership diversity, which addresses the relationship between investment in diversity and organizational performance and success; and
- leadership evaluation.

Thus, the current state of the leadership research, particularly in relation to academic libraries, provides a clear indication of an area of concern, central to the future of the profession, which requires further development, insight, and analysis.

References

1. George R. Goethals, Georgia Sorenson, and James MacGregor Burns, eds., *Encyclopedia of Leadership* (Thousand Oaks, CA: Sage. 2004).

2. Sharon Gray Weiner, "Leadership of Academic Libraries: A Literature Review," *Education Libraries* 26, no. 2 (2003): 5.

3. Ibid., 17.

4. Samuel E. Trosow, "Organizational Theory in Library and Information Science Education," *Journal of Education for Library and Information Science* 41, no. 2 (2000): 129–141; Beverly P. Lynch, "Theory and Practice," *Library Administration and Management* 18, no. 1 (2004): 30.

5. Certainly, it is important to note the aspect of leadership that has been somewhat extraorganizational and has included the writings of Aristotle, Plato, Machiavelli, and Tolstoy. While theory development has been influenced by these preindustrial studies of leadership and more recent studies of leadership that is extraorganizational, the primary focus here is leadership in the context of organizations and professions.

6. Jonathan P. Doh, "Can Leadership Be Taught? Perspectives from Management Educators," *Academy of Management Learning and Education* 2, no. 1 (2003): 54.

7. James V. Liberty and Jim Prewitt, "Professional Leadership Education: An Analysis," *Career Development International* 4, no. 3 (1999): 155.

8. Mark Winston and Deborah Fisher, "Leadership Education for Young Adult Librarians," *Public Library Quarterly* 21, no. 1 (2003): 32.

9. Lynch, "Theory and Practice," 33.

10. Kevin Dobbs and others, "Leadership Theories: A Top-10 List," *Training* 36 (1999): 26–27.

11. Ibid., 26.

12. Ibid.

13. Janet Z. Burns and Fred L. Otte, "Implications of Leader-Member Exchange Theory and Research for Human Resource Development Research," *Human Resource Development Quarterly* 10, no. 3 (1999): 225.

14. Daniel Goleman, "Leadership That Gets Results," *Harvard Business Review* 78, no. 2 (2000): 78–92; Boas Shamir and Jane M. Howell, "Organizational and Contextual Influences on the Emergence and Effectiveness of Charismatic Leadership," *Leadership Quarterly* 10, no. 2 (1999): 257–284.

15. Dobbs and others, "Leadership Theories," 26.

16. Reginald Shareef, "Ecovision: A Leadership Theory for Innovative Organizations," *Organizational Dynamics* 20, no. 1 (1991): 50–63.

17. Clayton M. Christensen and Michael E. Raynor, "Why Hard-Nosed Executives Should Care about Management Theory," *Harvard Business Review* 81, no. 9 (2003): 66–74.

18. Donald E. Riggs, ed., *Library Leadership: Visualizing the Future,* (Phoenix, AZ.:

Oryx Press, 1982).

19. Donald E. Riggs, "Libraries," in *Encyclopedia of Leadership,* ed. George R. Goethals, Georgia Sorensen, and James MacGregor Burns, vol. 2, pp. 908–911 (Thousand Oaks, CA: Sage Publications, 2004).

20. Donald E. Riggs, "The Crisis and Opportunities in Library Leadership," *Journal of Library Administration* 32, no. 3/4 (2001): 8.

21. Ibid., 7–8, 16.

22. Robert Renaud and Anne Murray, "Organizing for Leadership: How University Libraries Can Meet the Leadership Challenge in Higher Education," in *Leadership, Higher Education, and the Information Age,* ed. Carrie E. Regenstein and Barbara I. Dewey, 163–180 (New York: Neal-Schuman, 2003).

23. Rebecca T. Lenzini, "The Graying of the Library Profession: A Survey of Our Professional Association and Their Responses," *Searcher* 10, no. 7 (2002): 88–98; Stanley J. Wilder, "New Hires in Research Libraries: Demographic Trends and Hiring Priorities," *ARL Bimonthly Report* 221 (2002): 5–8.

24. Stanley Wilder, "The Changing Profile of Research Library Professional Staff," *ARL Bimonthly Report* 208/209 (2000), http://www.arl.org/news-ltr/208_209/chgprofile.html (accessed March 31, 2008).

25. Paula T. Kaufman, "Where Do The Next "We" Come From? Recruiting, Retaining, and Developing Our Successors," *ARL Bimonthly Report* 221 (2002): 1–5.

26. Ibid.

27. Kathryn J. Deiss and Maureen Sullivan, "The Shared Leadership Principle: Creating Leaders throughout the Organization," *Leading Ideas,* no. 2 (1998), http://www.arl.org/bm~doc/li2.pdf (accessed July 15, 2008).

28. Robert Kelley, "In Praise of Followers," *Harvard Business Review* 66, no. 6 (1988): 143.

29. Veronica Reyes, "The Future Role of the Academic Librarians in Higher Education," *portal: Libraries and the Academy* 6, no. 3 (2006): 301.

30. Debra L. Gilchrist, "Academic Libraries at the Center of Instructional Change: Faculty and Librarian Experience of Library Leadership in the Transformation of Teaching and Learning," (PhD diss., Oregon State University, 2007).

31. Dave Ulrich, Jack Zenger and Norm Smallwood, "Building Your Leadership Brand," *Leader to Leader,* no. 15 (2000): 40

32. Robert Barner, "Five Steps to Leadership Competencies," *Training and Development* 54, no. 3 (2000): 51.

33. Ibid.

34. Jim Intagliata, Dave Ulrich, and Norm Smallwood, "Levering Leadership Competencies to Produce Leadership Brand: Creating Distinctiveness by Focusing on Strategy and Results," *Human Resource Planning* 23 no. 3. (2000): 16

35. Christopher B. Bingham, Teppo Felin, and J. Stewart Black, "An Interview with John Pepper: What It Takes to be a Global Leader," *Human Resource*

Management 39 no. 2/3 (2000): 287–292; Bill J. Bonnstetter, "The DNA of Global Leadership Competencies," *Thunderbird International Business Review* 42, no. 2 (2000): 131–144.

36. Bingham, Felin, and Black, "Interview with John Pepper," 287.

37. Allen J. Morrison, "Developing a Global Leadership Model," *Human Resource Management* 39 , no. 2/3 (2000): 117–131; Margaret E. Alldredge and Kevin J. Nilan, "3M's Leadership Competency Model: An Internally Developed Solution," *Human Resource Management* 39, no. 2/3 (2000): 133–145.

38. Barner, "Five Steps to Leadership Competencies," 48.

39. Suzanne H. Mahmoodi and Geraldine King, "Identifying Competencies and Responsibilities of Top Management Teams in Public Libraries," *Minnesota Libraries* 30, no. 1/2 (1991/1992): 28.

40. Ibid., 27–28, 31.

41. Joan Giesecke and Beth McNeil, "Core Competencies and the Learning Organization," *Library Administration and Management* 13, no. 3 (1999): 158.

42. Debbie Schachter, "The Synthesizing Information Professional," *Information Outlook* 10, no. 3 (2006): 12.

43. Special Libraries Association, "Competencies for Information Professionals of the 21st Century," rev. ed., June 2003, Special Libraries Association, http://www.sla.org/content/learn/comp2003/index.cfm (accessed March 31, 2008); Young Adult Library Services Association, "Young Adults Deserve the Best: Competencies for Librarians Serving Youth," rev. ed., October 2003, Young Adults Library Services Association, http://www.ala.org/ala/yalsa/profdev/youngadultsdeserve.cfm(accessed July 15, 2008).

44. Peter Hernon, Ronald R. Powell, and Arthur P. Young, "University Library Directors in the Association of Research Libraries: The Next Generation, Part One," *College and Research Libraries* 62, no. 2 (2001): 116–145; Hernon, Powell, and Young, "University Library Directors in the Association of Research Libraries: The Next Generation, Part Two," *College and Research Libraries* 63, no. 1 (2002): 73–90.

45. Hernon, Powell and Young, "University Library Directors, Part Two."

46. Arthur P. Young, Peter Hernon, and Ronald R. Powell, "Attributes of Academic Library Leadership: An Exploratory Study of Some Gen-Xers," *Journal of Academic Librarianship* 32, no. 5 (2006): 489.

47. Ibid., 501.

48. Patha Suwannarat, "Library Leadership in Research University Libraries" (PhD diss., Peabody College for Teachers of Vanderbilt University, 1994).

49. Peter Hernon and Nancy Rossiter, "Emotional Intelligence: Which Traits Are Most Prized," *College and Research Libraries* 67, no. 3 (2006): 260–275.

50. Xuemao Wang and Chang Su, "Develop Future Library Leaders with Global Literacy in the Context of Cultural Intelligence," *Chinese Librarianship*, no. 22 (2006), http://www.iclc.us./cliej/cl22.htm (accessed March 31, 2008).

51. Suzie Allard and Bharat Mehra, "Intercultural Leadership Toolkit for Librarians: Building Awareness to Effectively Serve Diverse Multicultural Populations," *Education Libraries* 30, no. 1 (2007): 5.

52. Mark Winston and Gretchen Ebeler Hazlin, "Leadership Competencies in Library and Information Science: Marketing as a Component of LIS Curricula," *Journal of Education for Library and Information Science* 44, no. 2 (Spring 2003): 177–187; Mark Winston and Lisa Dunkley, "Leadership Competencies: The Issues of Development and Fundraising in Academic Libraries," *College and Research Libraries* 63, no. 2 (2002): 171–182.

53. Winston and Fisher, "Leadership Education."

54. Winston and Hoffman, "Leadership Competencies: Project Management."

55. Winston and Fisher, "Leadership Education."

56. Winston and Fisher, "Leadership Education"; Winston and Hazlin, "Leadership Competencies," 183.

57. Winston and Hazlin, "Leadership Competencies," 183.

58. Ria Newhouse and April Spizak, "Fixing the First Job," *Library Journal* 129, no. 13 (2004): 44–46; Tom Terrell, "Salaries Rebound, Women Break Out," *Library Journal* 127, no. 17 (2002): 30–34, 36.

59. Association of Research Libraries, Office of Leadership and Management Services, "ARL Research Library Leadership Fellows Program," Feb. 5, 2007, Association of Research Libraries Web site, http://www.arl.org/olms/rllf/ (accessed March 31, 2008).

60. David Bilyeu, Marianne Gaunt, and Maryruth Glogowski, "ACRL/Harvard Leadership Institute: Three Participants Share Their Rewarding Experiences," *College and Research Libraries News* 61, no. 2 (2000): 106–108, 120; Jennifer Franklin, "An Uncommon Experience—Northern Exposure to Leadership," *Feliciter* 42 (July/August 1996): 14–15.

61. Beverly P. Lynch, "Taking on the Issues in a Changing Environment: The Senior Fellows Program," *Journal of Library Administration* 20, no. 2 (1994): 5–15.

62. Teresa Neely and Mark Winston, "The Snowbird Leadership Institute: Leadership Development in the Profession," *College and Research Libraries* 60, no. 5 (1999): 412–425.

63. Janelle M. Zauha, "Turned On and Tuned In? Professional Side Effects of a Library Leadership Institution," *PNLA Quarterly* 71, no. 3 (2007): 8.

64. Peter Edward Sidorko, "Fostering Innovation in Library Management and Leadership," *Library Management* 28, no. 1/2 (2007): 5.

65. Lois Kuyper-Rushing, "A Formal Mentoring Program in a University Library: Components of a Successful Experiment," *Journal of Academic Librarianship* 27, no. 6 (2001): 440–446; Barbara Wittkopf, "Mentoring in Academic Libraries," *LLA Bulletin* 61, no. 4 (1999): 226–232.

66. Jerry J. Jasinowski, "Growth and the Imperative of Diversity in the Twenty-First Century," *Executive Speeches* 15, no. 3 (2000/2001): 58–61.

67. Richard Koonce, "Redefining Diversity: It's Not Just the Right Thing to Do. It Also Makes Good Business Sense," *Training and Development* 55, no. 12 (2001): 24.

68. Geoffrey Colvin, "The 50 Best Companies for Asians, Blacks, and Hispanics: Companies That Pursue Diversity Outperform the S&P 500. Coincidence?" *Fortune* 140, no 2 (1999): 53–54; Sherry Kuczynski, "If Diversity, Then Higher Profits? Companies That Have Successful Diversity Programs Seem to Have Higher Returns. But Which Came First?" *HR Magazine* 44, no. 13 (December 1999), http://www.shrm.org/hrmagazine/articles/1299div.asp (accessed March 31, 2008).

69. Colvin, "The 50 Best Companies," 54.

70. Kuczynski, "If Diversity, Then Higher Profits?"

71. Ibid.

72. Katie Dean, "Study: Women Good for Your Biz," *Wired News*, December 6, 2000, http://wired.com/news/women/0,1540,40438,00.html. (accessed March 31, 2008).

73. Patricia Schaeffer, "Annual HR Salary Survey," *Training and Development* 55, no. 12 (2001): 62–66.

74. Don Knight and others, "Top Management Team Diversity, Group Process, and Strategic Consensus," *Strategic Management Journal* 20, no. 5 (1999): 445–465.

75. Christine Y. Chen, and Jonathan Hickman, "America's 50 Best Companies for Minorities," *Fortune* 142, no. 2 (July 10, 2000): 190.

76. Mark Winston, "The Importance of Leadership Diversity: The Relationship between Diversity and Organizational Success in the Academic Environment," *College and Research Libraries* 62, no. 6 (2001): 517–526.

77. Judith Block McLaughlin, "James O. Freedman on Diversity and Dartmouth," *Change* 23 (1999): 25–31; Neil Rudenstine, "Why a Diverse Student Body Is So Important," *Chronicle of Higher Education* 42, no. 32 (1996): B1–B2.

78. Fay Hansen, "Diversity's Business Case Doesn't Add Up," *Workforce* 82, April 2003: 28–32. Thomas Kochan and others, "The Effects of Diversity on Business Performance: Report of the Diversity Research Network," *Human Resource Management* 42, no. 1 (2003): 3.

79. Stephanie Armour, "Debate Revived on Workplace Diversity," *USA Today* (July 20, 2003): 4B.

80. Ibid.

81. Mark Winston and Haipeng Li, "Managing Diversity in Liberal Arts College Libraries," *College and Research Libraries* 61, no. 3 (2000): 205.

82. Thomasina Kennedy, and Marilyn T. Okrent, "Managing Diversity: Some Practical Tips for Managers," *New Jersey Libraries* 26 (Fall 1993): 15–18.

83. Christopher J. Kertesz, "Asian Pacific Americans Do Some Consciousness-Raising through Libraries," *American Libraries* 31, no. 5 (2000): 11.

84. Joe Martin, "The Homeless: Adversity as Diversity," *Alki* 18, no. 1 (2002): 12–14.

85. Joan S. Howland, "Beyond Recruitment: Retention and Promotion Strategies to Ensure Diversity and Success," *Library Administration and Management* 13, no. 1 (1999): 4–14; Mark D. Winston, "The Role of Recruitment in Achieving Goals Related to Diversity," *College and Research Libraries* 59, no. 3 (1998): 240–247.

86. Reed Coats, Jane Goodwin, and Patricia Bangs, "Seeking the Best Path: Assessing a Library's Diversity Climate," *Library Administration and Management* 14, no. 3 (2000): 148–154.

87. Judy Rizzuti-Hare, Ruben Cavazos, and Gloria Garcia, "The Synergy in Diversity," *Alki* 18, no. 1 (2002): 28–29.

88. Mark Winston and Haipeng Li, "Diversity and Organizational Success: A Survey of Chief Academic Officers in Liberal Arts Colleges," (paper presented at the 11th National Association of College and Research Libraries Conference, Charlotte, NC, April 10–13, 2003), http://www.ala.org/ala/acrl/acrlevents/winston.PDF (accessed March 31, 2008).

89. Deborah R. Hollis, "Affirmative Action or Increase Competition: A Look at Women and Minority Library Deans," *Journal of Library Administration* 27, no. 1/2 (1999): 49–75; Marta Mestrovic Deyrup, "Is the Revolution Over? Gender, Economic, and Professional Parity in Academic Library Leadership Positions," *College and Research Libraries* 65, no. 3 (2004): 242–250.

90. Betty J. Turock, "Women and Leadership," *Journal of Library Administration* 32, no. 3/4 (2001): 111–132.

91. Mark Winston, "Education for Ethical Leadership," *New Library World* 106, no. 5/6 (2005): 234–235.

92. Intagliata, Ulrich, and Smallwood, "Leveraging Leadership Competencies."

93. Hernon, Powell and Young, "University Library Directors, Part Two."

94. Wallace Koehler, "Professional Values and Ethics as Defined by 'The LIS Discipline'" *Journal of Education for Library and Information Science* 44, no. 2 (Spring 2003): 99.

95. Ibid.

96. Michael Gorman, *Our Enduring Values: Librarianship in the 21st Century* (Chicago: American Library Association, 2000), 26–27; Wallace C. Koehler and others, "Ethical Values of Information and Library Professionals—An Expanded Analysis," *International Information and Library Review* 32, no. 3/4 (2000): 485–507; Ann Symons and Carla J. Stoffle, "When Values Conflict," *American Libraries* 29, no. 5 (1998): 56–58.

6 Usability Testing: Method and Research

Michael J. Prasse and Lynn Silipigni Connaway

With the advent of easy-to-use search engine Web sites such as Google, users now expect their library's Web sites to be as easy to use and retrieve information. However, many users indicate that searching library Web sites is difficult and cumbersome, and consequently they do not use them. Librarians can increase both amount of use and searcher's effectiveness by improving the ease of use and of learning of their Web sites, i.e., their level of usability. In the first section of this paper, one method of usability evaluation, the usability test, is discussed. Beginning with a definition of usability and how to recruit users and concluding with a brief discussion of remote testing, this section includes insights and tips garnered from testing experience in the OCLC Usability Lab. This section is followed by a review of studies related to usability testing of library Web sites, and the paper ends with a discussion of widely accepted usability testing methods. Usability testing can be an effective method for improving library Web sites.

Introduction

With the availability of electronic resources and the widespread use of Internet search engines and Web-based services such as Google, Yahoo!, and Amazon.com, users' needs for and expectations of retrieval systems and full-text electronic content have evolved. With the technologies currently available, academic libraries are presented with an unprecedented array of design decisions for the integration of catalogs and resources into their Web sites. Librarians with a basic knowledge of Web design and programming skills now can be major contributors to the "look and feel" of how their resources are presented to patrons.

In addition, there has been much discussion of whether there is a need for the traditional library catalog in the current Web environment. Dempsey comments on the increased interest in the catalog at a time "when the classic catalog may be fading in importance as a central venue of user activity."[1] Karen Calhoun makes a case for enriching the library catalog with discovery tools that will link the reader to full-text electronic resources as well as recommender services that include reviews and identify related sources.[2] Data gathered for a study of college and university information-seeking behaviors, funded by the Institute of Museum and Library Services (IMLS), Ohio State University (OSU), and OCLC,[3] indicate that an undergraduate student will "stay away from the library catalog, [because] it will give me a list of a thousand things, but there is really no ranking that I can understand."[4] Others state that they first use Amazon. com to find materials of interest and then use the bibliographic information provided by Amazon to find the item in the library catalog.

While librarians now have the skills needed to develop their own Web sites, users indicate library Web sites are too difficult to use or have too many limited features to be useful. One way for librarians to develop systems and services that meet user needs and expectations is to evaluate the Web site for usability. Such evaluations, combined with human-factors input, can support or refute developers' opinions about a system with data provided by users.[5]

Initially, few librarians had training or experience in graphic design, Web design, or human-computer interaction (HCI). Soon librarians began to borrow usability methods from HCI in order to develop and evaluate their Web sites. Today, evaluating usability has become widespread, particularly among larger academic libraries.

The need to make library Web sites and catalogs usable and easy to learn is a persistent and increasingly important consideration. Recognizing and correcting major usability problems in library Web sites is vital if the academic library is to continue to be relevant not only to the current academic audience, but also to prospective users of sources and services. Most prospective users are familiar with searching the public Internet and expect the academic library Web site to be at least as easy to use as Google, Yahoo!, or other Internet search engines.[6] Usability testing is a method that can help academic libraries meet this critical user expectation.

The Usability Test

Evaluating usability involves using research methods that measure the degree to which a person can successfully learn and use a system or service. One of these methods is usability testing, which is the observation and analysis of users' behavior while they interact with a system or prototype.[7] Usability testing is a relatively new method, which began with the testing of aircraft design and was first widely used in marketing research. The method evolved from human ethnographic observation, ergonomics, and cognitive psychology, and it can produce both qualitative and quantitative data. With the widespread access to computers in the 1980s, the method became popular in user-system interface design, the catalyst for HCI usability studies. The process involves the user from the initial design phase through system upgrades.[8] Usability testing should identify problem areas and "determine the fit of the design to the intended users."[9]

Usability testing can provide data for questions addressing human interaction with any system. Some suitable, basic library-related questions for the method include:

- What is the best layout for a Web page?
- How can reading from the screen interface be optimized?
- Which online fonts are the best?
- What makes a site difficult to use?

Usability testing also can accommodate more structured, detailed questions, such as:

- Can individual personality or cognitive skills predict Internet-use behavior?
- Can library collection holdings and library data be represented geographically in a way so that users can understand and manipulate the data?
- Can users easily customize and manage discipline-specific content available in an open-source library portal?
- Can users quickly and easily find serials, i.e., newspapers, journals, magazines, etc., from a library's Web site and online catalog?

Defining Usability and Usability Testing

There are many definitions of usability and usability testing; two seem to appear most often in the literature. One is provided by the International Standards Organization (ISO), which defines usability as the effectiveness, efficiency, and satisfaction with which specified users achieve specified goals in particular environments.[10] Using this definition, a measure of effectiveness would be the percentage of goals achieved, while a measure of efficiency would be the time it takes a user to complete a task. Satisfaction might be measured by a rating scale for satisfaction on a questionnaire.[11]

Prasse expands the ISO definition to define usability testing as a method to determine if a Web site allows users to use the site quickly, accurately, and enjoyably.[12]

The second definition of usability includes four measures identified by Dicks.[13] These measures are (1) ease of learning, (2) ease of use, (3) usefulness, and (4) pleasantness of use. A critical difference between the two definitions is that Dicks' version adds the concept of *usefulness*; i.e., Does the system do what it is supposed to do? A system's usefulness is determined primarily by having the right functionality built into the Web site. This depends on both gathering *and* implementing the correct design requirements.

Conversely, under the ISO definition, a Web site's usability is not determined by whether the functionality built into a Web site does what it is supposed to do. Instead, its usability is dependent on how quickly, accurately, and enjoyably a user can do predetermined tasks, such as those in a usability test. If the tasks require a user to do whatever the site is supposed to do (which they should), then some measure of usefulness might be determined. However, it is not a requirement of the ISO definition of usability that such tasks be done during a usability test.

To limit the scope of this paper to usability testing and not requirements gathering, the concept of usability testing will not include the task of evaluating usefulness. However, it is critical that library Web site teams understand that a useful Web site is at least as important as a usable Web site; usability testing does not inherently evaluate a Web site's usefulness, and both usefulness and usability are critical to creating a successful Web site.

Usability Testing Method

Usability testing is a design method that can be conducted in an artificial or natural environment. The natural environment provides a more holistic representation of real people doing real tasks. Alternatively, the laboratory environment gives the researchers more control over the tasks and environment and may provide more specific data on a particular feature.

There are four types of usability tests, each requiring the same rigorous process as experimental design studies. They include the exploratory test for early product development; the assessment test, which is the most typical test and is performed either early or midway in the product development; the validation test, which is used to verify a product's usability; and the comparison test, which compares two or more designs and can be combined with the other three types of usability tests.[14]

Recruiting Testers

Testers who will evaluate the Web site may or may not be randomly chosen. In addition, Campbell offers several suggestions for recruiting testers, including advertising and, most important, "selecting people who are representative of the library's user population."[15] This is indeed critical: Only a few tests will be conducted, so the most accurate data collected will be from the most representative testers available.

However, it is not unusual to find that the representativeness needed in a tester correlates with the maturity of the developing Web site. For example, in the earliest stages of Web site development, many usability problems, such as color combinations or visual organization, impact more on fundamental human attributes than on attributes specific to the ultimate target user population, such as user familiarity with cataloging terminology or expertise in information organization. As a consequence, it is possible to use less representative testers, e.g., library staff, when testing in the early stages of development, with the obvious restriction that they have no association with the development of the new Web site.

The value of testing with library staff is that they can be recruited very quickly. If library staff members are involved as testers, it is important not to identify staff observations as usability problems when they may not be problems for the target users. For example, a cataloger might advocate using technical terms that a noncataloger would not understand; therefore, it is also critical to test the Web site with representative target users before releasing it.

It is recommended to test between three and five users. Dickstein and Mills conducted nine iterations of testing, using between eight and twelve users per test, but they note, "It was usually apparent by the fourth or fifth test that the tested feature was either a problem or a success."[16] This finding has been reiterated in the literature. Four tests will usually identify approximately 80% of the site's usability problems, although some recommend up to 20 users. However, if different user groups are being tested, e.g., novice versus experienced searchers, three to five users *per group* should be tested.[17]

The Test Monitor

The monitor or administrator of the usability tests is also critical to the success of the evaluation. The monitor should be a good communicator who is able to react spontaneously and to continue with the plan regardless of the mistakes that occur or any on-the-fly changes in procedures.

Establishing What to Test

To determine what components of a Web site should be evaluated, a good first step is to "create a purpose statement and objectives."[18] This step is followed by determining which usability evaluation method would best achieve those objectives.

For a usability test, the purpose statement encapsulates the goals the team hopes to achieve in conducting the usability test. An example would be "to determine if users can easily search and navigate from search results to the display of a bibliographic record." This statement serves to focus the team on the most usable components of the site and also clarifies the goals for them.

While the purpose statement provides a general mission statement for the design team, it is rarely detailed enough to apply directly to the creation of test tasks. Detailed objectives need to be developed, and the tasks should be designed to answer a set of *usability questions* that are derived from these objectives.[19]

Campbell recommends establishing both *quantitative* and *qualitative* objectives for each task.[20] Quantitative objectives might include completing the task in a certain time period or with a minimum number of clicks. Qualitative objectives might include questions such as "Does the outcome message of moving a directory confuse or clearly explain what happened?" or "Are the items in the screens labeled clearly?" Developing the right objectives is key to creating the best tasks for the usability test.

One way to establish usability questions from the objectives is (1) to determine the component user behaviors needed to accomplish the purpose statement and (2) to identify which of those behaviors should be tested. For example, in the purpose statement "Determine if users can *easily search* and navigate from search results to the display of a bibliographic record," the behaviors required to "easily search" may involve setting search limits, entering the correct search terms, using Boolean operators, etc. One usability question could be "Can the user easily set search limits?"

Another way to determine the test objectives and usability questions is to base them on the goals the user will have when using the site. These *user goals* can be determined by using surveys or transaction log analysis, determining the most popular Web pages on the current site,[21] having Web team members play the role of a patron trying to find information on the Web site (i.e., a cognitive walkthrough),[22] or by conducting *contextual design* interviews.[23] In such an interview, observers are the apprentice to the user's expert, taking notes, asking questions, and following and observing the users while they actually use the library Web site for research. Such contextual interviews are particularly useful because user goals may be identified, leading to functional Web site innovations to support these goals.

King proposes another method to determine usability test objectives and tasks. He states, "[T]hink of your library website as a business ... of a single product: information."[24] For example, the library Web site version of a business plan might include these general and specific objectives:

- Our site should be user-friendly.
- Our stock needs to be inventoried. Keep your inventory (Web links) current.
- Make our catalog easier to find .(This specific goal supports the general goal that the site is user-friendly).[25]

Regardless of how the usability objectives and usability questions are determined, it is critical that they accurately reflect user needs. For example, the Web team may have set the ability to easily limit a search by date as a usability objective for an academic library Web site. This objective may have been based on interviews when students mentioned that their instructors always tell them that it is important to include new information in a report. The Web team interprets this as a user goal of limiting by date, resulting in a usability objective that the Web site should provide an easy way to limit by date. However, it is more likely that the actual user goal was to get the most recent information about a given topic. This goal could be achieved in several ways other than limiting a search by date, such as by adding a News button or providing the ability to rank results by date. The correct usability objective would be "Provide an easy way to get the most recent information about a topic," and the corresponding usability question would be, "Can users easily access the most recent information about a given topic?"

Understanding which usability objectives and questions to evaluate during a test is a key to an efficient usability test. Creating the usability questions also focuses the team on how the user is going to *interact* with the Web site's functionality. It is common at present to focus only on the *development* of that functionality.

Creating Tasks

After the usability questions are developed, rough drafts of tasks designed to answer each usability question should be created. These are the tasks the user will be asked to complete during the usability test. Research indicates that tasks that provide a reason for performing the task, not just a statement of instructions, improve user attention to task details, rigor of searches, and overall interest in the usability test;[26] therefore, King suggests using tasks that provide a *reason* to the user for doing the task, as well as the task itself., for example, "Your grades are slipping, and you need help with your coursework. Does our library have a Web site that will help you?"[27]

Another way to create tasks in an academic environment is to ask instructors to provide a list of research topics they have given to their students. This method also can provide a good snapshot of the potential usefulness of the Web site, such as: Do the functions implemented match the students' need to complete the tasks required by their instructors? The number of tasks in a test should be relatively small. Usability tests that have too many tasks can quickly wear out a user. For example, Chisman, Diller, and Walbridge included 45 questions and noted, "the test seemed grueling for both participants and observers... . Even though the test was completed within an hour ... fewer tasks (14 instead of 45) made the second test (iteration) less intense."[28]

It is very easy for Web team members to feel users *should* be able to complete a great number of tasks, not recognizing that users sometimes have a limited knowledge of the site. Fortunately, there are several ways to decrease the number of tasks and still get valuable information. One is for the Web team to prioritize their usability objectives from most to least important and to use only those tasks associated with the highest priority objectives and questions. Another way is to review the tasks for overlapping usability questions that could be combined and answered in a single task. For example, the following two tasks were developed to answer two usability questions:

- Do WSU Pullman libraries have a copy of the periodical *Audubon*?
  Usability Question: Can a user find a periodical by title?
- Did the Owen library receive the Sept/Oct 2008 issue?
  Usability Question: Can a user determine if the current issue of a periodical is located in a particular library?[29]

The two tasks might have been combined into a single task that could still answer the same usability questions:

- You need to find the Sept/Oct 2008 issue of the journal *Audubon* for a project in your Environmental Studies class. It may be in any of the WSU Pullman libraries, but you prefer the Owen library because it is near your dorm. Do any of the WSU Pullman libraries, in particular the Owen library, own this issue of *Audubon*?

Combining several tasks into one single task can result in a task that better represents a user's actions and help avoid questioning users in a linear pattern, which is often not "the process by which research is actually conducted."[30]

Quantitative Measures

The next step after creating a set of tasks is often to define for each task at least one quantitative measure that will be used to measure the level of usability for the Web site components to be tested. Although usability problems are often so obvious that quantitative measures are not needed to discern that a problem has occurred, there may be team members or those who will read the test reports who feel more comfortable with quantitative measures.[31]

Such measures might include categorizing user expressions, such as expressions of confusion or frustration.[32] However, more often it will include one or all of the following measures: (1) task completion (yes/no); (2) number of requests for help, e.g., the number of times users indicate they would contact a friend for assistance; (3) time to complete task; and (4) subjective satisfaction.

An example of a quantitative measure is: "The user must be able to set the Boolean operators needed to complete this task with no more than one help request." If a user makes more than one help request, the functions on the Web site that enable users to set Boolean operators are not at an acceptable level of usability. This indicates that a redesign of these Web site functions may be needed.

If using absolute task completion time as a quantitative measure, thinking aloud while doing a task will likely increase the time to complete the task.[33] However, this might be mitigated by using a percentage of total test time as the measure, e.g., "Task 1 should take 10% of the total time for the user to complete all the tasks."[34] Also, the median is often a better summary statistic than the mean for time measurements, since it is less affected by outliers, i.e., very short or very long task completion times.[35]

Another measure can be derived by tracking the user's path through the Web site. This can be done by logging the mouse clicks of users while they are carrying out each task.[36] Tasks not completed by a majority of users would be analyzed first, beginning with an analysis of the notes for that task for each test. The paths taken by each user in completing the task then can be compared. An alternative to documenting the click path of each user is to ask the Web team to identify the expected or optimal path to complete the task and to document whether a user took a particular step in the path. Although this method is much faster, it is potentially not as informative as noting all the steps in the exact path. However, since the Web team provides the click sequence, consistent user deviations from it may be more likely to be accepted by the team as indicative of a real usability or design problem.

Creating Post-test Questionnaires and Interview Questions

In addition to creating tasks for the user to conduct during the test, it is also valuable to develop a questionnaire and list of interview questions to be administered to the user after the test. The purpose of the *post-test questionnaire* is to gather consistent qualitative information and ratings from each participant. It allows the Web team to get answers to specifically targeted questions about the Web site that may not have been answered by the user's behavior during the test. Since the questions are the same for all users, the results may provide additional insight into usability problems that were observed consistently during the test for all or most users. The questionnaire can involve a rating scale, though the small sample size common to most usability tests prohibits any meaningful statistical analysis. Users also should be asked to provide written reasons for their ratings.

Talking to users in a *post-test interview* can help researchers to understand the rationale for the users' actions during the test and to answer any observer questions that arose during the test. To be useful and valid, it is critical that the interviewer be well-versed in asking questions objectively during the test.[37] For example, instead of asking, "Did you feel confused when you did Task 1?" an interviewer could ask the less biased question, "What were you feeling when you did Task 1?" The former question presumes knowledge about the users' method of expressing themselves, i.e., that what they were feeling could be expressed on some type of level of confusion continuum. As stated by Dumas and Redish, "Everyone expresses themselves differently, so we take a risk by trying to guess what they [the testers] are thinking," while a less biased question "allows the user to stop and think."[38]

The User Introduction

It is necessary to provide an introduction to the testing procedure to the user. In the 2001 test described by Marill, users read a description of the purpose and format of the test.[39] It may be read to the user by a member of the test team as well.[40] Such a description should provide the minimum amount of information about the Web site that the users would need to lead them to use the Web site in the real world.[41] This text is often just one or two descriptive sentences. Providing more than this level of knowledge could artificially bias the tests. It is not clear how the requirement for participants to read a user's guide prior to testing, for instance, might have affected the accuracy of the results reported by Marill. The introduction also should include a brief description of the testing procedures and how a user can get help during the test.

Conducting the Test

Prior to any test from which data will be collected, a pretest should be conducted to evaluate, and revise if necessary, the tasks and other test materials. Occasionally, the pretest also identifies critical usability problems in the Web site, which may require a postponement of the usability test.

When conducting usability tests, Campbell encourages making the test environment "as realistic and comfortable ... as possible."[42] Perhaps surprisingly, making the environment comfortable may be more important today than making it realistic. With the advent of laptops, any environment is potentially a realistic one for using a computer. However, being watched while using that computer is rarely comfortable, and nervous users may focus more on trying not to make a mistake than on using the Web site as they would in real life. To decrease the likelihood of such unrealistic behavior, it is a good idea to continually remind users they cannot make a mistake, are doing a great job, and are providing wonderful feedback.[43] By interjecting such reassurances to the testers, observers can make them feel more relaxed, and the test should run more smoothly.[44] If the users encounter a problem with the Web site so great that they cannot complete the task and their self-confidence is clearly slipping, the observers should move them on to the next task, and remind them that it is the Web site that has a problem, not them.

Collecting Data during the Test

A common procedure for collecting data during the test (in addition to observing the user) is the think-aloud protocol.[45] In a think-aloud protocol, the users are asked to verbalize the reasons for each of their actions during a test. They may optionally also be asked to comment on anything they like or find particularly confusing in the Web site. In a *concurrent* think-aloud protocol, the verbalization occurs during the test, i.e., the users explain their actions at the same time they are performing those actions. In a *retrospective* think-aloud, users recall what they were thinking during a test after the test (or test task) is completed. This recall may be supplemented by viewing a videotape of their test.

Each technique has advantages and disadvantages. The concurrent protocol has the advantage of being collected as it happens, with no intervening time period for memory to change the information reported. It is well documented that memories change over time, often in unpredictable ways.[46] The disadvantage of the concurrent protocol is that it may interfere with and alter the validity of the observed behavior since it may divert attention away from the task at hand and is in general an artifact of the testing situation. Many people do not talk aloud to themselves while working on a computer. Conversely, a retrospective think-aloud protocol cannot directly alter the observed behavior since it occurs after the task or test is completed. However, memories of what one was thinking at a particular time can get fuzzy very quickly, even with the recognition aid of a videotape. Testing also may take longer to complete because of the extra time needed to produce the retrospective commentary.[47]

Comparing the two methods, Van Den Haak, De Jong, and Schellens note that they do not differ in the total number of problems detected, but rather in how they were detected.[48] The retrospective group tends to reveal more problems via *verbalizations* after the test, while the concurrent group tends to reveal more problems through *observation* of their behavior during the test. This finding suggests that using both methods may be the best path to follow: a concurrent think-aloud during the test, followed by a post-test interview with the tested Web site in view.

When Is a Task Done?

Having the moderator of a test determine when a user is to go on to the next task is fairly common. Marill gave users approximately 10 to 15 minutes to find the answer to each question.[49] Similarly, the script in Battleson, Booth, and Weintrop instructed the moderator to intervene when the user had completed the task.[50]

Another approach, however, is to let the user, not the moderator, determine when a task is completed.[51] Users who think they have completed a task when they have not, or equally important, do not realize they have already completed a task and continue to work at it, provide additional insights into a Web site's usability problems. For example, did the user interface (UI) provide the wrong feedback and lead the user to think he had completed the task? Or perhaps the UI provides too much feedback, overwhelming the user to the point it was perceived more as noise than as information and therefore ignored, leading the users not to perceive the cues that the tasks were completed?

However, it is a good general rule to set an *expected* upper time limit for completing the task. This upper limit would be based on the expected time a user would work at a task before giving up entirely or going to another Web site if that user were performing the task in the real world. For example, it may be estimated that for a given task, users in the real world would have stopped or moved on to another Web site when they had spent three minutes trying to complete the task. Thus a user taking longer than three minutes to complete this task in the artificial situation of a usability test has most likely encountered a usability problem that would have led to the abandonment of the task in the real world. This does *not* mean the user should be stopped after the upper time limit is reached or that information gained during the time after the limit is reached should be discarded. Instead, it means that a task completed after the upper time limit is exceeded, even if it is completed correctly, is still indicative of a usability problem.

Providing Help during a Test

Providing users with the help they would have available in the real world is another part of making the test situation as real as possible. One approach would be to ask the user to read the documentation for the Web site prior to using it. For example, Marill asked users to read the MedlinePlus "Selection Guidelines," which describe its purpose and criteria for the inclusion of linked content, prior to evaluating the site.[52] Another approach is to assume that while users may have offline documentation in the real world, they rarely use it.[53] Consequently, it may be more realistic not to ask users to read any documentation prior to testing, but to make it available to the user during the test.

Users in the real world may also get help from friends, from the Web, and from librarians. One way to emulate this in a test is to have an observer in the room with the testers, available to answer questions as they arise. However, this very easy access to help may actually result in users seeking help at times when they would not in real life. One way to handle this is to require a little extra effort to get help by requiring the user to call a fictional help desk.[54] The users could be instructed prior to the test that in situations where they might seek any type of help in real life while doing one of the tasks, they should instead dial a number for a help desk. This strategy is particularly useful if the help desk is staffed by a member of the Web site design team: Not only do the team member and entire team learn what is causing difficulty for the user, they get to hear it phrased in nontechnical user terms. It also may be the first time team members have interacted with a user they do not know personally, making the entire conversation one the member is not likely to soon forget.

Regardless of how help is provided, one should be careful about two key issues: providing help the user will not have once the Web site goes live, and requiring users to access help that would be optional in the real world. For example, Chisman, Diller, and Walbridge report that a second iteration led to the observers being more "willing to offer suggestions when participants ran into difficulty."[55] While librarians often do offer unsolicited help, they cannot help everyone all of the time. Thus, an intentional intervention such as this one may have biased the results away from what would happen in the real world. It may be better to avoid offering such suggestions during a test and limiting comments instead to non–task-related reassurances and encouragement. After all data are collected, helpful suggestions could be made.

In a second example, Marill provided users with up to five minutes to explore MedlinePlus and ask any questions about it before testing began.[56] However, it may be more realistic to assume that users in a library setting do not actively explore a library Web site prior to using it, but have in mind a specific *user goal* that guides their actions from the moment they begin using the Web site. While trying to accomplish this goal, testers may learn how to use the Web site more effectively, even though that was not their intent. Asking a user intentionally to explore a Web site prior to a usability test may bias the results of the test away from what the user might do in reality.

In a third variation, Vaughn and Callicott suggest adding research hints to the usability task itself, instead of simply asking participants to find a magazine or journal article about a specific subject.[57] Again, one must ask whether such research hints would be available in reality. If the answer is no, then they should not be provided during a usability test.

In summary, it is very tempting to tell users something helpful when they are encountering numerous usability problems. However, unless the person providing the hint is expected to be available 24/7 to handle user problems with the Web site, such overt intervention would create serious questions about the validity of the usability test. It is more valid to assume that in the real world of libraries, users either will not have someone readily available to provide hints or will not access such help even if it is available and known to the user. A better approach might be to let users know during the introduction that help is available, but only if requested.

After the Test

After the test is completed, the user can be given a questionnaire and/or an interview. If a questionnaire is chosen, it is best if the user completes it immediately after a test, while the experience is still fresh and accurate in the user's mind.[58] Asking a user to complete a questionnaire hours or days after the test is finished can lead to less accurate results. For example,

Vaughn and Callicott gave users a questionnaire to complete at home and noted that users "were vague and evasive in their responses [to a take-home evaluation]."[59] Vague and evasive answers to a take-home evaluation are a known problem with retrospective recall.[60] Memories of what happened during the test change over time and become fuzzy, especially for something of such little importance to a user as a usability test. This reality does not mean it is not a good idea to encourage users to contact the Web team if they think of things after the test, but this information should be considered secondary to the information obtained in a questionnaire or user interview completed immediately after the test.

As noted previously, a post-test interview with the user is also a good way to get valuable information by discussing with the users how they might have completed tasks they could not finish or how they might use the Web site more effectively. As a bonus, one may get additional information during this part of the post-test debriefing that is very revealing with regard to what needs to be corrected or what functions might make the site easier to use. While it may also seem a good idea to get design ideas from the user during the post-test debriefing, it is too easy for a user's design suggestions to be taken literally, without looking fully at their overall Web site ramifications. As noted by Marill, "Users are poor designers but good refiners."[61]

However, if one does ask such questions, it is critical that they are asked with the screens or Web pages displayed. This practice allows users to provide design suggestions within their role as "good refiners." It is also recommended to conduct a debriefing with the observers after the test to get agreement on the results and to discuss possible solutions.[62] An equally important reason for a post-test debriefing with the Web site team is to help them emotionally handle the results, which often are quite disappointing and rarely what the team expected prior to the tests.

Analysis of Results

In general, the first analysis should be conducted on those tasks not completed by a majority of the users by comparing the notes for each test from each observer and aggregating for each task the number of observers who deemed it not completed by the user.[63] However, a usability test rarely requires a lengthy analysis to identify enough major usability problems to keep the Web team busy. Instead, many usability problems observed during a test pass the "interocular test" (i.e., they hit you right between the eyes). Such an analysis usually can be done quickly and is one of the benefits of the usability testing method.

In order to determine what to analyze first, one should also consider the effort required to correct the problem and the likely impact of the usability problem on the success of the site. For example, if four of five users do not understand the term *holdings,* but three of five users are unable to complete a successful search, the latter usability problem would have a greater impact on the success of the Web site, and its analysis should be considered first.

However, one must be cautious when determining the likely impact of a problem. It is easy to dismiss a problem that seems minor on the surface and to conclude that the usability test resulted in "only a few, minute changes made to the design of the library's website,"[64] while ignoring that those minute changes may have affected the usability of the site at a much deeper level. As Dicks states, "[W]e can design tests that … do not [clearly] uncover larger, more global problems, especially related to how users conceived of the overall product and its processes, what their mental maps are."[65]

Minute changes, however, can have major effects on the usability of a product. At OCLC, for example, a bibliographic-only Web site service used the term *index* as the label for a link to the database index. This seemingly minute component of the UI resulted in the first 11 users looking instead for online full text, often until the moderator intervened and reminded them it was a bibliographic-only service, because "indexes are something at the back of a book." One minute problem created a major usability issue. This result highlights one of the advantages of usability testing: the capability to identify components that are clear for those familiar with the Web site, but have the potential to cause major problems for those unfamiliar with it.

One challenge of this method is that the usability data obtained through observation, user verbalizations, questionnaires, and interviews may be contradictory. In particular, the users' performance as recorded via observation may be poorer than indicated by the users' verbalizations, questionnaires, and interview answers. The effect is sometimes known as the "preference over performance" phenomenon.[66] Users often rate a site higher in preference or speak more favorably about a site than their actual performance would indicate. It is not unusual for users who clearly had major usability problems during the test to express very few negative evaluative comments during or after the test and/or to blame themselves for any difficulties they had completing a task. As such, it is imperative *not* to focus on such positive Web site comments as indicating a lack of major usability issues with the Web site. A user having problems with a task who states, "This is a nice Web site, so I must be doing something wrong" is actually expressing a *negative* comment about the Web site's usability.

Implementing the Results

The tests and analyses are of little value if they are not used to implement change in the actual Web site. Campbell suggests that establishing a time line and creating an action plan for implementing test results can increase the chances of integrating results-based changes that will become part of the final product.[67] However, time lines and action plans are often the responsibility solely of the Web team, whose schedule may not include a formal phase for applying the results of usability testing. To prevent this, the usability analyst can sometimes offer usability fixes in a post-test debriefing with the Web team after each test. These would be changes that could be put into operation quickly and easily, but would never formally be stated in an official project document.

To be most effective, a test report, or minimally, a summary of the report, should have an easy-to-understand format and contain a description of the Web site and of the users who tested it, and the findings of the Web site team. Long reports, especially those that include verbose descriptions of the test methodology and results, can be exasperating to designers, who want only the information needed to make changes to the Web site. Consequently, a test report that immediately presents two or three key observations often can be more valuable and effective in instituting Web site revisions than a long, detailed report with involved and time-consuming analyses such as a keystroke or best path analysis.

For example, the first page of an effective report should include a brief description of the product or Web site and the users, and three or four of the most frequently occurring problems identified during the test. It also is helpful to present a brief list of the positive results of the test on the first page to provide perspective to the reader about the extent of the usability problems, as well as to provide encouragement for the Web team. More detailed information about the tasks performed, the success with which the users completed the tasks, and any quantitative findings might then be presented in the remainder of the report.

A final and often underestimated feature of an effective test report is a short turnaround time (24 hours or less) between the completion of the tests and the delivery of a report. The longer a report takes, the more likely it is that members of the Web team will design and/or institute fixes to correct problems they believe occurred during the one or two usability tests they observed. This severely decreases the value of any usability analysis provided post hoc. In addition, since these fixes are instituted by those who unknowingly created the usability problems in the first place, the revisions may not be as effective at improving the usability of the Web site as those based on a Web team analysis of all the usability tests conducted.

Post-test Evaluation of Test Procedures

After all the testing and analyses are completed and delivered to the Web team, it can be helpful to evaluate the effectiveness of the usability test with them. Items that should be covered during this evaluation might include the following questions:

- Were the right questions asked?
- Were the tasks unbiased and clearly worded?
- Was there too much or too little intervention during the test?
- Could the testing environment be improved?

This evaluation provides the opportunity to identify any procedures or methods that were not effective and to make the necessary revisions to future usability tests.

New Techniques: Remote Testing

A fairly new way of conducting a usability test is by remote usability testing. In remote usability testing, the user is not in the same location as the test team, e.g., in a usability lab. In Thompson's study, the observer was in a room adjacent to the test location.[68] However, with technology available on the Internet, users could participate in a test anywhere in the world if a telephone and an Internet connection are available. This development dramatically increases the size of the potential pool of testers and enables users to do the evaluation in the more comfortable confines of their home or office instead of in a usability lab with several cameras directed at them or with an observer looking over their shoulder. Of course, the users' facial expressions and gestures usually cannot be seen in the remote usability testing environment, which can be a disadvantage.

Remote testing was done for the California State University at San Marcos (CSUSM) library Web site.[69] To identify problems with the current interface, users were observed doing research on the library Web site. Researchers also conducted focus group interviews, distributed questionnaires, and examined activity logs to "identify high-use areas of the existing website."[70] This information was used to prototype a new library Web site, which was tested for usability with a facilitator and observer. The observer was not in the same room as the user, but viewed the user's screen from another room via a screen viewer, such as Timbuktu, PC Anywhere, or LiveMeeting. Remote tests were conducted "because we felt a silent observer behind the user's shoulder would be intimidating."[71] However, the observer was introduced to the user prior to the test. Knowing that someone is watching from another room could be as intimidating as being watched from within the same room. Unlike the observer, the facilitator remained in the same room as the user to maintain a "friendly, interactive relationship with the user."[72]

Thompson identified a number of problems with the CSUMC library Web site. She reported that the most serious usability problems were those concerning terminology.[73] To correct the problem, some terminology could be changed, and the use of mouse rollovers could be expanded. Thompson notes that some problems were identified too late in the development cycle and could not be incorporated into the new Web site. Thompson also discussed other issues associated with remote testing, including techniques to capture user comments and to record screen images. She notes that remote testing over a networked connection also allows remote observation, providing developers and designers with the ability to view the testing on their computers without having to be in the same location as the facilitator.[74]

Examples of Usability Testing in Academic Libraries

Dickstein and Mills report one of the first studies to document extensive user involvement in the design of a library Web site.[75] They discuss a number of usability evaluation techniques that were used, outline the process, and identify the problems encountered. The goal was to redesign SABIO, the library gateway for students at the University of Arizona. A team of five librarians, one systems expert, and a graphic designer were involved. The team began with a heuristic review of the new design,[76] which was reviewed for deviations from user interface design guidelines identified in the literature. In addition, the team used the cognitive walkthrough technique,[77] where Web team members emulate expected usage patterns to identify potential problems. Card sorting also was used to evaluate how users would organize the numerous databases and CD-ROM products in the Web site.[78] In this method, 3×5 cards are labeled with each link to appear on the Web site. Users are then asked to group the cards into related piles, and then to group these related piles into related areas. The result can be used as the basis for the Web site's hierarchical organization.

These methods were followed by a series of usability tests. Dickstein and Mills note that librarians may have been reluctant to use usability testing because "they may presume that these tests are difficult to conduct, costly, and time consuming."[79] They demonstrate that this need not be the case. A total of nine iterations of testing, using between eight and twelve users per iteration, proved to be sufficient.

The results of the SABIO testing indicate that "initial attempts at screen design proved almost totally ineffective."[80] This result is the best reason to do usability testing. Indeed, if initial testing does not identify any usability problems that need to be corrected, the testing process itself should be reviewed for possible biases or flaws. The authors also note that the most common problem was the terminology used on the Web site. They state, "Some of the problems ... [were] caused by librarians expecting users to understand how library information is organized and ... the meaning of standard library terminology."[81] For example, Augustine and Greene state, "[Users] struggle to interpret *commonly used terminology* (e.g., 'Webcat')"[82] [emphasis added]. While *Web* and *Cat* may be terms commonly used by librarians, the term *Webcat* is unlikely to be a part of a user's everyday vocabulary. To correct this problem, Dickstein and Mills changed some of the library terminology and added graphics to the Web site.[83] The major revision included the addition of a series of clever help functions to the SABIO site. Subsequent studies have resulted in the availability of more user-centered library terminology that can be used on library Web sites.[84] The authors conclude by noting some of the lesser known values of usability testing. In particular, they note that "testing allows designers to settle disagreements and differences."[85]

Marill discusses the development by the National Library of Medicine (NLM) of the MedlinePlus user interface, released in October 1998.[86] Researchers conducted both a heuristic evaluation and a series of three usability test iterations. Participants were considered typical users of the Medline system and ranged in age from 20 to 60 plus, with a wide range of experience levels with computer systems, but no previous experience using MedlinePlus. Prior to the test, users read a description of the purpose and format of the test. As mentioned previously, they also were told to read the MedlinePlus "Selection Guidelines" and were provided up to five minutes to explore MedlinePlus and to ask any questions about the service before testing began. This procedure features an unusual amount of pretest exposure to the Web site and likely exceeds what a "typical" user would experience prior to using the Web site in the real world. Consequently, the extent to which the usability test results are applicable to the real world may be limited.

After testing was completed, Marill indicates a report was distributed that contained an executive summary, an overview of user demographics, key observations, the amount of time it took the users to complete each task, and the results of a post-test questionnaire. The use of a short executive summary is an important component of the report since it increases the chance that test results will actually be read by those who have the power to make changes. Marill's results support the need for a more visible search engine. They also suggest using graphics to attract users' attention and terminology that is comprehensible to users.[87] In conclusion, the author notes some general tips, such as maintaining neutrality by not using test administrators who are also on the development team.[88]

Chisman, Diller, and Walbridge extensively detail the usability evaluation procedures used on the Washington State University (WSU) libraries' Online Public Access Catalog (OPAC), Griffin.[89] The authors' goal was to test users' ease in understanding and navigating the Griffin Web site. A questionnaire was used to assess the 10 usability testers' level of experience (novice or expert) with OPACs in general, and with Griffin specifically. Of the seven users whose profiles were discussed in the paper, four used the library at least once a week. The initial WSU tests consisted of 45 questions. During the second iteration, the test administrators were more "willing to offer suggestions when participants ran into difficulty."[90] As noted earlier in this paper, offering such suggestions may make the user more at ease, but must be done with caution, as they can easily bias the results of the test.

The results of this study indicate that novices and experienced users did not differ in their ability to use Griffin. In addition, while most users knew how to navigate Griffin via the standard Web controls, they often did not understand basic library concepts and terminology. For example, users concluded, after one or two failed searches, that the library did not have the item, when the real problem was that the Web site's search engine did not recognize the search formats of the users. Similarly, when users were asked to determine if the library owned a particular article published in a specific volume and issue of the journal *Advertising Age*, they searched for the title of the article, while Griffin was programmed to search for the title of the serial. Users finally did search for the title of the serial, but "often discovered [it] by trial and error."[91]

This gap between what the Web site expects the user to do and what the user expects the Web site to understand has been labeled the *Gulf of Execution*.[92] It is one of the major design issues underlying the usability of any Web site: How do you get the site and the user to think the same way? While some believe the answer is for the Web site to think like the user, others, such as Vaughn and Callicott (discussed below), take the view that the onus is primarily on the user to adjust to the Web site.[93] Chisman, Diller, and Walbridge conclude by noting that one should "test early and often ... keep the tests narrow in focus ... debrief promptly after each test ... communicate findings to system developers."[94]

In Battleson, Booth, and Weintrop, the goal of usability testing was to change the user interface so the user could make more effective use of what the system already provided, rather than to determine how the system could be made easier to use. The ultimate goal was to "determine how effectively the libraries' web site 'worked' when used for library research by undergraduates ... with little or no experience using the site."[95] They developed a set of 11 questions/tasks based on the following three used in Dickstein and Mills:

- Do the university libraries own the book *Alias Grace*?
- Find an encyclopedia article about French wine.
- Does the libraries' Web site have a guide to doing research in computer science?

In the study, a scribe took notes while a moderator interacted with each user based on a formal script. The script instructed the moderator to emphasize to the user that there were no right and wrong answers and to intervene when users had completed the task. As has been noted previously, an alternative would have been to let users indicate when they felt the task was completed. The authors qualitatively analyzed what the users *did*, rather than what they *said* they did. This type of behavior analysis is valuable and is recommended for data analysis of usability tests. The authors conclude by stressing that "the importance of usability testing … to library websites cannot be understated [sic]."[96]

Fagan evaluated two EBSCO user interfaces.[97] The *Basic Search* interface was a single input box. The *Visual Search* interface used a circular style interface to Groxis's Grokker concept-mapping software.[98] The major research question to be evaluated was, "To what extent does Ebsco's basic search interface and visual search interface support student research?"[99]

Twelve students from James Madison University in Virginia participated in the usability test. An interesting feature of the methodology was the use of the codiscovery technique,[100] with 8 of the 12 students working in four groups of two for the evaluation. The remaining four students worked individually (i.e., in "groups" of one). This design was used to simulate the educational environment, which requires students to work in groups for various projects.[101] No student had been at the university more than 2.5 years, with the median being 1.5 years. Each of the eight user groups was given the same three tasks. (Occasionally, a fourth task was given, but only if time permitted, and only to the Basic Search group.) The tasks always were initiated with the Basic Search. The same three research tasks then were attempted with the Visual Search. However, the groups could choose a different topic to research if they desired. Unfortunately, since Basic Search always preceded Visual Search, it is impossible to determine if any improvement with the Visual Search interface could be attributed to a better interface or to the users' familiarity and knowledge of the Basic Search interface gained while initially completing the tasks.

The author did not use time to complete tasks as a measure. Fagan attributed this to the variable user-facilitator interaction time and to the fact that longer search times to come up with subtopics "could as easily be a sign of exploration and interested inquiry as it might be of frustration or failure."[102] However, the facilitator can control the interaction time with the user and impose deadlines for the tasks to decrease the probability of task-unrelated exploration by prefacing a task with the statement, "You have a paper due tomorrow and have just started today." These controls also can make the task more realistic for many students.

The findings indicate that users had difficulty with searches defaulting to phrase-searching and not the more typical Boolean AND searching, and that "during task 2 ... students did go past the first page of results."[103] This research contrasts with Jansen and Spink's finding that "73 percent of Web searchers only view the first results page."[104] However, the first sentence of Fagan's Task 2 encourages the students to "Spend a few minutes just looking through your results."[105] Perhaps without this artificial encouragement to spend time reviewing their results, users would not have reviewed their search results beyond the first page of those results. The study also reports that of the eight groups, four did better with Basic Search, two did equally well with both user interfaces, and only two did better with the Visual Search interface. The results indicate that students did better in the Basic Search condition in the quality of the subtopics they identified, the improvement of the chosen subtopic over the one originally selected, and the quality of the search results. The author concludes by stating, "If you take away one conclusion from this study, let it be this: Do not hesitate to try Visual Search with your users!"[106] However, this conclusion does not seem to be supported by the results of the study.

Manzari and Trinidad-Christensen used both a heuristic review and traditional usability testing to evaluate a prototype Web site.[107] The Web site was intended to be used by postgraduate library and information science (LIS) students at Long Island University. The evaluation began with a heuristic review by three faculty members and students with "expertise in Web-site design and human-computer interaction."[108] The review was exhaustive and not scenario-based. This protocol indicates that the evaluators were not asked to do a set of tasks, which is generally preferred to ensure the most important components of the user interface are evaluated.[109] The results of the review were a number of recommendations, although all reviewers "were in agreement that the Web site was well-designed."[110] A number of recommendations were to clarify terminology, e.g., to include the descriptor *library catalog* to explain the term *LIUCAT* instead of just *LIUCAT* as a menu label and to be consistent across screens, for example, to use the same menu options on each page instead of including only those options considered essential to each specific page.

The redesign resulting from the findings of the heuristic review was then subjected to a usability test. Ten students participated in the study, including nine master's degree–level students and one doctoral candidate, who was recruited at a later time. Users were given eight tasks that reflected "both the type of assignment a student might receive in class and the type of information they might seek on the LIS website on their own."[111] It is unclear how the type of assignments and user self-selected information was determined.

The results suggest that problems occurred mostly when "subjects left the LIS page to use a non-library science database located on the main Web site … [and] had problems getting back to the LIS site."[112] The authors attributed this to the design of the main Web site, since "no one expressed a preference for the design used by the main library Web site … the design of the LIS Web site was preferred over the main campus Web site by both the heuristic evaluators and the students in the usability test."[113] While this conclusion may be true, the preference versus performance phenomenon[114] suggests caution in accepting it in lieu of a usability evaluation of the main Web site. The authors concluded by noting, "The subjects barely read any of the site's text, so it can be difficult to make some points clearer."[115] However, this conclusion seems to assume that only through on-screen text can something be made clearer, whereas a more user-centered graphic and interactive design of the Web site might be equally effective.

Ascher, Lougee-Heimer, and Cunningham conducted a usability evaluation of the Web site for the health sciences library (HSL) at the New York Medical College (NYMC).[116] The purpose was to improve the usability of the Web site, but also to "provide the tools and a framework for conducting testing specific to the tasks identified as important by the health sciences faculty, students, residents, and fellows themselves."[117] Prior to the evaluation, a survey was distributed to 161 potential users who had responded to a variety of postings about the evaluation. The survey asked the users to report their level of experience using the Web site, to indicate their most common tasks when using the HSL Web site, and to identify their most frustrating tasks when using the Web site. The top five responses were used to develop five usability tasks. It is interesting to note that the most common task reported was at the same time the most frustrating—finding and viewing journal articles. From this group, nine participants were eventually selected who were considered representative of "various patron groups."[118]

Data collected during the sessions included audio, video, and key-stroke recordings, as well as notes taken by two observers. Tasks were considered completed when the user gave up or when the *observers* concluded that either a task was completed or a "reasonable amount of time had been exceeded."[119] As previously mentioned, it would be more informative for users to determine and indicate when a task is completed, either by verbalizing a success (e.g., "I am done with this task") or by showing behaviors clearly indicating failure (e.g., repeating actions that have already failed previously for the task).

The results indicated that users were very good at finding information about the library, such as hours of operation, and about the library's journals, such as a list of e-journal passwords. However, users were less successful retrieving articles about a topic (67% completion rate), and performed even more poorly using a citation to retrieve a specific article (44%). The authors concluded that the site needed to be more "Task oriented ... have headings such as *Find an Article* or *Find a book* rather than ... menu items such as *e-journal Portal* or *Databases*."[120] This result reinforces that of other studies that found that terminology, specifically the use of library jargon , e.g., *e-journal Portal*, is a frequent problem in library Web sites.

Wrubel and Schmidt conducted usability tests to compare two types of federated search systems.[121] *Quick Search* allowed users to select a database topic from a list of topics preselected by library staff. Users did not select individual databases in Quick Search. Alternatively, *Cross Search* allowed the user to again select a database topic area, but then also to select the individual databases to search within the topic. Eighteen students from four campuses in the University System of Maryland and Affiliated Institutions (USMAI) participated. All students completed tasks in both the Quick and Crossearch types. The tasks were based on sample test questions and research topics from actual courses in the USMAI system. The first task for each search type was identical for every user. However, the second task allowed the user to select one of several topic areas. It is not clear if the order of testing of each search type was randomly assigned, counterbalanced across users, or identical for each user. This design would be important as a means of avoiding carry-over learning from the first search type tested to the second search type tested.

Results indicated that overall users both preferred the Quick Search to the Cross Search user interface and performed better on it. However, users had difficulty with both search types, and surprisingly, their success rate did not improve as they worked more with each user interface. The authors concluded by noting that at least some of the difficulties encountered by users could be attributed to the poor response time for doing real-time metasearches, which can take significantly longer than other search services such as Google. However, the authors also noted that "discovering results from disparate resources can present ... usability challenges. Improving the design of search screens and the display of results lists would help increase students' success."[122]

From a usability evaluation viewpoint, Wrubel and Schmidt demonstrate what can be accomplished with a well-documented plan and sufficient time. They developed a coding scheme to categorize both verbal and nonverbal comments as well as screen actions. They also had three levels of task completeness (where overall completion was defined by the participants) and transcribed all audio from the 18 evaluations. Post-test interviews were extensive, as was the overall granularity of the data recorded.

The studies above are representative of the many library usability studies conducted. There is a large body of literature describing the use of this methodology in libraries.[123]

Cautions

Van Den Haak, De Jong, and Schellens utilized the think-aloud protocol, which is one of the primary techniques for acquiring usability information.[124] The test site was the online library catalog of the Vrije Universiteit in Amsterdam, the Netherlands. Users performed seven tasks written in the "find this, find that" format. The users were given no reason or explanation for performing the tasks. All users were novice users of the university's catalog, but had experience with other library catalogs. The users in the concurrent group were given the instruction to think aloud while performing the tasks and to pretend that the facilitator was not present. Users in the retrospective group were instructed to "simply carry out the tasks in silence."[125] Unfortunately, the exact instructions given to this group were not provided. Thus, it is not clear if the authors might have instructed the users that they would be asked to recollect their experience at the completion of the test. Such an instruction probably would have a major impact on the results of the study.

The results indicate that the two methods did not differ in the total number of problems detected, but they did differ in *how* problems were detected. The retrospective group revealed more problems through verbalizations after the test, while the concurrent group revealed more problems through observation of their behavior during the test. The researchers also report the most common finding in usability studies of library Web sites: "Terminology and data entry clearly presented most problems to the participants in both conditions."[126] In addition, users in the retrospective group completed significantly more tasks on average (47%) than those in the concurrent group (37%). The low rate of completion for both groups suggests the tasks were very difficult and may have imposed a high cognitive load, a situation in which the act of concurrent verbalization and the ability to complete a task may result in users expressing difficulty completing a task.[127]

Unfortunately, Van Den Haak, De Jong, and Schellens do not define how an incomplete task was determined, i.e., after a set time, when users seemed to give up, or based on an observer's evaluation.[128] As a consequence, the interpretation of this result is unclear. The authors conclude that "[t]he [retrospective method] … proved significantly more fruitful in revealing problems that were not observable, but could only be detected by means of verbalization."[129] This conclusion does raise the issue of whether a nonobservable problem is a problem at all. Most important in practical terms, trying to convince a Web site team to fix a problem that no one observed, even if a user mentioned it verbally, would be very difficult.

Vaughn and Callicott take a much less positive view of usability testing than the previously discussed studies. In their paper, "Broccoli Librarianship and Google-Bred Patrons, or What's Wrong with Usability Testing?" the authors question the use of usability testing to develop library Web sites. They cite definitions of ease of use and usefulness from Dicks: "Ease-of-use refers to efficiency, to how quickly we can use a product to complete tasks. Usefulness refers to … does it do what it is supposed to do? Is it usable at all? Does it work?"[130] Using these definitions, the authors suggest that changing the design of a Web site based solely on usability tests with the naive library user and a small set of tasks can result in systems that are not useful. They state, "This inability to measure site usefulness is ... an inherent and often overlooked limitation of usability testing."[131] According to the authors, tasks used in library Web site testing often also reflect a "linear pattern of questioning [that] is rarely the process by which research is actually conducted."[132]

They proceed with a discussion of a usability test of their library's Web site. They comment that the result of the testing was that "only a few, minute changes were made to the design of the libraries' website."[133] The authors conclude their analysis by indicating two types of problems were generally found, "poor web design and participant's lack of research skills."[134] As evidence of "poor research skills," they state:

> [Asked to] find a magazine or journal article about *The Great Gatsby* ... 8 of 15 users were unable to complete this task... . By watching and listening ... it was clear that when the terms 'magazine', 'journal' or 'article' did not appear on the libraries home page (but did in the tasks), their confidence to complete this task was lowered. This lack of confidence when it came to basic library function gave the authors pause.[135]

They conclude that "it is simply essential that researchers ... learn and understand the meaning, functions, and limitations of the catalog, indexes, and databases,"[136] i.e., that it is the user that needs to change, not the Web site design. In conclusion, Vaughn and Callicott argue:

> Hopefully, novice patrons will visit or call the reference desk, ask a question via email or engage in a virtual reference conversation ... but librarians must raise students to a rudimentary level of research skills so that they understand library terminology ... only then will library web site usability studies be truly effective.[137]

Students should have a basic understanding of fundamental research skills and how to use their library effectively. However, to assume that basic research skills entails an understanding of library terminology, or that using a library Web site effectively requires knowledge of such terminology, is questionable. The goal of a user is rarely to learn library terminology and organization so he or she can use a library Web site. Instead, the goal is to use the library Web site as a tool to reach their individual research goals. Like any tool, the site should allow users to do what they need to do as quickly as possible with minimum interference from, and knowledge about, the tool itself. Usability testing is one of the most effective ways to make the library web site such a tool, but only when its results are not used to determine how to change the user to accommodate the Web site, but rather when they are used to change the Web site "tool" to accommodate the user.

Conclusion

Building a Web site with the right functionality is only part of the development process. The Web site must meet the needs of its users. One method for testing and developing Web sites is to conduct usability evaluations. Although there are many methods of evaluating usability, this review discusses a single method—the usability test. Usability testing involves watching users try to do a set of predesignated tasks on the Web site, often commenting while they attempt the tasks.

Usability testing has been around for many years, at least since the 1964 study by Johnson.[138] The design of the Star interface at Xerox in the early 1980s is often credited with being the first use of user-centered design and usability evaluation for computer software. For the library community, the methodology is relatively new, often said to have begun in the mid-1990s with work at the University of Arizona and Washington State University.

A review of methods used also identifies a number of variations in usability testing. Most studies have at least one observer in the same room as the user, often to answer questions, to moderate the test, or simply to help the user relax. However, other tests have used remote testing where one or more observers are in another location, be that another room or another country. Some methods simply ask the user to find information or sources, while others provide scenarios or situations for the searches. Some studies have questioned the validity of common techniques such as the think-aloud protocol. Even the most commonly accepted purpose for usability testing—to test, change, and improve a Web site—has been questioned, suggesting that not only the Web site needs to be changed, but also the user.

The results of many library Web site usability studies converge on several key results. Foremost among these is that the most common usability problem with a library Web site is its terminology. Too often, this terminology reflects librarians' jargon rather than the language of the user. It is also important to continually question the current methods, looking for better ways to do usability testing. Van Den Haak, De Jong, and Schellens suggest that the common method of the talk-aloud approach, which requires the user to talk while doing tasks, has drawbacks of which the practitioner should be aware.[139] Vaughn and Callicott go one step further, questioning not only the classic usability testing methods, but suggesting that the usability problems identified by this method are usually not the result of a poorly designed Web site, but of a poorly designed user.[140]

Regardless of the method or viewpoint, the introduction of usability testing into the development of library Web sites is an effective, quick, and relatively inexpensive method of testing and refining Web sites based upon user behavior. This methodology also can identify topics for library information literacy programs, therefore influencing the content and design of these programs. Hopefully, the trends of increased usability evaluation and testing will continue as new technologies and innovations, such as Web 2.0, RSS (Really Simple Syndication), blogs, and wikis, are introduced into the construction of library Web sites. Regardless of the technology integrated into a library Web site, if a user cannot use it, it does not work.

References

1. Lorcan Dempsey, "The Owl of Minerva," Lorcan Dempsey's Weblog: On Libraries, Services and Networks, June 1, 2006, http://orweblog.oclc.org/archives/001035.html (accessed March 31, 2008).

2. Karen Calhoun, *The Changing Nature of the Catalog and Its Integration with Other Discovery Tools: Final Report* (Washington, DC: Library of Congress, 2006) http://www.loc.gov/catdir/calhoun-report-final.pdf (accessed March 31, 2008).

3. Brenda Dervin, Lynn S. Connaway, and Chandra Prabha, "Sense-Making the Information Confluence: The Whys and Hows of College and University User Satisficing of Information Needs," http://imlsosuoclcproject.jcomm.ohio-state.edu (accessed March 31 2008).

4. Lynn Silipigni Connaway, "Mountains, Valleys, and Pathways: Serials Users' Needs and Steps to Meet them, Part I: Identifying Serials Users; Needs: Preliminary Analysis of Focus Group and Semi-structured Interviews at

Colleges and Universities," *Serials Librarian* 52, no. 1/2 (2007): 226.

5. Susan L. Fowler, "Appendix B: Usability Tests," in *GUI Design Handbook* (New York: McGraw-Hill, 1998), 283–298 .

6. See Michael E. Casey and Laura C. Savastinuk, "Library 2.0: Service for the Next Generation Library," *Library Journal* 131, no. 14 (2006): 40–42; Beth Evans, "Your Space or MySpace?" *netConnect Library Journal* (October 15, 2006) http://www.libraryjournal.com/article/CA6375465.html (accessed March 31, 2008); Dorothea Salo, "Design Speaks," *netConnect Library Journal* (October 15, 2006) http://www.libraryjournal.com/article/CA6375469. html (accessed March 31, 2008).

7. Joseph S. Dumas and Janice Redish, *A Practical Guide to Usability Testing* (Norwood, NJ: Ablex Publishing Corporation, 1993), 283.

8. Elaina Norlin and C. M. Winters, *Usabilty Testing for Library Websites: A Hands-On Guide* (Chicago: American Library Association, 2002).

9. Ibid., 5.

10. ISO 9241-11, *Ergonomic Requirements for Office Work with Visual Display Terminals* (Geneva: International Organization for Standardization, 1988).

11. Alan Dix and others, *Human Computer Interaction* (Englewood Cliffs, NJ: Prentice-Hall, 1998).

12. Michael J. Prasse, "Evaluating Usability," in "People Count: User-Centered Interface Design" (panel session, American Library Association Annual Conference, Chicago, IL, July 6–12, 2000).

13. R. Stanley Dicks, "Mis-usability: On the Uses and Misuses of Usability Testing," in *Sigdoc 2002: Proceedings of the 20th Annual International Conference on Computer Documentation,* ed. Michael Priestly, 26–30 (New York: ACM Press, 2002).

14. Jeffrey Rubin, "Overview of Usability Testing," in *Handbook of Usability Testing: How to Plan, Design, and Conduct Effective Tests* (New York: Wiley, 1994), 31–46.

15. Nicole Campbell, "Conducting a Usability Study," in *Usability Assessment of Library-Related Web Sites: Methods and Case Studies* (Chicago: ALA Press, 2001), 13.

16. Ruth Dickstein and Vicki Mills, "Usability Testing at the University of Arizona Library: How to Let the Users in on the Design," *Information Technology and Libraries* 19, no. 3 (2000): 147.

17. Robert Virzi, "Refining the Test Phase of Usability Evaluation: How Many Subjects Is Enough?" *Human Factors* 34, no. 4 (1992): 457–486; Jared Spool and Will Schroeder, "Testing Web Sites: Five Users Is Nowhere Near Enough" (paper presented at Conference on Human Factors in Computing Systems, Seattle, WA, March 31–April 5, 2001).

18. Campbell, "Conducting a Usability Study," 11.

19. Prasse, "Evaluating Usability."

20. Campbell, "Conducting a Usability Study.".

21. David King, "The Mom-and-Pop Shop Approach to Usability Studies," *Computers in Libraries* 23, no. 1 (2003):12–15.

22. Peter G. Polson and others, "Cognitive Walkthroughs: A Method for Theory-Based Evaluation of User Interfaces," *International Journal of Man-Machine Studies*, 36, no. 5 (1992): 741–773.

23. Hugh Beyer and Karen Holtzblatt, *Contextual Design* (San Francisco: Morgan Kaufmann, 1998).

24. King, "Mom-and-Pop Shop," 13.

25. Ibid.

26. Christine Perfetti Landesman, Erik Ojakaar, and Jared Spool, "Do You Know What Your Users Do? New Techniques in Task Design," in *Proceedings of the 10th Annual Usability Professionals Conference (Las Vegas)*, (Chicago: Usability Professionals' Association, 2001), unp.

27. King, "Mom-and-Pop Shop," 14.

28. Janet Chisman, Karen Diller, and Sharon Walbridge, "Usability Testing: A Case Study," *College and Research Libraries* 60, no. 6 (1999): 554.

29. Ibid.

30. Debbie Vaughn and Burton Callicott, "Broccoli Librarianship and Google-Bred Patrons, or What's Wrong with Usability Testing?" *College and Undergraduate Libraries* 10, no. 2 (2003): 3.

31. Michael J. Prasse and R. Tigner, "The OCLC Usability Lab: Description and Methodology," in *13th National Online Meeting Proceedings—1992, New York, May 5–7, 1992*, ed. Martha L. Williams, 255–261 (Medford, NJ: Learned Information, 1992).

32. John Whiteside and Karen Holtzblatt, "Usability Engineering: Our Experience and Evolution," in *Handbook of Human-Computer Interaction,* ed. Martin Helander, 791–817 (Amsterdam: North-Holland, 1988).

33. K. Anders Ericsson and Herbert Alexander Simon, *Protocol Analysis: Verbal Reports as Data* (Cambridge, MA: MIT Press, 1984).

34 Michael J. Prasse, "Snapshot Problem Analysis, Dewey for Windows," OCLC internal report, October 1995.

35. William L. Hays, *Statistics for Psychologists* (New York: Holt, Rinehart and Winston, 1963).

36. Brenda Battleson, Austin Booth, and Jane Weintrop, "Usability Testing of an Academic Library Website: A Case Study," *Journal of Academic Librarianship* 27, no. 3 (2001): 188–198.

37. King, "Mom-and-Pop Shop."

38. Dumas and Redish, *Practical Guide,* 299.

39. Jennifer L. Marill, "Designing a Usable Health Information Portal: The MedlinePlus Experience from the National Library of Medicine," in *Usability Assessment of Library-Related Web Sites: Methods and Case Studies,* ed. Nicole

Campbell, 100–108 (Chicago: ALA Press, 2001).

40. Prasse and Tigner, "OCLC Usability Lab."

41. Michael J. Prasse, "The Politics of Usability" (invited presentation, Internet Librarian 2001 conference, Pasadena, CA, November 6–8, 2001).

42. Campbell, "Conducting a Usability Study," 14.

43. In fact, the OCLC Usability Lab's motto, which is posted in full view of users when they enter the lab, is "The user is always right."

44. Chisman, Diller, and Walbridge, "Usability Testing."

45. See Ericsson and Simon, *Protocol Analysis*.

46. Elizabeth Loftus, *Eyewitness Testimony* (Cambridge, MA: Harvard University Press, 1979).

47. Julie H. Birns and others, "Getting the Whole Picture: Collecting Usability Data Using Two Methods: Concurrent Think Aloud and Retrospective Probing" (paper presented at the 11th Annual Meeting of the Usability Professionals' Association, Orlando, FL, July 8–12, 2002).

48. Maaike J. Van Den Haak, Menno D. T. De Jong, and Peter Jan Schellens, "Retrospective vs. Current Think-Aloud Protocols: Testing the Usability of an Online Library Catalogue," *Behavior and Information Technology* 55, no. 5 (2003): 339–351.

49. Marill, "Designing a Usable Health Information Portal."

50. Battleson, Booth, and Weintrop, "Usability Testing of an Academic Library Website."

51. Prasse and Tigner, "OCLC Usability Lab."

52. Marill, "Designing a Usable Health Information Portal."

53. John M. Carroll and others, "The Minimal Manual." *Human-Computer Interaction*. 3, no. 2 (1987): 123–153.

54. Michael J. Prasse, "The User under the Lens: Analysis and Test Methods," in *Proceedings of the BiblioStar '99 Conference (Milan, Italy)*, ed. Ornelia Foglieni. 80–90 (Milano: Editrice Bibliografica, 2000).

55. Chisman, Diller, and Walbridge, "Usability Testing," 556.

56. Marill, "Designing a Usable Health Information Portal."

57. Vaughn and Callicott, "Broccoli Librarianship."

58. Loftus, *Eyewitness Testimony.*

59. Vaughn and Callicott, "Broccoli Librarianship," 7.

60. Ross Teague, Katherine De Jesus, and Marcos Nunes-Ueno, "Concurrent vs. Post-Task Usability Test Ratings," in *Conference on Human Factors in Computing Systems Seattle, WA*, ed. M. M. Tremaine, 289–290 (New York: ACM Press, 2001).

61. Marill, "Designing a Usable Health Information Portal," 107.

62. Campbell, "Conducting a Usability Study."

63. King, "Mom-and-Pop Shop."

64. Vaughn and Callicott, "Broccoli Librarianship," 7.

65. Dicks, "Mis-usability," 28.

66. As noted by John M. Booker, C. M. Chewar, and D. Scott McCrickard, "Usability Testing of Notification Interfaces: Are We Focused on the Best Metrics?" in *Conference Proceedings of the 42nd Annual ACM Southeast Regional Conference, Huntsville, Alabama*, ed. Seong-Moo Yoo and Letha H. Etzkorn 128–133 (New York: ACM Press, 2004).

67. Campbell, "Conducting a Usability Study."

68. Susan M. Thompson, "Remote Observation Strategies for Usability Testing: Redesigning the Web Site at California State University, San Marcos," *Information Technology and Libraries* 22, no. 1 (2003): 22–31.

69. Ibid.

70. Ibid., 25.

71. Ibid., 26.

72. Ibid., 24.

73. This was also among the findings of King, "Mom-and-Pop Shop."

74. Thompson, "Remote Observation Strategies," 31.

75. Dickstein and Mills, "Usability Testing."

76. See Jakob Nielsen, "Heuristic Evaluation," in *Usability Inspection Methods*, ed. Jakob Nielsen and Robert L. Mack, 25–62 (New York: John Wiley and Sons, 1994).

77. Polson and others, "Cognitive Walkthroughs."

78. Gerald L. Loshe and others, "Classifying Graphical Information," *Behaviour and Information Technology* 10, no. 5 (1991): 419–436.

79. Dickstein and Mills, "Usability Testing," 147.

80. Ibid., 148.

81. Ibid.

82. Susan Augustine and Courtney Greene, "Discovering How Students Search a Library Web Site: A Usability Case Study," *College and Research Libraries* 63, no. 4 (2002): 360. Emphasis added.

83. Dickstein and Mills, "Usability Testing."

84. See John Kupersmith, "Library Terms Evaluated in Usability Tests and Other Studies," updated June 2, 2006, John Kupersmith's Webspace, http://www.jkup.net/terms-studies.html (accessed March 31, 2008), for a good summary.

85. Dickstein and Mills, "Usability Testing," 149.

86. Marill, "Designing a Usable Health Information Portal."

87. Ibid., 106.

88. Ibid., 107.

89. Chisman, Diller, and Walbridge, "Usability Testing."

90. Ibid., 554.

91. Ibid.

92. Donald A. Norman, and Steven W. Draper, *User Centered System Design: New Perspectives on Human-Computer Interaction* (Hillsdale, NJ: Erlbaum, 1986).

93. Vaughn and Callicott, "Broccoli Librarianship," 13, 15.

94. Chisman, Diller, and Walbridge, "Usability Testing," 559.

95. Battleson, Booth, and Weintrop, "Usability Testing," 190.

96. Ibid., 197.

97. Jody Condit Fagan, "Usability Testing of a Large, Multi-Disciplinary Library Database: Basic Search and Visual Search," *Information Technology and Libraries* 25, no. 3 (2006): 140–150.

98. Groxis, Inc., "Groxis and EBSCO Publishing Partner to Provide Visual Search Technology," March 14, 2006, Grokker News & Events, www.groxis.com/service/grokker/pr29.html (accessed March 31, 2008).

99. Fagan, "Usability Testing," 141.

100. Sue Kennedy, "Using Video in the BNR Usability Lab," *SIGCHI Bulletin* 21, no. 2 (1989): 92–95.

101. Fagan, "Usability Testing."

102. Ibid., 141.

103. Ibid., 143.

104. Bernard J. Jansen and Amanda Spink, "An Analysis of Web Documents Retrieved and Viewed," *Proceedings of the 4th International Conference on Internet Computing (Las Vegas, 2003)*, ed. H. R. Arabnia and Y. Mun, 67 (Athens, GA: CSREA Press, 2003).

105. Fagan, "Usability Testing," 143.

106. Ibid., 149.

107. Laura Manzari and Jeremiah Trinidad-Christensen, "User-Centered Design of a Web Site for Library and Information Science," *Information Technology and Libraries* 25, no. 3 (2006): 163–169.

108. Ibid., 164.

109. UsabilityNet, "Heuristic Evaluation," 2006, UsabilityNet Web site, www.usabilitynet.org/tools/expertheuristic.htm (accessed March 31, 2008).

110. Manzari and Trinidad-Christensen, "User-Centered Design," 164.

111. Ibid., 166.

112. Ibid., 167.

113. Ibid.

114. Booker, Chewar, and McCrickard, "Usability Testing."

115. Manzari and Trinidad-Christensen, "User-Centered Design," 168.

116. Marie T. Ascher, Haldor Lougee-Heimer, and Diana J. Cunningham, "Approaching Usability: Study of an Academic Health Sciences Library Web Site," *Medical Reference Services Quarterly* 26 no. 2 (2007): 37–53.

117. Ibid., 39.

118. Ibid., 44.

119. Ibid., 45.

120. Ibid., 50.

121. Laura Wrubel and Kari Schmidt, "Usability Testing of a Metasearch Interface: A Case Study," *College and Research Libraries* 68, no. 4 (2007): 292–311.

122. Ibid., 296.

123. Maryellen Allen, "A Case Study of the Usability Testing Of the University of South Florida's Virtual Library Interface Design," *Online Information Review* 26, no. 1 (2002): 40–53; Steve Brantley, Annie Armstrong, and Krystal M. Lewis, "Usability Testing of a Customizable Library Web Portal," *College and Research Libraries* 67, no. 2 (2006): 146–163; Frank Cervone, "What We've Learned from Doing Usability Testing on OpenURL Resolvers and Federated Search Engines," *Computers in Libraries* 25, no. 9 (2005): 10–14; Barbara J. Cockrell and Elaine Anderson Jayne, "How Do I Find an Article? Insights from a Web Usability Study," *Journal of Academic Librarianship* 28, no. 3 (2002): 122–132; Susan Goodwin, "Using Screen Capture Software for Web Site Usability and Redesign Buy-In," *Library Hi Tech* 23, no. 4 (2005): 610–621; John-Bauer Graham, Jodi Poe, and Kimberly Weatherford, "Functional by Design: A Comparative Study to Determine the Usability and Functionality of One Library's Web Site," *Technical Services Quarterly* 21, no. 2 (2003): 33–49; Sarah J. Hammill, "Usability Testing at Florida International University Libraries: What We Learned," *E-JASL* 4, no. 1 (2003), http://southernlibrarianship.icaap.org/content/v04n01/Hammill_s01.htm (accessed March 31, 2008); Judy Jeng, "Usability Assessment of Academic Digital Libraries: Effectiveness, Efficiency, Satisfaction, and Learnability," *Libri* 55, no. 2 (2005): 96–121; Judy Jeng, "What Is Usability in the Context of the Digital Library and How Can It Be Measured?" *Information Technology and Libraries* 24, no. 2 (June 2005): 47–56; Janice Krueger, Ron L. Ray, and Lorrie Knight, "Applying Web Usability Techniques to Assess Student Awareness of Library Web Resources," *Journal of Academic Librarianship* 30, no. 4 (2004): 285–293; Alexei Oulanov and Edmund J. Y. Pajarillo, "CUNY + Web: Usability Study of the Web-Based GUI Version of Bibliographic Database of the City University of New York (CUNY)," *Electronic Library* 20, no. 6 (2002): 481–487; Lutisoor Salisbury and Emilio Noguera, "Usability of E-Journals and Preference for the Virtual Periodicals Room: A Survey of Mathematics Faculty and Graduate Students," *E-JASL* 4, no. 2 (2003), http://southernlibrarianship.icaap.org/content/v04n03/Salisbury_l01.htm (accessed March 31, 2008); Elizabeth Stephan, Daisy T. Cheng, and Lauren M. Young, "A Usability Survey at the University of Mississippi Libraries for the Improvement of the Library Home Page," *Journal of Academic Librarianship* 32, no. 1 (2006): 35–51; Rom Stewart, Vivek Narenda, and Axel Scmetzke, "Accessibility and Usability of Online Library Databases," *Library Hi Tech* 23, no. 2 (2005): 265–286; Beth Thomsett-Scott, "Providing a Complete Menu: Using Comparative Usability in a Home Page Usability Study," *Technical Services*

Quarterly 23, no. 2 (2005): 33–47; Beth Thomsett-Scott, "Yeah, I Found It! Performing Web Site Usability Testing to Ensure That Off-Campus Students Can Find the Information They Need," *Journal of Library Administration* 41, no. 3 (2004): 471–483; Tiffini Anne Travis and Elaina Norlin, "Testing the Competition: Usability of Commercial Information Sites Compared with Academic Library Web Sites," *College and Research Libraries* 63, no. 5 (2002): 433–448.

124. Van Den Haak, De Jong, and Schellens, "Retrospective vs. Current Think-Aloud Protocols."

125. Ibid., 344.

126. Ibid., 345.

127. E. S. Johnson, "An Information Processing Model of One Kind of Problem Solving," *Psychological Monographs* 78, no. 4 (1964).

128. Van Den Haak, De Jong, and Schellens, "Retrospective vs. Current Think-Aloud Protocols."

129. Ibid., 349.

130. Dicks, "Mis-usability," 27.

131. Vaughn and Callicott, "Broccoli Librarianship," 6.

132. Ibid., 3.

133. Ibid., 7.

134. Ibid.

135. Ibid., 9.

136. Ibid., 13.

137. Ibid., 16.

138. Johnson, "Information Processing Model."

139. Van Den Haak, De Jong, and Schellens, "Retrospective vs. Current Think-Aloud Protocols."

140. Vaughn and Callicott, "Broccoli Librarianship."

Acknowledgement

The authors would like to thank Timothy J. Dickey, Ph.D., Postdoctoral Researcher at OCLC Programs and Research, for his assistance in preparing this chapter for publication.

Measuring the Quality of Library Service through LibQUAL+*

Martha Kyrillidou, Colleen Cook, and S. Shyam Sunder Rao

A review of the research on the concept of library service quality since 1990 reveals the rapid expansion and application of LibQUAL+ in academic libraries. LibQUAL+, a rigorously tested protocol, developed through a partnership between the Association of Research Libraries (ARL) and Texas A&M University Libraries, has been applied to more than 1,000 libraries between 2000 and 2007. This chapter examines applications of measuring library service quality across institutions and cultures. The authors present a review both of published articles that document how libraries have used LibQUAL+, as well as of library Web sites that demonstrate the local use of these results. The chapter raises questions about collaboration and standardization for improving library services across institutional and political boundaries on the basis of sound assessment and evidence-based methods.

Introduction

Library evaluation has a rich tradition, which Lancaster has documented extensively through the numerous studies undertaken for service-specific operations and specific functional areas.[1] Lancaster attempted to offer a theoretical framework of evaluation that links evaluation to the five laws of Ranganathan: (1) books are for use, (2) every reader his book, (3) every book its reader, (4) save the time of the user, and (5) the library is a growing organism.[2] In many respects, all five laws place a strong emphasis on the user approaches that have dominated the evaluation of library service quality from the 1990s.

Historically, libraries have measured their performance with the traditional input measures of collections, staffing, and expenditures.[3] Decades of descriptive data have been collected for academic and research libraries and published as the annual *ARL Statistics* and ACRL's *Academic Library Trends and Statistics*.[4] In the early 1980s, academic libraries began to place more emphasis on output measures and started collecting evidence on the number of service transactions, such as circulation and reference and

---

LibQual+ is a registered trademark of the Association of Research Libraries

interlibrary loans. Researchers propose that the library can be described in terms of both input and output measures as augmented indicators of library quality and impact:[5] "Analysis of the ARL Statistics data set showed that there was a relationship between the ARL Index and descriptive service measures; between the number of undergraduate students and services; and between instructional presentations and operating expenditures."[6] Pritchard acknowledges that input and output metrics are limited:

> The measurement of quality will come back to the questions of who are the users, what are the inputs, what are the outputs, do we produce the outputs in a way that meets the needs of the users, and what do those outputs contribute to the productivity and accomplishments of those users? The questions are not new, but the object we are measuring has changed in many dimensions.[7]

The concept of library service quality resonated in top administrative circles as a driving force for reshaping organizations tied to rapidly changing cultural and historical mandates that are magnified by technological innovation and increased competition for scarce resources.[8] Library service quality captured the imagination of librarians by focusing squarely on the library user. A series of OCLC reports documented the changing information-seeking user behavior patterns in a pragmatic wake-up call:

> College students are more aware of and use libraries' information resources more than other survey respondents. In addition, the more educated the respondents, the more they continue to use libraries after graduation. Awareness does not always translate into high usage. Overall, respondents have positive, if outdated, views of the 'library.' Younger respondents—teenagers and young adults—do not express positive associations as frequently.[9]

Results from another recently released study indicate that use of the library is highly related to the use of the Internet—information-rich people tend to use the multiplicity of resources available to them.[10]

A landmark publication on *Measuring Academic Library Performance: A Practical Approach* emphasized user-based assessment by providing an evaluation framework widely adopted by many libraries that were engaging in local user-based assessment efforts.[11] By the end of the 1990s, *Assessing Service Quality: Satisfying the Expectations of Library Customers* provided a thorough overview of the research and the theoretical and practical aspects of understanding service quality evaluation in libraries.[12] Leading researchers in the services marketing field influenced Hernon and Altman's work and also synthesized the library studies that had their basis in this field.[13]

Defining Service Quality

Business leaders define service quality as "the manner in which service is provided as it influences the degree of satisfaction with a good or service."[14] Service quality has roots in the total quality management (TQM) movement. In the library field, "service quality is typically defined in terms of gap analysis, or the gap between customers' expectations in general (for an ideal library and its services) and those perceptions relating to the particular library and its services."[15]

The emphasis on improving services is tied closely to the notion of organizational performance. The Balanced Scorecard (BSC)[16] is another framework that examines the organization from four perspectives: User, Finance, Internal Processes, and Learning and the Future.[17] The BSC provides another impetus for viewing organizational performance with a distinct emphasis on the user and the way the user experiences the quality of the services delivered. Both gap theory and the BSC have influenced the management of libraries in recent years and have shaped the ways in which libraries are describing and measuring organizational performance.

Understanding the needs and psychology of current users is an important element for generating and using customer-based data for service improvements and for engaging in evidence-based decision making. *Quality* is ultimately something personal, subjective, and distinct for each person and is shaped by prior experiences, word of mouth, and personal interactions. In the marketing services field, the SERVQUAL tool was developed to measure the gap between customer expectations and perceptions in for-profit service industries. A conceptual model that was tested in terms of both what is measured and how it is measured provided a robust basis on which libraries could experiment. The SERVQUAL instrument measures the following five dimensions of service quality: (1) tangibles—appearance of physical facilities, equipment, personnel, and communication materials, (2) reliability—ability to perform the promised service dependably and accurately, (3) responsiveness—willingness to help customers and provide prompt service, (4) assurance—knowledge and courtesy of employees and their ability to convey trust and confidence, and (5) empathy—caring, individualized attention the firm provides its customers.[18]

This framework was modified and tested in libraries across institutions and also in service-specific operations in single libraries. The basic SERVQUAL protocol is composed of 22 questions within the dimensions listed above. An important element of the SERVQUAL design is how these concepts are measured. In applying gap theory, or expectation confirmation-disconfirmation theory, the researchers developed and tested a variety of concepts and concluded that the best way to measure these concepts is in terms of both expectations and perceptions. Furthermore, there are two sets of expectations: minimum expectations and desired expectations. The area between minimum and desired expectations is the zone of tolerance. For the most part, the score on the organizational performance will fall within the zone of tolerance, though it is conceptually possible for performance to exceed desired expectations or fall below minimum expectations. The difference between perceptions and desired expectation is the service superiority gap, and the difference between perceptions and minimum expectations is the service adequacy gap.

The gap model in satisfaction assessment has been criticized from a number of different perspectives, which were briefly summarized by Roszkowski, Baky, and Jones:

- If after receiving the service, a customer experiences a discrepancy between a desired and an actual level of service, future expectations will probably be revised to be closer to the actual (perceived) performance.
- When expectations are assessed after an experience has occurred, as is the case with the SERVQUAL and the LibQUAL+, they are subject to contamination by the experience itself.
- Rarely do people rate the actual experience as higher than the desired level.
- Expectations are based on prior experiences with a particular service. People often have a difficult time formulating their expectations if they are novices to the given experience and may therefore assign an arbitrary or unrealistic rating to an expectation.

- There are statistical concerns with using a gap score because difference scores are notoriously unreliable.[19]

Nonetheless, library researchers have deployed gap theory successfully in assessing library services in an institution-wide perspective.[20] Other studies have explored whether disconfirmation theory can explain satisfaction formation processes in library users.[21] In one of these studies, "both library users' needs and expectations are investigated as disconfirmation standards. Overall library user satisfaction is predicted [and shown] to be a function of two independent sources: satisfaction with the information product received and satisfaction with the information system and library services used to retrieve the information product."[22]

Nitecki, in *Advances in Librarianship* and in *The Encyclopedia of Library and Information Science*, has published two thorough reviews of the service quality literature in libraries.[23] The need to move beyond the theoretical frameworks into implementing practical and effective measurements of user satisfaction has also been emphasized by library administrators.[24] More recent literature reviews attempt to examine service quality from a broader perspective, focusing on methods and models rather than the quality of the services. This tack has been an effort to incorporate objective approaches and place them within a program evaluation framework.[25]

A thorough review of the SERVQUAL literature was published by Heath and Cook in *The Encyclopedia of Library and Information Science* with an explanation of the elements that LibQUAL+ used from the gap theory model. Many of the user studies increasingly evaluate both physical and electronic library services, and many also address only electronic use. Troll reviewed the issues related to usage and usability assessment. Also, Tenopir completed a review of the use and user studies of electronic library resources soon after Troll's study; the Council on Library and Information Resources published both studies.[26]

Emergence and Refinement of LibQUAL

LibQUAL+ was initiated in 2000 as an experimental project of benchmarking perceptions of library service quality across 13 ARL libraries. It was created through collaboration between ARL and Texas A&M University, and both quantitative and qualitative methods were applied rigorously in an iterative fashion.[27] An early groundbreaking qualitative study reporting the results of the interviews that grounded the LibQUAL+ instrument was reported in a special issue of *Library Trends*.[28] This special issue published papers from of a symposium on measuring library service quality organized by ARL in 2000, with experts invited from all over the world.[29]

In parallel, a thorough quantitative study reported the results of the dimensionality of the first LibQUAL+ implementation (Figure 1) across the initial cohort of a dozen ARL libraries that implemented LibQUAL+.[30] These two pieces were the first two articles that reported a thorough iterative process between qualitative and quantitative methods for the development and refinement of LibQUAL+.

Figure 1. Dimensions

2000	2001	2002	2003-2006
41 items	56 items	25 items	22 items
Affect of Service	Affect of Service	Service Affect	Service Affect
Library as Place	Library as Place	Library as Place	Library as Place
Reliability	Reliability	Personal Control	Information Control
Provision of Physical Collections	Self-Reliance	Information Access	
Access to Information	Access to Information		

One of the recurrent themes in the library literature of the 1990s is the validation of dimensions measured by SERVQUAL. Calvert conducted a crosscultural study across China and New Zealand and reported that three common dimensions surfaced between these widely divergent populations: (1) access to collections, (2) the reliability and trustworthiness of services, and (3) physical space.[31] Calvert's dimensions were an early evocation of the three dimensions LibQUAL+ ultimately measured in 2003.

Issues related to the differences between the concepts of satisfaction and service quality also were explored in the articles presented at the ARL symposium.[32] For some survey researchers, the difference between satisfaction and service quality is hair-splitting and inconsequential. Others place stronger emphasis on the distinction between the immediate affective aspects of satisfaction and the more cognitive and long-term aspects of service quality expectations and perceptions. Researchers also studied the relationship between affective states and actual behavioral aspects, finding that the use of libraries relates to positive affect.[33]

In examining some of the performance measurement approaches used in Europe, two reports on measuring library service quality were presented at the ARL symposium. One of the reports focused on practices in the United Kingdom, and the other one explored practices in Germany. Issues of satisfaction and service quality measurement have a strong research and empirical base in the United Kingdom, as UK higher education institutions have become more involved in the quality audit processes established for academic institutions.[34] Research reporting the state of affairs in Germany indicated a stronger emphasis on objective and descriptive measures of library performance, focusing on efficiency aspects rather than the more psychologically "soft" aspects of user satisfaction and service quality expectations.[35]

LibQUAL+ is one of 11 ways of listening to users, called a *total market survey*. As Berry explained, "When well-designed and executed total market surveys provide a range of information unmatched by any other method.... A critical facet of total market surveys (and the reason for using the word *total*) is the measurement of competitors' service quality. This [also] requires using non-customers in the sample to rate the service of their suppliers." Although (1) measuring perceptions of both users and nonusers and (2) collecting perceptions data with regard to peer institutions can provide important insights, Berry recommended using multiple listening methods and emphasized that "ongoing data collection ... is a necessity. Transactional surveys, total market surveys, and employee research should always be included."[36]

Two of the libraries implementing LibQUAL+ during the initial formative years of 2000–2001, University of Arizona and University of Washington, also reported on their local organizational models and methods regarding user satisfaction measurement and how the local efforts complemented the total market survey perspective that LibQUAL+ was establishing.[37] From the very beginning, the point that LibQUAL+ is only one measure among the many tools and methods that libraries need to deploy was established by the practitioners in the early cohort.

Trends and Impact of LibQUAL+

Beginning in the1990s, the ground was fertile for building a rich literature on library service quality.[38] The developing of LibQUAL+ as a total market survey for measuring library service quality led to increased implementation.[39] LibQUAL+ has been applied to more than 1,000 libraries—primarily college and university libraries—between 2000 and 2007. LibQUAL+ initiated at least three kinds of partnerships: one between ARL and Texas A&M, a second among all the participating libraries and their staffs, and a third among the hundreds of thousands of users who have provided their valuable feedback over the years.[40] Has library service quality improved as a result of this work over the last two decades? As with every evaluative question, the operative question is "Compared to what?" The major trends and impact of LibQUAL+ will be presented through a review of the scholarly research.

Spurred by funding from Fund for the Improvement of Post-Secondary Education (FIPSE), LibQUAL+ grew rapidly, and by 2002, the LibQUAL+ Web-based protocol was completed by 20,416 participants representing 43 universities. A study examining the reliability of these scores and the dimensions underlying user perception showed that a shorter protocol could demonstrate very good reliability and that there were four basic dimensions of library service quality: *Affect of Service, Personal Control, Access to Information,* and *Library as Place.* The study concluded:

> Large collections do not, in and of themselves, insure that library users always have positive service experiences. Thus, librarians interested in improving service quality need tools to help them benchmark current user perceptions, identify needed areas of improvement, and locate peer institutions obtaining more favorable outcomes.... . LibQUAL+® satisfies the major reasons for conducting total market surveys. First, non-local information can reveal how well other libraries perform services and can provide a basis for comparison. Secondly, exemplary libraries can be identified as models for service improvement planning. Finally, total market surveys permit performance tracking over time. Systematic listening to users improves decision making in allocation of scarce resources.[41]

Additional research from the over 20,000 respondents showed that score norms could be developed, and such norm tables could help libraries interpret their scores with respect to typical profiles at other universities. Norms were developed for both *perceived* service scores and *gap* scores (i.e., perceived performance minus minimally acceptable performance). Norms such as these assist library managers in decision making by identifying (1) specific areas for needed improvement, (2) specific areas of needed additional service quality information (e.g., focus groups), and (3) peer institutions from which superior service practices can be modeled.[42] Recent research on the stability of the norms has shown that LibQUAL+ norms are remarkably stable across cohorts and time, so libraries that compare their institutional scores against group scores should be relatively certain that they are using a robust baseline.[43]

LibQUAL+ data were further mined to answer the following questions:

- How well do LibQUAL+ subscale (i.e., Service Affect, Library as Place, Personal Control, and Information Access) and total scores correlate with external validity scores (e.g., user ratings of service and satisfaction)?
- Which of the 25 LibQUAL+ item scores most differentiate the 43 institutional affiliations of the 20,416 study participants?
- Do mean ratings of perceived library service quality, as measured by LibQUAL+ T scores, differ with frequency of library use?
- Do mean ratings of perceived library service quality, as measured by LibQUAL+ total T scores, differ across user types (e.g., faculty members, graduate students)?
- To what extent are institutional mean LibQUAL+ subscale and total scores correlated with ARL Membership Criteria Index scores of the 35 participating libraries belonging to ARL?[44]

It was found that LibQUAL+ subscale and total scores correlated highly with satisfaction scores in two independent subsamples. As expected, respondents who reported never using the library systematically rated services lower than did other users. Also as expected, LibQUAL+ mean scores—intended primarily to measure perceived service quality—correlated less with institutional ARL Index scores. The relation of institutional characteristics and scores of service quality were explored in groups of libraries beyond the ARL member libraries.[45] Service quality indices, especially as measured by the service affect dimension, appear to have a slightly inverse relation to collection investments, reflecting the higher expectations and harder-to-meet demands of the research library user.

As a result of the iterative approach of applying qualitative and quantitative methods, the LibQUAL+ dimensions have been crystallized in measuring three essential aspects of library service quality: Affect of Service, Library as Place, and Information Control (Figure 2) after the 2003 LibQUAL+ implementation. That year, among the 300 participating libraries, a group of UK institutions joined the project;[46] a comparison was conducted between LibQUAL+ and other protocols used in the United Kingdom, such as the SCONUL Template for User Satisfaction Surveys and the Priority Research analysis service. Reliability and validity analysis of the UK results also show that the program provides useful evidence for improving service quality in that context. Furthermore, this study affirmed that the Access to Information and Personal Control dimensions are collapsed into an Information Control dimension. Users increasingly fail to distinguish between content and access mechanisms. These findings were confirmed by the results of the French language experience of applying LibQUAL+ in the French Canadian environment.[47] The question of whether the French translation produced scores equivalent to the English versions of the instrument (British and American English) was

Figure 2. Dimensions of Library Service Quality

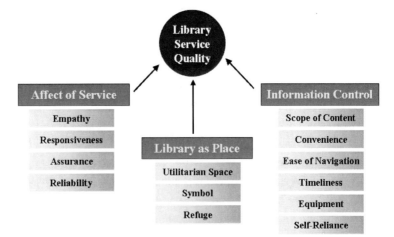

answered affirmatively. The process of validation provided confidence that the versions of the instrument are culturally relevant in the target language and conceptually equivalent to the original.

The protocol has since continued to expand internationally, followed with careful context-sensitive studies that inform its applicability to new environments. For example, Kyrillidou and Persson documented issues related to a Swedish implementation.[48] By 2008, the protocol was translated in 14 different languages and used in 17 different countries. Research regarding LibQUAL has appeared in many different languages describing aspects of the implementation and the lessons learned in new environments as well as relating the Anglo-American experience to non-English-speaking audiences.[49] In a recent study, the reliability of the scores was explored across hospital libraries in the United Kingdom and in the United States and at academic health science libraries in the United States. The findings revealed that the scores have high reliability coefficients in all these different settings.[50]

A set of important questions in the protocol ask about use of library premises, of library Web site, and of search engines like Google. The data have consistently showed the increasing dominance of Google and other search engines since 2000. During the 2006 library conference in Bielefeld, Anurag Acharya, principal engineer at Google Inc. and developer of Google Scholar, used LibQUAL+ data to demonstrate how often search engines like Google are used.

A detailed analysis of three years of data looked closely at the on premises versus Google-like information gateway usage patterns. Using LibQUAL+ data provided by 295,355 of the participants who completed the LibQUAL+ survey in 2003, 2004, and 2005, three research questions were addressed. First, what differences, if any, have occurred across time in the use by (a) undergraduates, (b) graduate students/postgraduates, and (c) faculty of on-premises library information resources versus non-library information gateways such as Google? Second, what differences, if any, have occurred across international regions in the use by (a) undergraduates, (b) graduate students/postgraduates, and (c) faculty of on-premises library information resources versus non-library information gateways such as Google? Third, what differences, if any, are there in perceptions of library service quality across four user types ("Nonusers," "Traditionalists," "Web Techies," and "Voracious Users") reflecting different on-premises and Internet gateway usage frequencies? The results shed light on information use trends and patterns around the world and show the increasing similarities of our global users. Undergraduates use library spaces, faculty use electronic resources, and graduate students tend to resemble more the faculty use patterns.[51]

As a tool for evaluating libraries, LibQUAL+ could not exist in the pre-Web world. The timing of the development of the tool coincided with the widespread emergence and adoption of the Internet. The tools that make Google possible make the need for LibQUAL+ imperative. Libraries need to know what their users think, to understand how it compares with the thinking of users in other libraries—not only within their own institution but also beyond.[52] LibQUAL is a grounded protocol that includes a standard set of items. Librarians have compared it with popular off-the-shelf Web survey tools like SurveyMonkey. LibQUAL+ is appropriate for those who want a standard solution with general questions that apply across institutions and allows benchmarking across different settings. For local survey development, tools like SurveyMonkey are more appropriate.[53] LibQUAL has also been compared with other similar efforts in Australia. It is found to be a more efficient and effective solution compared to the Rodski instrument, but considerations of investment already made in the Rodski instrument by many Australian institutions are important politically.[54]

Bruce Thomson documented the key elements of success by emphasizing the trustworthiness of the data and the various methodological approaches through which trustworthiness can be established. In particular, three questions need to be considered in evaluating the scores: Are the respondents representative? Do the scores measure anything? Do the scores measure the correct something? The more than 1,000 individual studies conducted between 2000 and 2007 show that results are representative for most institutions, that scores are reliable (i.e., they do measure something—service quality), and that they are valid (they measure the correct something). Furthermore, the integrity of the scores from a given user is evaluated with data screening criteria for excessive number of "not applicable" responses and excessive number of inconsistent responses. One of the most useful features of LibQUAL is the ability to triangulate quantitative with qualitative information in the form of comments:

These comments are at least as important as the ratings. Users tend to explain the basis for their views when they feel particularly strongly, either positively or negatively. Furthermore, when users are unhappy, they may feel compelled to be constructive in their criticisms, and they may say exactly what they would like done differently in the library.[55]

From 2003 to 2008, more than 200 libraries have conducted annual LibQUAL+ surveys. More than 100,000 users responded to the survey each year, and more than 50,000 users provided valuable comments about the ways they use the libraries.[56]

In 2005, libraries were able to conduct LibQUAL+ over a two-session period (Session I: January to May, and Session II: July to December). The balance of central administration and local customization has been a critical component of the success of LibQUAL+. As an option, for instance, libraries can customize their local LibQUAL+ survey with five survey items from a large pool of more than 100 items. Many of these items are related to the standard LibQUAL+ dimensions.[57]

The possibility of developing a short form of the LibQUAL+ instrument has also been explored using existing data.[58] Further research for introducing a LibQUAL+ Lite version is scheduled to take place to ensure that the equivalency of a short-form version to the full version will produce stable LibQUAL+ total and subscale scores. The development of the LibQUAL+ Lite environment within an assessment gateway branded as StatsQUAL also addresses issues of providing tools that are applicable to narrow local assessment needs.[59]

LibQUAL+ findings have engaged thousands of librarians in discussions with colleagues and ARL on what these findings mean for the local library, for its region, and for the future of libraries across the globe. As the information environment is changing rapidly, having current information on how academic users access information is critical.[60] Libraries led efforts to understand how the results can be used to alter resource allocation expenditures to improve customer satisfaction.[61] Consortia have supported their members' participation in LibQUAL+ to offer an informed understanding of the changes in their environment.[62]

Summary highlights have been published on an annual basis describing the rich array of information available through LibQUAL+. Among the findings, the performance of military libraries affiliated with graduate schools and academies is noteworthy. These libraries exceed desired expectations on all the dimensions and items measured by LibQUAL+. Professional military education (PME) libraries serve the students, staff, and faculty of the U.S. postgraduate military colleges. Six of these special libraries participated in the spring 2003 LibQUAL+ assessment. In every dimension of measured service quality, the military school libraries met or exceeded users' expectations. Participants involved in this study reviewed the military library environment to identify factors that may contribute to the positive perceptions of library service and examined practical applications for other special libraries.[63]

Sharing LibQUAL+ Results

LibQUAL+ findings indicate that users have an insatiable appetite for content, and no single library has content to satisfy a vast number of its users. A spirit of collaboration and willingness to view the world of libraries as organic, integrated, and cohesive are some of the ways that can help libraries move forward rapidly, spur major innovations, and break new ground. Innovation and more aggressive marketing of the role of libraries and the benefits they bring to their communities are some of the ways to flourish in the future.

In a spirit of collaboration, LibQUAL+ participants share their results within the LibQUAL+ community with an openness that respects the confidentiality of each institution and its users. LibQUAL+ participants organize ShareFair meetings to understand how data can be used. A community mechanism for improving libraries shaped by the active involvement of the participating libraries has been one of the most tangible outcomes of emphasizing library service quality assessment.

In addition to the peer-reviewed scholarly articles, there are two basic types of material documenting the emergence of LibQUAL+ over the recent years: (1) the articles reporting the practical ways that libraries have used LibQUAL+ to make service improvements, and (2) the Web-based gray literature. Of the more than 1,000 libraries that have implemented LibQUAL+, many have done so multiple times. As these libraries disseminate their assessment efforts and document their organizational commitments for service improvement, numerous reports are available through the library Web sites.

Through the Eyes of the Libraries: LibQUAL+ as Used by Library Practitioners
Trend analysis

Longitudinal studies using LibQUAL+ data are becoming possible. The University of Washington experience is initially described in "Assessing User Needs, Satisfaction, and Library Performance at the University of Washington (UW) Libraries." This article describes the results of the triennial faculty and student surveys since 1992 and compares some of these results with the 2000 LibQUAL+ pilot implementation, the first year of the LibQUAL+ pilot that included only 12 ARL libraries. The article views the evolution of SERVQUAL into LibQUAL+ as a positive step as "the underlying concept of developing a standard instrument to measure service quality across libraries is a powerful one deserving institutional support. However, it cannot supplant local efforts to work closely with faculty and students to assess user needs and library collections and services. There are local issues at each institution that probably cannot be effectively addressed in a standardized survey tool."[64]

The second article that traces the trajectory of the experience a couple of years later for the University of Washington identifies this institution as one of five institutions that participated in LibQUAL+ each year since its pilot phase in 2000, including 2001 and 2002. It discusses the integration of LibQUAL+ as another tool in the assessment toolbox. It points out that the local rich experience of UW lacked a sense of comparison with other institutions and LibQUAL+ provided a means to assess service quality in a broader context. In general, the experience continued to be viewed positively, and the article concludes that LibQUAL+ is not only useful for identifying deficiencies in service delivery but also for identifying service strengths: "Libraries need to understand what they do well as much as to discover what needs improvement."[65]

The University of Arizona experience is described through a collection of articles as well. The University of Arizona has a rich tradition in quality management and team-based management. It is an organization that has emphasized continuous customer focus and has attempted to integrate the customer perspective in the decision-making process, practicing the disciplines of the learning organization.[66] They have used the qualitative information collected as part of LibQUAL+ in the form of comments to inform strategic planning activities. They view the comments they get from LibQUAL+ as another piece of customer feedback that can be used to gauge the needs of the campus constituencies and to plan services to meet their needs.[67]

Analysis of Comments

LibQUAL+ literature includes reports of several qualitative analyses of data. An analysis of the spring 2001 LibQUAL+ comments using qualitative analysis software, Atlas.ti, was done to refine the instrument and reduce nonsampling error. Respondents' unsolicited e-mail messages were analyzed, and results showed that, at that time, there were issues with the length of the survey. The information helped the survey designers reduce the number of items and focus on resolving technical issues with the Web-based survey.[68] Another library followed their LibQUAL+ survey results with select focus groups of graduate and undergraduate students to identify satisfaction with specific service points. The data indicated general satisfaction with the professional staff but a perceived lack of knowledge and positive service attitude by student workers. The data were used to improve library directional tools and staff training.[69] Vanderbilt University also reported that analysis of the comments corroborated other evidence that there were issues with an aging and confusing main library building.[70] Overall about half of LibQUAL+ respondents provided comments, many of them readily actionable with specific, valuable suggestions. Libraries have real-time access to the comments provided by survey respondents. Additional analysis of the comments offers rich insights on the needs of faculty, undergraduates, and graduate students. An analysis of comments across a group of libraries is also underway by researchers in the LibQUAL+ project and expected to offer rich insights on qualitative trends that go beyond one single library.[71]

Transformative Nature

Tom Wall described LibQUAL+ as a "transformative experience," and Joseph Boykin as "a confirming resource." LibQUAL+ is seen as a new experience that creates opportunities for change as it provides the impetus for rethinking a library's service programs. Both articles suggest that participation in this survey protocol should be viewed as a long-term effort accompanied with strong commitment to listen to users and rethink operations.[72] It is an opportunity to confirm not only previously identified areas that need attention but also areas of strength within the library. Libraries have not only used these data to focus on the needs of faculty and students but have also explored other demographic issues, such as gender.[73] And, as was evident from the beginning, LibQUAL+ has applicability and interest outside the Association of Research Libraries, as both the Washburn University experience and the Miami University, Ohio, experience indicated.[74]

The applicability of LibQUAL+ protocol across groups of libraries has been documented by articles on the OhioLINK experience and the Association of Academic Health Science Libraries (AAHSL) experience.[75] The reports from consortia speak to the need not only for collective action in fulfilling traditional library purchasing functions, but also for providing library service, conducting library service quality assessments, and attempting to identify benchmarks of exemplary library service. Tom Sanville welcomes the appearance of a tool such as LibQUAL+, justifying it as the tool for scalable consumer research that is badly needed in libraries.[76] The experience of the health science libraries is described in more detail at Mercer University School of Medicine in Macon, Georgia,[77] the University of Colorado Health Sciences Center, Duke University, and the Galter Health Sciences Library at Northwestern University.[78] It is important to note that the problem-based learning environment of the medical school at Mercer University School of Medicine was pointed out as a best practice example; it provides a strong community-based component and a small student body, fostering an environment of service excellence.

In many institutions conducting LibQUAL+, there are immediate short-term actions resulting from LibQUAL+ results, such as the redesigning of public services at the University of Pittsburgh.[79] Two of the published articles explicitly link the implementation of LibQUAL+ to the strategic planning processes within the universities.[80] Several articles provide a framework for other libraries to follow as examples of best practice in data analysis. Wayne State analyzed the data in three different ways: (1) comparison with other institutions, (2) summary group analysis for local responses, and (3) analysis across disciplines. Similar in-depth analysis by discipline was also conducted at Vanderbilt.[81]

Overall, the outcomes of these early documented efforts regarding the application of LibQUAL+ indicate that libraries do act on their service quality findings, and the availability of LibQUAL+ services offers an additional platform where these actions can be shared for collective learning and improvement.

Additional articles continue to appear in the literature, giving us insights into the latest aspects of the implementations. The more recent reports of how LibQUAL+ results are offering a variety of increasingly diverse perspectives. As larger and larger numbers of libraries are implementing the protocol, interesting findings are being reported by small institutions even though the protocol was grounded in the research library environment.[82] In particular, higher survey response rates by faculty are observed in smaller institutions, and these institutions see the advantages of having a "turnkey" solution to gathering user feedback. In addition, there is a focus on specific user groups depending on the orientation and priorities of each institutions and a movement towards both the qualitative and quantitative evidence collected enhancing the end result of the decision making process.[83]

Library Assessment and LibQUAL+ on the Web: The Gray Literature

Much valuable information on using LibQUAL+ and interpreting results has appeared in the gray literature of the Web. These various Web resources often offer only a snapshot of a specific implementation in a specific institution within a year. The quality of Web resources and presentation may vary, and the information is presented for the most part to satisfy the needs of the local community and to demonstrate the service improvements and commitment of the library. Some institutions have placed LibQUAL+ within the context of the larger assessment and service-improvement efforts conducted by a library within a multiyear perspective.[84]

A special note should be made in relation to the confidentiality of the findings across institutions. Within the LibQUAL+ community, libraries have been asked to share their findings across institutions while maintaining the anonymity of the institutional identity of peer libraries when comparing themselves with each other. Many libraries, as the resources reviewed below indicate, opted to disclose their findings publicly on the Web and share openly their LibQUAL+ notebooks or interpretations of them. The resources described below are from the publicly available Web sites of the participating libraries, rather than the restricted-access Web site used by all participants. The publicly available resources spread the word about the application and usefulness of LibQUAL+.

Highlights in general indicate that there are deficits across libraries in the information-control dimension, while performance is more satisfactory in the affect of service area. From a few Web resources highlighted below, we see how libraries interpret and use their assessment and LibQUAL+ data in tangible and practical ways. From the publicly available information, we are highlighting a few findings to offer a perspective of how the data are used locally.

In the survey conducted in early 2005 among the eight colleges at University of North Texas, 560 respondents participated. Of the three dimensions measured by LibQUAL+, Affect of Service is viewed more positively by undergraduates, graduate students, and staff than the other two service dimensions, Library as Place and Information Control. For faculty, Library as Place slightly edges out Affect of Service as the dimension viewed with greatest satisfaction. Faculty and undergraduates are most dissatisfied with Information Control, graduate students and staff with Library as Place. In general, perceived scores for libraries participating in the survey tend to fall within the zone of tolerance, i.e., they tend to be less than desired scores and greater than minimum scores.[85]

The Clemson University Libraries participated in LibQUAL+ for a number of years. Overall, they seemed to be meeting the needs of undergraduates, who gave them high scores. Undergraduates have many services geared towards meeting their needs. Clemson is also improving electronic and print journal collections, especially for faculty and graduate students. Clemson initiated a follow-up activity called the University Summit, which has gradually spread to other institutions. The University Summit has been adopted by the University of Texas and is proving to be a useful framework for translating the data into actionable service improvement efforts.[86]

Florida A&M University Libraries conducted the LibQUAL+ survey in 2004. A total of 777 users completed their survey. Respondents have high expectations for library service quality. Mean values of minimal service quality for the group is 6.57 on a scale of 1 to 9. The desired mean is 7.83. The perceived mean is 6.10, representing an overall service gap of –0.47. Respondents were mostly satisfied with the willingness of staff to provide help as needed, the functionality of the library Web page, and the provision of a comfortable study environment. The libraries target staff development, customer relations, and iterative assessment of services as areas for improvement.[87]

Georgia Tech Library and Information Center, participated for a second consecutive year during spring 2004. There were 349 users responding. The key findings of the study are positive, with Library as Place being the area where users desire more urgent improvements. The library has taken a number of immediate actions in response to survey results and comments. The Library Council and other library working groups continue to monitor the results against other institution's results. In 2006, Georgia Tech led an effort to implement LibQUAL+ across a larger group of academic libraries throughout the state of Georgia.[88]

An example of a college library releasing LibQUAL+ data on the Web can be found at the Babson College Horn Library Web site.[89] The Babson College community has the highest expectations for Information Control. Comparisons to other participants in spring 2007 show Babson having slightly lower minimum requirements, slightly lower desired requirements, and except for Library as Place, slightly higher perceptions of quality of service overall.

The Penn State University Libraries was one of 202 libraries that participated in the 2004 LibQUAL+ survey. They received 2,426 completed surveys. In their analysis, they highlight the following findings:

Analysis of the general questions related to library usage (three), general satisfaction (three), and information literacy outcomes (five), suggests that users of the Libraries are generally satisfied with library services and resources. Overall, the survey responses to the three questions about general satisfaction were nearly identical. On a nine-point Likert scale, the average mean scores were 7.37 for University Park and 7.36 for the Campus Colleges. These numbers compare closely to the satisfaction levels reported in the Penn State 2002 Student Satisfaction Survey where 84% of University Park students and 88% of Campus College students reported satisfaction with library services, and in the 1991 and 1993 Libraries surveys at University Park where 82% and 83% (respectively) of the survey respondents reported being "satisfied" or "very satisfied" with library services. These numbers compare favorably to the average mean score of 7.33 for all ARL libraries. It is perhaps of interest to note that while faculty and graduate students reported higher general satisfaction levels of 7.76 and

7.48, respectively, than the undergraduate level of 7.20, the faculty and graduate students were generally more critical about service quality, primarily in the Information Control dimension.[90]

Queen's University, Kingston, Ontario, Canada, report from results from the LibQUAL+ survey conducted in 2004:

The results of the 2004 LibQUAL+® survey gave the Library a rich and interesting source of information about our many strengths and weaknesses, in the context of the Queen's community and in comparison with our peer Association of Research Libraries (ARL) institutions in Canada and the United States.

… Overall, Queen's scored higher than the average for all 2004 ARL participants and first among the Canadian participants. This relatively high rating is due to very high scores in the dimensions of Affect of Service and Library as Place. However, in the area of Information Control, Queen's rated below the ARL average.[91]

Geoffrey R. Weller Library of University of Northern British Columbia participated in 2003 and highlights areas of strength and improvement in their report. They report the following under areas for improvement:

The area of greatest concern is access to information, both books and journals. We believe this concern represents two issues. The first is that library users have difficulty accessing material that is located in storage and the second is that the library does not have or subscribe to all of the desired resources. An analysis of the survey and the comments indicates that all programs are affected by this concern and that graduate students are the group of library users who are the least satisfied with access to information. Weller Library users are also dissatisfied with the Library's hours of operation (especially on the weekend), the access to and availability of electronic resources and the cost and timeliness of inter-library loans.[92]

Leddy Library, University of Windsor, highlights the following summary findings: "Overall, the Library is performing slightly better than the minimum expected level of service in all areas. When respondents are asked to rate their satisfaction with the Library, the outcomes are fairly positive, with the mean responses being just above mid-range. Drawing from both the quantitative and qualitative results, there are some areas that respondents feel we might improve."[93]

The University of Liverpool Library was one of 20 UK libraries that participated in a study. They found from the survey that Affect of Service shows negative gap scores for undergraduates and positive scores for postgraduate students and staff. With regard to Information Control, all the users groups had negative gap scores. With regard to Library as Place, only postgraduate students showed positive scores. As in the 2003 survey, the level of satisfaction varies slightly between the three groups of respondents, with undergraduates and taught postgraduates again being marginally less satisfied than staff or research postgraduates.[94]

Edinburgh University Library participated in the LibQUAL+ survey in 2003 and 2005. The 2005 overall results were similar to 2003. Some of the desired scores are higher than in 2003, while the average scores for the general satisfaction questions are all slightly down from 2003. This interpretation highlights areas where there are "negative scores," i.e., where users score the service they receive below the minimum they would expect. Negative scores were received in the Library as Place items. The library is addressing some of the concerns, both through ongoing, incremental changes in libraries, as well as through more major changes that will take place in the future. The management team continues to monitor the results against other institution's results as they become available for further analysis.[95]

Glasgow University Library is one of two UK institutions that have conducted LibQUAL+ almost every year since 2003. Jacqui Dowd has created a rich resource on the Web with the findings over the years and how they have been used to improve library services. She highlights that "overall, users indicated that the service level of Library staff's attitude exceeds their minimum expectations. Undergraduate and post-graduate students indicated that on average their perceived service level of Library staff's attitude was higher than their 2003 ratings."[96]

A recent article explores similarities and differences on library users' desired service quality levels across undergraduate students, graduate students and faculty, across geographic regions, and across time. The sample consisted of 297,158 LibQUAL+ participants from the years 2004, 2005, and 2006 who completed the survey in American English and British English:

> "The stability in rankings is quite striking, given that the range of the mean values was so narrow. Usually, such stability in rankings occurs when ratings are more heterogeneous, because larger shifts in means must occur for rank orders to be altered. Thus, these 297,158 LibQUAL+ participants made very subtle differentiations across items with respect to desired service qualities, but these small differences were nevertheless invariant across time… . The findings of similarities internationally was not entirely unexpected. One recent global study was the Online Computer Library Center Report on *Perceptions of Libraries and Information Resources*. The report highlighted the existence of a strong international 'universal' library brand.[97]

The universal library brand is being marketed in innovative ways with the application of LibQUAL+ in all these different settings, especially as libraries share their results readily with their immediate community and the world at large openly through the gray literature seen on the Web. One of the major impacts of LibQUAL+ may be a loose, yet powerful social network where the voices of million library users are telling us their needs and wants through the survey box presented to them. Our individual and collective ability to share and act on this information in an effective way will ensure a stronger library brand and have a long term impact on libraries' abilities to meet users' desires.

Key Elements to the Success of LibQUAL+

The widespread application of LibQUAL+ is primarily due to the fact that it has reduced much of the labor and cost associated with survey management through the ease of the Web administration interface. Library staff may use their creativity and knowledge of the local context in the process of drawing the sample, managing the survey notification and reminder process, developing an effective marketing campaign, and translating the results into positive actions for their organization.[98] LibQUAL+ has demonstrated that it can handle large numbers, the survey can be turned around quickly with the delivery of results within days of the survey closing, and there is limited need for local expertise regarding mechanical aspects of survey research. Interpretations should be carefully implemented across chosen cohorts, and additional analysis can be conducted both in terms of the quantitative and qualitative data collected since there are opportunities to discern user behaviors across the various demographic categories.[99]

LibQUAL+ has made a number of important contributions to the measurement of effective delivery of library services. In particular, LibQUAL+

- Shifted the focus of assessment from mechanical expenditure-driven metrics to user-centered measures of quality
- Re-grounded gap theory for the library sector, especially academic libraries
- Grounded questions yield data of sufficient granularity to be of value at the local level
- Determined the degree to which information derived from local data can be generalized, providing much needed "best practices" information
- Demonstrated the efficacy of large-scale administration of user-centered assessment transparently across the Web
- Made little demand of local resources and expertise.

In summarizing the importance of LibQUAL+, Colleen Cook points out its contribution both at the local level and for crossinstitutional benchmarking:

> It has overcome the theoretical and practical obstacles that previously prevented large scale, multi institutional assessments in libraries. It assesses three overarching dimensions of library services ... from a user perspective. As a web delivered and managed survey, it is easy and cost effective in terms of time and money. A well crafted interactive management process for the survey is under continual refinement and allows the survey to be run simultaneously across hundreds of institutions throughout the world with a turnaround for data and analysis of only a few days.... LibQUAL® longitudinal data has also shown how quickly user perceptions, and desired and minimum expectations have changed over the five years of survey administration. Finally,

LibQUAL® data have yielded the first glimpses into how users assess the value added by libraries for higher education outcomes in teaching, learning and research.[100]

What LibQUAL+® Is Not

LibQUAL+ is not and should not be the only evaluation libraries deploy. It has a specific place in the library evaluation literature being a total market survey, but it does not provide the answer to all the questions libraries need to know. Libraries need to engage in transaction based surveys and multiple other ways of collecting evidence such as focus group interviews,[101] anthropological observations,[102] analysis of existing artifacts and documents, usability studies, and a multiplicity of quantitative and qualitative approaches that can enrich their presence and ability to describe their effectiveness.

Finding the right numbers in interpreting the LibQUAL+ data may be challenging. Within the framework of measuring minimum expectations, desired expectations and perceptions of library service, LibQUAL+ provides three scores directly derived from users and two calculated scores: the service adequacy gap (the difference between perceptions and minimum expectations) and the service superiority gap (the difference between perceptions and desired expectations). Finding out which figures one may use for what purposes is not intuitive to many librarians, but practitioners have published research that provides guidance in this area. Jim Self, for example, recommends the use of the zone of tolerance where you can see perceptions charted between minimum and desired expectations in a series of bar charts instead of the popular radar charts that summarize all 22 core questions.[103]

In many ways LibQUAL+ raises as many questions as it answers. These issues need to be addressed with collective and local actions. In particular, there is great concern that across all institutions, faculty respondents rate the library systematically low on issues regarding access to the full-text journals needed for their work. Such findings are calls for collective action and exploration of solutions for reversing these perceptions.[104]

As we have seen, libraries have used LibQUAL+ for strategic planning purposes. Yet limitations were expressed by one of these libraries in that the results do not map to the strategic goals:

What is evident is that libraries are using LibQUAL+ results as a repository of information from which aspects of the strategic plan can be implemented. What is more tenuous is using this information to actually map out the strategic plan. Purdue Libraries discovered this when it undertook to create a new strategic plan in 2006. LibQUAL+ was administered in 2005 with the idea that the results could be used to formulate the plan. As they progressed, the planning team realized that the shortfalls in library service as revealed by LibQUAL+ were focusing attention on the sins of the past and not on the possibilities of the future. This does not mean that LibQUAL+ was a futile exercise. On the contrary, its measures turn up frequently in the plan as a metric for determining progress toward the goals of the strategic plan; what LibQUAL+ did not do was set the goals of the strategic plan.[105]

In the future, more emphasis on understanding all the factors that positively influence teaching, learning, and research outcomes will need to take place. The relationship between different environments, personal and cultural variables, and success in educational endeavors will need to be explored to understand the mitigating effect of a library. Improvements may happen both from observing and studying users and from the creativity and innovation of library professionals.

Researchers recognize that users have a limited frame of reference and tend to offer incremental, rather than bold, suggestions. Stewart Saunders points out in a recent article that "only customers judge reality, all other judgments are essentially irrelevant" is not always the accepted perception: "[A]ll other judgments are not essentially irrelevant. Customers are best able to judge how a service is delivered through their own perceptions. With the professional training, however, librarians are in many ways better positioned than the customers to judge the overall quality of 'what' is delivered. That is, they can best judge the technical quality of the library."[106] So a distinction between technical quality and functional quality is drawn where technical quality is the actual objective service delivered and functional quality is how service is delivered.[107]

Other researchers have pointed the responsibility of the professional in developing innovation. Innovation is the professional responsibility of the staff working in an organization. Anthony Ulwick urges researchers to shift their focus to outcomes and truly understand the driving forces behind users' behavior. He uses the development of the ubiquitous "sticky note" as an example. Focusing on outcomes will help jump-start innovation: "When desired outcomes become the focus of customer research, innovation becomes a manageable, predictable discipline."[108]

An emphasis on outcomes has also been the latest focus of work done by Hernon and colleagues.[109] Service quality and satisfaction can be viewed from the perspective of outcomes as well. Appreciative inquiry techniques and the university summit that have been implemented by various institutions are among the frameworks libraries can use to foster positive outcomes in relation to quality service and satisfaction.[110] In studying the relation of the LibQUAL+ dimension to satisfaction and outcomes, there is a stronger relation between the Affect of Service dimension and satisfaction, as opposed to outcomes. Information Control, on the other hand, is more closely related to positive academic outcomes.[111]

A Special Note about Library Performance Measures in the United Kingdom

Library service quality was urgently pursued in the 1990s in the United Kingdom as well. Some researchers and administrators experienced a process quality improvement effort through an ISO 9000 certification process and foresaw the desirability and feasibility of implementing a SERVQUAL-like assessment effort across libraries. Extensive research conducted by Peter Brophy in the United Kingdom focused on "Performance Measures for 21st Century Libraries." Brophy presents performance measurement as an integral and important component of the management of academic libraries. He considers the need for alternative metrics for different library types, established as well as emerging.[112] Brophy's work has been applied to other countries within the European Union through a series of funded initiatives during the middle 1990s. For the most part, libraries in the United Kingdom seem to have been able to deploy effectively methods for measuring satisfaction and service quality perceptions from an affective and cognitive perspective.[113] The work of implementing LibQUAL+ across an increasing number of libraries in the United Kingdom is also fostering successful emphasis on the user needs.[114] Research in linking affective and cognitive states to behavioral outcomes and long-term impact of libraries to teaching and research is still in its infancy.[115]

Service Quality in the Electronic Environment

An increasing amount of work has taken place in the area of assessing networked services,[116] and its importance continues to grow.[117] The profession has a good sense of how much money libraries spend on electronic resources through descriptive data like the ACRL and *ARL Statistics,* but little is known about the products libraries buy, how they are used, and their impact. Efforts to formalize investigations related to e-metrics have been under way as part of the ARL New Measures effort.[118] Voices of dissent as to whether such efforts can yield successful outcomes have also surfaced.[119]

Recent studies have also examined closely the notion of e-service quality from a user's perspective and attempted to develop a survey instrument that measures the dimensions of e-service.[120] Their model builds on the E-S-QUAL model developed by Parasuraman, Zeithaml, and Malhotra.[121]

Evaluating the usage of library networked electronic resources may take place through vendor-supplied data on sessions, searches, and items requested and through Web survey data.[122] Terry Plum has pointed out the importance of the library web architecture accommodating the "infrastructure of assessment for web surveys, where much richer data can be collected through simple questions. The infrastructure of the gateway itself can be comprised of scripts, OpenURL servers, database-to-web architectures such as ColdFusion or php-MySQL, a referral server, a re-writing proxy server, or any other mechanism that the library can implement which assures that all requests by patrons for network resources and services go through a central gateway at which point the survey can be inserted."[123] There are clear limitations on the usage data supplied by vendors despite the continuing efforts to come up with more meaningful Web metrics. Tracking author and reader identities on the Internet is becoming increasingly more tempting as we are no longer able to observe physical behavior in classrooms and libraries the way we used to. A more accurate picture of how libraries are used in the electronic environment is being built gradually and in a way that positions libraries to determine the value added components of their operations.[124]

Complementary models of measuring the impact of networked electronic services approached the issue of understanding uses of networked electronic services by collecting data on the purpose of use and demographics of library users.[125] These methods allow libraries to differentiate between uses related to research and teaching and uses that are taking place from within the library, outside the library but on campus, and off campus. Currently, an ARL tool known as MINES for Libraries (Measuring the Impact of Networked Electronic Services) attempts to offer a concrete way for libraries to link uses of electronic resources to the needs of their users.[126] An implementation of MINES at the Ontario Council of University Libraries (OCUL) over a period of a year has been successful across a group of institutions and demonstrated the proportion of users who use resources from in the library, on campus, and off campus, demographics and purpose of use (research, teaching, or learning).[127] A similar study at OhioLINK has also been reported in the literature.[128] Tracking these behaviors across time is an important element in the assessment tool kit libraries deploy.

Understanding the impact of digital libraries is another aspect of emerging importance for libraries. Digital libraries are closely linked to their virtual presence as manifested by their Web sites. Libraries have engaged in usability studies for improving their Web sites. Usability studies have been an important transformative methodology and a catalyst for bringing the library closer to the needs of their users.[129]

In an effort to develop a deeper understanding of digital library service quality, a tool called DigiQUAL has been developed, grounded in the National Science Digital Library (NSDL) environment.[130] This effort, funded by NSDL at the National Science Foundation, developed a typology of the dimensions of a digital library Web site based on focus group interviews with DLESE (Digital Library for Earth Systems Education) and MERLOT (Multimedia Educational Resource for Learning and Online Teaching) users, both communities of educators. The qualitative model that emerged from this research indicates that community-building mechanisms are as important as content, trustworthiness, and reliability of the Web site, together with the virtual aesthetic aspects of the digital library presence.[131]

Organizational Climate Assessment

The assessment infrastructure that needs to be supported to expand evaluative studies beyond the local environment needs to combine and support the presentation of both quantitative and qualitative evidence.

The notion of an assessment gateway has been promoted by the ARL Statistics and Measurement Program, branded as StatsQUAL,[132] as a way to provide one entry into a variety of assessment tools such as the historical ARL Statistics, LibQUAL+, DigiQUAL, MINES for Libraries, and the latest addition to the tool kit being ClimateQUAL.

ClimateQUAL-OCDA (Organizational Climate and Diversity Assessment) is an organizational climate and diversity assessment survey of internal staff focusing on issues of organizational fairness and diversity. It provides a framework of comparison across different institutions, and it is currently being expanded to half a dozen institutions, doubling the initial pilot activities that took place across five ARL libraries. Issues of organizational diversity and climate are of major concern to many organizations because climate has an impact on the fulfillment of organizational goals and the delivery of services and products. The University of Maryland (UM) Libraries, as a team-based learning organization, initiated this project among ARL libraries. The notion of the healthy organization is emerging as a fundamental concept from this stream of research. The relation between organizational climate and improvements in service quality is empirically being investigated so that it can not only be measures but also influenced with the deployment of effective intervention activities.[133]

Conclusion

One may ask to what degree libraries have embraced service quality improvement. Quality, much like beauty, is in the eye of the beholder, as Nitecki and Olshen have articulated in the six-week online training they offered to hundreds of librarians through ARL.[134] In their study of online lyceum participants, they examined the following: expectations for staff development to prepare librarians to embrace service quality improvement as a management approach to delivering service; the perceived readiness of library organizations to support a culture of assessment; and the effectiveness of Web-based teaching and learning technologies in developing the requisite skills. At that time, they drew two conclusions: that library organizations are not ready to transform libraries into well-managed service quality operations and that the need is great for preparing librarians to lead this transformation.

The number of libraries implementing LibQUAL+ has continued to grow since then. The needs for developing more sophisticated assessment skills and building expertise within each organizational context is becoming urgent. For a number of years, ARL has sponsored the ARL Service Quality Evaluation Academy to aim at increasing the research and methodological skills to library professionals through an intensive one-week exposure to quantitative and qualitative research methods. More recently, in response to Nitecki and Olshen's admonition for developing "'communities of practice' in the area of service quality assessment,"[135] the first Library Assessment Conference was organized and offered in September 2006 in Charlottesville, Virginia. Post-conference discussion on library assessment issues takes place in the library assessment blog at http://www.libraryassessment.info/—a blog established in 2006 as a follow-up to sustain the community concerned with library assessment issues. Another forum is the ARL-ASSESS list, available at https://mx2.arl.org/Lists/ARL-ASSESS/List.html.

The conference proceedings offer a glimpse of the diversity of assessment approaches that are emerging in libraries, including service quality assessment,[136] qualitative analysis,[137] the building of assessment capacity in libraries,[138] return on investment,[139] information literacy assessment,[140] evaluation and research methodologies,[141] strategic planning,[142] assessment of learning spaces,[143] applications of the Balanced Scorecard,[144] assessment of internal organizational climate,[145] digital libraries,[146] and value and impact studies.[147] The multiplicity of approaches continues to emerge strongly in the papers and research at the second library assessment conference in Seattle, August 4–6, 2008.[148]

Building effective, sustainable, and practical assessment is an ongoing service established at ARL, based on extensive practical and thorough research across a group of 24 ARL libraries over the course of a two-year period. The major lessons learned from this effort and the driving forces of successful assessment stories were documented through the literature.[149] "After evaluating results from nearly all participating libraries, two elements emerged as key to effective, sustainable, and practical assessment: (1) library leadership and (2) a library that was customer-centered. Other related issues included aspects of organizational culture, assessment responsibility, link and integration with relations activities, presenting results and acting on results."[150] The findings are being updated regularly as experience is being built by visiting additional libraries every year. By 2007, it is evident that "the lack of a coordinated approach to research often results in a plethora of individual research studies, an over-reliance on surveys (especially with the advent of inexpensive Web surveys), and a lack of awareness of assessment activities in the library. At each library we visited we found instances of surveys conducted by members that our contact person and library administrators were not aware of."[151]

Corroborating studies have also looked into the inherent limitations of the traditional library environment when it comes to analytical critical thinking and called for a strengthening of the organizational culture of assessment.[152] Based on interviews with over 20 library directors, the latest work by Amos Lakos focuses on the role of leadership in fostering evidence-based decision making in libraries. The author focuses observations on the use of data in decision making in libraries, specifically on the role of leadership in making evidence-based decisions a reality, and reviews new opportunities for data analysis, assessment delivery, and decision making in libraries. Developments in the information technology (IT) area, especially the increased dominance of very large networked infrastructures and associated services, large-scale digitization projects, collaborative frameworks, and economic and market trends, may have a positive impact on library options for data use and analysis by library management.[153]

Where Next?

James Neal documents the plight of the field: "Librarianship is an 'information poor' information profession. Decisions are routinely not supported by the evidence of well-designed investigations. Research in the field is poorly communicated, understood, and applied. It is imperative that academic librarians and higher education libraries develop and carry out systematic research and development programs."[154] He lays out the challenge for continued commitment to research and development capacity so that decisions are based more on facts and less on opinion.

Measuring library service quality across institutions leads to the issue of whether improvements of library services can be facilitated by greater collaboration and resource sharing. Users' expectations of library service across the globe are converging, as they want to access seamlessly all information resources they need, irrespective of location. Can this translate into a successful implementation of universal and local standards for the provision of library services?[155] What levels of standards need to be applied to different types of educational institutions across the globe to harmonize and manage the expectations of library users for the benefit of improving research, teaching, and learning? Are there service attitudes that are specific to the different cultures, what they might be, and how can this knowledge be leveraged for providing excellent library services? How would these concepts be translated into library policies and procedures that can meet local needs, yet help establish and manage expectations of delivering quality library services across institutional and political boundaries?

Improving the quality of library services in the electronic environment offers unique opportunities for collaboration across institutions and the excitement of enhancing the library's role in lifelong learning. Sustaining a robust Research and Development (R&D) capacity and advocating the value of our services will remain an ongoing challenge as librarians are being called to answer probing and exciting questions in the years to come. Collaborative assessment based on sound research and methodological principles with technological insights are proving to be sound ways for libraries to improve services for the years ahead.

References

1. F. Wilfrid Lancaster, *If You Want to Evaluate Your Library* (Champaign: University of Illinois, Graduate School of Library and Information Science, 1998).

2. F. Wilfrid Lancaster and Shiyali Ramamrita Mehrotra, "The Five Laws of Library Science as a Guide to the Evaluation of Library Services," in *Perspectives in Library and Information Science,* ed. S. N. Agarwal, R. R. Khan, and N. R. Satyanarayana, 1 (Lucknow, India: Print House, 1982).

3. Kendon Stubbs, "University Libraries; Standards and Statistics," *College and Research Libraries* 42, no. 6 (1981): 527–538; Kendon Stubbs, "Lies, Damned Lies … and ARL Statistics?" in *Research Libraries: Measurement, Management, Marketing: Minutes of the Meeting of the Association of Research Libraries (108th, Minneapolis, Minnesota, May 1–2, 1986),* ed. Nicola Daval, 79–85 (Washington, DC: Association of Research Libraries, 1986); Kendon Stubbs, "Apples and Oranges and ARL Statistics," *Journal of Academic Librarianship* 14, no. 5 (1988): 231–235.

4. Association of Research Libraries, *ARL Statistics* (Washington, DC: Association of Research Libraries, annual); Association of College and Research Libraries, *Academic Library Trends and Statistics* (Chicago: American Library Association, annual).

5. Sharon A. Weiner, "Library Quality and Impact: Is There a Relationship

between New Measures and Traditional Measures?" *Journal of Academic Librarianship* 31, no. 5 (2005): 432–437.

6. Ibid., 432.

7. Sarah Pritchard, "Determining Quality in Academic Libraries—Perspectives on Quality in Libraries," *Library Trends* 44, no. 3 (1996): 572–594.

8. Carla Stoffle, Robert Renaud, and Jerilyn Veldof, "Choosing Our Futures," *College and Research Libraries* 57, no. 3 (1996): 213–225.

9. Online Computer Library Center, Web page offering download of *College Students' Perceptions* (Dublin, OH: OCLC, 2005), http://www.oclc.org/reports/perceptionscollege.htm; see also OCLC, *Perceptions of Libraries* (Dublin, OH: OCLC, 2005), http://www.oclc.org/reports/pdfs/Percept_all.pdf (accessed March 31 2008); *Environmental Scan: Pattern Recognition* (Dublin, OH: OCLC, 2003), http://www.oclc.org/reports/escan/introduction/default.htm; *Information Format Trends: Content, Not Containers* (Dublin, OH: OCLC, 2004), http://www5.oclc.org/downloads/community/2004infotrends_content.pdf.

10. Leigh Estabrook, Evans Witt, and Lee Rainie, *Information Searches That Solve Problems: How People Use the Internet, Libraries, and Government Agencies When They Need Help* (Pew Internet and American Life Project and the University of Illinois at Urbana-Champaign Graduate School of Library and Information Science, December 30, 2007), http://www.pewInternet.org/PPF/r/231/report_display.asp (accessed March 31 2008).

11. Nancy A. Van House, Beth Weil, and Charles R. McClure, *Measuring Academic Library Performance: A Practical Approach* (Chicago: American Library Association, 1990).

12. Peter Hernon and Ellen Altman, *Assessing Service Quality: Satisfying the Expectations of Library Customers* (Chicago: American Library Association, 1998).

13. Valarie A. Zeithaml, A. Parasuraman, and Leonard L. Berry, *Delivering Quality Service: Balancing Customer Perceptions and Expectations* (New York: The Free Press, 1990).

14. Robert W. Sexty, *Canadian Business in the New Stakeholder Economy* (Upper Saddle River, NJ: Prentice-Hall, 1998), 297.

15. Peter Hernon and John R. Whitman, *Delivering Satisfaction and Service Quality: A Customer-Based Approach for Libraries* (Chicago: American Library Association, 2001), 15.

16. Robert S. Kaplan and David P. Norton, "The Balanced Scorecard—Measures That Drive Performance," *Harvard Business Review* 70, no. 1 (1992): 71–79.

17. Jim Self, "Using Data to Make Choices: The Balanced Scorecard at the University of Virginia Library," *ARL Bimonthly Report* 230/231 (2003): 28–29, http://www.arl.org/bm~doc/balscorecard.pdf (accessed July 15, 2008).

18. Zeithaml, Parasuraman, and Berry, *Delivering Quality Service,* 26.

19. Michael J. Roszkowski, John S. Baky, and David B. Jones, "So Which Score on the LibQUAL+ Tells Me If Library Users Are Satisfied?" *Library and Information Science Research* 27, no. 4 (2005): 427–428.

20. Danuta A. Nitecki and Peter Hernon, "Measuring Service Quality at Yale University's Libraries," *Journal of Academic Librarianship* 26, no. 4 (2000): 259–273.

21. Ruth Maddox Swan, "Perceived Performance and Disconfirmation of Expectations as Measures of Customer Satisfaction with Information Services in the Academic Library" (PhD diss., Florida State University, 1998).

22. Xi Shi, Patricia J. Holahan, and M. Peter Jurkat, "Satisfaction Formation Processes in Library Users: Understanding Multisource Effects," *Journal of Academic Librarianship* 30, no. 2 (2004): 122.

23. Danuta A. Nitecki, "Quality Assessment Measures in Libraries," in *Advances in Librarianship,* vol. 25, ed. F. C. Lynden, 133–162 (San Diego: Academic Press, 2001); Nitecki, "Service Quality in Academic Libraries," in *The Encyclopedia of Library and Information Science,* vol. 65, ed. A. Kent, 216–232 (New York: Marcel Dekker, 1999).

24. Danuta A. Nitecki and Brinley Franklin, "New Measures for Research Libraries," *Journal of Academic Librarianship* 25, no. 6 (1999): 484–487.

25. Danuta A. Nitecki, "Program Evaluation in Libraries: Relating Operations and Clients," *Archival Science* 4 (2004): 17–44.

26. Fred Heath and Colleen Cook, "SERVQUAL: Service Quality Assessment in Libraries," in *The Encyclopedia of Library and Information Science,* 2nd ed., vol. 24, ed. M. A. Drake, 2613–2625 (New York: Marcel Dekker, 2003); Denise Troll, *Usage and Usability Assessment: Library Practices and Concerns* (Washington, DC: Council on Library and Information Resources, 2002); Carol Tenopir, *Use and Users of Electronic Library Resources* (Washington, DC: Council on Library and Information Resources, 2003), http://www.clir.org/PUBS/reports/pub120/pub120.pdf (accessed March 31 2008).

27. Colleen Cook and Fred M. Heath, "Users' Perceptions of Library Service Quality: A LibQUAL+™ Qualitative Study," *Library Trends* 49, no. 4 (2001): 548–584; Colleen Cook and Bruce Thompson, "Psychometric Properties of Scores from the Web-Based LibQUAL+ Study of Perceptions of Library Service Quality," *Library Trends* 49, no. 4 (2001): 585–604; Colleen Cook, Fred Heath, and Bruce Thompson, "Users' Hierarchical Perspectives on Library Service Quality: A 'LibQUAL+' Study," *College and Research Libraries* 62, no. 2: 147–153; Colleen Cook and others, "LibQUAL+: Service Quality Assessment in Research Libraries," *IFLA Journal* 27, no. 4 (2001): 264–268; Colleen Cook and others, "The Search for New Measures: The ARL LibQUAL+ Study—A Preliminary Report," *portal: Libraries and the Academy* 1, no. 1 (2001): 103–112; Bruce Thompson, Colleen Cook, and Fred Heath, "How Many Dimensions Does It Take To Measure Users' Perceptions of Libraries? A LibQUAL+ Study," *portal: Libraries and the Academy* 1, no. 2 (2001):

129–138; Bruce Thompson and Colleen Cook, "Stability of the Reliability of LibQUAL+™ Scores: A 'Reliability Generalization' Meta-Analysis Study," *Educational and Psychological Measurement* 62, no. 4 (2002): 735–743; Bruce Thompson, Colleen Cook, and Fred Heath, "Structure of Perceptions of Service Quality in Libraries: A LibQUAL+ Study," *Structural Equation Modeling* 10, no. 3 (2003): 456–464; Youhua Wei, Bruce Thompson, and Colleen Cook, "Scaling Users' Perceptions of Library Service Quality Using Item Response Theory: A LibQUAL+™ Study," *portal: Libraries and the Academy* 5, no. 1 (2005): 93–104.

28. Cook and Heath, "Users' Perceptions of Library Service Quality."

29. Martha Kyrillidou and Fred M. Heath, "Measuring Service Quality: Introduction," *Library Trends* 49, no. 4 (2001): 541–547.

30. Cook and Thompson, "Psychometric Properties of Scores."

31. Philip J. Calvert, "International Variations in Measuring Customer Expectations," *Library Trends* 49, no. 4 (2001): 732–757.

32. Nitecki and Hernon, "Measuring Service Quality"; Rowena Cullen, "Perspectives on User Satisfaction Surveys," *Library Trends* 49, no. 4 (2001): 662–686.

33. Patience L. Simmonds and Syed S. Andaleeb, "Usage of Academic Libraries: The Role of Service Quality, Resources, and User Characteristics," *Libraries Trends* 49, no. 4 (2001): 626–634.

34. Ian Winkworth, "Innovative United Kingdom Approaches to Measuring Service Quality," *Library Trends* 49, no. 4 (2001): 718–731.

35. Roswitha Poll, "Performance, Processes, and Costs: Managing Service Quality with the Balanced Scorecard," *Library Trends* 49, no. 4 (2001): 709–717.

36. Leonard L. Berry, *On Great Service: A Framework for Action* (New York: The Free Press, 1995), 37, 54.

37. Shelly Phipps, "Beyond Measuring Service Quality: Learning from the Voices of the Customers, the Staff, the Processes, and the Organization," *Library Trends* 49, no. 4 (2001): 635–661; Steve Hiller, "Assessing User Needs, Satisfaction, and Library Performance at the University of Washington Libraries," *Library Trends* 49, no. 4 (2001): 605–625.

38. Martha Kyrillidou and Kaylyn Hipps, "Symposium on Measuring Library Service Quality," *ARL Bimonthly Report* 215 (2001): 9–11, http://www.arl.org/bm~doc/octsymp.pdf (accessed July 15, 2008); Kyrillidou and Heath, "Measuring Service Quality."

39. Julia C. Blixrud, "Mainstreaming New Measures," *ARL Bimonthly Report* 230/231 (2003): 1–8, http://www.arl.org/bm~doc/mainstreaming.pdf (accessed July 15, 2008).

40. C. Colleen Cook, "A Mixed-Methods Approach to the Identification and Measurement of Academic Library Service Quality Constructs: LibQUAL+™" (PhD diss., Texas A&M University, 2001); abstract in *Dissertation Abstracts International*, publ. nr. AAT3020024, 62 (2001), 2295A.

41. Bruce Thompson, Colleen Cook, and Russel L. Thompson, "Reliability and Structure of LibQUAL+ Scores: Measuring Perceived Library Service Quality," *portal: Libraries and the Academy* 2, no. 1 (2002): 10.

42. Colleen Cook, Fred Heath, and Bruce Thompson, "Score Norms for Improving Library Service Quality: A LibQUAL+ Study," *portal: Libraries and the Academy* 2, no. 1 (2002): 13–26.

43. Bruce Thompson, Colleen Cook, and Martha Kyrillidou, "Stability of Library Service Quality Benchmarking Norms across Time and Cohorts: A LibQUAL+™ Study" (paper presented at the Asia-Pacific Conference of Library and Information Education and Practice [A-LIEP], Singapore, April 4–7, 2005), http://www.coe.tamu.edu/~bthompson/libq2005.htm#1 (accessed March 31 2008).

44. Fred M. Heath and others, "ARL Index and Other Validity Correlates of LibQUAL+ Scores," *portal: Libraries and the Academy* 2, no. 1 (2002): 27–42.

45. Martha Kyrillidou and Fred M. Heath, "The Starving Research Library User: Relationships between Library Institutional Characteristics and Spring 2002 LibQUAL+™ Scores," in *Libraries Act on Their LibQUAL+™ Findings: From Data to Action*, ed. Fred M. Heath, Martha Kyrillidou, and Consuella A. Askew, 1–11 (New York: Haworth Press, 2004), co-published simultaneously in *Journal of Library Administration* 40, no. 3/4 (2004): 1–11.

46. J. Stephen Town, "Filling the Void or Bridging the Deep? LibQUAL+ in the UK," in *Proceedings of the 5th Northumbria International Conference on Performance Measurement in Libraries and Information Services, Durham, UK, July 28–31, 2003*, ed. Sandra Parker, 212–219 (Bradford, UK: Emerald, 2004), available online at http://www.libqual.org/documents/admin/Town-Filling_the_void.doc (accessed March 31 2008).

47. Martha Kyrillidou and others, "Cross-Cultural Implementation of LibQUAL+™: The French Language Experience" (paper presented at the 5th Northumbria International Conference, Durham, UK, July 28–31, 2003); Colleen Cook, Fred Heath, and Bruce Thompson. "LibQUAL+™ from the UK Perspective" (paper presented at the 5th Northumbria International Conference, Durham, UK, July 28–31, 2003).

48. Martha Kyrillidou and Ann-Christin Persson, "The New Library User in Sweden: A LibQUAL+™ Study at Lund University," *Performance Measurement and Metrics* 7, no. 1 (2006): 45–53.

49. Ann-Christin Persson, "AddedLibQual+ Synliggor den Vilde Anvandaren," *InfoTrend: Nordic Journal for Information Specialists* 60, no. 2 (2005): 46–53; Martha Kyrillidou and others, "La Mise en Œuvre Interculturelle de LibQUAL+MC: Le Cas du Français," *BBF 2005 Paris* 50, no. 05 (2005): 48–55; Ann-Christin Persson, "Mätning av Tjänstekvalitet i Bibliotek: Användning av LibQUAL+™ i Sverige," (Measuring service quality in libraries: The use of LibQUAL+™ in Sweden; master's thesis, University College of Borås, 2005; Eva Alopaeus and Britt Omstedt, "Jag Har Kommit Hit För Att Låna

Böcker, Inte För Att Bli Ompysslad Försök Med LibQual+™ Vid Två Svenska Bibliotek," *InfoTrend: Nordic Journal for Information Specialists* 60, no. 2 (2005): 39–45; Jos Smelik, "Een Ander Gebruikersonderzoek," *Informatie Professional* 8, no. 1 (2004): 28–31; Rosa Flor Tello Santos, "Propuesta de Evaluación del Servicio de la Sala de Referencia de la Biblioteca Central Pedro Zulen de la UNMSM: Experiencia Piloto con LibQUAL+ de la Association of Research Libraries", thesis, Universidad Nacional Mayor de San Marcos, Lima, Peru, 2004, available online at http://sisbib.unmsm.edu.pe/bibvirtualdata/Tesis/Human/tello_sr/T_completo.PDF; Maria I. C. Sampaio and others, "PAQ—Programa de Avaliação da Qualidade de Produtos e Serviços de Informação: Uma Experiência No SIBi/USP," *Ciência da Informação* 33, no. 1 (2004): 142–148 (written by a research team in Brazil in Portuguese); Pehlke Rainer, "LibQUAL+: Ein Instrument zur Messung der Servicequalitat in Bibliotheken" *BuB-Journal* 54, no. 10/11 (2002): 654–657; Colleen Cook, Fred Heath, and Bruce Thompson, "A New Culture of Assessment: Preliminary Report on the ARL SERVQUAL Study" (paper presented at the 66th IFLA Council and General Conference, Jerusalem, Israel, August 13–18, 2000), http://www.ifla.org/IV/ifla66/papers/028-129e.htm (English), http://www.ifla.org/IV/ifla66/papers/028-129f.htm (French), http://www.ifla.org/IV/ifla66/papers/028-129r.pdf (Russian), http://www.ifla.org/IV/ifla66/papers/028-129s.htm (Italian), http://www.ifla.org/IV/ifla66/papers/028-129g.htm (German; all accessed March 31, 2008).

50. Bruce Thompson, Martha Kyrillidou, and Colleen Cook, "User Library Service Expectations in Health Science vs. Other Settings: A LibQUAL+ Study," *Health Information and Libraries Journal* 24, supp. 1 (2007): 38–45.

51. Bruce Thompson, Martha Kyrillidou, and Colleen Cook, "On-Premises Library versus Google-Like Information Gateway Usage Patterns: A LibQUAL+® Study," *portal: Libraries and the Academy* 7, no. 4 (2007): 463–80.

52. Richard Groves, "Sharing Best Practices by Disseminating Assessment Results via the Web," *ARL Bimonthly Report* 236 (2004): 6, http://www.arl.org/bm~doc/lqweb.pdf (accessed July 15, 2008).

53. Frances M. Brillantine, "Using Surveys to Improve Service to Students: A Comparison of LibQUAL® and SurveyMonkey," *Law Library Lights* 50, no. 1 (2006): 5–9.

54. University of Technology, Sydney, "Report Comparing the UTS Experience with Client Surveys Using Rodski in 2003 and the LibQUAL Survey 2004 for CAUL September 2004," http://www.caul.edu.au/best-practice/caul20042RodskiLibQual.doc (accessed March 31, 2008).

55. Bruce Thompson, "Research and Practice: Key Elements of Success for LibQUAL+®," in *Library Assessment Conference: Thessaloniki 13–15 June 2005*, ed. Mersini Moreleli-Cacouris, 50 (Washington, DC: Association of Research Libraries, 2006).

56. MaShana Davis, Richard Groves, and Martha Kyrillidou, *LibQUAL+® Procedures Manual* (Washington, DC: Association of Research Libraries, 2006).

57. Bruce Thompson, Colleen Cook, and Martha Kyrillidou, "Using Localized Survey Items to Augment Standardized Benchmarking Measures: A LibQUAL+™ Study," *portal: Libraries and the Academy* 6, no. 2 (2006): 219–30.

58. Bruce Thompson, Colleen Cook, and Fred Heath, "Two Short Forms of the LibQUAL+™ Survey Assessing Users' Perceptions of Library Service Quality," *Library Quarterly* 73, no. 4 (2003): 453–465.

59. E. Steward Saunders, "The LibQUAL+ Phenomenon: Who Judges Quality" *Reference and User Services Quarterly* 47, no. 1 (2007): 21–24.

60. Sarah Lippincott and Martha Kyrillidou, "How ARL University Communities Access Information: Highlights from LibQUAL+™," *ARL Bimonthly Report* 236 (2004): 7–8, http://www.arl.org/bm~doc/lqaccess.pdf (accessed July 15, 2008).

61. John H. Heinrichs, Thomas Sharkey, and Jeen-Su Lim, "Relative Influence of the LibQUAL+™ Dimensions on Satisfaction: A Subgroup Analysis," *College and Research Libraries* 66, no. 3 (2005): 248–265.

62. Jeff Gatten, "The OhioLINK LibQUAL+™ 2002 Experience: A Consortium Looks at Service Quality," in *Libraries Act on Their LibQUAL+™ Findings: From Data to Action,* ed. Fred M. Heath, Martha Kyrillidou, and Consuella A. Askew, 19–48 (New York: Haworth Press, 2004), co-published simultaneously in *Journal of Library Administration* 40, no. 3/4 (2004):19–48; Jeff Gatten, "Measuring Consortium Impact on User Perceptions: OhioLINK and LibQUAL+™," *Journal of Academic Librarianship,* 30, no. 3 (2004): 222–228; Tamera Lee, "Exploring Outcomes Assessment: The AAHSL LibQUAL+™ Experience," in *Libraries Act on Their LibQUAL+™ Findings: From Data to Action,* ed. Fred M. Heath, Martha Kyrillidou, and Consuella A. Askew, 49–58 (New York: Haworth Press, 2004), co-published simultaneously in *Journal of Library Administration* 40, no. 3/4 (2004): 49–58.

63. J. Gail Nicula and Shirley B. Laseter, "LibQUAL™ and the Professional Military Library" (paper presented at the Special Library Association annual conference: Putting Knowledge to Work, Nashville, TN, June 5–10, 2004), http://www.sla.org/documents/libqual.doc (accessed March 31, 2008).

64. Hiller, "Assessing User Needs," 623.

65. Steve Hiller, "Another Tool in the Assessment Toolbox: Integrating LibQUAL+™ into the University of Washington Libraries Assessment Program," in *Libraries Act on Their LibQUAL+™ Findings: From Data to Action,* ed. Fred M. Heath, Martha Kyrillidou, and Consuella A. Askew, 137 (New York: Haworth Press, 2004), co-published simultaneously in *Journal of Library Administration* 40, no. 3/4 (2004).

66. Phipps, "Beyond Measuring Service Quality."

67. Wendy Begay and others, "Quantifying Qualitative Data: Using LibQUAL+™

Comments for Library Wide Planning Activities at the University of Arizona," in *Libraries Act on Their LibQUAL+™ Findings: From Data to Action,* ed. Fred M. Heath, Martha Kyrillidou, and Consuella A. Askew, 111–119 (New York: Haworth Press, 2004).

68. Julie Anna Guidry, "LibQUAL+™ Spring 2001 Comments: A Qualitative Analysis Using Atlas.ti," *Performance Measurement and Metrics* 3, no. 2 (2002): 100–107.

69. Gwyneth Crowley and Charles Gilreath, "Probing User Perceptions of Service Quality: Using Focus Groups to Enhance Quantitative Surveys," *Performance Measurement and Metrics* 3, no. 2 (2002): 78–84.

70. Flo Wilson, "LibQUAL+ at Vanderbilt University: What Do the Results Mean and Where Do We Go from Here?" *Journal of Library Administration* 40, no. 3/4 (2004): 197–240.

71. Yvonna Lincoln, Colleen Cook and Martha Kyrillidou, "Evaluating the NSF National Science Digital Library Collections" (paper presented at the Multiple Educational Resources for Learning and Online Technologies [MERLOT] Conference, Costa Mesa, CA, August 3–6, 2004), http://www.libqual.org/documents/admin/MERLOT%20Paper2_final.pdf (accessed March 31 2008).

72. Tom Wall, "LibQUAL+™ as Transformative Experience," *Performance Measurement and Metrics* 3, no. 2 (2002): 43–47; Joseph F. Boykin, "LibQUAL+™ as a Confirming Resource," *Performance Measurement and Metrics* 3, no. 2 (2002): 74–77.

73. Eileen Hitchingham and Donald Kenney, "Extracting Meaningful Measures of User Satisfaction from LibQUAL+™ for the University Libraries at Virginia Tech," *Performance Measurement and Metrics* 3, no. 2 (2002): 48–58.

74. Wanda Dole "LibQUAL+™ and the Small Academic Library," *Performance Measurement and Metrics* 3, no. 2 (2002): 85–95; Judith Sessions, Alex Schenck, and Aaron Shrimplin, "LibQUAL+™ at Miami University: A Look from Outside ARL," *Performance Measurement and Metrics* 3, no. 2 (2002): 59–67.

75. Gatten, "OhioLINK LibQUAL+™ 2002 Experience"; Lee, "Exploring Outcomes Assessment."

76. Tom Sanville, "Defending and Expanding Library Turf—The Need for Scalable Consumer Research," in *Libraries Act on Their LibQUAL+™ Findings: From Data to Action,* ed. Fred M. Heath, Martha Kyrillidou, and Consuella A. Askew (New York: Haworth Press, 2004), 13–18, co-published simultaneously in *Journal of Library Administration* 40, no. 3/4 (2004): 13–18.

77. Jan H. LaBeause, "LIBQUAL+ in a Problem-Based Learning (PBL) Medical School: The Case Study of the Medical Library and Peyton T. Anderson Learning Resources Center (LRC) at Mercer University School of Medicine in Macon, Georgia." *Journal of Library Administration* 20, no. 3/4 (2004): 59–72.

78. Rick B. Forsman, "The Evolution and Application of Assessment Strategies at the University of Colorado Health Sciences Center," 73–82; Richard B. Peterson and others, "The LibQUAL+™ Challenge: An Academic Medical Center's Perspective, Duke University," 83–98; James Shedlock and Linda Walton, "An Academic Medical Library Using LibQUAL+™: The Experience of the Galter Health Sciences Library, Northwestern University," 99–100; all in *Libraries Act on Their LibQUAL+™ Findings: From Data to Action,* ed. Fred M. Heath, Martha Kyrillidou, and Consuella A. Askew (New York: Haworth Press, 2004), co-published simultaneously in *Journal of Library Administration* 40, no. 3/4 (2004).

79. Beth McNeil and Joan Giesecke, "Using LibQUAL+™ to Improve Services to Library Constituents: A Preliminary Report on the University of Nebraska-Lincoln Experience," *Performance Measurement and Metrics* 3, no. 2 (2002): 96–99; Amy E. Knapp, "We Asked Them What They Thought, Now What Do We Do? The Use of LibQUAL+™ Data to Redesign Public Services at the University of Pittsburgh," *Journal of Library Administration* 40, no. 3/4 (2004): 157–171.

80. Stephen Shorb and Lori Driscoll; "LibQUAL+™ Meets Strategic Planning at the University of Florida," 173–180; Lorraine Haricombe and Bonna Boettcher, "Using LibQUAL+™ Data in Strategic Planning: Bowling Green State University," 181–196; both in *Libraries Act on Their LibQUAL+™ Findings: From Data to Action,* ed. Fred M. Heath, Martha Kyrillidou, and Consuella A. Askew, (New York: Haworth Press, 2004).

81. Barton Lessin, "Mining LibQUAL+™ Data for Pointers to Service Quality At Wayne State University," in *Libraries Act on Their LibQUAL+™ Findings: From Data to Action,* ed. Fred M. Heath, Martha Kyrillidou, and Consuella A. Askew, 139–156 (New York: Haworth Press, 2004); Wilson, "LibQUAL+ at Vanderbilt University."

82. John B. Harer, "LibQUAL+™ in Lilliput: Assessment Benefits for Small Academic Libraries" *Performance Measurement and Metrics,* 7, no. 3 (2006): 193–204.

83. Maria Anna Jankowska, Karen Hertel, and Nancy J. Young, "Improving Library Service Quality to Graduate Students: LibQual+™ Survey Results in a Practical Setting," *portal: Libraries and the Academy* 6, no. 1 (2006): 59–76; William J. Hubbard and Donald E. Walter, "Assessing Library Services With LibQUAL+: A Case Study," *The Southeastern Librarian* 53, no. 1 (2005): 35–45; Michelle M. Foss, Amy Buhler, and Lenny Rhine, "HSCL LibQUAL+ 2004: From Numbers and Graphs to Practical Application," *Medical Reference Services Quarterly* 25, no. 1 (2006): 1–15.

84. Rachel Lewellen, "University of Massachusetts: Assessment and Statistics," n.d., University of Massachusetts, http://www.library.umass.edu/assessment/index.html (accessed October 29, 2006); Fred Heath, "Service Quality Assessment and Improvement." n.d., Austin: University of Texas. http://

www.lib.utexas.edu/vprovost/assessment/index.html (accessed March 31, 2008).

85. Diane Wahl, "LibQUAL+™ Library Service Quality Survey: Results," February 1, 2008, University of North Texas Libraries, http://www.library.unt.edu/libqual/results (accessed March 31, 2008).

86. Jan Comfort, "Results of Spring 2004 LibQUAL+™ Survey," August 14, 2007, Clemson University, http://www.lib.clemson.edu/GovDocs/LibQUAL/LibQUAL+%202004.htm (accessed March 31, 2008).

87. Ruth Swan, "Florida A&M University Libraries: LibQUAL 2004 Survey Results—Executive Brief," July 2004, http://www.famu.edu/index.cfm?a=library&p=LibQUAL2004 (accessed March 31, 2008).

88. Kathy Tomajko, "LIBQUAL Survey Results," Spring 2008, Georgia Tech Library and Information Center, http://www.library.gatech.edu/about_us/libqual/index03.html (accessed March 31, 2008).

89. Babson College, "Horn Library LibQUAL+™ Survey," October 9, 2007, http://www3.babson.edu/library/libqual/libqual.cfm (accessed March 31, 2008).

90. Laura Probst, "LibQUAL+™ Survey: Executive Summary," November 2004, Pennsylvania State University Libraries, http://www.libraries.psu.edu/admin/stratplan/rev_final_libqual_2004_exec_summary.pdf (accessed March 31, 2008), 3.

91. Sam Kalb, "Library Service Quality Survey 2007," September 22, 2007, Queen's University Library, http://library.queensu.ca/webir/libqual.htm (accessed March 31, 2008), 3.

92. Heather Empey and Jo Ann Murphy, "Analysis of the Results of Participation in the LibQUAL+ Survey 2003," University of Northern British Columbia Library, http://library.unbc.ca/Libqual/LibQualAnalysis.htm (accessed March 31, 2008).

93. Katherine Ball, "LibQUAL+ Spring 2004: Leddy Library," September 2005, University of Windsor Library, http://www.uwindsor.ca/units/leddy/leddy.nsf/LibQUALspring2004LeddyLibrary!OpenForm (accessed March 31, 2008).

94. Carol Kay, "LibQUAL+ ™ Liverpool University Library User Surveys," Liverpool University Library, http://www.liv.ac.uk/library/info/libqual04.html (accessed March 31, 2008).

95. Richard Battersby, "LibQUAL+ 2005 Survey," May 2005, Edinburgh University Library Committee, http://www.lib.ed.ac.uk/about/libcom/Papers-Jun05/a10jun05.pdf (accessed March 31, 2008).

96. Jacqui Dowd, "The LibQUAL+™ Library Service Survey," December 7, 2006, Glasgow University Library, http://www.lib.gla.ac.uk/libqual/ (accessed March 31, 2008).

97. Bruce Thompson, Martha Kyrillidou, and Colleen Cook, "Library Users' Service Desires: A LibQUAL+ Study," *Library Quarterly* 78, no. 1 (2008):

8–10.

98. Davis, Groves and Kyrillidou, *LibQUAL+® Procedures Manual*.

99. Amy E. Hoseth. "We Did LibQUAL+®: Now What? Practical Suggestions for Maximizing Your Survey Results," *College and Undergraduate Libraries* 4, no. 3 (2007): 75–84.

100. Colleen Cook. "The Importance of the LibQUAL+® Survey for the Association of Research Libraries and Texas A&M University," in *Library Assessment Conference: Thessaloniki 13–15 June 2005*, ed. Mersini Moreleli-Cacouris, 6 (Washington, DC: Association of Research Libraries, 2006).

101. Eric C. Shoaf, "Using a Professional Moderator in Library Focus Group Research," *College and Research Libraries* 64, no. 2 (2003): 124–132.

102. Nancy Foster and Susan Gibbons, eds., *Studying Students: The Undergraduate Research Project at the University of Rochester* (Chicago: Association of College and Research Libraries, 2007).

103. Jim Self, "LibQUAL+: Finding the Right Numbers" (presentation, LibQUAL+® Meeting, Stellenbosch, South Africa, August 13, 2007), http://www.libqual.org/documents/admin/LQ_PM7gr2.ppt (accessed March 31, 2008).

104. Jim Self, "Bound for Disappointment: Faculty and Journals at Research Institutions" (presentation, 7th Northumbria International Conference on Performance Measurement in Libraries and Information Services [PM7], August 13–16, 2007, Stellenbosch, South Africa), http://www.libqual.org/documents/admin/jim_PM7f.ppt (accessed March 31, 2008).

105. Saunders, "LibQUAL+ Phenomenon," 23.

106. Ibid., 24.

107. William B. Edgar, "Questioning LibQUAL+™: Expanding Its Assessment of Academic Library Effectiveness," *portal: Libraries and the Academy* 6, no. 4 (2006): 445–465.

108. Anthony W. Ulwick, "Turn Customer Input into Innovation," *Harvard Business Review* 80, no 1 (2002): 97.

109. Peter Hernon and Robert E. Dugan, *An Action Plan for Outcomes Assessment in Your Library* (Chicago: American Library Association, 2002); Peter Hernon, R. E. Dugan, and D. Schwartz, eds., *Revisiting Outcomes Assessments in Higher Education* (Westport, CT, and London: Libraries Unlimited, 2006).

110. Martha Kyrillidou, "Service Quality: A Perceived Outcome for Libraries," in *Revisiting Outcomes Assessment in Higher Education*, ed. Peter Hernon, Robert E. Dungan, and C. Schwartz, 331–366 (Westport, CT, and London: Libraries Unlimited, 2006).

111. Bruce Thompson, Colleen Cook, and Martha Kyrillidou, "Concurrent Validity of LibQUAL+™ Scores: What Do LibQUAL+™ Scores Measure?" *Journal of Academic Librarianship* 31, no. 6 (2005): 517–522.

112. Peter Brophy, "Performance Measures for 21st Century Libraries," in *Proceed-

ings of the 4th Northumbria International Conference on Performance Measurement in Libraries and Information Services, ed. Joan Stein, Martha Kyrillidou, and Denise Davis, 1–8 (Washington, DC: Association of Research Libraries, 2002).

113. John Crawford, *The Culture of Evaluation in Libraries and Information Services* (Oxford: Chandos Publishing, 2006).

114. Stephen Town, "Academic Library Performance, Quality and Evaluation in the UK and Europe," in *Library Assessment Conference: Thessaloniki 13–15 June 2005,* ed. Mersini Moreleli-Cacouris, 29–39 (Washington, DC: Association of Research Libraries, 2006); Selena A. Lock and J. Stephen Town, "LibQUAL+ in the Local Context: Results, Action and Evaluation" (paper presented at the 6th Northumbria International Conference on Performance Measurement in Libraries and Information Services, Durham, UK, August 22–25, 2005), http://hdl.handle.net/1826/950 (accessed March 31, 2008); J. Stephen Town and Selena A. Lock, "LibQUAL+ ™ in the UK: A Brief Report on the UK Pilot," *SCONUL Newsletter,* no. 29 (2003): 8–10, http://hdl.handle.net/1826/953; Frankie Wilson and J. Stephen Town, "Benchmarking and Library Quality Maturity," (paper presented at the 6th Northumbria International Conference on Performance Measurement in Libraries and Information Services, Durham, UK, August 22–25, 2005), http://hdl.handle.net/1826/948 (accessed March 31, 2008).

115. Peter Brophy, "The Development of a Model for Assessing the Level of Impact of Information and Library Services," *Library and Information Research* 29, no. 93 (2005): 43–49.

116. John C. Bertot and Denise Davis, *Planning and Evaluating Library Networked Services and Resources* (Westport, CT, and London: Libraries Unlimited, 2004); Charles McClure, "Challenges and Strategies for Evaluating Networked Information Services: Introduction," *Library Quarterly* 74, no. 4 (2004): 399–402; John C. Bertot, "Measuring Service Quality in the Networked Environment: Approaches and Considerations," *Library Trends* 49, no. 4 (2001): 758–775; Charles McClure and John C. Bertot, eds., *Evaluating Networked Information Services: Techniques, Policy and Issues* (Medford. NJ: Information Today, 2001).

117. Andrew White and Eric Djiva Kamal, *E-Metrics for Library and Information Professionals: How to Use Data for Managing and Evaluating Electronic Resources Collections* (New York: Neal-Shuman, 2006).

118. Rush Miller, Sherrie Schmidt, and Martha Kyrillidou, "New Initiatives in Performance Measurement," in *Global Issues in 21st Century Research Librarianship,* ed. S. K. Hannesdottir, 161–177 (Helsinki: NORDINFO, 2002); Wonsik Shim, Charles R. McClure, and John C. Bertot, *ARL E-Metrics Project: Developing Statistics and Performance Measures to Describe Electronic Information Services and Resources in ARL Libraries: Phase One Report* (Washington, DC: Association of Research Libraries, 2000); Martha Kyrillidou and Sarah Giersch, "Qualita-

tive Analysis of ARL E-Metrics Participant Feedback about the Evolution of Measures for Networked Electronic Resources," *Library Quarterly* 74, no. 4 (2004): 423–440.

119. J. Stephen Town, "E-Measures: A Comprehensive Waste of Time?" *VINE* 34, no. 4 (2004): 190–195, http://hdl.handle.net/1826/954 (accessed March 31, 2008).

120. Peter Hernon and Philip Calvert, "E-Service Quality in Libraries: Exploring its Features and Dimensions," *Library and Information Science Research* 27, no. 3 (2005): 377–404.

121. A. Parasuraman, Valarie A. Zeithaml, and Arvind Malhotra, "E-S-QUAL: A Multiple Item Scale for Assessing Electronic Service Quality," *Journal of Service Research* 7, no. 3 (2005): 213–233.

122. Don Dillman, *Mail and Internet Surveys: The Tailored Design Method 2007 Update* (Hoboken, NJ: Wiley, 2007); John C. Bertot and Paul T. Jaeger, "Survey Research and Libraries: Not Necessarily Like in the Textbooks," *Library Quarterly* 78, no. 1 (2008): 99–106.

123. Terry Plum, "Evaluating the Usage of Library Networked Electronic Resources," in *Library Assessment Conference: Thessaloniki 13–15 June 2005,* ed. Mersini Moreleli-Cacouris, 103 (Washington, DC: Association of Research Libraries, 2006).

124. Joe Zucca, "E-Use Measurement: A Detour around the Publishers" (presentation at ALCTS meeting, ALA Annual Conference, Chicago, IL, June 23–29, 2005), http://www.libqual.org/documents/admin/ZUCCAalcts05.ppt (accessed March 31, 2008); Joe Zucca, "Building Frameworks of Organizational Intelligence" (presentation at ARL Library Assessment Forum, University of Pennsylvania, January 11, 2008), http://www.libqual.org/documents/admin/zuccaarl08.ppt (accessed March 31, 2008).

125. Brinley Franklin and Terry Plum, "Networked Electronic Services Usage Patterns at Four Academic Health Sciences Libraries," *Performance Measurement and Metrics* 3, no. 2 (2002): 123–33; Franklin and Plum, "Documenting Usage Patterns of networked electronic services," *ARL Bimonthly Report* 230/231 (2003): 20–21; Franklin and Plum, "Library Usage Patterns in the Electronic Information Environment," *Information Research* 9, no. 4 (2004):187, http://informationr.net/ir/9-4/paper187.html (accessed March 31, 2008); Franklin and Plum, "Successful Web Survey Methodologies for Measuring the Impact of Networked Electronic Services (MINES for Libraries™)," *IFLA Journal* 32, no. 1 (2006): 28–40, http://www.ifla.org/V/iflaj/IFLA-Journal-1-2006.pdf (accessed March 31, 2008).

126. Brinley Franklin, "Measuring the Impact of Networked Electronic Service (MINES): The North American Experience," in *Library Assessment Conference: Thessaloniki 13–15 June 2005,* ed. Mersini Moreleli-Cacouris, 75–94 (Washington, DC: Association of Research Libraries, 2006).

127. Brinley Franklin, Martha Kyrillidou, and Toni Olshen. "The Story behind the

Numbers: Measuring the Impact of Networked Electronic Services (MINES) and the Assessment of the Ontario Council of University Libraries' Scholars Portal(paper presented at the 6th Northumbria International Conference on Performance Measurement in Libraries and Information Services, Durham, UK, August 22–25, 2005), http://www.libqual.org/documents/admin/Northumbria_2005MINES_sept20.doc (accessed March 31, 2008).

128. Tschera H. Connell, Sally A Rogers, and Carol P. Diedrichs, "OhioLINK Electronic Journal Use at Ohio State University," *portal: Libraries and the Academy* 5, no. 3 (2004): 371–390.

129. Steve Hiller, Martha Kyrillidou, and Jim Self, "Assessment in North American Research Libraries: A Preliminary Report Card," *Performance Measurement and Metrics* 7, no. 2 (2006): 100–106.

130. Colleen Cook and others, "Developing a National Science Digital Library (NSDL) LibQUAL+™ Protocol: An E-Service for Assessing the Library of the 21st Century" (submitted for the NSDL Evaluation Workshop, October 2003), http://www.libqual.org/documents/admin/NSDL_workshop_web1.pdf (accessed March 31, 2008).

131. Lincoln, Cook, and Kyrillidou, "Evaluating the NSF National Science Digital Library Collections"; Yvonna Lincoln, Colleen Cook and Martha Kyrillidou, "User Perspectives into Designs for Both Physical and Digital Libraries: New Insights on Commonalities/Similarities and Differences from the NDSL Digital Libraries and LibQUAL+™ Data Bases," in *Proceedings of the 7th ISKO-Spain Conference: The Human Dimension of Knowledge Organization, (Barcelona: July 6–8, 2005)*, 380–404, available online at http://bd.ub.es/isko2005/lincoln.pdf (accessed July 25, 2008).

132. Martha Kyrillidou, "Library Assessment: Why Today and Not Tomorrow?" in *Library Assessment Conference: Thessaloniki 13–15 June 2005*, ed. Mersini Moreleli-Cacouris, 9–27 (Washington, DC: Association of Research Libraries, 2006).

133. Charles Lowry and Paul Hanges, "What is the Healthy Organization? Organizational Climate and Diversity Assessment: A Research Partnership," *portal: Libraries and the Academy* 8, no. 1 (2008): 1–5.

134. Danuta A. Nitecki and Toni Olshen, "Developing Service Quality Measurement Skills through an Online Course for Librarians," in *Proceedings of the 4th Northumbria International Conference on Performance Measurement in Libraries and Information Services,* ed. J. Stein, Martha Kyrillidou, and D. Davis, 235–244 (Washington, DC: Association of Research Libraries, 2002).

135. Ibid., 243.

136. Duane Webster, "Library Assessment: Demonstrating Value-Added in a Time of Constrained Resources and Unique Opportunities," 1–4; J. John V. Lombardi, "On the Research Library: A Comment" 5–8; Sayeed Choudhury and others, "LibQUAL®, ProSeBiCa (Development of New Library Services by Means of Conjoint Analysis), and CAPM (Comprehensive Access to Printed

Materials)," 9–14; Bruce Thompson and others, "How You Can Evaluate the Integrity of Your Library Service Quality Data: Intercontinental LibQUAL® Analyses Used as Concrete Heuristic Examples," 15–32; all in *Proceedings of the Library Assessment Conference: Building Effective, Sustainable, Practical Assessment, September 25–27, 2006, Charlottesville, VA,* ed. Francine DeFranco and others (Washington, DC: Association of Research Libraries, 2007).

137. Agnes Tatarka and others, "Wayfinding in the Library: Usability Testing of Physical Spaces," 33–42; Margi Jantti, "Assessing the Service Needs and Expectations of Customers—No Longer a Mystery," 43–52; Terri L. Holtze and others, "Frequently Noted: Approaches to Analyzing Qualitative Research," 53–62; all in *Proceedings of the Library Assessment Conference: Building Effective, Sustainable, Practical Assessment, September 25–27, 2006, Charlottesville, VA,* ed. Francine DeFranco and others (Washington, DC: Association of Research Libraries, 2007).

138. Lisa J. Hinchliffe and Tina. E. Chrzastowski, "Getting Started with Library Assessment: Using Surveys to Begin as Assessment Initiative," 63–68; Melissa Becher and Mary Mintz, "A Leap in the Right Direction: How a Symbiotic Relationship between Assessment and Marketing Moves the Library Forward," 69–82; Susan Bailey and Charles Forrest, "Assessment in the Emory University Libraries: Lurching toward Sustainability," 83–90; Eric Ackerman, "Library Assessment on a Budget: Using Effect-Size Meta-Analysis to Get the Most out of the Library-Related Survey Data Available across Campus," 117–126; all in *Proceedings of the Library Assessment Conference: Building Effective, Sustainable, Practical Assessment, September 25–27, 2006, Charlottesville, VA,* ed. Francine DeFranco and others (Washington, DC: Association of Research Libraries, 2007).

139. Brinley Franklin, "Return on Investment," in *Proceedings of the Library Assessment Conference: Building Effective, Sustainable, Practical Assessment, September 25–27, 2006, Charlottesville, VA,* ed. Francine DeFranco and others, 127–130 (Washington, DC: Association of Research Libraries, 2007); along the lines of the economics in higher education, also see by the same author: "The Privatization of Public University Research Libraries," *portal: Libraries and the Academy* 7, no. 4 (2007): 407–414.

140. Joseph A. Salem and Carolyn J. Radcliff, "Using the SAILS Test to Assess Information Literacy," 131–138; Louise R. Fluk and others, "The Fourth 'R': Information Literacy in Institutional Assessment," 177–200; Megan Oakleaf, "The Right Assessment Tool for the Job: Seeking a Match between Method and Need," 201–214; all in *Proceedings of the Library Assessment Conference: Building Effective, Sustainable, Practical Assessment, September 25–27, 2006, Charlottesville, VA,* ed. Francine DeFranco and others (Washington, DC: Association of Research Libraries, 2007).

141. Neal. K. Kaske, "Choosing the Best Tools for Evaluating Your Library," 215–224; John T. Snead and others, "Developing Best-Fit Evaluation Strategies" 225–232, both in *Proceedings of the Library Assessment Conference: Building Effective, Sustainable, Practical Assessment, September 25–27, 2006, Charlottesville,*

   VA, ed. Francine DeFranco and others (Washington, DC: Association of Research Libraries, 2007).

142. Dan O'Mahoney and Rayanna Bowlby, "Accountability to Key Stakeholders," 233–245; E. S. Saunders, "Drilling the LibQUAL® Data for Strategic Planning," 245–250; both in *Proceedings of the Library Assessment Conference: Building Effective, Sustainable, Practical Assessment, September 25–27, 2006, Charlottesville, VA,* ed. Francine DeFranco and others (Washington, DC: Association of Research Libraries, 2007).

143. Joan K. Lippincott, "Assessing Learning Spaces," 251–258; Rachal Lewellen and Gordon Fretwell, "Combining Quantitative and Qualitative Assessment of an Information Common," 259–262; Kimberly B. Sweetman and Lucinda Covert-Vail, "Listening to Users: The Role of Assessment in Changing Library Space to Meet User Needs," 263–284; Aaron K. Shrimplin and Matthew Magnuson, "Net Generation Students and the Library as Place," 285–292; all in *Proceedings of the Library Assessment Conference: Building Effective, Sustainable, Practical Assessment, September 25–27, 2006, Charlottesville, VA,* ed. Francine DeFranco and others (Washington, DC: Association of Research Libraries, 2007).

144. Joseph R. Matthews, "Balanced Scorecard in Public Libraries: A Project Summary," 293–302; Susanna Pathak, "The People Side of Planning and Implementing a Large Scale Balanced Scorecard Initiative," 303–318; both in *Proceedings of the Library Assessment Conference: Building Effective, Sustainable, Practical Assessment, September 25–27, 2006, Charlottesville, VA,* ed. Francine DeFranco and others (Washington, DC: Association of Research Libraries, 2007)..

145. Myra Sue Baughman and others, "From Organizational Assessment to Organizational Change: The University of Maryland Experience," 319–330; Laura Lillard, "Diversity and Organizational Culture Survey: Useful Methodological Tool or Pandora's Box?" 331–348; Nancy Slight-Gibney, "Looking In and Looking Out: Assessing our Readiness to Embrace the Future," 349–358; Paul Hanges and others, "Diversity, Organizational Climate, and Organizational Culture: The Role they Play in Influencing Organizational Effectiveness," 359–358; Carol Shepstone and Lyn Currie, "Assessing Organizational Culture: Moving towards Organizational Change and Renewal," 369–380; Yvonne Belanger, "Tools for Creating a Culture of Assessment: the CIPP-Model and Utilization-Focused Evaluation," 381–386; Irma F. Dillon and Maggie Saponaro, "The Use of Outcome-Based Evaluation (OBE) to Assess Staff Learning Activities at the University of Maryland Libraries," 387–392; all in *Proceedings of the Library Assessment Conference: Building Effective, Sustainable, Practical Assessment, September 25–27, 2006, Charlottesville, VA,* ed. Francine DeFranco and others (Washington, DC: Association of Research Libraries, 2007).

146. Judy Jeng, "Usability Assessment of Academic Digital Libraries," 393–408; Maribeth Manoff and others, "All That Data: Finding Useful and Practical Ways to Combine Electronic Resource Usage Data from Multiple Sources," 409–416; both in *Proceedings of the Library Assessment Conference: Building Ef-*

fective, Sustainable, Practical Assessment, September 25–27, 2006, Charlottesville, VA*, ed. Francine DeFranco and others (Washington, DC: Association of Research Libraries, 2007).

147. Sarah E. Aerni and Donald W. King, "Contingent Valuation of Libraries Including Examples from Academic, Public, and Special Libraries," 417–424; John T. Snead and others, "Web-Based Evaluation Instructional Systems: Design, Development, Issues, and Considerations," 425–436; Stephen Town, "Value and Impact Measurement: A UK Perspective and Progress Report on a National Programme (VAMP)," 437–448; all in *Proceedings of the Library Assessment Conference: Building Effective, Sustainable, Practical Assessment, September 25–27, 2006, Charlottesville, VA*, ed. Francine DeFranco and others (Washington, DC: Association of Research Libraries, 2007)..

148. Lizabeth A. Wilson, "Seattle to Charlottesville and Back Again: Building a Library Assessment Community," in *Proceedings of the Library Assessment Conference: Building Effective, Sustainable, Practical Assessment, September 25–27, 2006, Charlottesville, VA*, ed. Francine DeFranco and others, 449–452 (Washington, DC: Association of Research Libraries, 2007).

149. Hiller, Kyrillidou, and Self, "Assessment in North American Research Libraries."

150. Steve Hiller, Martha Kyrillidou, and Jim Self, "Keys to Effective, Sustainable, and Practical Assessment," in *Proceedings of the Library Assessment Conference: Building Effective, Sustainable, Practical Assessment, September 25–27, 2006, Charlottesville, VA*, ed. Francine DeFranco and others, 171–176 (Washington, DC: Association of Research Libraries, 2007).

151. Steve Hiller, Martha Kyrillidou and Jim Self, "When the Evidence Isn't Enough: Organizational Factors that Influence Effective, Sustainable and Practical Assessment" (paper presented at the 4th International Evidence Based Library & Information Practice Conference, Chapel Hill-Durham, NC, May 6–11, 2007), http://www.libqual.org/documents/admin/HIller2.pdf (accessed March 31, 2008).

152. Susan Beck and Wanda Dole, "Data Policy Action: The Continuous Improvement Cycle—Cases from ARL and Carnegie MA I Libraries," 139–158; Amos Lakos, "Evidence-Based Library Management: A View to the Future," 159–170; both in *Proceedings of the Library Assessment Conference: Building Effective, Sustainable, Practical Assessment, September 25–27, 2006, Charlottesville, VA*, ed. Francine DeFranco and others (Washington, DC: Association of Research Libraries, 2007).

153. Amos Lakos, "Evidence-Based Library Management: The Leadership Challenge," *portal: Libraries and the Academy* 7, no. 4 (2007): 431–450.

154. James G. Neal, "The Research and Development Imperative in the Academic Library: Path to the Future," *portal: Libraries and the Academy* 6, no. 1 (2006): 1.

155. Kyrillidou, "Service Quality."

About the Authors

Mary F. Casserly has a master's in library and information science from Drexel University, and a PhD from Rutgers University. Before joining the staff at the University at Albany—SUNY, where she serves as the Assistant Director for Collections and User Services, she was Head of Collections at the University of Maine and the William Paterson University of New Jersey. Dr. Casserly has authored articles on self-study, planned change, and accreditation; she conducted studies of material availability and collection development personnel training and evaluation.

Lynn Silipigni Connaway, Senior Research Scientist at OCLC Programs and Research, received a PhD in library and information science from the University of Wisconsin-Madison and a master's in library science from the University of Arizona. Previously she served as Director of the Library and Information Services department at the University of Denver and was on the faculty of the School of Library and Informational Science at the University of Missouri, Columbia. Her current research projects include data mining using WorldCat holdings and use data to facilitate library decision making. Dr. Connaway is the co-author of the fourth edition of *Basic Research Methods for Librarians* and the co-principal investigator of an IMLS-funded project to study and evaluate the sustainability and relevance of virtual reference service. Dr. Connaway has authored numerous published papers and given presentations at both national and international venues.

Colleen Cook, Dean, Texas A&M University Libraries, and Evans Chair in Librarianship was one of the principal investigators in the development of LibQUAL+. She holds a PhD in higher education administration and an MA in European history from Texas A&M University and an MLS in library science from the University of Texas at Austin. Dr. Cook has published journal articles and book chapters and made numerous presentations in the fields of library science, history, and research methodology. She specializes in qualitative and quantitative methodologies and has served on both ARL and IFLA statistics committees.

Martha Kyrillidou has been directing the ARL Statistics and Measurement Program since 1994. She has a master's in library science and an MEd in educational psychology—evaluation and measurement from Kent State University. Formerly editor of the *ARL Statistics* and the ARL Annual Salary Survey, she is one of the principal investigators in the development of LibQUAL+. She has been involved in projects regarding the evaluation of electronic resources such as MINES for Libraries, DigiQUAL, and E-metrics. Prior to joining ARL, she was affiliated with the Library Research Center of the Graduate School of Library and Information Science at the University of Illinois at Urbana-Champaign, the Bureau of Education Research at Kent State University, and the Aristotle University of Thessaloniki in Greece.

Lorri M. Mon, assistant professor at Florida State University, College of Information, received a PhD in information science from the Information School at the University of Washington and an MS in information and library science from the University of Michigan. Her scholarly interests and activities combine topics in library and information science and computer-mediated communication in the areas of reference and information services, online intermediation, digital libraries, e-government, and evaluation of information services. She has conducted research on digital reference question answering in chat and e-mail reference services, with a focus on evaluation from the user perspective.

Anita Ondrusek holds a PhD in instructional systems development from the Pennsylvania State University, an MLS from Pratt Institute, and an MEd from Elmira College. She is currently an associate professor in the MLIS program at Valdosta State University in Georgia. Dr. Ondrusek has developed instruction and assessments for various information literacy projects, including a quiz for the VOILA! project during her tenure as a reference librarian at Hunter College in New York City.

Michael J. Prasse, Consulting User Interface Designer at OCLC, is the founder and manager of the OCLC Usability Lab and Human-Computer

Interaction (HCI) Team. He holds a PhD in psychology from the Ohio State University. Prior to joining OCLC, he was a consultant to AT&T on user interface design. He joined OCLC in 1989 as the postdoctoral fellow in the OCLC Office of Research, where his postdoctoral project was the development of the usability lab and HCI team. He was the primary user interface designer for several OCLC products, including FirstSearch 1.0, FirstSearch Web 1.0, and WorldCat Collection Analysis 1.0, and has published a number of articles about user interface design and usability testing.

Marie L. Radford is an associate professor at the Rutgers University School of Communication, Information and Library Studies. Previously she was acting dean and associate professor at Pratt Institute's School of Information and Library Science. She holds a PhD from Rutgers and an MSLS from Syracuse University. Before arriving at Pratt, she was Head of Curriculum Materials at the Cheng Library of the William Paterson University of New Jersey. Her research interests are interpersonal communication in traditional and virtual reference encounters, evaluation of digital resources and services, cultural studies, and media stereotypes of librarians. Dr. Radford has given numerous presentations at communication and library conferences and published many scholarly articles in these areas. She is the author of *The Reference Encounter: Interpersonal Communication in the Academic Library* (1999) and *Web Research: Selection, Evaluation, and Citing* (2006). Her editorial board memberships include *The Library Quarterly* and *The Atlantic Journal of Communication*.

S. Shyam Sunder Rao is senior librarian at Siva Sivani Institute of Management in India. He holds a master of philosophy degree in library and information sciences from Alagappa University, a master of library and information sciences from Indira Gandhi National Open University, and an MCom from Osmania University. Currently, he is pursuing a doctor of philosophy from Indira Gandhi National Open University on "Users' Perception about Service Quality in Select University Libraries of Hyderabad: A LibQUAL+™ Approach." He has worked for over a decade across all operating environments and has presented and published six technical papers at seminars and conferences.

Pamela Snelson has held the position of College Librarian at Franklin and Marshall College since 1998. Previously she served as assistant director and in various other positions at Drew University. She earned a PhD degree and an MLS at Rutgers University. Dr. Snelson was president of ACRL (2006–2007) and a senior fellow at UCLA's Graduate School of Library and Information Science. She has published in *College and Research Libraries* and the *Journal of Academic Librarianship*. Her editorial board memberships have included *EDUCAUSE Quarterly*, *College and Research Libraries News*, and *The Journal of Academic Librarianship*.

Sherry L. Vellucci is professor and Dean of the University Libraries, University of New Hampshire. While on the faculty at Rutgers University, School of Communication, Information and Library Science, she taught courses in information organization, metadata, and cataloging and classification. Dr. Vellucci has also served as associate professor and director of the Division of Library and Information Science at St. John's University, a cataloger at Princeton University, and director of the Library and Media Center at Westminster Choir College. She holds a PhD in library science from Columbia University and a master's degree in library science from Drexel University. She is an international conference speaker and has taught courses and workshops in New Zealand and Vietnam. She has published books and articles in the area of bibliographic relationships, authority control, cataloging, and metadata. Dr. Vellucci serves on the editorial board of the journal *Cataloging and Classification Quarterly*.

Mark Winston is assistant chancellor and director, John Cotton Dana Library, Rutgers University at Newark. He earned his master's in library science and PhD at the University of Pittsburgh. Prior to his current position, Dr. Winston taught at the University of North Carolina at Chapel Hill, School of Information and Library Science, and at Rutgers University, School of Communication, Information and Library Science. In addition to having held positions in banking and auditing, he has served as Assistant University Librarian at Valdosta State University in Georgia, Visiting Program Officer at the Association of Research Libraries, and Coordinator of Instruction and Business and Undergraduate Services Librarian at the University of Arizona. He has presented extensively and published more than 25 articles in peer-reviewed journals on various aspects of leadership, management, and diversity, as well as two books, *Managing Multicultural-ism and Diversity in the Library: Principles and Issues for Administrators* (1999) and *Leadership in the Library and Information Science Professions: Theory and Practice* (2001). His editorial board memberships have included the journals *College and Research Libraries, Library Administration and Management* and the *Journal of Library and Information Science.*

Subject Index